FAMILY AND ENVIRONMENT
An Ecosystem Perspective

GAIL FREEDMAN MELSON

Department of Child
Development and Family Studies
Purdue University

Burgess Publishing Company
Minneapolis, Minnesota

Copyright © 1980 by Burgess Publishing Company
Printed in the United States of America
Library of Congress Catalog Number 79-56585
ISBN 0-8087-1395-7

Burgess Publishing Company
7108 Ohms Lane
Minneapolis, Minnesota 55435

0 9 8 7 6 5 4 3

For my family: Parents Isaac and Eva Freedman; husband Robert; children Sara and Joshua; and sisters Carol and Susan.

Contents

Preface

About five years ago, I was invited to teach a course entitled "Family as Ecosystem" at Purdue University's School of Consumer and Family Sciences (then the School of Home Economics). The course was to be interdisciplinary and broad in focus. It was to address the family as its members interacted not only with each other, but with the physical and social environments to which the family was linked. This was to be a course in which majors in such diverse fields as interior design, dietetics, early childhood education, and family studies might see how their fields of study met together on the common ground of concern with the complexity of family life.

In my attempt to translate these lofty goals into a coherent course structure with relevant readings, it soon became apparent that no integrative text existed. At the same time, there was growing public and academic concern with issues affecting the family as an actor in the global ecosystem of energy exchanges, issues such as fossil-fuel shortages, family violence and abuse, crowded housing, consumer education, and the stresses of rapid social and technological change.

After I had taught the "Family as Ecosystem" course for several years, a conceptual framework emerged that seemed to provide for a persuasive approach. It viewed the family as neither a victim of larger environmental forces nor the creator of its own destiny, but rather as a *transactor*, exchanging and transforming energy and information. This framework also moved easily from macro- to micro-levels of analysis, viewing the family in the former as a unit of analysis in transaction with outside environments; in the latter, taking the individual family member as the unit and the family as the larger environment with which he or she transacts.

This book together with the companion *Instructor's Manual* is the result of the fleshing out of such a conceptual framework. I expect it will be most useful for undergraduates but might be used in more advanced courses if supplemented with substantial readings.

When an author completes a book manuscript and surveys the people involved with the project from germination of the idea to its final typed version, what first appeared as a mostly solitary enterprise ends as a group endeavor. Particularly, I must single out Beatrice Paolucci, who reviewed numerous versions of the manuscript and offered guidance and support whenever shoals threatened this fragile craft. Norma H. Compton's assistance was invaluable, helping me first refine the conceptual framework, later carefully reviewing earlier drafts and suggesting new avenues to explore. My thanks to Hamilton McCubbin, Janice Hogan, and several anonymous reviewers for their helpful comments on portions of earlier drafts. Naturally, any shortcomings in the resulting work are entirely my own. Kay Kushino, Home Economics editor at Burgess Publishing Company, was a steadfast beacon of encouragement throughout. I would like to thank Dena Targ, Assistant Professor and Extension Specialist at Purdue University, for her volunteer role as resource person.

I particularly appreciate the assistance that Burgess, my department—Child Development and Family Studies—and my department head—Donald Felker—extended to me, enabling me to concentrate energy at critical junctures of the writing. A year's leave of absence at the Hebrew University in Jerusalem was invaluable both for its intellectual stimulation and for the luxurious stretches of writing time it provided. I am indebted to the Department of Education at the Hebrew University for graciously allotting me work space and to the staffs of the Department of Education and Department of Psychology libraries at the Hebrew University for opening their excellent facilities to me.

At Purdue University, I owe much to the students of the undergraduate course "Family as Ecosystem" who willingly read draft versions of the book as their required text. A special note of thanks to Rita McCoy, Jan Roberts, and Calla Wooldridge, who cheerfully typed what seemed to be innumerable drafts of the manuscript. My husband Robert, daughter Sara, and son Joshua remain in this, as in all else, the *sine qua non*.

Introduction

Here is Nawa. . . . As she turns the spoon in the pot she tells her daughters that they are lazy and their husbands will scold them. But this is just talk. A man never speaks to his wife, even when they lie down together on the mat at night during the first ten or fifteen years of marriage. He cares little for what she likes or what she may be thinking, any more than she cares for what he likes, beyond the likes of a normal man: a hot couscous when he comes home and healthy children. Theirs are two separate worlds, which pass without touching.

(Duvignaud, Change at Shekiba, p. 16)

Morris Rappaport and his wife Annie live in the 400 block of Clymer Avenue. Their apartment is on the third floor in the rear of the building. It is always dark in all of their three and a half rooms. The building is always poorly heated and to get plumbers to fix the main water pipes in the basement seems to be an impossible chore for the owners of the building. At sixty-eight, Morris and Annie Rappaport, who came to this country almost fifty years ago, feel they have nothing left to live for except a grandson, the only child of their only child. The boy is fifteen and lives in Cleveland. His one dream is that he be allowed to come to Boston someday and attend MIT.

(Cottle, A Family Album, p. 167)

From modernizing Tunisia to contemporary Boston, the universal dramas of family life keep playing. The cast varies, the stage setting and props are sure to be richly distinctive, and the script is a marvel of continuous improvisation. Nevertheless, all families, as part of the Family of Man, share a universality of experience. Each family appears in a special relationship to its environment. The life of the family often seems to be organically part of its setting, to have grown up out of its nurturing soil. At the same time, the family exercises all the power and creativity in its grasp to fashion an environment that will reflect its aspirations, values, and means.

This book studies the complex interweaving of family and environment. The concept of the family as an ecosystem reflects the belief that family life and its immediate environment—its space, food, clothing, and artifacts—form a complex, dynamic, living system of which family members are a part. By viewing the family as an ecosystem, one can begin to understand how family life may be both the product of environmental forces and a significant creative force itself. The ecosystem approach allows students of the family in an era of rapid change to focus on the relationships between a changing environment and a changing family. The concepts of system stability, homeostasis, and feedback, all cornerstones of ecosystem theory, may be invoked to answer pressing contemporary family issues. When does change produce stress in a family? How much stimulation is best for family members? When should families seek to adapt to a rapidly changing environment; when should they attempt to control environmental change itself? How may families learn about and articulate their environmental needs?

Interest in the family ecosystem is not new. At the beginning of this century, Ellen Richards defined the ecosystem approach as "the study of laws, conditions, principles and ideals which are concerned on the one hand with man's immediate physical environment and on the other hand, with his nature as a social being and the study especially of the relation between these two factors" (Lake Placid Conference on Home Economics, 1902, pp. 70-71). Almost seventy years later, in a time of rapid change and "future shock," this definition is receiving renewed interest (Hook and Paolucci, 1970; Marshall, 1973). Home economists now urge that the family be viewed as "an interdependent life support system" (Hook and Paolucci, 1970, p. 316). The family, sustained by the resources of both the natural and the social-emotional environments, uses these materials to pursue its goals. The ecosystem approach explores the relation between humans as social beings and their near environment in an effort to understand and manage better the impact of change upon families (East, 1970).

Mannino (1974) has called attention to three important components of such an ecosystem approach to the family: (1) variations in family life styles, (2) the relationship between family behavior and certain environmental situations, and (3) the interrelatedness of family and environment. Differences in family values and interaction patterns can be better understood if the links between the family and its near environment are kept in mind. But it is also true that despite variations in family organization and life style, families share many common concerns. For example, throughout much of the world family members agree on the basic components of the concept of "quality of life." A study reported by Wallace (1974) considered the following four types of indicators of quality of life: economic (e.g., gross national product and average income), environmental (air, water quality), social (education, health), and psychological (opportunity to realize one's potential). Wallace found that people from contrasting cultures agreed that a high quality of life for their families consisted of such things as hope for the future, land, adequate food, clothing, shelter, income, employment opportunities, maternal and child health, and family and social welfare. Thus, while differences in family life style are reflected in different environmental needs, families share many of the same basic goals.

Of necessity, the study of the family as an ecosystem cannot examine all facets of family life. The fields of psychology, sociology, anthropology, and family history have all laid claim to important territory. Literature, from the Old Testament to *Anna Karenina* to *Buddenbrooks*— and each reader will want to add his or her favorites—continues to provide insights that illumine the meaning of the family drama for its universal participants. In addition, fiction often generates for the social scientist new hypotheses concerning the family. In short, hardly any inquiry into the human condition will fail to deal in some way with the family, that most basic and central of human experiences.

One may well ask at this point: Why yet another approach to the family? Why in particular an ecosystem approach? For one thing, the family's near environment often receives little attention from disciplines with other questions in their collective minds. Psychological and psychosocial approaches to the family focus on interpersonal dynamics, communication, conflict resolution, and individual development. Evidence comes often from the family's words, via interviews, standard tests, or responses to experimental manipulations. While this approach recognizes that the immediate environment of the family gives important clues about interpersonal relations, the root and flowering of these relations are seen in the family history of interactions. For example, Hess and Handel's excellent psychosocial study of five families (*Family Worlds: A Psychosocial Approach*) devotes only one paragraph to the physical setting of each family.

Similarly, the sociology of the family views the family as a social institution tied into the economic, political, and educational systems of the complex web of society. The internal workings of family life—its formation, growth, and development—are often treated as dependent upon forces outside the family. Clearly, the family's immediate environment is influenced by, and in many ways reflects, larger societal forces. For example, the economy of many American small farms often means that farmers spend long hours at work away from their wives. One study of Michigan farm wives and city wives (Blood, 1968) found that 58 percent of the farm wives, as compared with 30 percent of the city wives, did nearly all housework unassisted. This difference in family interaction pattern may well be reflected in the organization of the family's space, the planning and securing of the family's food, clothing and household objects, and the arrangement and care of the family home. Because of her longer labors, does the farm wife see the farmhouse as her domain, the fields as his? Are the movements of both husband and children more restricted than the wife's inside the farmhouse? What household objects are most highly valued and desired by all family members? The sociological approach does not address itself to the translation of societal forces into the everyday language of the family setting.

Students of cultural contrast, whether geographical or historical, often pay close attention to the mundane details of family setting as they seek clues to an initially mysterious family behavior pattern. The common cooking pot becomes a reaffirming act of common identity; the arrangement of wives' huts in the family compound visually depicts social organization for the observer. Yet, in the context of the apparently familiar, the family's immediate environment may lose much of its explanatory flavor for social scientists.

Disciplines most closely focussed upon the family's environment are those found in departments of home management, family economics, consumer studies, nutrition, clothing, and child development. Together, they have always been concerned with the effect of the family's environment on its quality of life. Too often, however, each discipline's concerns have gone uncommunicated to the others, and enhancement of the quality of life is urged without clear understanding of the concept. The need is presently felt for theoretical integration of disciplines into a unified approach to the family as an ecosystem. Such an integration is the goal of this volume.

THE CONCEPT OF THE FAMILY

Perhaps the thorniest issue for any book about the family is the deceptively simple question: What is a family? As Jane Howard remarks in her book *Families* (1978): "Nothing is or ever was more wonderful, more dreadful or more inescapable than families, nor are there many words more perplexing to define" (p. 24). In an age of alternative life styles, perhaps the path of least resistance might be the answer: "A family is anything two or more individuals say it is." However, the very importance of the family as a group within which people find a sense of membership and identity, the very insistence of atypical groupings to wear the mantle of "family," should signal the reader that no society takes the term *family* lightly. All members of a society see the formation, continuance, and dissolution of a family as basic life experiences and thus will confirm or undermine a group's sense of "family-ness."

The family is the most important group within which people find a sense of membership and identity. (Photo by Natalie Leimkuhler.)

At the same time, in rapidly changing, mass-communication societies like contemporary America, the distinct life styles of subgroups as well as the changing behaviors of the majority are quickly disseminated, permeating society's view of what a family is and how it should behave. Thus, much recent writing on the family bears such titles as *Marriage and Family in a Decade of Change, Adaptation and Diversity,* and *Is Marriage Necessary?* These books echo a raucous national debate on the very worth of the contemporary nuclear family as a viable institution. Many in the women's movement decry the housewife as an economically dependent, childlike servant, while those alarmed at population growth and concerned about the personal growth of adults see children as threats to both societal and individual well-being. At the same time, often the brightest of our youth urge abandonment of the rat race for a sense of community with others and a sense of accomplishment by work completed with one's own hands.

This societal discord is itself evidence of social concern for the nature of the family. Therefore, varied definitions of the family sparkle with that multi-faceted concern. Sociologists emphasize the fact that societal expectations, or norms, occur in interrelated combination as roles. Roles represent precepts about how actors in the family ideally should behave; their actual role behavior may be quite another matter. In addition, roles carry penalties to encourage appropriate performance. These penalties—legal, social, and psychological—exert pressure upon the person to carry out a suitable performance.

Another definition of the family emphasizes the fact that families have histories. The developmental approach to the family particularly emphasizes the idea of family life-cycle stages—the common passage of families through the onset of the relationship, possible expansion with children, contraction as children leave the "nest" or grandparents die. Some of these happenings are anticipated, some unexpected, but none is unique to one family alone. As Rodgers (1973) puts it, "Though each family's history is unique, it is also common. Furthermore, it has a certain quality of inevitability, though not necessarily of predictability" (p. 13). This means that while one may not be able to predict the specific developmental crises of a particular family, the fact of change itself is assured. Furthermore, the biological timetables of family members imply that many crises will be shared widely. A couple will grow old, their children will reach adolescence and then adulthood, and their parents will eventually die. As a family passes through these life stages, their environment changes as societal expectations shift to take into account the family's developmental stage. Modern America broadcasts incessant messages about the "Pepsi generation" and Mrs. Folger's puzzled housewife friend, all cameo portraits of modal family types—the young (in love) couple; the busy, somewhat harried housewife with small children; the elderly isolated grandparents tearfully grateful for a call via Ma Bell. These media messages are the result of advertising's best attempt to identify societal expectations concerning family developmental stages. Since advertising and television situation dramas represent the results of the most lavishly funded research efforts in identifying such norms, their implied conclusions provide invaluable raw material for the student of family life.

The notion that families have histories also suggests that societal norms concerning family roles are rooted in a particular moment. The work of Philip Aries in *Centuries of Childhood* has shown how modern views of family life and human development represent not eternal verities but the complex product of social change. Using art, family records, and biographies, Aries argues that medieval Europe failed to distinguish childhood as a separate stage in development, integrating people of all ages into work and recreation. The family was far less important then as the basic unit of social organization; the life of the family merged gradually into the life of society. By contemporary standards, the medieval family seems shameless in its lack of individual or family privacy. Accounts of the period illustrate how changes in the constitution of families and in the definition of significant age divisions radically affected household organization, creating a physical and psychological environment designed to support the medieval family form.

Still another approach to the family has grown out of viewing human relationships as a process of social exchange. Increasingly, many (Homans, 1961; Gouldner, 1960; Thibaut and Kelley, 1959) have argued that social relations involve the exchange of costs and benefits. Put another way, interaction tends toward a norm of equity and reciprocity. In many cultures, marriages are arranged with literal exchanges of valued goods, such as cattle and jewels. In our own society, the norm of equity is also often used in practice. A handsome man is seen with a woman of mediocre attractiveness. "I wonder what he sees in her?" may be the quizzical question of a bystander. Although social exchange theory generally is applied only to pair relationships, the family may be viewed as a group of individuals who seek to maximize material and psychic resources in order to achieve personal and group goals.

Both in their relations with each other and in their transactions with their environment, family members use personal resources such as interpersonal competence, intelligence, attractiveness, and coping skills. In addition, the family as a group varies in its store of such resources as stability, cohesiveness, and trust. Finally, the environment in which the family functions furnishes additional resources and incurs additional costs. A new job brings income, prestige, and power, but may require that family members pay costs in terms of adjustment to new surroundings, loss of old friends, and loss of old satisfactions. The family constantly makes entries in its "balance sheet," however unconsciously.

In summary, the family has been viewed from three vantage points: The sociological view emphasizes the family as a constellation of roles. The developmental view stresses the changing nature of the family life-cycle. The social-exchange view depicts the family as a goal-setting and value-seeking group out to maximize benefits and reduce costs.

Elements of each of these perspectives have been integrated into a family systems approach. This view incorporates ideas of the family as a set of interrelated roles, as changing with time, and as actively pursuing goals. In addition, the following points are stressed:

1. The family is more than a collection of interacting individuals. It is a whole greater than the sum of its parts.
2. The family consists of interdependent individuals whose behavior mutually affects one another.
3. Family systems tend toward equilibrium or balance so that changes in one family member cause reciprocal changes in others to restore the old balance or stabilize at a new equilibrium level.

FAMILY AS ECOSYSTEM

This book unites a systems approach to the family with the perspective of ecology to view the family as an ecosystem. In this view, family members not only are linked to one another by patterns of reciprocal influence but also are embedded in a network of physical and social environments. Family behavior may be understood in terms of energy exchanges with environments. Ultimately, all energy is derived from solar sources; some energy is transformed into fossil fuels, which in turn make agricultural and industrial environments possible. To make matters more complex, humans have developed elaborate regulatory systems—educational, political, cultural, and religious—that provide rules about how such energy exchanges are to be carried out. For example, religious dietary restrictions, such as the Moslem injunction against the eating of pork, specify how nutrient energy is to be converted into caloric fuel to fuel human behavior.

Within this global ecosystem, the family may be thought of as an environment producing resources in the form of human energy. It is the family that creates, nurtures, and largely prepares new human material to function in the global ecosystem as producers, consumers, and regulators of energy. Moreover, in traditional agricultural societies, which still make up the majority of the world's population, the family functions directly as the primary unit of agricultural production. In industrialized societies like the United States, the functioning of agricultural and industrial sectors rests upon the ability of the family to produce future workers, nurture their early growth, instill attitudes toward work, authority, and consumption, and provide continuing emotional support.

The family then is an important link in the global ecosystem. Family functioning profoundly affects this web of energy exchanges. At the same time, the family itself is affected by the forces acting upon it. Thus, the family is in *transaction* with environments surrounding it.

THE CONCEPT OF THE ECOSYSTEM

The term *ecosystem* originated with A. G. Tansley in 1935, when he wrote:

> The more fundamental conception is . . . the whole system. . . including not only the organism-complex, but also the whole complex of physical factors forming what we call the environment. . . . We cannot separate them from their special environment with which they form one physical system. . . . It is the system so formed which . . . are the basic units of nature on the face of the earth. . . . These *ecosystems,* as we may call them, are of the most various kinds and sizes.

It is interesting to note that the *eco-* prefix of ecosystem comes from the Greek *oikos,* meaning household. The household, as this book will show, represents the basic environment for the organism *homo sapiens.*

The term *system* needs a closer look also, Webster defining it as "a group of units so combined as to form a whole and to operate in unison." Thus, an ecosystem approach considers organisms as they exist in nature and studies their interdependence with each other and with the environment. One writer on ecology put it succinctly: "Ecology is the new name for a very old subject. It simply means scientific natural history" (Elton, 1927).

The term *ecosystem* emphasizes the regular interdependence of organisms within their environment. Basic to the concept of the ecosystem are energy flow and the cycling of nutrients (Smith, 1972). The ultimate energy for all ecosystems is, of course, solar radiation. Solar radiation reaching the earth is fixed in plant photosynthesis. Much of this energy must be used by the plants for their own respiration; what remains will appear in the accumulation of plant growth, or *biomass.* This biomass is the energy source for all other living organisms on earth, from one organism to the next via food chains. Herbivores feed directly on plant growth, converting only a small percentage of what they eat to animal tissue. Much of it is used to maintain respiration and metabolic needs, much is excreted in feces, urine, and other waste materials, much is simply lost. When a steer grazes on short grasses, only about 9 to 10 percent of the forage is converted to animal tissue.

Carnivores, including man, likewise are able to convert only a small portion of the animal energy they consume into growth. At each step in the food chain, as carnivore feeds on carnivore, most of the energy available is lost or used up in maintaining body heat, respiration, and metabolism. Many animals function as omnivores, feeding on both plant and animal energy, and thus a food chain tends to be a complex, nonlinear affair.

Intertwined with the food chain is a detritus, or waste chain, a series of steps in which the waste products of energy fixation are broken down for reuse. When a mature ecosystem like a pine forest is studied, it becomes evident that no single food or detritus chain can account for its stable functioning. Numerous food chains exist interwoven in food webs.

The diverse complexity of food webs indicates another characteristic of ecosystems, their development from immature to mature form. A good example of ecosystem development, or *succession,* has been reported by Keever (1950). An abandoned corn field is first covered by crabgrass, then horseweed, and by the third summer, broomsedge, a perennial bunchgrass. The grasses support the life of crickets, grasshoppers, seed-eating birds, and meadow mice. The grass stage ends with the advent of pine seedlings, which begin to shade out the grasses within five to ten years. Amid the pines are now seen rabbits, pine warblers, and sparrows. Finally, oaks and sweet gums, longer-rooted and more shade tolerant, crowd out the pine seedlings and finally establish a stable hardwood deciduous forest. Now downy woodpeckers, flycatchers, grouse, and squirrel are among the inhabitants.

The early stages of succession in this abandoned corn field were characterized by small total organic mass, low diversity of plant and animal species, and clear dominance of a few species, like broomsedge. Because energy transactions passed through fewer steps than in complex multi-species ecosystems, less net energy loss was experienced and production of biomass was relatively high. Because there were few species and low species populations, it is not surprising that organisms in this young, immature ecosystem were not highly specialized with respect to their environment. The place of an organism within the ecosystem is called its *ecological niche* and niche specialization in immature ecosystems is generally broad. This production efficiency and low specialization is not without its dangers, however, for an immature ecosystem, like the abandoned corn field gone to grasses, is highly susceptible to environmental disturbance. Disruptions in the food chain at one point quickly send shock waves reverberating through it.

The stable, mature ecosystem by contrast has a rich diversity of species with energy transactions passing through many steps. With maturity, the size, complexity of life history, and niche specialization of organisms all tend to increase. Dominance of a few species is less likely. Defining efficiency as the ratio between energy consumption and biomass increase, the mature ecosystem is, of necessity, less efficient than the young system. Species diversity means that energy transactions go through many steps, with a loss of energy at each point. However, lowered efficiency is accompanied by greater resistance to environmental disturbance. Disruption at a single point will be less severely felt when many long food chains exist intertwined in food webs.

These changing attributes of ecosystems as they develop are neither uniform nor inevitable (Odum, 1972). Many events may counteract the tendency toward species diversity in mature ecosystems. Increased species size may be accompanied by greater inter-specific competition, squeezing out some species. Despite such exceptions, the development of the mature ecosystem is a trend toward homeostasis within complexity. As Odum puts it, "The overall strategy is directed toward achieving as large and diverse an organic structure as is possible within the limits set by the available energy input and the prevailing physical conditions of existence" (p. 33).

Maintaining a steady state or homeostasis assumes a feedback mechanism to ensure continued *fit* with the environment despite stimulus variation. All organisms thus must have means of getting information about the environment, of determining appropriate action, and of carrying it out. In the evolution of man, selection pressures have favored the creature able to anticipate environmental change and foresee necessary adaptations.

HUMAN ECOLOGY

While ecologists were calling attention to the importance of the distribution and interdependence of all living systems, it struck social scientists of the period, like McKenzie (1924), that humans, as individuals and in groups, are also fundamentally affected by their spatial and temporal distribution. In addition, the distinctively human capacities to contrive and adapt the environment to one's needs mean that the field of human ecology must consider both environmental influences on humans and human perception and creation of that environment.

Early writers on human ecology emphasized spatial and temporal distance as their most significant area of inquiry. McKenzie put it this way: "Human institutions and human nature itself become accommodated to certain spatial relationships of human beings. As these spatial relationships change, the physical basis of social relations is altered, thereby producing social and political problems" (1924). Five decades later, the importance of spatial distributions is undiminished, but placed within a larger context.

The field of human ecology has attracted psychologists, home economists, architects, and designers to form a rich mosaic of approaches and methods. In a recent review, six major approaches to human ecology were identified (Moos, 1974). The first consists of a search for ecological variables by which the environment may be classified. Many architects and designers, whose job it is to create environments, are increasingly concerned with the behavioral consequences of these settings. For example, Deasy (1973) advocates behavioral plans, or inventories, of expected behaviors in a planned environment as adjuncts to the blueprint. Focussing on semipublic and public institutions like psychiatric wards, lounges, and classrooms, Sommer (1969) has shown that user behavior is strongly affected by such factors as setting arrangement, building materials, and window placement. Despite a wealth of evidence, the usefulness of this approach has been hampered by lack of consensus on the relevant dimensions of environments for user behavior. Thus, it is not clear how one may apply existing research on public places to the identification of ecological variables in the family's habitat.

The second approach, represented by the ecological psychology of Barker and his associates (1968), consists of a theory of behavior settings. Over more than twenty years, Barker has explored the interweaving of behavior patterns and environmental settings in a small Midwestern community. He has shown that the drugstore, school, and basketball game, to cite a few, are distinctive settings for behavior patterns appropriate to them. The components of such settings (the stands, basketball court, etc.) are essential to the execution of environment-bound behaviors. In this clear application of ecosystem principles, organism behavior and environmental factors form one interdependent system.

Barker's behavior setting analysis has not been widely employed by others, however. Some (Hutt and Hutt, 1970) have criticized his molar, naturalistic accounts as imprecise and unreliable, since each observer may impute differing emotions and motivations to those he observes. Despite this, the work of Barker and his associates has been enormously important for the field of human ecology in showing the significance of environmental supports for behavior. His work suggests that an understanding of family behavior and attitudes may be enriched by study of its behavior settings.

The third approach relates dimensions of organizational structure, such as size, degree of centralization, span of control, or size of organizational subunits, to job attitudes and behavior. In family research, parallels may be drawn with work on family size (Bossard, 1956), on authoritarian versus democratic family structures, and on kinship networks (Hsu, 1972). In applying this approach to family-environment interactions, one may ask how the physical setting of the family helps support (or undermine) its organizational structure. For example, among polygamous Hausa families in Northern Nigeria, autonomy for wives is supported through separate sleeping huts within the larger family compound. Similarly, doing your own thing in an affluent American family may be supported by separate bedroom-living areas for family members.

A fourth approach, somewhat related to the study of organizational structure, investigates the social climate of an organization. The dimensions of the climate, such as organization, order, clarity, and control, all elicit expected behaviors from their participants. In the novel *Something Happened,* Joseph Heller gives a chilling account of the organizational climate of one modern corporation:

> The company is having another banner year. . . . We have twenty-nine officers now, twelve in this country. We average three suicides a year. . . . People in the company like to live well and are usually susceptible to nervous breakdowns. . . . Everybody is divorced. . . . Everybody drinks and takes two hours or more for lunch. The men all flirt. [The salesmen] . . . are always on trial, always on the verge of failure. . . . (pp. 17-22)

The scientific study of organizational climate has attempted to measure its important dimensions largely by means of rating scales. The College and University Environment Scale (CUES) (Pace, 1969) may be taken as an example of a number of scales currently in use. Five dimensions of college environments are assessed: (1) emphasis on academic competition, (2) concern for self-understanding and personal involvement, (3) sense of community, (4) emphasis on decorum, and (5) practicality. CUES and other scales ask participants in a setting to rate it in the light of their own perceptions; thus, it measures what are likely to be the critical components of an environment for the actors within it. As Moos (1974) points out, such scales are particularly useful in measuring personality-environment congruence.

Although less attention has been paid to the home, some efforts have been made to assess the effects of what may be called "habitat" climate on the family. Hess and Handel (1959) used lengthy interviews and story-telling devices* with five families to uncover each family's themes, significant issues as perceived by the family. Ruesch and Kees (1956) bring together photographic montages of six houses to illustrate through their settings dominant family concerns. This work is imaginative and suggestive of fruitful areas of research, but little systematic work has been done to determine how family members perceive and rate the important dimensions of their immediate environments.

A fifth approach to human ecology takes average background characteristics of individuals in a particular setting as components of that environment and investigates their effect on new recruits to the setting. One example given is that of a new student entering a college with high academic standards (Astin, 1968). The average characteristics of students there—intellectual argument, intense competition for grades, and intellectual recognition—will strongly affect the novice's behavior and psychological adjustment.

Lastly, a sixth approach to human ecology is an outgrowth of the animal ethology field. Sparked by Lorenz (1965) and Tinbergen (1951), ethology studies animal behavior patterns as they occur in natural environments. This approach has led to the discovery of specific aspects of the environment that act as triggering mechanisms, or releasers, for behavior patterns. The gosling follows its mother solely because of the patch of color on her tail, baby chicks peck at anything small and square, and migratory birds fly north when daylight lengthens. In this way, aspects of the environment function to support and maintain adaptive behaviors. The animal is "in sync" with precisely those environmental stimuli it is most likely to encounter.

---

* Story-telling devices include sentence-completion measures and responses to TAT-type (Thematic Apperception Test) pictures.

In recent years, both the method and conceptual framework of animal ethology have been applied to human behavior. In particular, the human infant's long period of helplessness and extraordinary need for social interaction to stimulate growth and learning have sparked interest in uncovering adaptive mechanisms that make the process of giving and getting care function at all. Human infants prefer faces, and particularly eyes, over other equally complex visual patterns, and this preference is seen as a way of ensuring proximity by caregivers. At the same time, the "cute baby-face" of the human infant (and infants of other species as well) is felt to function as a releaser of nurturant behaviors. Thus, helpless infant and (sometimes) harried caregiver are mutually aided by their predisposed reactions to each other.

Ethologists carefully distinguish their method of observing behavior in natural settings from other ecological approaches. One hallmark of the ethological method is the insistence on behavior categories containing no inferences about the motivational state of the actor. Why some behavior sequence occurs must be determined by its regular occurrence with other behaviors or environmental releasers and not assumed. The ethologist is more interested in asking "What is the function of this behavior sequence for the adaptation of the species?" It is obviously adaptive for goslings shortly after birth to follow any bright red patch, since in their natural state, this patch will belong only to their mother. It is also adaptive for human infants to prefer faces to other interesting displays, since faces alone bring nourishment and cuddling.

The tradition of ethology has been enormously useful to students of human adaptation to the environment in showing how such adaptation is mediated by specific environmental cues. With respect to the family's immediate environment, we may ask: Are there environmental cues which help "release" cooperation among family members, or privacy needs, or feelings of control over one's setting? Of course, one cannot assume that ethological concepts can be taken over wholesale and applied to the family in its environment. However, looking at an old scene from a new vantage point can often generate interesting new hypotheses.

All six approaches to human ecology share an interest in how individuals exchange stimulation with one another and with their environment. They illustrate how the application of ecosystem concepts to human relationships may illuminate family-environment relations. For example, ecological studies show that organisms have ranges of tolerance for specific environmental factors, like temperature or salinity. Within the range of tolerance, a smaller optimal range exists within which normal activity is carried out, while above and below this optimum, stress will occur (Darnell, 1973). The activity range of each individual and each species is intricately intermeshed with the others in the ecosystem, so that each individual occupies an "ecological niche . . . defined both in terms of the surrounding environment, the habitat, and the role played by the organism within it" (Darling and Dasmann, 1972, p. 40).

As Darling and Dasmann point out, every human being may be characterized within his ecological niche. Each individual is located within enlarging concentric circles of environmental forces, from the immediate physical space around him or her to the neighborhood, community, region, and nation. But the ecosystem enthusiast must be wary of letting applications of the ecological niche concept degenerate into an apologia for the *status quo*. If individuals are found in such complex interdependence, it is tempting to conclude that everyone has his allotted function in some grand ecosystem scheme not to be disturbed. As we will show, it is crucial to specify adaptation in terms of the perceptions and aspirations of the occupants of ecological niches, so that we may understand why destabilizing a human ecosystem may be ardently desired by some of its participants.

Those advocating an ecological approach to the study of human behavior (Barker, 1968) are concerned with laying the groundwork for family ecosystem theory and research. They point out that before determinants of the family ecosystem can be studied, one must first specify as completely as possible the range of normal human activity within a specific environment, thereby illustrating how certain environmental features support activity patterns, while at the same time these patterns require an environmental complex for their execution.

A basic assumption of ecosystem research states that organisms must have feedback mechanisms in order to adapt successfully to changes in environment. Similarly, they must have adaptive mechanisms that build in flexibility of behavior. Searching for feedback and adaptive mechanisms in the family leads to such questions as: (1) How does a family get information about environmental change? (2) How much control does a family have over environmental variation? (3) What kinds of adaptive mechanisms do families have? (4) Does family stress occur when the family must adapt to environmental forces outside their optimum range? (5) Is there an optimum range of environmental stimulation of a set of family behaviors?

For example, Mr. Jones, an upwardly mobile junior executive in a large corporation, is informed one Monday morning that he is to be promoted (and relocated), for the third time in two years. His wife, teenage daughter, and young son are delighted with his rapid rise but dismayed by another move so soon after the last one. Several weeks later, his wife begins to develop splitting headaches whenever she so much as contemplates packing up again, his son tries to run away, and his teenage daughter's already volatile temper begins to shade into unqualified hostility. Since such stress is not very unusual in a highly mobile, work-oriented society, a clearer understanding of its components may emerge from the application of ecosystem concepts. In the case of Mr. Jones and his family, environmental variation is precipitous and large-scale. Control over such change lies outside the family, a fact which may engender feelings of helplessness. Although this family has had some prior practice in adapting to the far-reaching changes involved in physical relocation, past experience is now only of minimal help. Perhaps the roles articulated in this family are not flexible enough for successful adaptation. It is likely that all three factors—extent of environmental variation, control over change, and flexible adaptive mechanisms—are at work. Understanding how environmental changes and family relations interact will aid others to minimize their stress, often the most lasting legacy to families caught up in rapid change.

FAMILY ENERGY NEEDS

Ranges of adaptation, feedback, and adaptive mechanisms are concepts readily applicable to family-environment relations. The ecosystem approach also deals with the fixing and exchanging of energy. The family ecosystem approach considers the energy sources available to a family. Studies of natural ecosystems have described how solar energy is fixed and transmitted via food chains. The family ecosystem, like all living systems, ultimately depends upon solar energy fixation transformed into nutrient energy. But nutrient energy composes only one level, albeit a basic one, of the energy needs and uses of the family.

It is appropriate to consider family energy needs as forming a hierarchy, similar to Maslow's hierarchy of needs (1954). Nutrient energy is basic to survival and must be fulfilled at some minimum level before other, higher-order needs are activated. Once felt, however, these higher-order needs are no less real and pressing because they are founded upon the satisfaction of more basic needs. What are these higher-order needs? Although one might postulate a limitless number of perceived needs, most families' concerns fall into several categories. Once survival needs are satisfied through nutrient energy, safety needs become dominant. The family needs to maintain its integrity as a unit, to exercise some control over the environment, and to feel itself in some sense not the victim but the master of both its physical and psychological setting. Once such safety needs are satisfied at an acceptable minimum, stimulation needs are activated. *Stimulation needs* means an optimal level of stimulation from the environment. At the lowest levels are stimulation-deprived environments, where options do not exist and where tolerable adaptations to change are not possible. At the other end lie information overload and "future shock"; stimulation levels are here too high for rational processing. Thus, stimulation needs involve both minimal and maximal levels of tolerance. Finally, *support needs* occur at the highest level of the hierarchy, the needs for interpersonal warmth, love, and commitment that family members feel both within the family and between the family and valued others in the environment. Thus, a hierarchy of needs—survival, safety, stimulation, and support—means that different sources of energy become important for the family as it articulates its needs.

Such a hierarchy requires that one consider the family ecosystem as considerably more complex an energy-exchange system than natural ecosystems. Establishing energy needs requires an understanding of the perspectives of family members, of perceived requirements as well as observer-defined minimums. The question "What are the energy sources for the family?" quickly becomes "How does the family perceive its environment and articulate its energy needs?" The distinctly human characteristics of the family ecosystem, in the importance of its perceptions and its hierarchy of needs, imply that the family's environment is always an active construction of family members. As the family perceives its world and articulates its needs, it attempts to create and maintain a supporting environment. At the same time, the family's environment exerts profound effects upon it, environmental change constantly requiring family adaptation. Thus, viewing the family as an ecosystem requires consideration of the family in both active and reactive roles. In its active role, the family attempts to achieve an optimal level of stimulation from the environment in order to satisfy a hierarchy of energy needs from survival to support. In its reactive role, the family must constantly adjust to environmental change and adapt to environmental constraints.

The organization of the text reflects this dual nature of the family as an ecosystem. The first section deals with the family and the individual family member as active agents in the creation of environments. Chapter 2 sets out in detail the conceptual framework of the ecosystem approach to the family, while Chapter 3 examines current trends in the American family in order to sketch a brief portrait of our subject. Chapters 4, 5, 6, and 7 consider four processes—perceiving, spacing, valuing, and deciding—by which family systems transact with their environments.

Later chapters consider applications of this conceptual framework to such issues as nutrition (Chapter 8), resource management (Chapter 9), consumer behavior (Chapter 10), and housing (Chapter 11). Here I show how the transactional framework may be applied usefully to our understanding of contemporary environmental issues. Finally, Chapters 12 and 13 address the dynamic interplay of changing family and changing environments by looking at sources of stability, change, and stress.

REFERENCES

Aries, P. *Centuries of Childhood.* New York: Knopf, 1962.

Astin, A. W. *The College Environment.* Washington, D.C.: American Council on Education, 1968.

Barker, R. *Ecological Psychology.* Palo Alto: Stanford University Press, 1968.

Blood, R. O. The division of labor in city and farm families. *Marriage and Family Living* 20 (1958): 170-174.

Bossard, J. *The Large Family System.* Philadelphia: University of Pennsylvania Press, 1956.

Cottle, T. J. *A Family Album.* New York: Harper & Row, 1974.

Darling, F. F., and Dasmann, R. F. The ecosystem view of human society. In R. Smith, ed., *The Ecology of Man: An Ecosystem Approach.* New York: Harper & Row, 1972.

Darnell, R. *Ecology and Man.* Dubuque: Wm. C. Brown, 1973.

Duvignaud, J. *Change at Shekiba.* New York: Pantheon Books, 1970.

Deasy, C. M. People patterns in the blueprints. *Human Behavior,* August 1973, pp. 8-15.

Duvall, E. *Family Development.* Philadelphia: Lippincott, 1971.

East, M. Family life by the year 2000. *Journal of Home Economics* 62 (1970): 13-18.

Elton, C. *Animal Ecology.* New York: Macmillan, 1927.

Encyclopedia Americana. New York: Americana, 1923.

Gouldner, A. W. The norm of reciprocity: A preliminary statement. *American Sociological Review* 25 (1960): 161-179.

Heller, J. *Something Happened.* New York: Knopf, 1974.

Hess, R., and Handel, G. *Family Worlds: A Psychosocial Approach.* Chicago: University of Chicago Press, 1959.

Homans, G. *Social Behavior: Its Elementary Forms.* New York: Harcourt, Brace & World, 1961.

Hook, N. C., and Paolucci, B. The family as an ecosystem. *Journal of Home Economics* 62 (1970): 315-318.

Howard, J. *Families.* New York: Simon & Schuster, 1978.

Hsu, F. Kinship and ways of life: An exploration. In F. Hsu, ed., *Psychological Anthropology.* Cambridge, Mass.: Schenkman Press, 1972.

Hutt, S. J., and Hutt, C. *Direct Observation and Measurement of Behavior.* Springfield, Ill.: Charles C Thomas, 1970.

Keever, C. Causes of succession on old fields of the Piedmont, North Carolina. *Ecological Monographs* 20 (1950): 229-250.

Lake Placid Conference on Home Economics. Proceedings of Conferences 1 to 10, 1899-1908. Washington, D.C.: AHEA Proceedings of 4th Annual Conference, 1902, pp. 70-71.

Lorenz, K. *Evolution and Modification of Behavior.* Chicago: University of Chicago Press, 1965.

McKenzie, R. D. The ecological approach to the study of human community. *American Journal of Society* 30 (1924): 3.

Mannino, F. An ecological approach to understanding family and community relations. *Journal of Home Economics* 66 (1974): 9-13.

Marshall, W. Issues affecting the future of home economics. *Journal of Home Economics* 65 (1973): 8-10.

Maslow, A. *Motivation and Personality.* New York: Harper & Row, 1954.

Moos, R. H. Systems for the assessment and classification of human environments: An overview. In R. H. Moos and P. M. Insel, eds., *Issues in Social Ecology.* Palo Alto, Calif.: Note Press Books, 1974.

Odum, E. P. The strategy of ecosystem development. In R. Smith, ed., *The Ecology of Man: An Ecosystem Approach.* New York: Harper & Row, 1972.

Pace, R. *College and University Environment Scales.* Princeton: Educational Testing Service, 1969.

Rodgers, R. H. *Family Interaction and Transaction: The Developmental Approach.* Englewood Cliffs: Prentice-Hall, 1973.

Ruesch, J., and Kees, W. *Non-Verbal Communication.* Berkeley: University of California Press, 1956.

Smith, R. *The Ecology of Man: An Ecosystem Approach.* New York: Harper & Row, 1972.

Sommer, R. *Personal Space.* Englewood Cliffs: Prentice-Hall, 1969.

Tansley, A. G. The use and abuse of vegetational concepts and terms. *Ecology* 16 (1935): 284-307.

Thibaut, J., and Kelley, H. *The Social Psychology of Groups.* New York: Wiley, 1959.

Tinbergen, N. *The Study of Instinct.* Oxford: Clarendon Press, 1951.

Wallace, S. Quality of life. *Journal of Home Economics* 66 (1974): 6-9.

Basic Concepts

Let us stop off on our way to the family to take a look at a small patch of seashore on the North Atlantic coast of the United States. Here all is sand, rocks, and tall marsh grasses. The quiet is soon broken by the screeching swoops of gulls as they dive down for breakfast. Low tide pools teem with life; little blow-holes in the mud mark the addresses of clams and fiddler crabs. If this book were about the family life of the typical clam, it would immediately become apparent that clam behavior cannot be understood except within the ecological context of its seashore setting. The climate, the rhythm of high tide–low tide, the behavior of all other living things form, with the clam, an ecological system, in which all parts are interdependent. Change in any one component, for example, average temperature during a season, will prompt changes in all others.

Up to now, we have been considering the clam an element in the complex web of elements called the North Atlantic seashore environment. But closer examination of the clam itself indicates that it, too, may be viewed as an environment, in which cells making up body organs are interdependent. And for that part, the cell itself turns out to be the same kind of complex environment composed of interdependent parts. So, depending on how closely the camera zooms in, this wide stretch of beach in our imagination is really a nested series of environments, all in intricate balance.

Humans are most assuredly not clams. Indeed, humans differ so dramatically from all other living things in their ability and propensity to direct their own will, symbolize, and think about themselves and their world, that the linkages among humans and their environments sometimes seem of little importance. After all, humans are masters and creators of environments, are they not? People are determiners of their own destinies, are they not?

Despite the undeniable differences between humans and other living systems, there is growing appreciation that ecological principles govern our lives, too. We are more aware now that life on the small spaceship earth rests upon a limited supply of natural resources in delicate balance. Human social organization and culture cannot be divorced from their ecological settings. Just as we zoomed in on the clam and found it, too, to be a complex, interdependent environment, so closer examination of the family unit reveals it to be a mini-world in which family members are in dynamic interaction. And the individual himself is an environment in which millions of cells organized into organs are linked by reciprocal relationships. Individual psychology, though often studied in terms of discrete processes such as perception, cognition, motivation, and the like, in reality is an interconnected whole.

Thus, an ecological perspective emphasizes on different levels common themes, among them system-environment relations, interdependence, and reciprocal change. These concepts, and others to be introduced shortly, form a structure for viewing the family as interconnected *within* and *without*. This chapter will erect the scaffolding of such a structure, which subsequent chapters will complete.

SYSTEM AND ENVIRONMENT

A *system* is simply some part of the world singled out for attention whose parts interact. Hence, a system is an *organized whole*. When the term *system* is used to refer to a set of components in interaction, the *environment* is simply all other factors (outside the system) that impinge upon it. Hence, we may consider the individual as a system and other family members as environment. Or moving to a broader level, we may consider the nuclear family unit as a system and the immediate physical setting or community or kin network as the *environment,* depending on the focus.

No matter what we take as the system of interest and its surrounding environment, the same principles may be used to think about their interrelationship. Systems may be thought of as *open* or *closed.* Closed systems exchange no information or energy with their surrounding environments, while open systems do. Clearly, all living entities are open systems. Thus, living systems may be said to have *boundaries* or *interfaces* with environments through which information and energy are exchanged. In open systems, there is a continuous exchange and flow of component materials.

Although living systems are open with permeable boundaries, they are not totally so. They take in information and energy selectively, so that the integrity or wholeness of the system is preserved. For example, despite dizzying cultural variety in diet, the human system takes in nutrients not randomly, but selectively.

Systems consist of interdependent components. Elements mutually affect one another, maintaining a balance of forces. Change in one component prompts reciprocal changes in other components, keeping the system in *equilibrium* or homeostasis.

Homeostasis may be defined as a *set of regulating mechanisms which act to maintain the steady state of the system* (von Bertalanffy, 1962). Homeostasis may be illustrated by the regulating mechanisms that maintain human temperature at 98.6° F. Decreases in temperature trigger centers in the brain which turn on heat-producing mechanisms. Metabolic rate goes up, and body temperature remains constant.

The body-temperature example also illustrates another characteristic of living systems, one related to homeostasis, namely *feedback mechanisms*. The simplest feedback model is illustrated in Figure 2.1. In feedback mechanisms, the effects of some change in the system, such as decreased temperature, are registered or fed back to the system, causing it to adjust in the direction of maintaining the steady state of the system. In general, feedback consists of the following components: (1) the sensing of information, (2) comparison of this information with certain

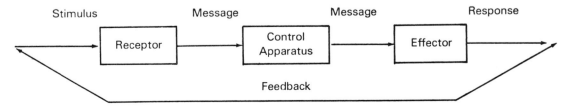

Figure 2.1. Simple feedback model. (Reproduced with permission from von Bertalanffy, 1962, p. 16.)

criteria or goals, (3) corrective action (Black and Broderick, 1972). Therefore, central to the idea of feedback mechanisms is purposive, goal-seeking behavior. Such feedback loops have been called *constancy feedback loops* since their goal is to maintain the stability of the system (Kantor and Lehr, 1975).

This view implies that developmental changes in individual family members will exert pressure for changes throughout the family. It implies, too, that marital relationships can never be evaluated as if untouched by parent-child relationships. Finally, it means that development is not a matter of parents *raising* or *bringing up* children with the implicit notion that parents mold their children to be what they become. Rather, an ecosystem approach sees the development of children within the family as a set of mutual influences, with children as active forces for change in their own right. In short, all members of the family are enmeshed together in a web of mutual influence.

Systems need not remain in equilibrium, however. Disequilibrium also occurs, system components may be in conflict, system breakdown may ensue. Change in a system does not necessarily result in corrective action to return the system to its original state. Sometimes change stimulates still further change. The technical term given to such a process is *deviation amplifying causal loop* (Maruyama, 1963). The *vicious cycle* is an example of this. A child feels ugly and unloved, eats to feel better, becomes fat, feels even more ugly and unloved, eats even more, and so on (Wilkinson, 1973).

Too often, system models of family life assume it resembles a smoothly functioning clock, each part ticking along, exquisitely attuned to the others, forever maintaining a steady state. But families are anything but smoothly functioning clocks. In fact, it often appears as if conflict, breakdown, and reconstruction are the hallmarks of families. Family forms themselves are no longer unquestioned verities, but subject to the flux of experimentation and innovation. In short, for both the individual and the family system, components will sometimes be in equilibrium, sometimes not.

Deviation amplifying loops allow a system to change its structure. They build in variety and change as integral system characteristics. This is why some analysts of family systems advocate the term *variety feedback loops* for deviation amplifying ones. They see such loops as the vehicles by which systems grow, create, and innovate (Buckley, 1968). One of the purposes of the following chapters is to indicate conditions making for stability, change, conflict, and disequilibrium in families.

Finally, it is important to emphasize that equilibrium is not necessarily a positive characteristic of family systems. Imagine a self-destructive, alcoholic husband married to a sadistic wife who takes great pleasure in hounding her sick mate into deeper misery. The abused children become alcoholics themselves. The external environment further reinforces this family's condition by labelling the husband as a misfit and denying him employment. The children are typed in the early grades of school as "no good." This stable family system is in equilibrium; each member's behavior supports that of the others. The external environment further encourages stability. Indeed, the family system is being perpetuated in the next generation. Yet, such a family not only burdens and threatens the larger environment, but also persistently stunts human potential.

Reciprocal influence operates also when we look at boundary exchanges between system and environment. Dynamic, open systems exchange information and material with their environments in such a way as to maintain equilibrium, or a balance of forces within the system. In addition, living systems are *growing* ones. They take in energy from the surrounding environment and transform it for internal use. Growing systems, while seeking to maintain equilibrium, have change built into them. They are *self-organizing,* not merely responding to external forces. They are also *self-differentiating;* they evolve toward greater complexity (von Bertalanffy, 1962). They actively seek out change in order to foster growth. The one-year-old seems driven by the need to manipulate, explore, and experience. The adolescent often questions the whole fabric of family life; the adult at midlife sometimes radically shifts direction. The dictates of autonomous growth may impel a living system toward conflict and disequilibrium. The individual and family systems are seen not as responding to external stimulation, but as internally motivated and spontaneously active.

Growth does not take place at the same rate throughout the life history of a system. Periods of rapid expansion alternate with stretches of relative stability. When individual human growth is considered, the first three years of life, along with early adolescence, emerge as critical periods of change along the route to adulthood. Recently, we have come to appreciate how much the same rocky road of change characterizes adulthood itself. The crises of later life, while not closely tied to physiological transformation, often occur at junctures of multiple psychological, occupational, and familial changes.

Just as the individual system is punctuated by rapid growth periods, so too is the family system. It is common to view the family life cycle, from marriage to the death of both spouses, in terms of periods of expansion with the advent of children and contraction as they leave home and spouses die. Increasingly, many families do not fit such neat patterns. Childless families, divorced family members who later remarry, and others show jagged peaks and valleys of expansion-contraction rather than a smooth curve. Despite the great diversity of family history, however, it is likely that all family systems are characterized by some periods of rapid growth and change.

Human systems not only are growing, autonomous systems but also are purposeful and self-directed. They should be thought of as acting *on* their environments to create as well as react to energy and information. Humans are unique in the central importance of self-image and self-esteem to their behavior. They differ from nonhumans in their propensity to symbolize and reflect about their functioning. This important property of human systems means that we can never talk about environmental impact on humans without understanding the *meaning* of such impact for those experiencing them. This self-reflective quality of human life also implies the possibility of abrupt, self-initiated change. People can be "born again"; they may radically reorganize their lives. In short, for any student of family-system functioning, surprises are in store. Human systems have their own indeterminacy principle whose source is the sense of self.

Let us summarize to this point. Human systems have been described as selectively open to the surrounding environment with permeable boundaries, in dynamic equilibrium, using feedback mechanisms, yet also self-directed and growing. Such system-environment relations characterize the individual as a system within the family environment, as well as the family system within larger environments.

Having described system characteristics, let us turn to the notion of environment. The term *environment* has gotten such heavy use in recent years that its meaning has become rather fuzzy. Air and water pollution are considered environmental issues that threaten the quality of our environment. Poor minority children are thought to experience a disadvantaged "environment." Schools are urged to provide a stimulating "environment" to enhance student learning. The term *environment* has been used and many feel abused to refer to natural or man-made physical objects, to social relations, and to qualities of change and novelty in both physical and social objects.

What are the defining characteristics of the term *environment?* Recall that earlier we defined the term *environment* relative to "system," with the former being all objects and relations among objects outside of but affecting a system of interest. Hence, the referent of environment may change as the system of interest changes. For example, if we are interested in how the individual transacts with other family members, that individual becomes the system while the remaining family members are considered the environment. If the focus shifts to transactions between the family unit, taken as a whole, and perhaps other families, the wider kin network, or the natural setting or social structure, each of these becomes an environment.

The immediate physical environment is of special interest in this book. The physical setting of the family includes its housing environment, clothing, and all the objects and resources at its disposal. Furthermore, family members' nutrition may be thought of as their internal environment.

In thinking about a family system's relations to such an environment, it is important to distinguish between the terms *object* and *environment*. Objects are "out there"; a system may see, handle, relate to them, but it is impossible to be the subject of an environment. As one writer (Ittelson, 1973) put it, the environment *surrounds* and engulfs; it is the context in which behavior occurs. Environments *involve* the system and make it a participant. Roger Barker (1954) has used the concept *behavior setting* to emphasize that physical settings carry with them expectations for proper behavior by those who enter them. Contrast a college basketball game with a college classroom. Proper spectator screaming in the behavior setting of the game would be unacceptable in the classroom.

Environments, or behavior settings, are *multimodal.* They engage the senses, bombarding the eyes, ears, nose, skin, and muscles simultaneously with stimulation. They provide *visual* stimuli (color, shape), *auditory* stimuli (pitch, intensity), and *somesthetic* stimuli (texture, temperature). Moreover, such stimulation is *redundant;* that is, the senses are provided with more information than can be processed. Therefore, part of experiencing an environment includes the selection and organization of sensory information.

It is easy to visualize the sensory bombardment of an environment like a discotheque with loud rock, flashing and pulsating strobe lights, weaving legs and arms. It is more difficult, perhaps, to realize the high levels of sensory information potentially there to be perceived in even the quietest, dullest situation. Let us imagine the dentist's waiting room as an effective contrast to the disco. The ticking clock, the background music, the softer but still alarming sound of the drill, the soft whisper of the receptionist into the phone, the murmurs of other patients, the rustle of magazines, the muted traffic noises outside, the dim whirr of air conditioning—this partial listing of just auditory stimulation indicates how much is really happening in the quietest of settings.

Another characteristic of environments is the *quality,* not just the extent of sensory information. Environments always present *contradictory, conflicting, ambiguous,* and *confusing* information, so that selection and organization of stimulation is always a complex process. The hallmarks of environments are change and variation (Buckley, 1968).

Furthermore, environmental information is never neutral, but loaded with the *symbolic meanings* of past history and present experience. To return to the dentist's office, it may be the much-feared site of painful memories. As such, everything is experienced with alarm and foreboding. The meaning of the setting is colored by all previous experiences with it, both directly and indirectly.

Despite the confusing bombardment of stimulation that any environment represents, there is at the same time a *wholeness.* Behavior settings are learned holistically as units in which physical objects, peoples' behavior and expectations, as well as the intensity and rate of stimulation, all go together.

In summary, immediate physical environments, or behavior settings, are involving, multimodal, redundant, ambiguous, symbolically meaningful, and experienced as wholes.

What implications do such environmental characteristics have for relations between environment and system? Whether the system is considered the individual or the family unit, a central system-function is to *monitor, interpret, exchange, and store recalled and synthesized* environmental information. Buckley (1968) has called this function the *mapping* of environmental variety.

DEFINING THE FAMILY'S ENVIRONMENT

Although we will be interested primarily in the near physical environment, there are a number of different ways we may conceptualize the family's environment. First, since the family is embedded in a *social structure,* this may be the environment of interest. Inkeles (1968) has identified four major dimensions of social structure: *economic, political, cultural,* and *ecological.* The *economic* dimension considers the allocation of resources such as money to the family. In this context, a family-environment issue might be how family behavior is affected by its social class. The *political* dimension considers the distribution of power in a society and how it affects the family. From this perspective, one might be interested, for example, in how political attitudes are developed within the family or in how characteristics of the political system influence family values. In the first case, the family's effect on the political system is highlighted, while in the second, the system's impact on the family is the major concern.

The *cultural* dimension focuses attention on values. Different cultures have differing conceptions of the ideal citizen and ideal family member. Traditional Hopi culture, with its docile, cooperative, and nonaggressive ideal, may be contrasted to the culture of the traditional Iroquois warrior, fearless in his boundless aggression and daring. It is thought that the family plays a crucial role in transmitting such expectations to young children.

Finally, the *ecological* dimension directs attention to the immediate physical setting, particularly the density of individuals, the arrangement of houses, the amount and type of space available to the individual and the family unit. It also considers the family's setting as a configuration of stimulation which is processed, organized, and transformed. This perspective gives rise to questions like: What is the impact of crowding on family relations? What is the relation between amount of space per individual and behaviors such as aggressiveness and compromise?

None of these dimensions—economic, political, cultural, or ecological—exists independent of the others. When one discusses the geographical setting of the family, as in studies of urban versus rural families, one is also talking about possible differences in social class and value system coinciding with the urban-rural difference. Thus, each reference point is part of an interacting system of influences, all of which impinge upon the family. For example, a family's social class (economic dimension) is largely defined in terms of the husband's occupational status and income, although the combined incomes derived from the rapid increase in recent years of employed wives often make possible a higher family social status. The husband's occupational status is largely derived from his educational background. In turn, cultural values of personal achievement, delay of gratification, and independence (transmitted through childrearing) all help to make educational attainment likely by teaching habits conducive to achievement.

Not only may one differentiate family environments in terms of the above reference points, but also in terms of differing levels of analysis. On the macro level, the family is considered as an institution in relation to other institutions in a society, such as the educational system, political system, stratification system (class structure), or religious system, and the environment is then specified in terms of issues affecting such large systems, such as population, technological change, housing availability and policy, and nutritional supply.

When the family is viewed on the micro level, on the other hand, it is seen close up, as through a microscope. The fact that the family is composed of individuals in interaction is emphasized.

Now the family is the environment and individual members are unit systems. What is this family environment? The picture which may come to many minds contains a husband, wife, and one or more natural children. As Chapter 3 will show, this family structure is but one of many forms— childless couples, divorced families, single parent families, reconstituted families, and alternative family forms like the commune. Moreover, most nuclear families maintain close and important ties with other relatives, notably grandparents. Kin-like relationships may develop with friends who become "like one of the family."

It is best, perhaps, to think of the family as a kind of *social network* characterized by intimate, long-term reciprocal relationships. This definition leaves room for a diversity of family and family-like arrangements. The interdependence and reciprocal influence of relations within the family are stressed. Each family member is viewed as a purposeful, open, information-exchanging and resource-transforming system. The family system is characterized by equilibrium or homeostasis-seeking tendencies on the one hand, and drives to maintain and enhance self-esteem on the other.

On this level, we might describe how individual development involves the child's influences on the parent as much as parental influences on the child. We might analyze how individual problems, such as mental illness or alcoholism, must be understood within the context of the family system and not as a product solely of individual psychology. On the micro level, we might also show how the effects of extrafamilial environments are mediated by family interaction patterns. Thus, while a macro approach might consider how housing quality and supply are related to family structure, a micro approach might examine how family members' needs for and perceptions of space influence adjustment to a particular housing situation. The ecosystem view of the individual within the family considers the family environment to be composed not of family members with their reciprocal relationships but rather of *family members within settings.* Thus, many family interactions take place within the context of the household in which management of space, services, machines, and products becomes important.

More systematically, in defining the environment, Bronfenbrenner (1976) has described four different levels of analysis. These levels may be thought of as a nested arrangement of structures, each contained within the next. (1) The *microsystem* is an immediate setting containing the actor (e.g., home, classroom, office). The elements of a specific place in which individuals engage in specific activities as part of their roles during specified times are integral to the notion of the microsystem. (2) The *mesosystem* consists of the microsystems regularly involving an individual. For example, a mythical Mr. Jones may divide his days between home, bus, factory, bowling league, and church. (3) The *exosystem* may be thought of as an extension of the mesosystem. The former consists of those social structures that impinge on or encompass the microsystems that involve the individual. These social structures represent the actions of major institutions operating on the local level and include the neighborhood, work world, mass media, government agencies, distribution of goods and services, and transportation facilities. These larger forces will affect the manner in which individuals function in their microsystems. (4) Finally, *macrosystems* may be defined as the overarching institutions of the culture, such as religious, political, economic, and educational systems. These represent not only the structural characteristics of the society, but also the carriers of ideology and symbolic meaning that give character to life at the micro-, meso-, and exosystem levels.

Thus, each level of analysis is more inclusive than the preceding one. Furthermore, we think of each system as linked to the others in terms of mutual influence. This is easier to understand when influence is pictured as flowing "downward" from macro- to microsystems. For example, it is clear that the educational system of a society (macrosystem) affects the organization of the community schools (exosystem), which in turn affects the individual family in relation to a particular school setting (microsystem). What goes on in this school setting, finally, will be felt in the other microsystems of the family, such as home and work settings because of the connections among microsystems (mesosystem). If a child is defined as a behavior problem at school, his behavior may undergo change at home as well. He may begin to fight with his brothers and sisters and throw tantrums or, just as likely, he may exhibit conspicuously model behavior at home, as if to say to the world, "The trouble is in the setting, not in me."

While it is easy to understand the "downward" flow of influence from macro to micro levels, the flow of influence in the opposite direction, from micro to macro, is given less attention and seems less intuitively obvious. This is because *power* differences among systems produce uneven exchanges of influence. The individual family finds it cannot change school policy. Lacking a bureaucratic structure of its own, the family is often cowed by the massive institutions impinging upon it. Nonetheless, the nested systems of the environment are in transaction with one another. Changes in behavior by individuals or small groups like the family at the micro level will be felt in other related microsystems (mesosystem).

For example, a family may begin to change expectations concerning the educational setting of its children. They may now view it as stressing achievement goals for their children at the expense of meeting expressive needs. These changed expectations may be reflected in the encouragement of emotional expression at home and during recreation as well as in the school setting (mesosystem). The new demands this family will begin to make of the school setting, if shared by even a minority of influential others, may introduce change in the allocation of community resources, the planning of school curricula, and the hiring of teachers (exosystem). These changes, in turn, may subtly affect the climate of the educational system on the macro level as a carrier of ideology. Thus, grassroots change in social institutions may come about because individuals and small groups become dissatisfied with the functioning of the institutions as they operate on the local level.

Just as consideration of differing reference points for defining the family's environment led to the conclusion that each focus was interrelated in one large transactional system, so, too, one must emphasize the connections between macro and micro levels of analysis. The family environment as perceived and acted upon in the micro level is itself related to macro forces. Family members may be in conflict because of crowded housing conditions reflected in their low social class in an urban slum. This geographical setting itself must be understood in terms of housing policies and priorities and opportunities for geographical mobility affected by the political system.

Perhaps the most important way that the individual family affects its larger environments is through *socialization*. This term refers to the process by which a culture's values and attitudes are transmitted, particularly to children. The family is considered the most important *agent of socialization*. This means that changes in society are likely to be reflected in changes in preferred styles of rearing children. It also implies that changes in family practices concerning socialization will later bear fruit in somewhat different young adults who will, in turn, put their stamp on the society's attitudes. Thus, change flows both down to the individual family and out from the family to larger environments.

The dynamic interaction of family members as individuals in the family group is never merely a pale reflection of larger macro forces. Family members are also individuals with needs, personality predispositions, and histories, which motivate them. In family interaction and transaction with the environment, they seek to maximize their own potentialities within the range of macro-derived environmental forces.

Studying the family is always complex because it requires that we consider both individual needs and personality, on the one hand, and group and institutional relations on the other. This is because the family is at the same time a collection of individuals, a small group, a part of the social system, a major transmitter of cultural values, and a basic regional entity located in space and time. As all these things, the family can only be fully understood by continually shifting levels of analysis.

Does this mean one can never reduce the complexity of the family as an object of study to manageable proportions? While keeping in mind the larger transactional system of which the family is a part, one can focus on particular transactions. Thus, one can consider the transactions of family members with each other, the purview of family dynamics, or the transactions of family members with their physical, geographical, and social environments. On the macro level the family unit itself is the system viewed within surrounding environments, while on the micro level, the individual is considered the system in transaction with the family environment. Again, it is well to emphasize that this shifting of focus should not obscure the fact that all environments, from individual cell upwards, are interdependent.

With this general picture in mind, some broad principles emerge that will guide the discussion of the family as ecosystem. First, cause-and-effect relationships are not an appropriate way to describe family functioning. The reciprocal influence and interdependence that characterize component parts within a system and system-environment relations do not permit simplistic thinking in terms of environmental attribute X causing family behavior Y. Rather than action and reaction, the term *transaction* will here be used to indicate simultaneous mutual influence. Instead of arrows of cause and effect, the explanatory analogy will be the circle. Of course, it sometimes helps to see a complex picture in terms of artificially separated segments. Thus, we will at times consider how parental behavior or values, for example, influence children's behavior, or how nutritional habits affect family interaction patterns at mealtimes. But these relationships will repeatedly be placed within the context of transactions.

Secondly, the self-directed, self-reflective nature of human systems leads us to emphasize their active, goal-seeking nature. The individual within the family is seen as striving to realize goals, to create as well as react to the family environment. Similarly, the family system is viewed as a resource extractor and transformer in relation to the environment. Such an accent on the active does not deny the existence of many times in family life when confusion and passivity reign in the place of vigorous goal-directed behavior. Rather, it alerts us to the potentialities of family functioning.

Finally, because human systems are self-aware, transactions with environments may attempt to preserve and even enhance *autonomy* and self-esteem. When families search for a way to respond to an environmental challenge, such as an economic depression, some try to choose strategies that maintain, at the same time, their inner sense of worth. One implication of this principle is the destructive impact of environmental demands that challenge feelings of self-worth.

Families, however, do not inevitably seek autonomy and the enhancement of self-esteem. Disturbed, even pathological patterns of family interaction exist in which individuals seem driven to punish and degrade themselves. If self-enhancement is a powerful motivating force, then self-destruction must also be considered, in some cases, its dark underside.

A PROCESS APPROACH

Recall that earlier we defined living systems in general as open, information-exchanging, and dynamic. Human systems in particular were characterized as being, in addition, self-aware and self-driven. These attributes refer to processes by which human systems and environments interconnect, by which, in other words, human *eco*systems operate. How precisely is environmental information extracted, transformed, and exchanged?

This approach emphasizes four major components or processes—perceiving, valuing, decision making, and spacing. In each case, the gerund word form, e.g., *perceiving* rather than the noun *perception*, is deliberately used to convey the central meaning of activity and process.

Perceiving. This is the process by which environmental information is registered by the senses, organized meaningfully, and made available for use. Perceiving is the process of deriving meaning from environmental stimuli. Hence, each individual is likely to perceive an environment somewhat differently from the way others do. Each family member relates to the family as it appears through the prisms of his or her own perceiving process. Each family, to shift to a macro level, perceives environments impinging upon it, in the light of its own history, predispositions, and interacting individual propensities.

Valuing. This process refers to the use of standards by which perceived information is selected and used. Values are rules by which environmental information and planned action are judged, both for oneself and others. The process of valuing, furthermore, underscores the importance of self-direction in family ecosystem behavior. In contrast to the clam visited earlier, the goal is not merely adaptation and equilibrium, but the maximization of values, a goal that may stimulate change, conflict, and disharmony. Valuing as a process structures the relations among individual family members. The transmission of values to children is a central family activity. The family as a system in interdependence with outside environments filters its transactions through values. Environmental influences can prompt value changes in the family. At the same time, environmental impact is mediated by family valuing.

Decision making. The family as an information-exchanging system is directed toward goals. Information is always *for* something. We may think of information as inputs into the system whose outcomes are behavior. Decision making is then the process by which information, filtered by perceptual and valuing processes, is transformed into actions. It is continuous and characterized by *appraisal* and later reappraisal of potential hazards, potential benefits, and possible alternatives (Lazarus, Averill, and Opton, 1974). Yet decision making is never wholly so rational that families make lists of anticipated pros and cons, look at the balance sheet, and act accordingly. Both rational and emotional features are an integral part of decision making. Some have suggested that rational features are likely to dominate when the decision is a "low-stakes" one, while emotional features play a greater role in "high-stakes" situations (Paolucci, Hall, and Axinn, 1977). Obviously, it is easier to be rational about a decision to replace the family car than the problem of how to deal with a terminal illness in the family.

On the micro level, decision making is a central process of family interaction, reflecting and itself influencing patterns of power, authority, communication, and conflict resolution. Individual styles of decision making are powerfully influenced by life in the family. On the macro level, when the family unit is taken as the system, family decision making in relation to the use of environmental resources, and involvement in larger, impinging environments is emphasized.

Spacing. This term refers to the importance of spatial-temporal arrangements in regulating distance and contact between family members and between the family and outside family influences. Most fundamentally, spacing refers to the process by which *autonomy,* the sense of separateness balanced by connectedness, is maintained. The individual within the family juggles these two tendencies, striking a personal balance between forces pulling toward and forces pushing away. Central to the process of spacing is self-direction and self-control. Autonomy imposed from without becomes enforced isolation (Laufer, Proshansky, and Wolfe, 1975). The concepts of privacy, crowding, and territoriality are relevant here in describing different aspects of this separateness-connectedness dimension as it is given spatial expression. The sense of autonomy is rooted in what has been called "place identity ' (Proshansky, 1973). The physical settings that are the stage sets of an individual's life are inextricably tied to his or her sense of self.

The family unit, too, has a sense of itself. Like the individual, the family is motivated to retain its separateness while remaining involved in the outside world. As freedom of choice is an important component of individual spacing, so is self-direction for the family. The spatial expression of family autonomy is most vivid in the importance of the middle-class family home as the embodiment of family identity. The importance of a psychological sense of control over one's dwelling for all families is now being appreciated. Urban public housing design often leaves occupants feeling at the mercy of a huge, impersonal setting. Some research suggests that public housing that facilitates a sense of territorial control is associated with lowered crime rates.

These four processes, for both individual and family, may be viewed together as *stimulation regulation* and *environmental control*. Spacing, for example, is stimulation regulation, because in the tendencies to separateness and connectedness are respectively movements away from or toward the stimulation provided by others. Spacing means that one strikes a personal balance between such taking-in and shutting-out so that stimulation is at a desired level. Indeed, some students of family process identify *distance-regulation* as the central activity of family interactions (Kantor and Lehr, 1975).

Environmental control refers to the important component of self-direction in processing stimulation. As one author put it (Mechanic, 1974), people approach the environment with *plans*, seeking information, shielding themselves from unwanted stimulation, keeping options open for future changes in direction. Family interactions, rather than being random, fall into recurrent patterns which have been termed *family strategies*. This term highlights the fact that family behavior is purposive. This does not mean that family members behave rationally, as they often do not, but simply that some goals underlie their actions, even if they cannot clearly state them (Kantor and Lehr, 1975). Thus, autonomy and family identity are important motivating forces.

FEEDBACK

These four processes—perceiving, valuing, decision making, and spacing—are interwoven and extended over time. Families act on decisions, things happen to them in an unplanned fashion, the development of family members makes new demands. As the family reacts to and acts on the environment in the context of daily trivia or major crises, it obtains *feedback* concerning the effects of actions taken. Suppose, for example, a family decides to move from what it feels to be cramped quarters into a larger dwelling. Perhaps the advantages of additional space and the desire to move up in the world have been weighed against increased financial burden, school changes, and other possibly negative effects. The decision itself reflected family perceptions about the needs of their family, the environmental resources at their disposal, and the supports (loans) or constraints (housing discrimination) they might encounter. The decision, too, reflected underlying family values about the importance of the family dwelling, individual autonomy, and social standing. The protracted decision-making process itself was structured by family communication patterns and decision-making styles.

Now the family has moved. The consequences of this decision are fed back to the family, filtered, of course, through the same lenses of perceiving, valuing, deciding, and spacing. Did the move realize the values articulated by the family? Did it confirm the family's perception of what needed to be done? Soon, perhaps, the bigger house feels just as crowded, the financial burdens greater than anticipated, the children miserable in the new school. Information about each family action is fed back to the family to modify the next family transaction with the environment. This information loop from environment to family to environment and back to family ensures a method of monitoring the state of the family as a system in transaction with other environmental systems.

Let us take another example, this time illustrating feedback relations between the individual system and the family as environment. A husband and wife, feeling "they never talk any more," decide to set aside one evening a week just for each other, hoping that this will revitalize their sense of intimacy. After several weeks, each appraises the new arrangement. Perhaps during the first evening they erupted into a bitter quarrel full of mutual recriminations. How the feedback of this information will affect future actions depends, of course, on its meaning in terms of the individual's values and perception. The husband may be appalled at the harvest of hatred this experiment in closeness has reaped, while the wife concludes that finally they are communicating, bringing out into the open what has been hidden too long. Each may make a very different assessment of preferred future action based on feedback.

The feedback loop has been portrayed in its ideal form. Too often families have inadequate access to information about their actions, or fail to use such information when available to inform future decisions. Most decisions are made with limited information and under stressful conditions (Janis and Mann, 1977). Nevertheless, by portraying the transactional relations between system and environment in terms of this ideal model, one can understand more clearly how and by what mechanisms families inevitably deviate from the ideal. The model provides a framework within which to understand the family in its active role as shaper of its environment and in its reactive role, as a system continually affected and limited by its environment.

In Figure 2.2, each of the feedback loops, between individual and family, family and environment, individual and environment, symbolically depicts how the four system-processes described earlier act on an environment, which in turn, changes (or fails to change) and thus constitutes a new environment within which further actions will be taken.

ADAPTATION AS SYSTEM-ENVIRONMENT FIT

As stated earlier, change within a system component, or between system and environment, stimulates reciprocal changes in other components. In other words, systems tend toward *adaptation* to their environment, a system-environment "fit" in which functioning is supported by and attuned to the environment.

A good definition of *fit* in the literature on adaptation is *the discrepancy between demands and supplies* (French, 1974). The lower such a discrepancy, the better the fit. For example, one might measure how much intelligence seems to be required for success in a particular school (environmental demand) compared to the intelligence of a given student (individual-system supply). If the difference is small, we could conclude that a good fit exists between student and educational environment, in this respect. Taking a family example, one could ask a wife: How much sharing and emotional support do you need (individual-system demand)? Her answer could be compared to the amount of free time, companionship, and intimacy her husband and children have to give (environmental supply). Suppose we found that while the wife, at home with several small children, felt isolated and lonely, her husband, burdened by career demands, had little time to spare for her. Here, system-environment fit is relatively poor.

Adaptational processes are most evident when sudden change in system or environmental properties occurs. For example, sudden unemployment requires new family decisions, attempts to

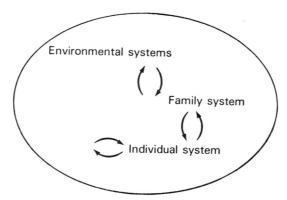

Figure 2.2. System-environment transactions.

increase resource level by seeking alternate means of income, changes in demands by devaluing some consumer items that are no longer affordable, new family actions to tighten belts. Each of these actions may be viewed as the family system's effort to stabilize at a new adaptation level. Similarly, divorce sets off a chain of changes in the relationships between parent and child, parent and grandparent, parent and friends, parents and work colleagues. Divorce also stimulates a kind of psychological overhaul of the individual systems involved. Divorcing husband and wife often find themselves changing drastically through the experience.

This view does not portray adaptation as adjustment to the *status quo.* We define adaptation as including fit between *system demands* and *environmental supplies.* System demands include needs for growth, variety, stimulation, and change. Hence, adaptation can also mean *acting on* the environment to bring about a new reality in contrast to adjusting passively to an existing one.

Furthermore, since the environment is characterized by change and novelty above all else, *environmental demands* make it necessary for family systems to be change-oriented. Family systems must be capable of *morphogenesis,* change in basic structure, organization, and values (Buckley, 1968).

STRESS

The perceived demands of sudden change in environment are termed *stress.* Stress is not something "out there," but depends upon the meanings people attribute to their experiences. What is stress for one is the spice of life for another. Responses families make to stress situations indicate their adaptational efforts in the form of coping, defense, mastery, or retreat. These terms have been used in a variety of often confusing ways. Defensive behavior, such as denying the reality of crisis, is to some an example of positive coping when it gives time for "strategic withdrawal" to gather one's strength for later action. One often sees such denial when family members first confront their own or another's death. Others distinguish sharply between positive, reality-engaging coping techniques and denial, withdrawal, and the like (Haan, 1977). Leaving the terminology quarrel aside, we will follow White's (1974) description of coping, defense, mastery, retreat, and other actions as examples of different strategies for adaptation, and emphasize that the normal business of living involves all of them.

Following the earlier definition of adaptation as system-environment fit, such strategies are used to reduce the felt discrepancy between demands and supplies. To take a previous example, if I perceive that my intelligence is not equal to the demands of my school, I might consider switching educational institutions (reducing environment demand) or sharpening my cognitive skills through extra tutoring (increasing individual-system supply). If a wife sees that her needs for intimacy (individual-system demand) are not being met by her family's willingness to share (environmental-system supply), she may seek companionship outside the family or lower her demands in some way. She may also attempt to make her husband aware of her need by discussing the problem and trying to convince him to spend more time at home (increasing environmental supply). Both reduction of demands and increase in supplies may occur at the same time.

It is important to emphasize here that the concepts of adaptation and stress do not mean that systems seek to maintain the *status quo* and resist change. Indeed, earlier in the chapter living systems were described as self-directed, growth-oriented entities. Thus, for example, a baby's need for manageable variety and exploration (individual-system demand) should be met by a home environment providing opportunities for safe manipulation of varied objects. The baby, as a human system, needs to grow, test itself, and assert its autonomy, and these demands must be met by environmental challenges, not quietude. Similar needs for self-growth, or in Maslow's terms, *self-actualization,* remain dominant throughout the life-span. This fact leads to the conclusion that stress may be as much associated with too little challenge, too little variety, or too little conflict as with too much. The key concept is fit, an *optimal* rate of stimulation. Thus, dealing with stress does not necessarily mean reducing challenge, but matching it to needs.

Moreover, stress may be actively sought out in order to reach long-range goals. When a housewife enters the labor force after many years of working at home, new system demands are often generated. Her husband and children are expected to change their behavior patterns, taking on new tasks and, perhaps, new attitudes as well. In the short run, this may increase family strain. Yet return to the old equilibrium is not the goal. In this example, stress is *intentionally* generated as part of systems change.

Another characteristic of human systems, the need to maintain self-esteem, has important implications for stress management. Strategies of dealing with stress may be chosen selectively to maintain or enhance feelings of self-esteem. As one writer (Vickers, 1959) put it: "It is the *idea of ourselves* which guides our valuations and hence our compromises." When other options are open, few students will want to conclude that because a school makes high performance-demands, they are dummies. Perhaps they have chosen the wrong subject or the wrong school. Perhaps the school faculty is unrealistic in its demands. Perhaps study habits could be improved. All these assessments have in common the need to preserve self-esteem while dealing with stress.

Adaptation may be guided, not only by the need for self-esteem and self-growth, but also by constitutional predispositions. Individuals come into the world with differing styles of processing stimulation. The active, high-energy infant may be contrasted to the quiet watcher. Some infants, too, have an imbalanced physiological system with, for example, both high activity and high sensitivity to stimulation. Thus, their style of extracting information from the environment invariably results in conflict. Such an early temperament, it has been suggested, may be at the root of the development of ambivalence (Murphy and Moriarty, 1976). Such early predispositions are, of course, affected by experience and need and can never be separated from the child's experiences with the world.

PREDICTABLE CRISES

It is common to think of stress in terms of isolated crises—death, serious illness, divorce, natural disasters, war. Such crises may be mass events or may involve only the individual family. While their importance is not denied, stress is here treated as a nearly continual feature of all family life. In the ever-changing balance between demands and supplies, stress is the perception of discrepancies in fit, and stress management is what one does about it. Of course, there are many environmental demands for which almost no one has adequate supplies. We are none of us really at peace with the death of a loved person. The full impact of a tornado cannot be experienced in advance, despite public awareness and rehearsal. Such crises are different in degree, but not in kind from the daily stresses of life. These disasters are composed of environmental stimuli of such intensity, novelty, or ambiguity that the individual or family system invariably perceives them as stressful.

Despite our emphasis on adaptation and stress as more constant than unusual features of family life, it is possible to pinpoint periods relatively more stressful than others. In the development of the individual within the family, early adolescence is a time when rapid biological changes temporarily deplete the child's stock of supplies for coping with environmental change. Late maturation relative to peers may dampen self-esteem. Raging hormones may drastically affect energy level and activity rate. At the same time, this developmental period is precisely the time when the shift from primary to junior high school brings about a whole new set of environmental demands—escalation of academic expectations, increased impersonality, more independent work habits. Parents often take this transition as the signal that their child has moved into a new role, the adolescent, and treat him or her in a drastically different manner (Hamburg, 1974). This coming together of increased environmental demands with decreased system supplies causes a predictable crisis of adolescence.

Similarly, in the development of the family system, the advent of young children during the early years of marriage has been identified as a predictable crisis. The young couple may have had too little time to resolve differences in values, communication style, needs for separateness and intimacy, or views about household management. Simply, they are just beginning to learn how to live together. Their supply of emotional and physical energy is likely to be inadequate to the demands made by the advent of young children. The early years of marriage often coincide with periods of greatest occupational struggle when the husband feels most insecure about succeeding, when a wife may have just withdrawn from employment to an unpracticed style of life. Financial supplies are likely to be lowered.

Moreover, the environmental context does not provide the young family with small children with much emotional or material support. While adolescence is culturally defined as a crisis, having a baby is not. In the United States new parents are rarely given extended leaves from work with full pay. Their work schedules are not adjusted to permit both child care and employment. Occupational demands are expected to take precedence over family needs, yet ensuing difficulties in family functioning are often analyzed in terms of personal failings. Indeed, new parents are apt to feel guilty about their stress reactions in the midst of such an unqualifiedly joyous event. Here we see how society may close off avenues of coping with crisis while maintaining self-esteem.

This brief sketch of young parenthood as a predictable crisis indicates that environments may chronically tax adaptive capacities by failing to provide ways of coping while safeguarding self-esteem. Environments may also be unpredictable, with extremely high rates of change. As Alvin Toffler describes it, modern technological societies produce "future shock" in their citizens. The only stable characteristic of their lives is change itself. The need for self-direction and growth in family systems is thwarted in repressive environments that deny self-expression. The totalitarianism of many governments is an obvious and extreme example. More subtle manifestations of environmental coercion lie in social censure of alternative family forms, discrimination against minority families, typing of poor children as future failures, or social rejection of the aggressive career woman.

The advent of young children during the early part of marriage has been identified as a predictable crisis. (Photo by Natalie Leimkuhler.)

In addition, environments, through their educational institutions and general cultural milieu, train individuals to certain styles of adaptation, teaching resignation or active manipulation, communicating powerlessness or a sense of efficacy. Class differences in adaptational style reflect very real differences in life experiences. The poor child is apt to be taught the lessons of obedience to authority his parents must practice daily. The middle-class child is shown the way of questioning, manipulation, and independence. In large part, parents prepare children for the different worlds they live in.

Throughout life, environments support certain adaptational strategies and discourage others. In complex technological societies, action on the environment by the individual family to modify environmental demands is usually impossible. The young family in the crisis of new parenthood is powerless to make the occupational policy of their employers more responsive to its needs as parents. Environmental change of this type can only come about through social action on a large scale. Thus, the new parents are forced to adapt largely by adjusting their own demands. In all these ways, environments close off options for adaptation and make others more likely.

SUMMARY AND PREVIEW

A broad sketch of the family-ecosystem approach can now be drawn. The concepts of transacting system and environment are used to talk about, on the micro level, the interdependent relationship between individual and family, and on the macro level, the interdependent relationship between family and larger environments. The latter are conceived as a set of nested environments, based upon solar energy and fossil fuels that support agricultural and industrial environments regulated by educational, legal, political, and religious environments. Transactions between system and environment are characterized by mutual change. Human systems, as open, dynamic, growth-oriented, self-directed, and self-reflective, extract energy and information from environments and transform them into system products. Human systems monitor the effects of these actions on the environment in the form of feedback and adjust their functioning so that goal direction is maintained. The goal is a fit between system demands and environmental supplies, between system supplies and environmental demands.

Such a fit is also called *adaptation*. Lack of fit is perceived as stress, and system efforts are mobilized to change demands or supply level in such a way that fit is once again obtained. Strategies of adaptation depend on both system and environment characteristics. Adaptation styles reflect constitutional predispositions. Physiological functioning varies widely in ease of stimulation processing. Thus, some individuals are initially resilient while others are vulnerable. However, early experience determines the lessons learned from such predispositions—that stress can be overcome with determined effort or perhaps that the world is unpredictable and fearful. One's entire developmental history adds its store of such lessons.

The environment affects adaptational strategies by the intensity and predictability of stimulation, by the coping styles encouraged, by the magnitude and intractability of environmental demands. Importantly, environments differ in the extent to which they encourage adaptational strategies that maintain self-esteem and family integrity.

Transactions between system and environment to maintain adaptation may be viewed as a set of four interrelated processes: perceiving, valuing, deciding, and spacing. Together these processes refer to ways in which the individual or family system actively extracts and transforms environmental stimulation to further system growth under conditions of adaptive fit. The chapters to follow consider each of these processes in detail. The analysis will focus sometimes on the individual as a system in relation to the family environment or other environments, sometimes on the family as a system transacting with other environments. While the components shift, the relationships remain the same.

In the second part of the book, the workings of these processes in system-environment transactions are illustrated by looking at environmental resource management, nutrition, housing, and consumer behavior. "Resource Management" and "Nutrition" examine how both individual and family systems extract and transform fossil fuels and nutrient energy, since the ability to develop "high-order" human resources depends upon this ecological base. In "Housing," the transactional processes are applied to questions concerning the impact of the spatial environment on families. Issues such as crowding, substandard housing, and geographical mobility are placed within the context of the family's active, though not necessarily successful, efforts to maximize its environmental control. Finally, "Change and Stability in Family Ecosystems" examines the adaptation process in detail. In the chapter entitled "Stress," both family and environmental sources of change and stability are described in the context of stress and how families deal with it. The central questions are: How may the full development of the individual within a well-functioning family environment be enhanced? How may the family system transact most effectively with its environment?

REFERENCES

Barker, R., and Wright, H. F. *Midwest and Its Children: The Psychological Ecology of an American Town.* Evanston, Ill.: Row, Peterson, 1954.

Black, D., and Broderick, C. Systems theory vs. reality. Paper presented to annual meeting of the National Council on Family Relations, Portland, 1972.

Bronfenbrenner, U. The experimental ecology of education. *Educational Researcher* 5 (1976): 5-15.

Buckley, W., ed. *Modern Systems Research for the Behavioral Scientist.* Chicago: Aldine, 1968.

French, J. P., Rodgers, W., and Cobb, S. Adjustment as person-environment fit. In G. V. Coelho, D. A. Hamburg, and J. A. Adams, eds., *Coping and Adaptation.* New York: Basic Books, 1974.

Haan, N. *Coping and Defending: Processes of Self-Environment Organization.* New York: Academic Press, 1977.

Hamburg, B. Early adolescence: a specific and stressful stage of the life cycle. In G. V. Coelho, D. A. Hamburg, and J. A. Adams, eds., *Coping and Adaptation.* New York: Basic Books, 1974.

Inkeles, A. Society, social structure and child socialization. In J. A. Clausen, ed., *Socialization and Society.* Boston: Little, Brown, 1968.

Ittelson, W. H. Environment perception and contemporary perception theory. In W. H. Ittelson, ed., *Environment and Cognition.* New York: Seminar Press, 1973.

Janis, I., and Mann, L. *Decision-making.* New York: Macmillan, 1977.

Kantor, D., and Lehr, W. *Inside the Family.* San Francisco: Jossey, Bass, 1975.

Laufer, R. S., Proshansky, H. M., and Wolfe, M. Some analytic dimensions of privacy. Paper presented at the Third International Architectural Psychology Conference, Lund, Sweden, 1975.

Lazarus, R. S., Averill, J. R., and Opton, E. M., Jr. The psychology of coping: Issues of research and assessment. In G. V. Coelho, D. A. Hamburg, and J. A. Adams, eds., *Coping and Adaptation.* New York: Basic Books, 1974.

Maruyama, M. The second cybernetics: Deviation amplifying mutual causal processes. *American Scientist* 51 (1963): 164-179.

Mechanic, D. Social structure and personal adaptation: Some neglected dimensions. In G. V. Coelho, D. A. Hamburg, and J. A. Adams, eds., *Coping and Adaptation.* New York: Basic Books, 1974.

Murphy, L., and Moriarty, A. E. *Vulnerability, Coping and Growth From Infancy to Adolescence.* New Haven: Yale University Press, 1976.

Paolucci, B., Hall, O. A., and Axinn, N. *Family Decision-Making: An Ecosystem Approach.* New York: Wiley, 1977.

Proshansky, H. M. Theoretical issues in environmental psychology. *Representative Research in Social Psychology* 4 (1973): 93-107.

Vickers, G. Is adaptability enough? *Behavioral Science* 4 (1959): 219-234.

von Bertalanffy, L. General systems theory—a critical review. *General Systems* 6 (1962): 1-20.

White, R. W. Strategies of adaptation: An attempt at systematic description. In G. V. Coelho, D. A. Hamburg, and J. A. Adams, eds., *Coping and Adaptation.* New York: Basic Books, 1974.

Wilkinson, M. Systems theory vs. tradition; vive la différence? Paper presented at the annual meeting of the National Council on Family Relations, 1973.

The Contemporary American Family: A Capsule Portrait

3

Out from the glossy pages of a magazine beams the all-American family—Father home from the office grind, Mother fresh from some baking in the kitchen, Sis and Junior with Rover nipping at their heels. Is this the typical American family or a warmed-over fantasy of the obsolete? Are we rearing an endangered species or a robust specimen? This all-American family is smiling, but many view it as beleaguered and on the defensive. Its critics charge that the really satisfactory marriage (and by implication, family) hardly exists. Most common, they say, is the couple locked in deadly contentment, civil, polite, measuring out their lives, in Eliot's phrase, with coffee spoons. In the words of one author: "Marriage has provided . . . a convenient mechanism for maintaining the physical, emotional and sexual status quo, blocking personal growth" (Leonard, 1972). The divorce rate statistics are the most common weapon in the arsenal of the nay-sayer. However, there is other more indirect but still equally gloomy evidence. For example, during the period 1964-66, fully one-third of all first-born children were conceived illegitimately, thereby creating many unwanted marriages. In addition, marriage specialists estimate that about half of all marriages are "subclinical," that is, needing marital counseling.

Others charge that the family has lost all function, abdicating its authority over socialization to schools, over protection to social agencies, over production to the world of work. The remaining function of providing emotional support is too frail a foundation to support the institution of the family. This very emphasis on interpersonal relations within the family is seen by some as pernicious (Sennett, 1970). The middle-class family, they contend, has withdrawn from the world to monotonous suburbia, intense in its internal relations, rejecting of all diversity outside its orbit. Such heavy investment in family relations makes family members guilty over conflict as unacceptable evidence that all is not well in the haven of home.

Yet others point to the contemporary travails of families as labor pains before a brave new birth. Many are seen to be actively searching for the ideal of marriage, a family unwilling to settle for deadly contentment. The search for alternative family structures in communes and other arrangements, the growth of marriage counseling, marriage enrichment, family life education, and parent education all point to the serious concern of many to enhance the quality of the family. Against this background of debate let us consider the characteristics and concerns of recent trends and future predictions.

THE SHRINKING FAMILY

The first thing one notices is that the magazine picture contains too many people. If anything characterizes the American family it is decreasing size, or as one analyst put it, the "birth dearth" (Wattenberg, 1976), as illustrated in Figure 3.1.

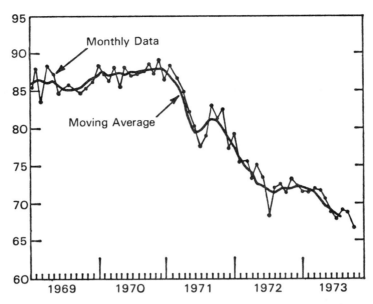

Figure 3.1. Seasonally adjusted fertility rate per 1,OOO women aged 15-44. (Excerpted from *The Real America* by Ben Wattenberg. Copyright 1974 by Ben J. Wattenberg. Reprinted by permission of Doubleday & Company, Inc.)

Women of childbearing age are delaying the onset of childbearing, and having fewer children. In addition, there is increasingly less likelihood that the household will include individuals outside the nuclear family—husband, wife and children. Hence, the net effect of both birth dearth and nuclear family units is a decreasing average household size (see Figure 3.2).

Those who speculate about the future of the American family see a continuation of these trends for several reasons. First, attitude surveys indicate that Americans are increasingly in favor of small family size, as can be seen by the figures in Table 3.1. During the last ten years there has been a precipitous drop in the number of families who feel that "four or more children is the ideal number."

Perception of overpopulation as a serious ecological problem may be contributing to this attitude shift. According to the Gallup poll (1971) 53 percent of of those in their twenties believe that "the present U.S. population is a major problem now," while only 38 percent of those in their thirties and forties agree.

Secondly, after a period of increasingly early marriage by both men and women, there are indications that average age at first marriage is again going up. In 1890, the typical groom was 26 years old and his bride 22. By 1960 he was likely to be 22 years old and she 20.3 years old. However, by 1976, the median age at first marriage had inched back up to 23.8 for men and 21.3 for women. If this trend continues, we are likely to again see marriage delayed until the mid-twenties. Since "fertility delayed is fertility denied," the later the marriage occurs the less likely that many children will be born to it.

One life-style change that has accompanied delayed marriage is the cohabitation of unmarried adults. Although the number of people in such an arrangement is still only a tiny minority of the populace, their ranks are growing. As of 1976, more than half a million unmarried couples were living together. This represents an increase of 200,000 such couples over a six-year period.

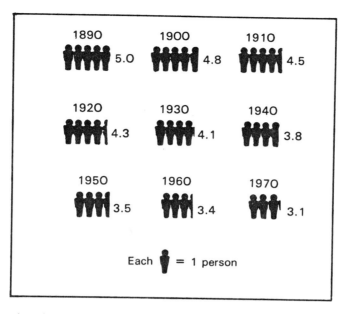

Figure 3.2. Average size of household: 1890-1970. Source: U.S. census of housing, U.S. Department of Commerce, Social and Economics Administration, Bureau of the Census. Excerpted from *The Real America* by Ben Wattenberg. Copyright 1974 by Ben J. Wattenberg. Reprinted by permission of Doubleday & Company, Inc.)

TABLE 3.1 THOSE SAYING, "FOUR OR MORE IS THE IDEAL NUMBER."

1936	34%
1941	41%
1945	49%
1947	47%
1953	41%
1957	38%
1960	45%
1963	42%
1966	35%
1967	40%
1971	23%
1973	20%
1974	19%

Source: Excerpted from *The Real America* by Ben Wattenberg. Copyright © 1974 by Ben J. Wattenberg. Reprinted by permission of Doubleday & Company, Inc.

This increase is particularly marked among younger couples. Among couples under forty-five, the number of unmarrieds living together has increased fivefold during this period. The growth of cohabitation as a life style has caused confusion about the appropriate name for such a relationship. A young woman obviously can't refer to her mate as "husband," nor is he simply a "friend," and "lover" seems too theatrical. One mock-serious suggestion has been to coin the term "spoze," derived from "spouse" to be sure, but short for the phrase often heard on the lips of parents: "We s'poze they'll get married."

For some, living together is a prelude to marriage, a kind of shakedown cruise during which the couple assesses whether their craft is truly seaworthy. For others, cohabitation is a substitute for marriage, which is not planned. There is some evidence that women tend to view such arrangements as preludes to matrimony more frequently than do men (Arafat and Yorburg, 1973; Lyness, Lipetz, and Davis, 1972).

Another life style that has gained new respectability with the trend toward delayed marriage is *singleness*. Traditionally, the single man and, even more, the single woman or "spinster" were viewed with emotions ranging from disdain to downright suspicion of evildoings. Both men and women belonged in the married state and it was "unnatural" of them to be otherwise, with, of course, some specific exceptions such as the Catholic clergy. Marriage has not lost its popularity, but increasingly being single is a respectable, if not for most an enviable, state. Not only delayed marriage but also the increased life span has swelled the ranks of the single to include, along with the never married, the widow and widower. Among whites under thirty-five, the percentage of singles has increased about 4 points (men) and 7 points (women) from 1960 to 1974, while among those over thirty-five the rate has actually decreased about 1–2 points. The latter figure may be explained by the fact that those formerly married have higher rates of remarriage than those never married. It appears that marriage is so attractive an institution that some can't resist rushing into it again and again! Among those in the singles statistics, it is not known how many are merely waiting to marry later or plan lifelong single status.

With singleness in general being more accepted, it should not be surprising that single parenthood is also gaining ground. While widespread belief still persists that a single parent is detrimental to the development of the child, some adoption agencies are beginning to permit single-parent adoptions.

Another important deterrent to increased family size is the widespread use of contraception, particularly the pill, and the increased though still controversial use of abortion as a means of ending unwanted pregnancies. Finally, the influx of married women into the labor market during the last fifty years may be deterring large family size by providing women with occupational roles incompatible with large families. Census data also support this relationship. In 1969 among employed wives aged thirty-four to fifty-four, the fertility rate was 27 percent lower than among nonemployed wives (Wattenberg, 1976).

The trend toward decreasing family size should be interpreted with caution. Despite the current preference for smaller families, most Americans still do not value childlessness or even the one-child family. Expectations about family size have fluctuated during the past fifty years; hence, a backlash swing in favor of larger families should not be ruled out. The phenomenon of rapidly rising out-of-wedlock teenage parenthood despite the availability of abortion and contraception may be the beginning of such a change.

DUAL EMPLOYMENT

Take off Mom's apron and tuck a typewriter under her arm—she's likely to be employed outside the home. A second dramatic trend has been the increase in employed wives, up from 15

Women have been entering employment in record numbers. (Photo by Natalie Leimkuhler.)

percent in 1940 to 31 percent in 1960 to 43 percent in 1974. (Note: The following discussion of female employment and the family avoids the terms *working wife* or *working mother* which imply that the full-time homemaker does not really work. The terms *maternal employment* and *wife's employment* are used.)

When rates of employed mothers, even mothers of young children, are examined, similar substantial increases are evident. In the past, childbearing and childrearing brought a complete withdrawal from the labor force. The changing trend is illustrated by the fact that in 1978, 40 percent of children under six had employed mothers or those looking for employment, an increase of 12 percent since 1970. Fifty percent of all school-age children have mothers employed outside the home, an 11 percent rise since 1970. One out of five children with employed mothers was, in 1978, in a family headed by a woman, compared with one out of seven in 1970.

In short, no matter what category of women are considered, the general picture is one of increasing rates of employment outside the home. The employed wife usually contributes about one-quarter of the family's combined income. For example, in 1977 the median income of dual-employed families was almost $20,000 compared with $8,100 in a family in which the employed mother was head-of-household.

Among the many reasons for this massive influx into the labor force are increased numbers of single-parent families—a consequence of the divorce rate—increased numbers of families in which a woman is head-of-household, and increased educational attainment for women. The women's movement has stimulated changes in legislation and public policy to extend opportunity and ensure equal treatment of women in the labor force. The overall effect of these efforts has been to create a climate of opinion in which "women's work" assumes new importance. Although most media attention has been given to expanding career opportunities for professional women and maximizing women's personal growth in achievement areas, it is well to keep in mind that 70 percent of all employed women are either single, divorced, or in families with incomes under $10,000. (The U.S. government considers a low income to be $12,000.) Thus, for most employed women, economic necessity is the major motivating force.

The effects of this increase in employed women have been the subject of great interest in recent years. When substantial segments of the population shift their behavior within a short span of time, it is likely that a host of policy issues will be created and that family relationships will be pressured to change. Thus, related to the employed-mother phenomenon is renewed debate over alternate child-care arrangements, from publicly funded infant day care to time-sharing plans that enable both parents to jointly participate in child care while employed. Since about half of all children aged three to thirteen have mothers in the labor force, it is important to ask: Who is caring for the kids? Arrangements include relatives, self-care (latch-key children), day-care home, or day-care center. Surprisingly, the use of a day-care center is the least reported child-care arrangement (Current Population Reports, 1976). The United States is the only advanced technological society without a comprehensive national child-care program (Bronfenbrenner, 1977).

When changes in child-care arrangements are proposed as national policy, they are hotly debated, some decrying the "working mother trap" (Gratz and Van Gelder, 1974) as the abandonment of children to impersonal institutional care. Others point to research showing no difference between children receiving *high-quality* care and those receiving *high-quality* care at home. It is well known that the quality of existing day care varies alarmingly. The quality of care by full-time homemakers also varies widely. They may spend only a small portion of their time in interaction *with their children,* with the rest of the day devoted to household chores and other activities. For example, one study of Michigan families (Thorpe, 1957) found that families spent only about an hour a day together, usually at meals, and farm families averaged even less time. Similarly, on examination of maternal attitudes, it appears that satisfaction with one's role, whether full-time homemaker or employed mother, is more important than the role itself. In one study of dissatisfied full-time homemakers (Birnbaum, 1971), childrearing was perceived as a sacrifice, involving duty and responsibility, with the independence strivings of their children viewed with ambivalence. By contrast, a comparison group of professionally employed women (presumably by choice) stressed enrichment and self-fulfillment in childrearing and were more accepting of the independence needs of their children. Although no direct evidence on child behaviors was provided, it is likely that the dissatisfied mothers in this study would encounter difficulties in their childrearing role, particularly as their children approached adolescence.

While much research has been directed at showing the *absence* of negative effects due to maternal employment, some feel that the long-range consequences of increased rates of maternal employment may be beneficial for both childrearing and family functioning in general. For example, it has been suggested (Hoffman, 1976) that increasing participation of mothers in the labor force will tend to make maternal and paternal roles more similar, with both involving caretaking and bread-winning functions. The wife's outside obligations make it more likely that the husband will help out at home, in both household chores and child care, although this does not usually imply equal sharing of tasks (Blood and Hamblin, 1958; Hall and Schroeder, 1970; Holmstrom, 1972). For example, studies of employed mothers indicate that an average of 26 hours weekly are still spent in household tasks in addition to their full-time work load, while the husband's time allotted to household help is much smaller. Nonetheless, it appears that college students with employed mothers are more likely to perceive their fathers as nurturant and their mothers as instrumental than are children with full-time homemakers (Vogel, et al., 1975).

Thus, the dual-career family in which both work and nurturing roles are a source of satisfaction presents the child with a multi-faceted parental model. This has been shown to affect self-esteem positively, particularly that of daughters (Kappel and Lambert, 1974). Of course, when outside employment is not satisfying, undertaken only out of necessity and without adjustments in the family division of tasks or adequate child-care arrangements, such positive effects cannot be anticipated. Unfortunately, the real-life situation of many dual-career families with young children is often a struggle to cope with the possible, not to attain the ideal.

In addition, caution must be exercised in interpreting existing research, which has focussed almost entirely on school-age and college students, neglecting the infant and preschool child (Hoffman, 1974). Moreover, since the effects of maternal employment have not been assessed over time, we do not know whether observed differences between employed and nonemployed mothers, or between their children, would persist over time.

Moreover, since the family must be thought of as a system of interacting individuals, effects of maternal employment on the child cannot be assessed independent of the marital relationship. Does the husband support his wife's decision to seek outside employment, and is he willing and able to participate in household tasks and childrearing? Is the wife's employment perceived by the husband as a threat to his bread-winning role? A marital relationship in which maternal employment becomes a thorny issue is likely to affect the wife's feelings of job satisfaction, worthiness as a parent, and guilt. Since as noted earlier, morale and satisfaction appear as factors in assessing effects on children, the husband-wife relationship is crucial.

OCCUPATIONAL PRESSURES

Just as forces drawing wives and mothers outside the home are viewed as potential dangers to family stability, so the preoccupation of men with the work world is viewed with alarm.

Particularly among middle-class career professionals, work is seldom a nine-to-five routine. The career demands a commitment of time and energy far beyond that. Many professionals work fifty-five hours per week, including frequent out-of-town trips, work brought home from the office, and preoccupation with work problems during leisure time. Those who commute from suburbs to their jobs must often add two hours daily to their working day. In short, work never stops, and the family is often squeezed in for brief, inadequate snatches of time. Daddy arrives after the children have eaten supper and is then too tired to give them much attention. Such professionals often plan a family vacation, two weeks at the seashore or on the ski slopes, designed to make up in quick doses of intensive family interaction for a year of relative absence. Such vacations, however, are often invested with too much emotional intensity and usually fail to achieve their goals.

The blue collar husband-father has other equally serious work pressures that affect his family life. He may have to take two jobs to make ends meet and thus work as long as the career professional. Although he is rarely as personally committed and preoccupied with his job, he may be even more irritated, exhausted, and unfulfilled by what he does. The deadly routine of the factory may leave him angry or apathetic. He comes home not wanting to be "bugged."

On a more hopeful note, the inroads that work can make on family life are receiving new attention from not only family practitioners, but also from those in government and industry. Flex-time arrangements, which allow a worker flexibility in putting in the required number of working hours, provide more opportunity for husbands and employed wives to find time for each other and the children. Time-sharing plans permit two workers to take joint responsibility for one full-time position; this may be an ideal solution for the dual-employed parents who feel it essential for their children to be with a parent all day. Finally, awareness in government has grown of the importance of "family-impact" statements accompanying every piece of proposed legislation. Just as environmental impact statements are now required to show how proposed programs might inadvertently affect the natural environment, it is important to evaluate before their implementation some of the potential effects upon the family of new legislative programs.

DIVORCE

In addition to the shrinking size of the family, dual employment, and work pressures, a related change is divorce. It is commonplace to cite rising divorce rates as a symptom of a deep-seated malaise in the institution of the family. Others counter with the argument that dissatisfaction with marriage has not risen, only the willingness to do something about it. It is, in this view, precisely because people are concerned about the quality of marriage that they are unwilling to tolerate an unsatisfactory one.

Let us look at the divorce statistics themselves (Figure 3.3). First, one should note that apart from the period following World War II, the divorce rate has been fairly stable from the early 1900s to the 1960s. From the postwar period to 1960, it had levelled off at about 2.2 per 1,000 persons per year. But by August 1975 it had more than doubled to 4.6 per thousand. This increase, one must remember, reflects divorces resulting from second marriages as well as first marriages. It is estimated that among first marriages only, the divorce rate is 25-29 percent. Thus approximately one in four new marriages will end in divorce, with the marriage lasting, on the average, seven years (Wattenberg, 1976). This real increase in divorce does not portend the demise of marriage and family as institutions, for most of those who divorce turn right around and marry again. It is not marriage per se which is in danger, but the assumption that married life is to be spent with one person

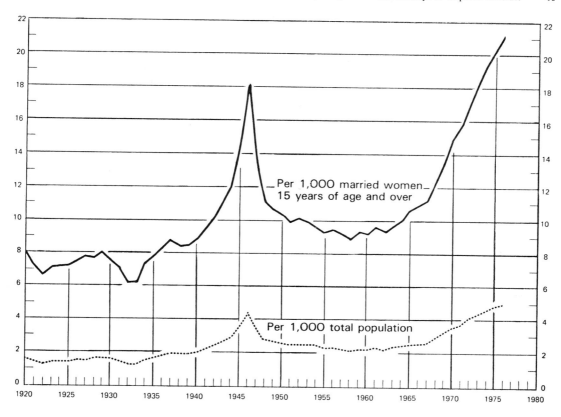

Figure 3.3. U.S. divorce rates per 1,000 population, 1920-1976. (Reprinted from U.S. Department of Health, Education, and Welfare, Vital Statistics Report, vol. 27, no. 5 [August 16, 1978].)

Largely as a spin-off from these divorce statistics, another family form on the increase is the single-parent household, particularly that headed by a female. As Figure 3.4 shows, this family form has been steadily increasing since 1930. As of March 1978, there were 8.2 million families (or one out of seven) headed by a woman who either had never married or was widowed, divorced, or separated. There are substantially more nonwhite female-headed households than white (in 1967, about 30 percent nonwhite compared to 19 percent white). However, the trend from 1960 has been for percentages of white female-headed households to increase at a *relatively* greater rate than nonwhite, which have actually decreased. Thus, the gap in racial differences appears to be narrowing. This overall increase in female-headed households is significant for several reasons. First, such families are disproportionately represented in the ranks of families in poverty. Secondly, economic necessity requires most of these women to seek outside employment, often without adequate child-care arrangements or educational preparation.

In a minority of single-parent families, the father may have custody of his children. When all single-parent households are considered, including those resulting from separation, widowhood, and single-parent adoption, about 10 percent are headed by men (U.S. Census, 1975). This represents nearly half a million families in which the father is the only parent present. Furthermore, there is evidence that the proportion of male single-parent households resulting from

Percent

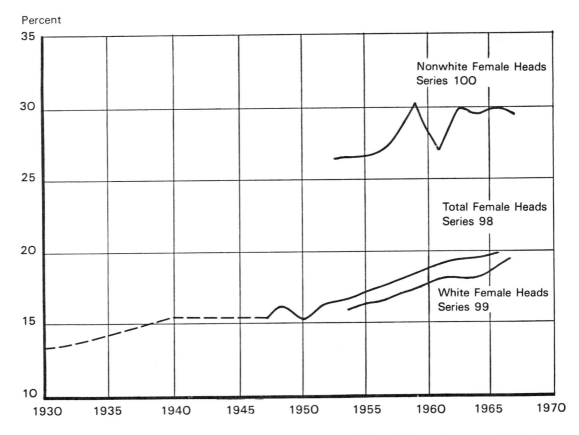

Figure 3.4. Percent of households with female heads, total, 1930-1967, and by color, 1954-1967, Series 98-100. (From *Indicators of Change in the American Family*, by Abbott L. Ferriss. Copyright 1970 Russell Sage Foundation, New York.)

separation and divorce is increasing, while that due to widowhood is declining (Orthner, Brown, and Ferguson, 1976). Some predict that the incidence of male single-parent heads of household will increase in the future, as courts no longer routinely award child custody to mothers but weigh the merits of each case. No-fault divorce legislation often includes increased rights to negotiation for children by fathers.

However, little is known about the experience of these single-parent fathers. In an exploratory study, (Orthner, Brown, and Ferguson, 1976) twenty of such fathers in North Carolina were interviewed. Most were affluent men in responsible professional or managerial positions. They had been awarded custody only after their former wives had shown inability or unwillingness to keep the children. While these fathers maintained active social lives, their nurturant role as carers for and protectors of their children assumed greater importance after their divorce.

One of the single fathers interviewed in this study provided a graphic illustration of this changed perspective. As the president of a textile firm, he had never been concerned with child-care provisions available to his female employees. He had assumed that adequate facilities had existed. After gaining custody of his preschool child, problems in finding suitable day care became a personal reality, and the interviewers reported that he is now planning a child-care center at his plant.

Divorce probabilities do not operate randomly, like throws of the dice. There are certain factors which make a family "at risk" for divorce, for example, social class, race, age, religion, and personality characteristics. The lower the social class and the younger the couple, the more likely the divorce. Clearly, lower-class families are subject to more intense financial pressures, a common source of marital dissatisfaction. Young couples may also have less to lose in terms of status, networks of friends, and organizational involvements when the marriage breaks up. Families whose religion discourages divorce (e.g., Roman Catholics) are less likely to divorce. Divorce and desertion rates are higher among blacks than whites even when social class is controlled.

It is well known that families in which the husband has an "at risk" career are more likely to become divorced than in other families. Such "at risk" jobs often include personal danger, long working hours, frequent trips away from the family, and the presence on the job of attractive, interested females. One such profession is police work, and the divorce rate for families of police officers ranges from 60 to 85 percent, the highest of any profession. It is estimated that if a policeman and his wife have been married for three years, their chances of making it to ten years are only one in four. Wives report the constant strain of worrying about their husband's safety, husbands the difficulty in communicating their on-the-job problems to their wives. In addition, the profession of police officer, some argue, demands a high degree of commitment, so much so that such dedication begins to compete with the needs of the family. As the wife of one policeman put it,

> The strain on a marriage has to do with the commitment of police work. Often he's not at home; he's working late or going to court. A policeman can't spend a lot of time with his family. It's not a job you can leave after 40 hours. He has to be as committed to the job as to his family. That's the strain (Farnan, 1976).

Divorce may and sometimes does occur without any of these at-risk factors such as early marriage, class background, or demanding profession. After all, the most common reason given for divorce is lack of communication. Problems in relating to one another in such an intense, complex relationship as the contemporary family persist no matter how benign the circumstances.

Among those attitudes associated with divorce are thought to be lack of commitment, rigidity, and inflexibility. More generally, some have argued that the increased divorce rate reflects to a large extent the pervasive "me-first" attitude of an age of self-development, where commitments to others take second place to "doing your own thing." One historian of the family (Shorter, 1975) describes how the traditional family of the seventeenth and eighteenth centuries, with its emphasis on duty, community links, and responsibility, gradually gave way to the modern notion of family centered on romantic love, privacy from community intrusion, and emphasis on childrearing. One consequence of this stress on the emotional underpinning of the family is to place the institution on a shaky foundation, for emotions are notoriously labile. Romantic ecstasy may give way quickly to indifference, even hostility. Moreover, with education and experience, people acquire a sophisti-cated understanding of the alternatives available to them in other potential unions or outside marriage entirely. These alternatives are not closed off by community shame or the weight of tradition, but represent real choices lying just beyond the present.

This greater fragility of particular marriages should not be automatically decried as a symptom of sickness in the institution of family. The historically traditional family, while stable as a rock, has been described as brutal toward children and wives, lacking totally in concepts of companionship or caring within the family nexus. Moreover, there is no contemporary evidence that remaining in an unhappy marriage out of a sense of duty and commitment has any beneficial effects on spouses or children. In one study (Nye, 1957) children from intact but unhappy homes were found to have poorer adjustment than those in broken homes.

Nevertheless, the feeling is widespread that divorce is "bad for the children." Young children often feel that they are somehow the cause of marital breakup and feel a strong sense of responsibility and guilt for the situation. Piaget tells us that the young child's world is largely *egocentric;* that is, events are seen only from the child's perspective. This is illustrated in a five year old's eager suggestion for his Daddy's birthday gift: "That big red truck!" The egocentric child has difficulty in understanding that the cause of divorce may have nothing to do with him or her. Hence, unrealistic fantasies may grow of bringing the parents back together.

Separation and divorce precipitate a host of changes in the family. Mothers who retain custody of their children (as is still the rule) are likely to find themselves in severe economic straits within a few years after divorce. Less than 10 percent of divorce cases award alimony (Weitzman, 1974). Child-support payments dwindle to nothing within a few years, and it is very difficult to prosecute defaulting ex-husbands. Sixty-two percent fail to comply within the first year and 42 percent make no payment at all. After ten years, 79 percent of all ex-husbands are in noncompliance (Weitzman, 1974). The single mother's precipitous fall in economic status is translated for the child into a new neighborhood and new school, fewer toys, treats, and outings, and perhaps communication of abiding resentment against the one-time provider.

Meanwhile, women who have failed to sharpen marketable skills during their years of work as full-time homemakers find that this "work" is not perceived as much by the outside world. A painful retraining process must begin if the "displaced homemaker," as she is now being called, is to get on her own feet again.

While the divorced husband-father has been neglected in research, the adverse effects of divorce upon him may be gleaned from descriptive accounts. The divorced father must find a way to retain an effective role as a "weekend parent," if he is lucky enough to live fairly close to his children. Otherwise, he must endure long absences. Time spent with his children tends to acquire the intensity and urgency earlier described as characteristic of busy executive fathers who set aside a week or two vacation for the family. The father may lack adequate quarters to make his children feel at home. Outings with them may assume an unrealistic holiday air rather than reflect daily emotional highs and lows. Finally, if remarried, the divorced father may feel pressures from his new family not to spend so much time with the old. The strains that divorce inflicts upon both men and women are reflected in reports of lowered happiness and satisfaction with life. A major national survey (Campbell, Converse, and Rodgers, 1976) concluded that marital status was one of the most important predictors of satisfaction. Both the divorced and never married felt much bleaker about their lives than their married cohorts.

When the family is viewed as a system of interacting individuals, it is clear that tensions felt by both divorced mother and father will have repercussions on the children. For example, in one study of husbandless mothers in a housing project (Kriesberg, 1967), these women were more demanding of their children but also more dissatisfied with them than mothers with husbands at home. At the same time, the single mothers used more inappropriate means of encouraging their children, urging the child to do better rather than using specific helping techniques.

Some research has indicated that boys raised by single mothers may fail to achieve a strong masculine identification. However, other studies show that when the single mother is able to take on some of the traditional functions of the absent father, her child's (particularly her son's) development will not be hampered. For example, in several studies by Biller (1969, 1971) single mothers who encouraged masculinity in their boys, by engaging in rough and tumble play, had boys whose masculine identification was no different from boys in dual-parent homes.

While the negative impact of divorce has been emphasized, it is perhaps worth repeating that no evidence exists to suggest that remaining in an unsatisfactory union is in any way superior.

Moreover, in one examination of remarriages (Bernard, 1956), over 80 percent of the sample studied made satisfactory unions the second time around. In these cases, during the second marriage, the couple reportedly had greater maturity and "will to succeed."

Hence, the divorce rate per se cannot be cited as direct evidence for the breakdown of the family as an institution. It does indicate, however, that increasingly the marriage union itself is considered fair game if the goals of marriage partners are not being met. Commitment to the institution of marriage has undoubtedly weakened if measured in terms of willingness to dissolve unsatisfactory unions.

EXPERIMENTS IN FAMILY ORGANIZATION

Questioning of the marriage institution is also reflected in recent interest in alternative family forms, such as the commune and other multiple-family arrangements. These forms may involve intentional experiments with the distribution of tasks and relationships, or may be accidental by-products of social change. The commune has been the most publicized intentional innovation in family organization in recent years. Such intentional communities have a long tradition in American history, stemming from the well-known nineteenth-century examples of New Harmony and Oneida. While few have endured, experiments in communal living have always been part of the American landscape.

The Israeli kibbutz, or collective settlement, has provided a contemporary model of multiple-family living. Although these historical and cross-cultural examples of intentional communities differ in ideology, goals, and organization, some fundamental similarities exist. For example, in each case the intentional community is seen as correcting some fundamental ills in family functioning. At the beginning of this century, the founders of the Israeli kibbutz movement wished to do away with authoritarian family structure. It was felt that an unhealthy parent-child relationship resulted when the father was the sole source of economic support. If children could be cared for by the whole community through trained child-care specialists, both parents would be released to work, and the child's love and discipline would no longer be concentrated in the same individuals, his parents, thereby creating ambivalence and neurosis. Women would be "emancipated" from housework and child care as exclusive preoccupations and freed to become productive contributors to the overall well-being of the community.

To achieve these ends, the kibbutz espoused communal ownership of all property according to the principle "from each according to his ability, to each according to his need." Child care would be a collective responsibility, with all children reared together in children's houses under the care of members specially trained in child care as a profession. Fragmentation into family groups would be discouraged through communal dining, decision making, and equality in income, dress, and general possessions.

Children nevertheless remained clearly attached to and identified with their parents, spending two hours daily with them after work and all day on the Sabbath, their parents' only leisure time. Parent-child harmony was emphasized at these times, with daily discipline left up to the *metapelet,* or child-care specialist. The entire kibbutz community took collective responsibility for the welfare of all the children so that there would be no question that, in the event of parental death or divorce, a child's needs, both material and emotional, would continue to be met.

Since the founding of the original *kibbutzim* (plural of *kibbutz*) at the beginning of this century, their numbers have grown to approximately two hundred communities, making up about 3 percent of the Israeli population. Over time both the philosophical underpinnings and the character of daily living have undergone change, and the kibbutz is now by no means a uniform institution. In some, children sleep with their parents, spending only their daytime hours in the children's houses. Family identity has grown strong and now poses to kibbutz ideologues a threat to the communal philosophy. Despite early emphasis on equality for women, their roles have become increasingly traditional. The *metapelet* is without exception a woman, and cooking, cleaning and ironing are still "women's work." While all individuals are granted equal voting rights as kibbutz members, those elected to important committees, such as the one which assigns work duties or handles the budget, are almost invariably male.

If the kibbutz experiment provides any lessons for the American family, one of them must be that ideological visions of radical reorganization of family life do not necessarily turn out precisely as planned. Another lesson, however, remains. The kibbutz in general has been a success. Most children reared there feel positively identified with its way of life and often remain to raise their own families. Moreover, kibbutz members, while only a small fraction of the Israeli population, are disproportionately found in the ranks of their society's leaders in government and military. Thus, while radical restructurings of family life may not take quite the intended form, they can be realized and can raise loving, competent members of society.

Like kibbutz founders, those involved in contemporary American communes (most of which are of short duration) are motivated in large part by dissatisfaction with alienating work, nuclear-family isolation, and lack of expressiveness in interpersonal relations. During the 1960s, dozens of hippie communes were formed as part of a youthful rebellion against parental values. Most sought not so much a restructuring of the family, as had the kibbutz, but a redefinition of society's values, away from a work ethic toward a person ethic, away from the city back to nature, away from aggression and assertiveness to nonviolence and calm. Often drugs such as LSD were used to achieve the desired personality changes.

The seventies, with the passing of the hippie movement as a mass phenomenon, have produced from these common motives a dizzying array of structures. In one investigative article (Kanter, 1973), the following communal arrangements were described: (1) a hippie-style family of twenty-seven adults and thirteen children, (2) a family of nine middle-class adults who planned to share living quarters, money, children, and sex, and (3) a cooperative arrangement between two families sharing everything *but* sex. *The Modern Utopian,* a journal of the commune movement, listed in 1969 about two hundred intentional communities in the United States, although the actual number was estimated to be substantially above that. They may be urban or rural; highly organized with a coherent philosophy or anarchistic, with high turnover. Students of the contemporary American commune movement (Berger et al., 1971; Berger, Hackett, and Millar, 1972; Kanter, 1973) feel that the urban-rural difference is a basic one. Urban communes are easier to start but require less commitment by their members. In an urban commune, a number of people

In congregate living arrangements, the elderly share cooking, housekeeping, and most important, companionship. (Photo by Natalie Leimkuhler.)

simply need to move into a large enough house and may retain their old jobs in the city, while the rural commune requires a geographical move, change of work, and immersion in a totally different life style.

While diversity among communes has been emphasized, Ogilvy and Ogilvy (1972), themselves members of an urban commune, feel that diversity similarly exists *within* the commune. The Ogilvys described two camps, the *monists* and the *pluralists*. The former stress a common core of shared values while the pluralists emphasize "doing your own thing." When monists and pluralists exist within the same commune, as the Ogilvys feel they often do, this is a source of intragroup tension not easily resolved.

In addition to tensions from within, communes often face problems from without. They may pose a threatening example to their more traditional neighbors, particularly if commune members themselves are convinced of their own superiority. In general, the intense interactions within the commune membership may make it difficult to sustain outside-group interactions.

The way children are raised may reflect a rebellion against what are perceived as uptight middle-class values. The emphasis is on letting the child "do his or her own thing." Communal responsibility and sharing are stressed, a sharp contrast to the values of independence, autonomy, and personal achievement that informed their own parents' childrearing. One study of rural California communes (Berger et al., 1971) depicted them as extended families, with one group even adopting the same surname. Aggression among "family" members was strongly discouraged; in fact, the suppression of aggression was the only area in which adults sought to control and modify children's behavior directly.

This emphasis on expressiveness and personal freedom means that most American communes, in contrast to the Israeli kibbutz, are not concerned about the continued existence and strength of their way of life. That is, they do not emphasize the importance of teaching their children to perpetuate the commune as a distinctive mode of family organization.

At present we do not know what long-term effect childrearing in the American commune setting will have. Will their children eventually reenter the "rat race" from which their parents sought to shield them? Will they infuse the "other America" with values of sharing and interpersonal caring? Will they remain to perpetuate the commune, perhaps in an altered form?

While these questions must await the future, the brief history of contemporary communes already indicates that a number of young Americans genuinely feel a lack of community, sharing, and acceptance in the world of their parents. Indeed, the notion of establishing intentional communities for isolated individuals and families is increasingly appealing in a climate of rapid social change that leaves many feeling isolated. For example, interest has developed recently in "congregate living" for some of the estimated 1.1 million elderly who could manage living outside institutions if they had an alternative. Just such an alternative is provided by Weinfeld Group Living Residence outside Chicago, a communal environment for about a dozen women, average age eighty-two (Wax, 1976), where cooking, household maintenance, and—most important—companionship are shared.

Some behavorial scientists concerned about the problems of the elderly have even begun discussing polygyny, the practice of having more than one wife for a single husband, for the aged as a means of alleviating the loneliness of many widows while at the same time providing mutual support for many elderly.

Though less common than intentional communities, some experiments with group marriage have been reported and studied. One study (Constantine, 1973), was able to locate only about forty such groups, of whom twenty-six agreed to be interviewed. Less than half of these twenty-six were still in existence after one year. The average age of these groups was about thirty and most came from professional occupations. In contrast to kibbutz founders and most commune members, those in group marriages did not see themselves as rebelling against the inadequacies of parental values or family organization. Rather, they wished to enhance their lives and expand their potential to experience intimate closeness, including sexual relations with more than one person. Such experiments tend to be short-lived because the usual tensions of "pair-bonding," the marriage of one man and one woman—jealousy, sexual incompatibility, lack of communication, conflict over decision making and division of labor—simply multiply as family members do.

Experts on marriage and the family are also exploring ways of providing group supports to nuclear families wishing to preserve their independent existence. For example, one suggestion (Stoller, 1970) has been the "intimate network of families." In this arrangement groups of three or four families meet regularly, sharing their innermost concerns, monitoring and counselling one another, and exchanging services. The advocate of such networks recognizes the strong American need for privacy but feels that balancing both privacy and connectedness enriches the family. In this way they form an encompassing wider circle of support while preserving the boundaries of their immediate nuclear families.

Communes, group marriage, intimate networks of families—to what degree do these experiments hold interest and appeal for the vast majority of Americans who remain in traditional family forms? Are these experiments merely bits of exotica or do they indicate growing trends? One study explored the preferences of nonparticipants for ten different family forms (Jurnich and Jurnich, 1975). Their results indicated that monogamy, both legal and nonlegal, was clearly the first choice. However, women ranked monogamy, affairs, and serial monogamy higher than did men who in turn found communal marriage and polygamy (here defined as one man with two wives) more appealing. University-affiliated people were much more receptive to experiments in family forms than those from the same social class but not university-affiliated.

Finally, those already married regarded traditional family forms as both more feasible and conducive to personal growth than did singles. One must conclude from this exploratory study that innovation in family forms is not of compelling interest to most Americans at present, although tolerance for diversity may be growing. In fact, the national survey of reported satisfaction with life mentioned earlier (Campbell, Converse, and Rodgers, 1976) emphasized the greater dissatisfaction of those outside traditional wedded existence.

Despite continued acceptance of the model nuclear family as an institution, unions with particular partners remain shaky. Hence, the pooling of families in new family forms may also be an unintentional by-product of other changes such as divorce. For example, as divorced persons with children marry each other, the "reconstituted" or "blended" family is becoming more common (Figure 3.5). When each child maintains a relationship with a biological parent living within another nuclear family unit, this creates a kind of extended family system.

To take a fictitious illustration, when Mr. Jones, a divorced parent of two boys, Bill and Tom, marries Ms. Smith, a divorcee with two girls, Jane and Mary, these six people form a nuclear family system. However, Bill and Tom continue to spend regular intervals with their mother who has remarried a widower with two children, while Jane and Mary maintain close ties to their biological father now remarried to a divorcee with several children. This by no means rare example illustrates that any one child may have sibling-like relations with as many as seven other children, although he has only one full sibling. Similarly, each adult has a relationship with five other adults. Research is needed to uncover the special problems and potential strengths of this new family organization.

Other unintentional changes in family structure are by-products also of divorce and remarriage rates. One example is serial monogamy. Since most of those who divorce remarry within four years, the rising divorce rate is breeding a new type of family structure characterized, like musical chairs, by different partners at successive stages of the life cycle.

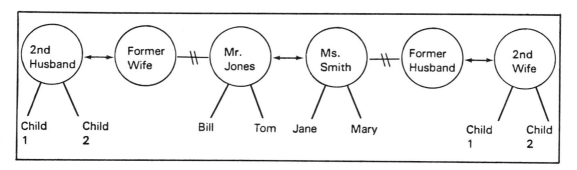

Figure 3.5. The complexities of a reconstituted or blended family.

There is another experimental departure from the traditional definition of marriage as a union between at least one man and one woman, namely union between members of the same sex, gay marriage. Although not legally recognized, gay marriage has become more common as part of a recent trend toward greater homosexual assertiveness and demand for tolerance, if not acceptance. A small faction of the women's movement has also espoused lesbianism as the path toward total liberation from men.

Looking over the experiments in family organization on the contemporary American scene, the key word is *diversity*. Increasingly, individuals are recognizing that they have choices about the timing, form, and permanence of the unions they make with others. While long-lasting heterosexual pair relationships remain overwhelmingly the norm, some by intention or accident find themselves in other arrangements. As their numbers swell, so does interest in the options they represent. If one were to hazard a guess about the future, a not-too-distant time might be envisioned when individuals who speak of getting married or starting a family are routinely asked which kind.

Yet this picture can also be overdrawn. The family still has primary responsibility for sexual expression, reproduction, and nurturance. In addition, it plays a prominent role in the socialization of children, particularly during the early years. The family has come to assume increased importance as an emotional refuge from the harsh world of work and the heavy demands of external institutions. Because of this increased emphasis on the function of the family as haven, emphasis on the expression of love and insistence that marriage be emotionally satisfying may be underlying causes for greater willingness to dissolve unions which fail to fulfill these needs.

EMERGING FUNCTIONS OF THE FAMILY

It is a misconception to view the family's only remaining functions as emotional support, sexual expression, and early nurture. The family, while no longer a major production unit, has emerged as the major *consuming* unit in a consumer-oriented society. Individual family units consume most of the nation's fossil-fuel energy in the form of heating and automobile fuel. Shopping for food and other purchases absorbs the entire family and serves as an organizing structure for much of their nonworking time. Indeed, one might almost say that the contemporary family *exists* to consume.

Consumption may also be viewed as a strategy for effectively manipulating one's environment. Family members must perceive their options amid a dazzling array of choices, rank them, relate these possibilities to their goals and underlying values, develop some procedure for arriving at decisions, be able to translate plans into actions effectively, and finally be able to monitor the effects of such actions.

The development of consumer skills is an important family function. Gartner and Riessman (1974), in their book *The Service Society and the Consumer Vanguard,* argue that economic development has passed from an agricultural through an industrial into a new service phase. Basic values are now service values that emphasize the humanization of work; improved quality of life and the environment; expansion of consciousness; reduction of hierarchy, bureaucracy, authority, and centralization; and the development of the self. The consumer wants not merely more but better. For the consumer vanguard at least, the focus has shifted from material resources to human services.

If the dawning of a new consumer age is upon us, it may be the family that is most able to adapt to such changes in society. As children are raised, societal changes are translated to the next generation, and children are thus provided with coping techniques for dealing with change (Vincent, 1966). At the same time, further social change is stimulated as families produce individuals with a new and different outlook.

Thus, the functions of the family have not disappeared but changed. The family unit itself has shrunk and centered upon its consumer and interpersonal functions as a miniworld, a haven from the outside. At the same time, alternate family forms indicate the need some feel to establish broader linkages in order to restore feelings of connectedness with others and to bring isolates into family systems.

The character of the contemporary American family is one in which environmental transactions play a central part. The family is a translator of societal change, is the major consumer of environmental products, and is seen as the chief source of stability in a world of rapid change.

REFERENCES

Arafat, I., and Yorburg, B. On living together without marriage. *Journal of Sex Research* 9 (1973): 97-106.

Bernard, J. *Remarriage*. New York: Rinehart and Winston, 1956.

Berger, B., Hacket, B., Cavan, S., Zickler, G., Miller, M., Noble, M., Theiman, S., Farrell, R., and Rosenbluth, B. Child-rearing practices of the communal family. In A. S. Skolnick and J. H. Skolnick, eds., *Family in Transition*. Boston: Little, Brown, 1971.

Berger, B., Hackett, B., and Millar, R. M. The communal family. *The Family Coordinator* 21 (1972): 419-427.

Biller, H. B. Father absence, maternal encouragement, and sex-role development in kindergarten age boys. *Child Development* 40 (1969): 539-546.

Biller, H. B., and Bahm, R. M. Father absence, perceived maternal behavior, and masculinity of self-concept among junior high school boys. *Developmental Psychology* 4 (1971): 178-181.

Birnbaum, J. A. Life patterns, personality style and self esteem in gifted family oriented and career committed women. Unpublished doctoral dissertation, University of Michigan, 1971. Cited in L. Hoffman, Effects of maternal employment on the child: A review of the research. *Developmental Psychology* 10 (1974): 204-228.

Blood, R., and Hamblin, R. L. The effect of the wife's employment on the family power structure. *Social Forces* 36 (1958): 347-352.

Bronfenbrenner, U. Nobody home: The erosion of the American family. *Psychology Today* 10 (1977): 40-47.

Campbell, A., Converse, P. E., and Rodgers, W. L. *The Quality of American Life*. New York: Russell Sage Foundation, 1976.

Constantine, L., and Constantine, J. *Group Marriage*. New York: Macmillian, 1973.

Current Population Reports Population Characteristics. U.S. Department of Commerce, Bureau of the Census. 298, October 1976.

Farnan, J. Policeman's career takes toll of marriage family life. Gannett News Service article, February 12, 1976.

Ferriss, A. L. *Indicators of Change in the Family*. New York: Russell Sage Foundation, 1970.

Gartner, A., and Riessman, F. *The Service Society and the Consumer Vanguard*. New York: Harper & Row, 1974.

Gratz, R. B., and Van Gelder, L. Double jeopardy: The working motherhood trap. *Redbook,* October 1974, pp. 38-42.

Hall, F. T., and Schroeder, M. P. Time spent on household tasks. *Journal of Home Economics* 62 (1970): 23-29.

Hoffman, L. Effects of maternal employment on the child: A review of the research. *Developmental Psychology* 10 (1974): 204-228.

————. Address to National Council on Family Relations, New York, 1976.

Holmstrom, L. L. The two-career family. Paper presented at the conference of women: Resources for a changing world, Radcliffe Institute, Radcliffe College, Cambridge, Mass., 1972.

Jurnich, A., and Jurnich, J. Alternative family forms: Preferences of nonparticipants. *Home Economics Research Journal* 3 (1975): 260-265.

Kanter, R. M. *Communes: Creating and Managing the Collective Life.* New York: Harper & Row, 1973.

Kappel, B. E., and Lambert, R. D. Self worth among children of working mothers. Unpublished manuscript, University of Waterloo, 1972. Cited in L. Hoffman, Effects of maternal employment on the child: A review of the research. *Developmental Psychology* 10 (1974): 204-228.

Kriesberg, L. Rearing children for educational achievement in fatherless families. *Journal of Marriage and the Family* 29 (1967): 288-301.

Leonard, G. The man and woman thing. In G. Carr, ed., *Marriage and Family in a Decade of Change.* Reading, Mass.: Addison-Wesley, 1972.

Lyness, J., Lipetz, D., and Davis, K. Living together: An alternative to marriage. *Journal of Marriage and the Family* 34 (1972): 305-311.

Manpower Report of the President including reports by the U.S. Department of Labor and U.S. Department of Health, Education and Welfare, transmitted to the Congress, April 1975.

Nye, I. Children in broken and unhappy unbroken homes. *Marriage and Family Living* 19 (1957): 356-361.

Ogilvy, J., and Ogilvy, H. Communes and the reconstruction of reality. In S. Teselle, ed., *The Family, Communes and Utopian Societies.* New York: Harper & Row, 1972.

Orthner, D. K., Brown, T., and Ferguson, D. Single parent fatherhood: An emerging family life style. *The Family Coordinator,* October 1976, pp. 429-437.

Rossi, P. *Why Families Move.* Glencoe, Ill.: The Free Press, 1955.

Sennett, R. *The Uses of Disorder.* New York: Knopf, 1970.

Shorter, E. *The Making of the Modern Family.* New York: Basic Books, 1975.

Stoller, F. The intimate network of families as a new structure. In H. Otto, ed., *The Family in Search of a Future.* New York: Appleton-Century-Crofts, 1970.

Thorpe, A. C. Patterns of family interaction in farm and town homes. Michigan Agricultural Experiment Station, Technical Bulletin No. 260, 1957.

Vincent, C. E. Familia spongia: The adaptive function. *Journal of Marriage and the Family* 28 (1966): 29-36.

Vital Statistics Report. U.S. Department of Health, Education and Welfare. Vol. 27, No. 5, August 16, 1978.

Vogel, S. R., Broverman, I. K., Broverman, D. M., Clarkson, F. E., and Rosenkrantz, P. S. Maternal employment and perception of sex roles among college students. *Developmental Psychology* 3 (1970): 384-391.

Wattenberg, B. *The Real America.* New York: Capricorn Books, 1976.

Wax, J. "It's like your own home here." *New York Times Magazine,* November 21, 1976.

Weitzman, L. J. Legal regulation of marriage: Tradition and change. *California Law Review* 62 (1974): 1169-1186.

Perceiving

4

The family's knowledge of the world comes from the active process of perceiving. In a real sense, what *is* is what is perceived. Family perceptions provide the raw materials of environmental information upon which family decisions and family actions will be based. If we consider the family ideally as actively trying to maximize its goals, then ability to do this will depend upon the perceiving process. Does the family accurately perceive its resources and how such resources are related to reaching goals? For example, if one family goal is to move to a new home within the year, does the family perceive how their income and savings will or will not facilitate the move? How does the family perceive the environment itself? Can they foresee change and adapt to it? How receptive is the family to new information?

Before one can talk about a *family's* perception of the environment, it is important to consider briefly the nature of perception, individual perceptual styles, and cultural influences on perception.

Let us consider the nature of perception itself. Perceiving may be defined as the *process by which meaningful information is extracted from physical stimulation.* Perceiving is a complex experience, involving organization and action as well as sensory input. Perceiving must be understood within the total environmental network within which it takes place, both as a source of information and as an arena for action.

All organisms, including man, live as part of a larger environmental context. Information concerning this context is received through the sense organs. Thus, perceiving is critical as the informational link with the environment, the means by which the adaptive functioning of the organism is made possible.

THE NATURE OF PERCEPTION

Traditional views of perception considered the stimulus as the determinant of what was perceived. A stimulus such as a light was received by an appropriate sensory receptor, in this case the eye, and transmitted in the form of impulses along the optic nerve to the brain where it was perceived by the individual as "light." Recent evidence, however, requires us to reject this simplistic model of perception. We now know that while the stimulus is involved as a source of information, perception is never wholly determined by the stimulus but in fact is surprisingly free of it. Perception is a process of *interpretation* based on what has been previously perceived.

This idea of stimulation as information means that the total context in which a stimulus occurs is important. Knowledge of the environment as a whole and of the probabilities of one type of information versus another is also crucial. The traditional view of the stimulus as determinant of perception might be summed up by the phrase "seeing is believing." It it tempting to consider recent evidence for interpretation and modification of the meaning of stimulation by the perceiver as indicating an opposing truth: "believing is seeing" (Ittelson, 1973). Yet neither statement is true. The perceiver brings interpretative capacities to the stimulation received, which in turn affects the perceiver, so that mutual influence is involved.

Emphasis on the relative freedom of perception from the stimulus itself implies that perceivers with differing needs and personalities will view the same stimulation differently. Research to be discussed later in this chapter on perceptual-cognitive styles illustrates this idea. A second implication is that perceivers in environments that differ in significant ways will come to perceive their world differently. Indeed, cross-cultural studies of perception (Allport and Pettigrew, 1957; Antonovsky and Ghent, 1964; Deregowski, 1968; Hallowell, 1957; Segal, Campbell, and Herskovits, 1966) have shown this to be true. Other studies have created artificial environments through the use of distorting lenses (Rock, 1966), and their wearers show long-term adaptation to such visual distortions.

Thus, it appears that the environment does color the inhabitants' perception. But exactly how does the environment shape the way perceivers think, feel, and act? One way the effects of the environment upon thinking, perceiving, and valuing may be studied is through investigation of cognitive or mental maps, mental representations of the environment. A discussion of cognitive maps follows later in this chapter.

In summary, from a view of perception as sensory stimulation of receptors have evolved several principles. (1) The perceiver affects what is perceived. (2) The environment within which stimulation occurs is important. Perceivers in differing environments will perceive the same stimulus objects differently. (3) Perception is the processing of environmental information; hence, the particular sensory organs affected are less important than the integration and processing functions themselves.

Current thinking about environmental perception has come far from the stimulus-sense organ —impulse-perception model. A recent formulation (Ittelson, 1973) has identified five processes that occur simultaneously and in an interrelated fashion during perception: affect, orientation, categorization, systematization, and manipulation. *Affect* may be defined as the emotional impact of perception. Examples of *orientation* are the identification of escape routes in novel negative environments. A move to a new neighborhood is usually accompanied by the need to orient oneself to important features such as the grocery store, laundry, school, shopping center, and playground. The third process, *categorization,* involves developing categories for understanding the environment. *Systematization* refers to the identification of regularities in the environment so that despite a constantly shifting perceptual world in which nothing is exactly the same twice, the world appears relatively stable. Finally, the active relationship of the perceiver to the environment emphasized earlier implies that the process of *manipulation* will be important. The perceiver always asks implicitly what kinds of interventions can be brought about in this environment.

Following this, the best way to evaluate the appropriateness of a family's perceptions of the environment would be to ask how such perceptions facilitate achieving family goals. Many of those involved in the study of man-environment relations through design of environments, through the study of families in interaction, and through an exploration of environmental issues, feel that the perceptions of those using an environment in terms of their goals and intentions must be understood in evaluating the person-environment "fit" of any setting. It is not enough for designers to agree on aesthetic beauty or economy of design if users are not able to realize their goals within that setting. Thus, this pragmatic view of perception requires the union of psychologists, family specialists, and others in the social sciences with those in design fields, and this growing cooperation has been reflected in the recent establishment and growth of multi-disciplinary organizations such as the Environmental Design Research Association (EDRA) and the Association for Man-Environment Relations (ASMER).

HUMAN PERCEPTUAL APPARATUS

Having briefly discussed the nature of perception, let us turn to the human perceptual apparatus. It is an interesting evolutionary fact that the perceptual equipment of an organism is uniquely adapted to the environment in which the organism lives and from which information must be gleaned. While this basic fact is true for humans as well, an important difference sets off *homo sapiens* from all the rest. Humans have the capacity to extend and modify their receptor system through cultural and technological innovation. Television lets us "see" on Mars. The gourmet has exquisitely functioning taste buds. Cultural variation may emphasize one receptor and discourage another as sources of information about the environment. This plasticity and variability in human receptor use means that one may observe not only receptor adaptation to the environment but also adaptation *of* the environment to conform to receptor capacities and uses.

It has been suggested that this ability to amplify and modify the human receptor apparatus carries dangers as well as benefits. Chermayeff and Alexander (1963), in their book *Community and Privacy,* contend that mechanized, industrialized civilization has led to a focus on the exciting and the extreme. Indifference to average dimensions, the dimensions of humankind, has taken hold, so that only the supercolossal, such as a manned vehicle on the moon, or the shocking, such as a ghastly mass murder, rivets attention. Loud noises and fast movement crowd out the soft and the slow. The dangers of physical damage from noise pollution are gradually becoming widely appreciated. For Chermayeff and Alexander, among others, the very instruments that give increased mobility, communication, and mastery are destroying the equilibrium of the human habitat.

Perceiving as the active process of extracting information from the environment may be more closely examined through a discussion of the significance of one mode of perceiving, namely *touch.* Touch itself is a powerful source of information about the world and others in it. The surface area of the skin has an enormous number of sensory receptors. It is estimated that there are at least fifty receptors per hundred square millimeters of skin, by far the largest organ system of the body. In addition to its size, its importance as a receptor system may be illustrated by our frequent linguistic references to touch and its significance. We like to get the "feel" of things, we are "touched" by a kindness but consider rudeness "tactless." Some things "rub us the wrong way" but we certainly want friends to "keep in touch."

These expressions and many more the reader can add are not merely linguistic conventions. They illustrate the importance of touch as a source of information, particularly interpersonal information. Furthermore, there is some evidence for a distinction between active and passive touch as sources of information. In the former, there is active searching out for sensation. There is a difference between these two forms of touch in terms of accuracy of information received. A study (Gibson, 1961) showed that when subjects used passive touch to try and identify abstract objects screened from view they could do so with 49 percent accuracy, but when active touch was employed, they were successful 95 percent of the time.

The world of early childhood is one in which a primary means of feeling good about the world and ourselves is derived from the loving touch of caregivers. Although some young children appear to delight in being cuddled and handled more than others (Schaffer and Emerson, 1964), for all children the frequent handling that is part of adequate caregiving permits important postural body adjustments to others. The latter are indications of interpersonal responsiveness. For example, studies of institutionalized children who receive minimal care and very little handling have reported the stiff, stick-like body posture of these children when picked up by a researcher. They appear to lack the ability or interest to adapt their body posture to that of others.

The glazed, withdrawn, and unresponsive appearance of institutionalized children who receive minimal tactile stimulation may be related to the fearful, cringing, poorly socialized Rhesus monkeys that Harlow demonstrated need contact-clinging to their mother for normal development. In a classic experiment, he provided some Rhesus babies with wire mesh "mothers" and some with soft cloth-covered "mothers." Though neither group fared as well as babies reared with live monkey mothers, the babies who were able to cling to a soft surface were significantly better adjusted and less fearful as adults than the babies denied this clinging opportunity (Harlow and Harlow, 1966; Harlow and Zimmerman, 1959).

Although ethical considerations do not permit the withholding of tactile stimulation from human babies, it is possible to see indirect support for Harlow's findings among humans. One study, for example, which sought to resolve the controversy between breast- and bottle-feeding, found that the "warmth" of the caregiver and the quality of the feeding experience were more important than the mechanism used for transmitting nutrients (Heinstein, 1963). The cold caregiver, whether breast- or bottle-feeding, appeared to have the most dissatisfied infant. Again, notice in the use of the terms *warm* and *cold* the importance of thermal communication during touch.

While up to now the general importance and need for stimulation of these receptor systems has been emphasized, it is clear that individuals and whole cultures differ in the importance they assign to certain receptors, in their need for stimulation, and in their interpretation of incoming information. These differences may be termed "perceptual-cognitive styles."

PERCEPTUAL-COGNITIVE STYLES

Perceptual-cognitive styles may be thought of in several ways. First, one may consider differences in preference for one receptor system over another. It is common to think of some people as more visual than others, of some people as always touching, others keeping a tactile distance and relying on distance receptors. Although the origins of such perceptual styles are unknown, some evidence suggests very early beginnings. As mentioned earlier, some research has suggested that babies may be classified as cuddlers and noncuddlers. Although only a minority in one study fit the category of children who actively resisted attempts at handling, it appeared that these children, highly active and exploratory, preferred to rely on the distance receptors of sight and sound to keep in touch with their caregivers. One must caution that this study used only mothers' reports and not direct observation. Hence, mothers of noncuddlers may in fact be less responsive and less interested in handling their babies than mothers of cuddlers. They may attribute this lack to interest to the babies themselves.

While the results of this study must be considered inconclusive, the more thorough longitudinal research of Stella Chess and her colleagues (Thomas, Chess, and Birch, 1970) provides clearer evidence of early perceptual style. *Longitudinal* research is the investigation of characteristics of the same individuals over time, as contrasted to *cross-sectional* research, which compares characteristics of a group of individuals of a certain age with another group of different individuals at a different age. For example, if preference for touch were the behavior of interest, the longitudinal study might follow a group of infants over several years to determine if such a preference is stable or undergoes change, while the cross-sectional method might compare touch preferences of several age groups. Differences among these groups might lead to the inference that preference for touch undergoes changes during early development. While longitudinal research is obviously more time-consuming, it does provide more direct evidence concerning the development of behaviors than the cross-sectional method.

Let us return to the research of Stella Chess and her associates. They observed differences in temperament during the early months of life that showed remarkable stability for several years. By temperament the investigators had in mind such dimensions of behavior as attention span, activity level, threshold for pain, and distractability. Thus, they observed what any parent can confirm: that some infants appeared more restless and irritable than others. Despite the wide variability characteristic of all individuals, the fussy and irritable infant turned out to be the restless toddler with a short attention span. Similarly, the placid baby of six months had a similar temperament at three years.

These findings of early temperament do not deny the importance of environmental influences on young children. Instead, they caution us not to assume that the infant is a "blank slate." Rather, the infant appears to come equipped not only with perceptual equipment for gathering information about the world, but also initial preferences for the pace and style of discovery. The dimensions of temperament affect not only the level of receptor information considered optimal for the individual but also the emphasis given particular receptor systems. In the mothers' reports of noncuddler babies, the high activity level and exploratory needs of these babies prevented them from sitting still long enough to enjoy the relative confinement of being held. Thus, temperament, which Chess suggests is to some extent congenital, or present at birth, affects both receptor choice and perceptual style.

In addition to receptor preferences, the above research indicates another important dimension of perceptual style—variation in amount of perceptual stimulation considered optimal. The research on early temperament illustrates that individuals vary in the amount of stimulation they appear to need and that these differences do not necessarily disappear but may remain as predispositions, preferred ways of knowing the environment. For example, the active, restless, easily distractible infant was observed to be the active, exploratory dynamo in nursery school. These temperamental differences, then, signal the need for differing levels and tempos of stimulation. Failure to appreciate such individuality may cause difficulties between child and caregiver. Thus, Chess and her associates found that mismatches between child and caregiver temperament—the active dynamo baby with the slow, phlegmatic mother, for example—were most often associated with children identified as having adjustment problems in nursery school.

Similarly, the existence of such temperamental differences indicates that the perceptual styles of some individuals will spell difficulty in their dealings with others. The easily adapted child with the easygoing temperament will be correctly perceived as an easy baby and hence receive more positive feedback from the environment than the child with the "difficult" temperament.

Research on *augmenters* and *reducers* of stimulation (Compton, 1972) supports this view. The augmenter may be defined as one who is able to make a lot out of a little stimulation, while the reducer may be viewed as one who makes a little out of a lot of stimulation. Thus, the augmenter is adapted to a lower level of stimulation than is the reducer. These terms of course describe only the extreme ends of a continuum along which most individuals will be found. Anyone strolling down a college dorm corridor before exam time will be able to recognize augmenters and reducers, however. One student may be seen (the door is ajar) in a mound of books and notes, with the radio and stereo blaring simultaneously, a knot of friends happily visiting in the corner. Next door, and the door is firmly shut, quiet reigns, as another student sits before a cleared desk silently focussed on a page of notes for hours. While the augmenter's study habits may make for better grades, the difference between these two styles stems not so much from ignorance or bad habit, but from differences in needed level of stimulation.

The origins of augmenter-reducer styles is not clear. Nor do we have much direct research illustrating what affects the development and persistence of such styles. However, one study found that in a comparison of delinquent with nondelinquent girls, significantly more delinquent girls were reducers in perceptual style. They appeared to need larger amounts of stimulation for optimal functioning than did most of the nondelinquent girls (Compton, 1972). It has also been suggested that homes which contain very high levels of visual, auditory, and tactile stimulation do not facilitate early verbal development as well as homes in which verbal stimulation is distinctive. In the latter, relatively quiet atmosphere, the words "mommy is coming" said in response to the baby's cry come distinctively to represent the mother and to carry important meaning to the baby. In the home filled with radio, television, the sights and sounds of others, tickles and touches, words do not loom as distinctively important. In the view of some researchers, this high but indiscriminate stimulation home may provide the setting in which reducer perceptual styles are born. This style may interfere with learning as the ability to attend to distinctive stimuli and may also raise the general level of minimal necessary stimulation.

Analogous to the augmenter-reducer distinction is a *leveling versus sharpening* dimension (Gardner et al., 1959; Gardner, Jackson, and Messick, 1960), defined as the tendency of the individual to minimize or maximize differences among environmental stimuli. In a line-length judging task, the leveler will fail to perceive differences as successive pairs of lines become less discrepant in length, while the sharpener will pick up very slight differences. The leveler is treating two different stimuli as functionally equivalent, responding to both as if they were the same. The perceived environment is less variegated for the leveler than the sharpener, and this is similar to the reducer who finds a given level of stimulation more inadequate than the augmenter.

Other research has focussed on the distinction between *impulsive* and *reflective* styles (Kagan and Kogan, 1970). Viewing these terms again as two extreme points on a continuum, one may define the impulsive style as one which, in a problem-solving situation, seizes on the first available stimuli, while the reflective style scans and considers all available stimuli before using them to make a judgment.

Reflective and impulsive styles may be viewed in their extreme form by observing individuals taking a test that demands choice of a correct alternative among an array of possibles. The impulsive approach is to fasten on to the first likely choice and quickly write it down. The reflective approach, on the other hand, involves careful consideration of each alternative, matching it against a criterion of "most appropriate response" and only after such thorough investigation, making a choice.

From the vantage point of academic learning, it is clear that the reflective style will pay more dividends. Thus, while reflectivity and impulsivity can be identified in children as early as three years of age, in general schooling gradually encourages reflective habits. Interesting research has shown, however, that impulsive teachers can by their unintentional modeling alone increase their pupils' impulsivity levels by the end of the school year (Kagan, Pearson, and Welch, 1966; Yando and Kagan, 1968). Class differences in reflectivity-impulsivity have also been found among young children. Middle-class children tend to be more reflective, taking more time before choosing a correct alternative and making fewer errors. Furthermore, they appear to take greater pleasure in the mastery of choosing the right answer than do lower-class children who, in one study, spontaneously smiled less often when making a correct choice (Kagan, Pearson, and Welch, 1966). It is felt that middle-class parents communicate to their children in both words and deeds the high valuation they place upon mastery of intellectual tasks. Thus, reflectivity-impulsivity appears strongly susceptible to modification through modelling and reinforcement (reward and punishment).

Reflective individuals do better academically, partly because of a greater fear of failure than their more impulsive counterparts. It is this fear that motivates them to scan carefully all alternatives in order to be doubly sure that no mistake will be committed.

Still another perceptual-cognitive style that has been the focus of much research is *field independence-dependence* (Witkin et al., 1962). Field dependence may be defined as *the tendency to use external cues in making a judgment based on conflicting perceptual evidence from the environment and from within oneself.* Field dependence refers to reliance on the environment external to oneself. The field-independent response, by contrast, relies upon attention to internal cues. This can be illustrated by describing two commonly used tests of field independence-dependence, the rod-and-frame test and the tilted room test. In the former, a rod is suspended in the air inside a similarly suspended empty picture frame. The perceiver must indicate when the rod is vertical. If this is done by using kinesthetic or body cues, the individual is considered field-independent; if the relation between the rod and constantly moving frame is considered, the individual is scored as field-dependent.

In the tilted room test, the subject sits on a chair which is in a small room. Both the chair and the entire room can be tilted independently. The subject is asked to indicate when he or she is sitting upright. Again, if the position of the chair relative to the room (which is tilted) is the criterion, the individual is using a field-dependent strategy, while the use of internal body cues for uprightness signals a field-independent approach.

While these tests may seem rather exotic, scores on these measures and others like them apparently do tap an important perceptual style. Field-dependent people, those who use context in making perceptual judgments, are also more social, more interested in other people, more easily influenced by persuasion, while field independents are more task-oriented and resistent to persuasion. This style, like the others discussed earlier, also appears to have early roots. Modified tests of field independence-dependence for young children (Coates, Lord, and Jakabovics, 1975) have found evidence of the style as early as three years. As with adults, the field-dependent child shows less task-orientation and more social interest in play when compared to the field independent children.

Sex differences in this style have also been found. Cultural emphasis on female social graces, on sensitivity to the needs of others, on women as people-oriented rather than task-oriented, is seen in repeated findings that women and girls are significantly more field dependent on the average than men and boys. This phrase "on the average" is important to keep in mind, however. This means that highly field-independent women will be found as will highly field-dependent men. *More* women will be field dependent, however, than men.

It is also important to point out that measures of field independence are highly correlated with IQ. This means that tests of field independence seems to be measuring something closely akin to what is measured on IQ tests. It is clear that the field-independent person will do better, on the average, on IQ tests, and since IQ tests predict success of academic achievement, it is not surprising that field independence is related to academic success as well.

The field independent-dependent dimension, then, illustrates a style based on preference for certain perceptual information. The field-dependent perceiver is strongly attuned to the context or perceptual field for cues in making a judgment, while the field-independent individual feels it relatively easy to ignore context.

In summary, the perceptual styles of reducer-augmenter, reflective-impulsive, and field independence-dependence illustrate differences in level of perceptual information needed, and in the use of perceptual information to make judgments. In addition, research on differences in temperament suggest that individuals may vary in receptor preferences. One problem with the evidence for

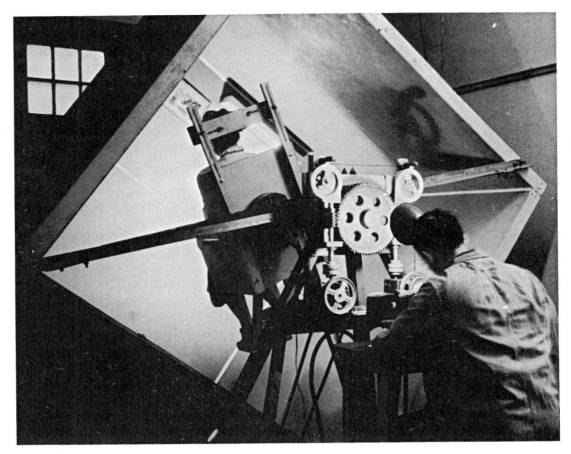

The tilting room-tilting chair test measures field independence—dependence perceptual style. (Photo by David Linton.)

perceptual styles is that there is so much of it. Different investigators working within differing frameworks have uncovered a dizzying array of perceptual-cognitive styles. Is the field-dependent individual also an augmenter? Is the leveler apt to be impulsive? No evidence currently exists to answer these questions. It has been suggested (Santostefano, 1964; Santostefano and Paley, 1964) however, that all these styles may be viewed as part of a single dimension of *cognitive differentiation*. Reflectivity-impulsivity, leveling-sharpening, field independence-dependence share a common reference to the relative simplicity or complexity of one's perceptual-cognitive involvement with the environment.

CULTURAL DIFFERENCES IN PERCEIVING

In addition to these perceptual styles, broader cultural differences in receptor use have been identified and studied in recent years. The existence of such cultural differences have long been the source of anecdote among foreign travelers. For example, American travelers and diplomats in the Arab countries of the Middle East have reported discomfort at the close contact and frequent touch during conversation. The paper-thin walls of the traditional Japanese house indicate a surprising lack of concern with noise levels and auditory privacy that a German accustomed to much thicker walls would find unacceptable, while he does not share the Japanese emphasis on visual beauty and serenity.

The anthropologist Edward Hall, in his book *The Hidden Dimension* (1966), was the first to call attention to such cultural differences in receptor emphasis as a source of information concerning variations in styles of perceiving the environment and in adapting it for the perceivers' use. Since the use of the distance and immediate receptors implies spatial differences between people and the environment, Hall felt that cultures emphasizing the immediate receptors such as touch would engage in closer interpersonal distances. He termed such cultures "contact-cultures" and felt that the source of much international misunderstanding lay in the attempted dialogue between members of contact and noncontact cultures. Since participants are usually unaware of these cultural differences in receptor use, vague feelings of discomfort and tension ensue.

A number of researchers were eager to test his hypotheses concerning contact and noncontact cultures in the laboratory and in field work. The evidence has been mixed. One study (Watson and Graves, 1966) verified that Arab students living in the U.S. did engage in more contact and close distance than American students. But another study, using Latin Americans (also considered a contact culture) found that the topic of conversation rather than culture alone determined the amount of interpersonal involvement. When Latin Americans discussed politics they remained as distant as American students. Thus, differences in culture are complicated and sometimes overshadowed by a host of factors, such as topic of conversation, the relationship between the individuals, and individual perceptual styles.

Despite this, it is felt that cultural differences in receptor use are real and must be transmitted to children as part of their cultural learning. Hence, research has also been directed at the roots of these differences in childhood. One study (Aiello and Jones, 1971), conducted on white, black, and Puerto Rican children in New York City, found that white first graders, observed during recess play, keep larger distances from each other than black or Puerto Rican children. However, a later study which investigated possible social class differences as an explanation concluded that more interpersonal involvement could be observed in encounters between lower-class as compared to middle-class children, no matter what the racial or ethnic identification. Hence, it appears that more interpersonal closeness characterizes class differences, not cultural differences per se in the United States.

Although this finding needs to be replicated (reproduced) in other studies, it is intriguing. One explanation that needs exploring illustrates the relation between receptor use and environmental context. Although the study cited did not report this, it is generally true that school settings provided the urban poor have significantly higher density than the school settings provided the middle class. It is possible that this greater density was related to the closer interpersonal distances and greater sensory involvement among lower-class children.

Thus, an environmental characteristic, density, may be associated with a perceptual style of close interpersonal sensory involvement. It is impossible to say, however, that environmental characteristics *cause* cultural differences in perceptual style. After all, people with high sensory involvement in one another may tend because of this to live in densely populated areas which permit such involvement.

In summary, perceptual styles may be considered as individual and group characteristics, related in ways not now entirely clear to environmental characteristics. They illustrate that when people are compared, the process of extracting information from the environment is infinitely varied.

DEVELOPMENTAL CHANGES

In addition, individuals themselves change as they develop. Perceptual capacities grow, styles are to some extent learned and modified, and receptor capacities themselves undergo change. For example, studies of aging show a reduction in the amount of environmental information processed as age increases. Each receptor system appears to show an age decrement (Birren, Bick, and Fox, 1948; Chapanis, 1950; Schaie, 1964). The gradual aging process makes adaptation to this lower level of perceptual information possible. Several studies, however, illustrate the dislocation that can occur when this perceptual decrement comes about sharply without time to adapt. In one (Pastalan, n.d.), architecture students wore diffusing lenses, ear plugs, and fingertip film designed to simulate the sensory loss of the average eighty-year-old person. This procedure directly affected the mood of the volunteers, one of whom became so depressed he had to drop out of the experiment. In another study, "old age" lenses were worn. These were designed to reflect the view of some investigators that the aged rely more on peripheral vision as they age. Again the wearers reported discomfort at not being able to get close to or to be in touch with their environment (Lawton and Nahemow, 1973).

Thus far, individual differences in perception (perceptual styles), cultural differences, and developmental changes have been described. Each provides an illustration of the manner in which perception is affected by the perceiver. Since perception is viewed here as the process of extracting, interpreting, and using environmental information, it is important to consider how the information provided by perceptual processes is integrated and organized into mental representations of the environment.

THE ENVIRONMENT IN OUR HEADS: COGNITIVE MAPS

It is well known that designers and users often perceive the same environment differently. For example, in one study three factors—friendliness, coherence, and character—were important to architecture students while only the first two factors mattered to other students (Canter, 1969). Recently, the importance of considering "people patterns in the blueprints" (Deasy, 1973), that is, users' needs, values, and attitudes, has been urged in the design professions. This is especially important in light of evidence that aesthetic evaluation may be relatively unimportant in assessing satisfaction with one's environment. Instead, the user's perception that the environment is meeting his/her needs is the primary consideration. Thus, environments that enhance rather than limit activity, achievement, complexity, and variety have been urged (Perrin, 1970; Steinitz, 1968).

Natural environments as well as designed ones are perceived through the prisms of needs, values, and attitudes. Studies of campsite preferences have emphasized the role of individual needs (Shafer, 1969), while on a more general level, observer characteristics are seen as an important dimension in understanding responsiveness to landscapes (Craik, 1968). Because of this emphasis on users' perceptions and the discrepancy often found when compared to those of a design elite, interest has burgeoned in strategies for uncovering potential users' perceptions, needs, and values through mapping techniques, interviews, and game simulations.

An important method of tapping environmental perception is the *cognitive map* or cognitive-mapping process by which "an individual acquires, codes, stores, recalls and decodes information about the relative locations and attributes of phenomena in his everyday spatial environment" (Downs and Stea, 1971). When considered as product rather than process, cognitive maps are mental representations of the environment. These "maps within our heads" provide the structure by which environmental information is organized and made available. Although the term *cognitive map* is widely used, it is sometimes misleading, since recent research on mental representations of the environment indicate that they are not really map-like at all (Siegel and White, 1975). Different units of the environment are tapped when an individual is asked to draw his home, street, neighborhood, town, region, country. For some units, information for the map comes totally from direct experience, while for others, maps of large regions such as the country and the world, formal schemata based on experience with maps and atlases are used rather than direct experience.

Cognitive maps or mental maps, as some (Gould and White, 1974) have called them, also reflect the emotional meaning of a setting. This was shown graphically in a study in which poor black inner-city children were asked to draw maps of their neighborhood, which also included a white residential housing project. One little boy's map depicts the project as a large blank space. From conversation it emerges that he is literally afraid for his life there and has never set foot in it. Another boy draws the street dividing his area from the white project as a wide band setting off "us" from "them" (Ladd, 1967).

The basic question about cognitive maps, of course, is how do they influence behavior? If mental representations remain locked in brains powerless to affect actions, they are of no consequence. It is only as they serve as impetus to behavior that they become important. It is the assumption of those interested in the cognitive mapping technique that such maps do have psychological importance and do influence behavior. But in what way? They have been depicted as filters controlling the flow of stimulation from the environment and giving it meaning (Gould and White, 1974).

One thinks of some individuals and families as having broad horizons. Others are felt to have an insular mentality. One approach to the family (Hess and Handel, 1974) in fact defines as a major family task that of "defining the boundaries of experience." Are such differences in outlook reflected in cognitive maps and if so, how is this information related to other aspects of psychological functioning? Is the family with broad horizons of experience more open in general to information about the world and about each other?

Do cognitive maps tell us something about the opportunities available to families? For example, a study of the cognitive maps of black city residents in Los Angeles (Orleans, 1967) indicated a very restricted view of the options available in their environment, while their wealthy, white counterparts had richly detailed maps of the sprawling city.

How do people come to learn about their environment? It appears that mental mapping develops in sophistication with age (Blaut, McCleary, and Blaut, 1970). It begins surprisingly early; preliterate children are able to perform relatively complex mental mapping tasks. Factors such as environmental enrichment and experience affect this type of spatial learning in children (Stea and Blaut, 1970). Spatial environments are largely learned through action. A three-step process has been suggested. First, the child's attention is drawn to significant landmarks because of their emotional importance in his life: home, school, the corner store. Then, routes connecting these landmarks are learned through action, and details are gradually filled in. Nevertheless, the mental map remains distorted, overlapping, and inaccurate. Only when the child reaches the final stage of subsuming his landmarks-plus-routes within an overarching framework (e.g., "my neighborhood") does the mental image become objectively accurate.

Analysts of the child's development of spatial representations have been struck by close parallels with the adult's method of learning new environments (Figure 4.1). In similar fashion, significant landmarks are linked to routes, although the role of action is less paramount than in children. Distortions also occur as the adult attempts to fit his landmarks-plus-routes into a larger

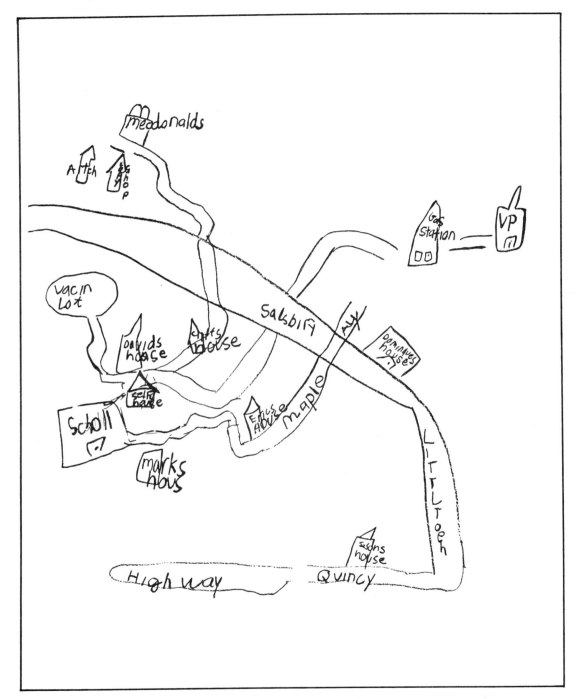

Figure 4.1. An eight year old's cognitive map.

schema. Because of these parallels, a "main sequence" for learning spatial representations has been posited by some who feel that humans may be programmed genetically to learn new environments (Siegel and White, 1975).

How is this process of spatial learning tapped? One approach to this knowledge is to ask new residents to keep a log indicating shopping activities (Golledge and Zannaras, 1970), services, landmarks, recreation areas, etc. Study of the logs over time illustrates the process of acquiring knowledge about the environment. It appears that after a period of consumer search in which different shopping possibilities are sampled, a funnelling process occurs by which choices are narrowed to the selection of two or three alternatives (Nicosia, 1966). For example, one study found that grocery shopping became a habitual routine after approximately four to six weeks of experimentation; another interesting method used game simulations of the environment, like the journey-to-work game (Golledge and Zannaras, 1970), in which participants map out a route to work with penalties associated with traffic lights and stop signs. After a few trials, most develop a habitual course. Interestingly, the students who participated in the journey-to-work game were shown modified maps of their own campus with the starting point at the apartments where most of them lived. While no student recognized the map as familiar, each duplicated his actual preferred route.

Taken together, these studies indicate that the environment is learned by a sequential decision-making process in which information derived from exploration is used to narrow the range of possibilities, thereby making behavior predictable. Of course, this predictability will hold only when conditions are constant; changes in either the environment or the individual will be processed as new information and may require changes in behavior. Cognitive maps illustrate how environmental images are built up through an interaction between observer and environment, the observer selecting, organizing, and interpreting a limited number of environmental features.

FAMILY PERCEPTION OF THE ENVIRONMENT

The family is both a collection of individuals and a small group. Thus, one can speak of individual modes of perceiving in the family and the family as a unit with its own perceptual style born out of group interaction and not reducible simply to its individual components.

We can consider the family as a set of individuals in intimate, long-term interaction. Then if the family is to remain intact, a major task is the reconciling of individual modes of perceiving. Each individual may be characterized by a preferred perceptual style that yet is responsive to changing developmental needs and to environmental influences.

The sensory needs of family members are not the same, of course. The young child's need for support, closeness, and tactility (touch) gradually declines with age if it has been nurtured when at its peak. The aging individual may live in a sensory world increasingly less sharply defined and more slowly paced. While the sensory needs of both young children and old people have received most scientific attention, the changing nature of sensory involvement throughout human development has been less carefully scrutinized. Moreover, each individual reflects the influence of the culture in which he or she was reared. Thus, each person will "see" a somewhat different world, and a central challenge for the family lies in integrating these separate worlds into a family world.

Family members have been described (Hess and Handel, 1974) as each having *images* of themselves and one another. These images might be thought of as *meaningfully organized perceptions*. Family members hold such images not only of each other, but also of the family as a whole. For one member the family is a haven from the stresses of the work world; for another it is

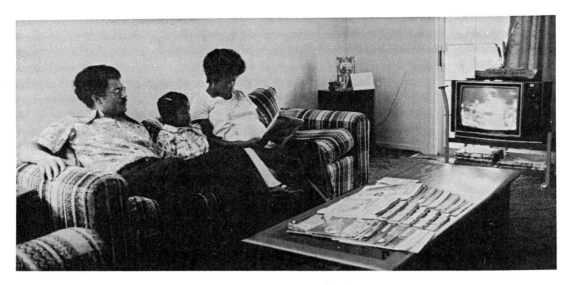

The family gleans information from many sources. (Photo by Natalie Leimkuhler.)

an arena of tension and conflict from which any escape is welcome. Besides such images of self, other, and family group, members have images of the external environment outside the family. Such images determine how much of the environment is perceived as relevant to the person. From this *relevant* environment, information will be extracted and transformed into personal and family goals.

Another way of describing the relevant environment is to ask the question: What are the boundaries of family members' experience (Hess and Handel, 1974)? Is information gleaned from many sources, television, radio, newspapers, friends? Are events outside the neighborhood, community, region, nation felt to touch personal concerns? Is information sought to bolster preexisting perceptions or is the relevant environment open to divergent views? What are the important landmarks by which perception of the environment is organized? Hess and Handel (1974) refer to the boundaries of experience as varying in *extensity* and *intensity*. By *extensity* is meant the range of experiences considered relevant; by *intensity* is meant the depth of feeling brought to these experiences.

When we shift focus from the family as only a collection of individuals to an interacting group, it becomes clear that these images of self, family, and environment that each individual holds must be integrated in some fashion into group images. In their daily interaction, family members share with one another what has been called "testimony" (Hess and Handel, 1974) concerning the images they hold. In simpler terms, we might say they communicate these images to one another. This sharing does not eliminate differences in perception. Its goal is to achieve a level of congruence satisfactory to family members (Hess and Handel, 1974). Some families tolerate wide divergence of world views, others demand greater uniformity. Some degree of congruence, however, is probably necessary to all families. If perceptual images were completely contradictory, it is unlikely that family members could remain together, each enclosed in a separate world.

Thus, when the family is considered as a group, we may say that a *family perceptual style* emerges that varies in distinctiveness depending on the extent of individual diversity and family tolerance for it. Certain factors operate to minimize extreme diversity. For example, individuals from similar cultures, religions, and regions tend to meet one another and eventually marry. This is the principle of *homogamy* or "like marries like." The greater the homogamy, the more likely also is the marriage to remain intact. Homogamy means that congruence of images probably already exists to a certain extent at the start of family formation and provides the groundwork for establishing a family perceptual style. The socialization of children is another source of commonality in families. Parents transmit to their children cultural values as they perceive them. They also present the child with their own perceptions of reality and these are absorbed as part of the child's emerging concept of the environment. The socialization process is one in which the child is brought into the parental world; hence, pressures toward congruence of perception are built into childrearing. Thus one is apt to see powerful continuities between parent and child in styles of perceiving.

Despite such common ground, individual differences persist because of differences in history, experience, and temperament. While the emergence of a family style indicates what family members share, much remains that they do not. Differences in temperament mean that one person may be distractible, process information at a rapid rate, and need a high level of environmental stimulation, while another is slow, methodical, attentive, and attuned to a lower level of stimulation. The emergence of a family perceptual style is a dynamic balancing of individual differences and group needs.

As we earlier defined perception as information extraction from the environment for action, we may also characterize famiy members in terms of their styles of information processing. Similarly, the family may be viewed as a group needing to evolve methods of information processing that characterize the unit as a whole. Style of information processing will differ in complexity of cognitive information, overload, and level of desired risk or uncertainty contained in new information.

Perceptual categories are ways *of organizing and giving meaning to new information from the environment.* The individual with few such categories can handle less information, see fewer distinctions than the one with complex cognitive categories. Stereotypes are examples of simplistic categories—the "ins" versus the "outs"—that prevent prejudiced people from seeing real differences and similarities. Archie Bunker provides a graphic illustration of a man with an impoverished set of perceptual categories for information processing. The number and complexity of cognitive categories influence the degree to which an individual can be open to new stimulation.

This chapter has emphasized individual and family differences in range of desired environmental stimulation. Stimulation exceeding this adaptation range is perceived as *overload.* While overload for one person may be just right or even too little for another, the concept is not completely relative. It has been shown that humans are inherently limited in their capacity to process information (Miller, 1956). Levels of environmental stimulation can rise so high as to bombard virtually everyone. Toffler (1970) argues that contemporary American life is characterized by runaway change so complex that it overwhelms our capacity to understand it. While this may be too strongly stated, it is undoubtedly true that modern society makes severe demands on information-processing abilities.

How is information overload handled? Milgram (1970) argues that people develop strategies for adapting to such overload, such as withdrawal from interaction, filtering stimulation, or cognitive structuring. In *withdrawal,* information is tuned out, as when another person or bit of information is ignored. *Filtering* involves selective attention to only parts of the stimulation being offered. *Cognitive structuring* does not modify informational input, but restructures the categories used to process this information, perhaps by creating new categories.

Can such strategies be observed? Milgram (1970) argues that city life is more likely to subject inhabitants to information overload than rural existence. Hence, city residents are less likely to come to the aid of strangers (withdrawal from interaction), and perhaps more likely to be sophisticated (cognitive structuring) than rural residents. In other research (Filipovitch), children in high-density housing environments (information overload) compared with those in lower densities were observed to ignore interactions with other children in their home environments (withdrawal from interaction). They also perceived higher density levels as uncrowded (cognitive structuring).

Finally, information-processing style also consists of attitudes toward risk or uncertainty. People who dislike taking risks will not attend to information that might increase their sense of uncertainty. They will evaluate information for the amount of risk involved. Sometimes, one must choose between information which promises high gain but involves greater risk and information offering more modest rewards but lesser risk. Changing from a safe job with little advancement to a more insecure one promising rapid promotion is just such a dilemma. No matter what the choice, intelligent risk-taking requires accurate assessment of the costs and gains attached to different options. In turn, such accurate assessment depends on the other dimensions of information processing discussed earlier: the level of desired stimulation, strategies for handling information overload, and the complexity and flexibility of cognitive categories.

All these dimensions of information processing not only characterize individual family members but also challenge the family as a small interacting group. Just as family members share perception of images with each other to form a family perceptual style, so do they share styles of extracting environmental information. Parents transmit to their children their own level of cognitive complexity, their openness to new information and their adaptation level for stimulation. They indicate how much risk and uncertainty they are willing to entertain. They exhibit preferred strategies for coping with informational overload. Although children do not become carbon copies of their parents, they remain strongly affected by parental models, particularly by experiences in early childhood. Indeed, Burton White, an expert on early child development, is convinced that environmental stimulation provided by the parents to the children during the first three years of life largely determines life-long patterns of processing information and relating to others (1975).

Perhaps less dramatically, but in like fashion, siblings affect one another and couples influence each other. Just as all family members share "testimony" about perceptual images, so they share information-extracting styles. Just as families differ in their tolerance for diversity of images, so do they differ in tolerance for diversity of information-processing styles. Families emphasizing cohesiveness, togetherness, and uniformity would be less likely to accept both high-risk and low-risk members, for example, than would a more "hang-loose" family. To my knowledge, however, no research has tested this hypothesis directly.

Styles of perceiving and extracting information from the environment have been portrayed in this chapter as active modes of relating to the environment. This emphasis on the active nature of perception should not obscure the fact that families also react to environmental change. Perceiving also means monitoring the environment for changes and then taking account of new events in formulating and attempting to reach family goals. Thus, perceiving is both acting and reacting, a series of transactions with the environment.

Families may accent the reactive or active aspects of this transactional process. Family *A* may see environmental changes as things that happen to it, forces it can do little to control and harness to its own goals. Family *B* may view itself as an active doer, able to affect its destiny. Such a family tends to view environmental change as at least potentially under its control. The difference between these two families lies in a difference in what has been termed "locus of control" (Rotter, 1966). The members of family *A* have an *external* locus of control, interpreting environmental changes as largely beyond their influence, while family *B* members share a more *internal* locus of control, viewing change as susceptible to their power.

Differences in locus of control can be easily seen when these explanations for failing an exam are compared: (1) "I guess I didn't study long enough and I was up late last night and feeling tired. If I would have spent more time on it, I'm sure I would have done better," versus (2) "You never know what's going to happen on these tests. It doesn't seem to matter what I do. It always turns out the same anyway." Notice that the explanation reflecting external locus of control closes off all possibility of translating environmental changes into new strategies for maximizing personal goals.

Locus of control may be considered not only an individual predisposition, but a family characteristic as well. As with perception of family images and information-extracting styles, locus of control is communicated in all family interactions. Parents interpret the meaning of environmental change to their children, couples share their views with each other. Moreover, family members share a common environment, and hence experience together observed connections between their perceptions, actions, and environmental changes. They can observe whether attempts to direct the course of events to reach family goals are successful. Families with few resources discover that their desire to be efficacious, to control environmental change, is chronically unsatisfied. Events appear to happen to them. Despite their dissatisfaction with where they live, they lack the means to move. Despite diligent work habits, the husband is laid off at the plant. No one responds to their protests about deteriorating neighborhood services.

It is not surprising, therefore, that class differences have been found in locus of control, with middle-class families more internal than lower-class ones. Unfortunately, while this class difference arises out of differing rates of success at environmental manipulation, once an external outlook is formed, it can prevent a family from seeing later opportunities for action when they arise. A defeatist outlook is born, and this in turn further discourages an active approach.

It is easy to see how such "learned helplessness" can come about. For poor minority families particularly, attempts to change environmental conditions are often futile. The message coming loud and clear through feedback based on such actions is "Don't bother trying to change things: it just won't work." Unfortunately, such messages over a period of time build up a generalized expectation that external forces control change in one's life, and such an expectation may interfere with those instances when an active, problem-solving stance is possible. Thus, one's relation to the environment in some ways reflects one's level of self-esteem, a sense of mastery over the ship of life or a feeling that one is borne along on irresistible environmental currents.

Value-orientations also influence the family's response toward environmental change. As Chapter 5 discusses, value-orientations may be thought of as emphasizing present, past, or future time. Modern industrial societies generally emphasize future-time orientation. Particularly in America, the past holds no special nostalgia; mistakes can always be corrected, new technologies can be developed, the best is yet to come. The present is not there to be savored for what it is but to be used to ensure a brighter future. Steele (1970) believes that this future orientation often blinds Americans to their present experience so that they fail to see the impact of their behaviors in the here and now. Thus, it becomes difficult to articulate what the problems are. Hence, an active problem-solving stance becomes more difficult to assume.

Furthermore, families develop habitual ways of relating to the environment, and these habits acquire a force of their own. Changing habits then requires an extra exertion of energy.

Family responses to environmental change also arise from the nature of the family as a small group. Group norms, cohesiveness, and organization help determine the behavior of any small group, and the family is no exception. For example, the norms of a group may specify who has the power to make changes in general, particularly changes over the environment. In the family, the distribution of power will affect decisions ranging from residential moves to small purchases and furniture arrangement. As discussed more fully in Chapter 7, families develop rules, often unspoken, about who decides what and when.

Secondly, a family may not agree on desired goals and, hence, changes designed to implement these goals. For example, a working-class family may disagree internally on the goal of upward mobility, the husband strongly urging moving up in the world, the wife valuing her integration into the old neighborhood with close ties to her family. With such difference in goals, environmental change such as a move to a middle-class suburb would further the husband's goals but thwart his wife's. It is likely that the family will have difficulty agreeing on any initiation of change under these circumstances.

Thirdly, the degree of group organization affects family responses to environmental change and its ability to initiate and carry out active manipulation of its environment. For example, there is evidence that among large families (more than four children) it is difficult for the family to function as one cohesive group (Blood, 1972). Instead, a tendency toward group differentiation occurs, with subgroups forming. As a result, organization to fulfill goals is relatively lacking when compared to smaller families. Hence, one finds that large families are less likely to provide as much education and to have children in as good jobs as those in smaller families, even with social class controlled. Of course, differences in level of resources undoubtedly still operate since even at the same social-class level, the large family has to distribute its resources over more people, and hence any one individual is likely to get less than in smaller families. Nonetheless, the organizational capacity of the family also appears important in determining the ability to pursue environmental change for the family's betterment.

In summary, families as collections of interacting individuals and as small social units have perceptual styles, information-processing strategies, and characteristic ways of interpreting environmental change. These modes of perceiving are active processes designed to make sense out of the environment, to derive information to be transformed into goal-seeking behavior. Families monitor the effects of their actions upon the environment and assess the degree to which they are effective in bringing about desired change. A discouraging history in this regard is apt to breed a defeatist outlook that resists modification.

SUMMARY

Perceiving is an active process of interpreting and giving meaning to the environmment, not the passive imprint of sensation upon sensory receptors. This view of perceiving means that many kinds of individual and group differences will be reflected in perceptual style—cultural distinctiveness, developmental changes, historical change. The diverse perceptual styles identified—augmenter-reducer, field independent-dependent, reflective-impulsive, leveler-sharpener among others—share common differences in preferred level of stimulation or adaptation level.

Differences among individuals in their approach to extracting information from the environment are another way to consider the active role of the perceiver. Here, individuals vary in the complexity of their cognitive categories, in their openness to new information, in their responses to information overload, and in their preferred level of risk taking.

Perceptual styles and information-processing strategies may be applied to families in two ways. First, when the family is considered a set of interrelated individuals, the family task of reconciling individual perceptual styles is highlighted. Families differ in their tolerance for individual diversity, but some congruence of images is probably necessary in all families.

Family members achieve this congruence in a number of ways: (1) They share "testimony" about their perceptions though communication, (2) couples are likely to come together initially and thereafter stay together partially out of common interests and characteristics, and (3) socialization of children involves imparting parental ways of seeing the world.

In addition to a collection of individuals, the family is a small group with characteristics transcending those of any of its members. As such, the family may be said to evolve its own perceptual style, its own preferred modes of extracting environmental information. Thus, we may say that "Family X is open (or closed) to new experience."

Finally, families not only actively manipulate their environment in the perceiving process but also react to environmental changes. Such reactions may lead to a view that change comes largely from one's own efforts (internal locus of control) or largely from environmental forces beyond one's control (external locus of control). Low-resource families are likely to have experiences of defeat when trying to effect changes and hence develop external loci of control. Value-orientations, habits, and group characteristics such as cohesiveness and organization, all affect the family's ability to monitor environmental change and respond actively to it. Providing all families with opportunities for exercising influence and determining their own destiny is important not only for present well-being but also for shaping future outlook.

REFERENCES

Aiello, J. and Jones, S. Field study of the proxemic behavior of young children in three subcultural groups. *Journal of Personality and Social Psychology* 19(1971): 351-356.

Allport, G. and Pettigrew, T. Cultural influence on the perception of movement: The trapezoidal illusion among the Zulus. *Journal of Abnormal and Social Psychology* 55(1957): 104-113.

Antonovsky, H.F. and Ghent, L. Cross-cultural consistency of children's preference for the orientation of figures. *American Journal of Psychology* 77(1964): 295-297.

Birren, J.E., Bick, M.W., and Fox, C. Age changes in the light threshold of the dark adapted eye. *Journal of Gerontology* 3(1948): 267-271.

Blaut, J.M., McCleary, G.F., and Blaut, A.S. Environmental mapping in young children. Unpublished manuscript, Clark University, 1970.

Blood, R. *The Family*. New York: The Free Press, 1972.

Canter, D. An intergroup comparison of connotative dimensions in architecture. *Environment and Behavior* 1(1969): 37-48.

Chapanis, A. Relationships between age, visual acuity, and color vision. *Human Biology* 22(1950): 1-31.

Chermayeff, S., and Alexander, C. *Community and Privacy*. Garden City, N.Y.: Doubleday, 1963.

Coates, S., Lord, M., and Jakabovics, E. Field dependence/independence, social/nonsocial play and sex differences in preschool children. *Perceptual and Motor Skills* 40(1975): 195-202.

Compton, N. The focus is on the environment. *Journal of Home Economics* 64(1972): 6-12.

Craik, K.H. The comprehension of the everyday physical environment. *Journal of American Institute of Planners* 34(1968): 29-37.

Deasy, C.M. People patterns in the blueprints. *Human Behavior*, August 1973, pp. 8-15.

Deregowski, T.B. Difficulties in pictorial depth perception in Africa. *British Journal of Psychology* 59 (1968): 195-204.

Downs, R.M., and Stea, D., eds. *Cognitive Mapping: Images of the Spatial Environment*. Chicago: Aldine Press, 1971.

Filipovitch, A.J. Children and residential density: Adaptation to sensory overload. Unpublished manuscript.

Gardner, R.W., Holzman, P., Klein, G., Linton, H., and Spence, D. Cognitive controls: A study of individual consistencies in cognitive behavior. *Psychological Issues* 4(1959), no. 4.

Gardner, R.W., Jackson, D., and Messick, S. Personality organization in cognitive controls and intellectual abilities. *Psychological Issues* 2(1960), no. 8.

Gibson J. Pictures, perspective and perception. *Daedalus* 89(1960): 216-227.

Golledge, R.G., and Zannaras, G. The perception of urban structure: An experimental approach. In J. Archea and C. Eastman, eds., *EDRA 2: Proceedings of the Second Annual Environmental Design Research Association Conference*. Pittsburgh, Pa.: Carnegie Press, 1970.

Gould, P., and White, R. *Mental Maps*. Baltimore: Penguin Books, 1974.

Hall, E. *The Hidden Dimension*. Garden City, N.Y.: Doubleday, 1966.

Hallowell, A.I. *Culture and Experience*. Philadelphia: University of Pennsylvania, 1957.

Harlow, H., and Harlow, M.H. Learning to love. *American Scientist* 54(1966): 244-272.

Harlow, H., and Zimmermann, R.R. Affectional responses in the infant monkey. *Science* 130(1959): 421-432.

Heinstein, M.I. Behavioral correlates of breast-bottle regimes under varying parent-infant relationships. *Monographs of the Society of Research on Child Development* 28(1963), no. 4.

Hess, R., and Handel, G. *Family Worlds: The Psychosocial Interior of the Family*. Chicago: University of Chicago Press, 1974.

Ittelson, W.H. Environment perception and contemporary perception theory. In W.H. Ittelson, ed., *Environment and Cognition*. New York: Seminar Press, 1973.

Kagan, J. On cultural deprivation. In D. Glass, ed., *Environmental Influences*. New York: Rockefeller University Press, 1968.

Kagan, J., and Kogan, N. Individual variation in cognitive processes. In P. Mussen, ed., *Carmichael's Manual of Child Psychology*. Vol. 1. New York: Wiley, 1970.

Kagan, J., Pearson, L., and Welch, L. Modifiability of an impulsive tempo. *Journal of Educational Psychology*, 51(1966): 359-365.

Ladd, F. A note on "The world across the street." *Harvard Graduate School of Education Association Bulletin* 12(1967): 47-48.

Lawton, M., and Nahemow, L. Ecology and the aging process. In C. Eisdorfer and M. Lawton, eds., *The Psychology of Adult Development and Aging*. Washington: APA, 1973.

Milgram, S. The experience of living in cities. *Science* 167(1970): 1461-1468.

————Introduction in W.H. Ittelson, ed., *Environment and Cognition*. New York: Seminar Press, 1973.

Miller, G. The magical number seven plus or minus two. *Psychological Review* 63(1956): 81-97.

Nicosia, F.N. *Consumer Decision Processes: Marketing and Advertising Implications*. Englewood Cliffs, N.J.: Prentice-Hall, 1966.

Orleans, P. Urban experimentation and urban sociology. In *Science, Engineering and the City*. Symposium sponsored jointly by the National Academy of Sciences and the National Academy of Engineering. No. 1498. Washington, D.C.: National Academy of Sciences, 1967.

Pastalan, L.A. Toward an empathetic model in architecture. Mimeographed. Ann Arbor: Department of Architecture, University of Michigan, n.d.

Perrin, C. *With Man in Mind*. Cambridge, Mass.: MIT Press, 1970.

Rappaport, A., and Hawkes, R. The perception of urban complexity. *Journal of the American Institute of Banners* 36(1970): 106-111.

Rock, I. *The Nature of Perceptual Adaptation*. New York: Basic Books, 1966.

Rotter, J. Generalized expectancies for internal versus external control of reinforcement. *Psychological Monographs* 80(1966), no. 609.

Santostefano, S.G. A developmental study of the cognitive control 'leveling-sharpening.' *Merrill-Palmer Quarterly* 10(1964): 343-359.

Santostefano, S.G., and Paley, E. Development of cognitive controls in children. *Child Development* 35(1964): 939-949.

Schaffer, H.R., and Emerson, P.E. Patterns of response to physical contact in early human development. *Journal of Child Psychiatry* 5(1964): 1-13.

Schaie, K.W., Baltes, P., and Strother, C.R. A study of auditory sensitivity in advanced age. *Journal of Gerontology* 19(1964): 453-457.

Segal, M.H., Campbell, D., and Herskovits, M. *Influence of Culture on Visual Perception.* Indianapolis: Bobbs-Merrill, 1966.

Shafer, E.L., Jr. Perception of natural environments. *Environment and Behavior* 1(1969): 71-82.

Siegel, A., and White, S. The development of spatial representations of large-scale environments. In H. Reese, ed., *Advances in Child Development and Behavior.* Vol. 10. New York: Academic Press, 1975.

Sprout, H., and Sprout, M. *The Ecological Perspective on Human Affairs.* Princeton: Princeton University Press, 1965.

Stea, D., and Blaut, J.M. Notes toward a developmental theory of spatial learning. In J. Archea and C. Eastman, eds., *EDRA 2: Proceedings of the Second Annual Environmental Design Research Association Conference.* Pittsburgh, Pa.: Carnegie Press, 1970.

Steele, F. Problem-solving in the spatial environment. In H. Sanoff and S. Cohn, eds., *EDRA 1: Proceedings of the First Environmental Design Association Conference,* 1970.

Steinitz, C. Meaning and the congruence of urban form and activity. *Journal of the American Institute of Planners,* 34(1968): 233-248.

Thomas, A., Chess, S., and Birch, H.G. The origin of personality. *Scientific American* 223(1970): 102-109.

Toffler, A. *Future Shock.* New York: Random House, 1970.

Watson, O.M., and Graves, T.D. Quantitative research in proxemic behavior. *American Anthropologist* 68(1966): 971-985.

White, B. *The First Three Years of Life.* Cambridge, Mass.: Harvard University Press, 1975.

Witkin, H.A., Dyk, R.B., Faterson, H.F., Goodenough, D.R., and Karp, S.A. *Psychological Differentiation.* New York: Wiley, 1962.

Wohlwill, J.F. The physical environment: A problem for the psychology of stimulation. *Journal of Social Issues* 22(1966): 29-38.

Yando, R.M., and Kagan, J. The effect of teacher tempo on the child. *Child Development* 39(1968): 27-34.

5

Spacing

In recent years, considerable interest has developed in how we perceive and experience space. The child builds up body boundaries and a sense of self as distinct from others. He or she develops expectations concerning closeness to and distance from others and from nonhuman objects in the environment. Space becomes filled with meaning. This spatial meaning or *personal space* helps to structure the individual's physical and social environment, regulating the flow of information and maintaining the individual system's sense of autonomy.

The concept of *territoriality*, adapted from studies of animal behavior, describes how individuals and groups regulate their interactions spatially. This regulation appears to serve important functions such as structuring social relations and maintaining a stable population level. Recent work suggests that *privacy* is a far more complex and important matter than had previously been supposed, playing a central role in both individual development and group behavior. By understanding these related concepts of territoriality, personal space, and privacy, a picture emerges of the wide-ranging significance of space regulation in humans. Against this background, the impact of the spatial environment on the family—crowding, housing conditions, geographic mobility— can be more clearly assessed. This chapter describes the process by which family members act on and in their spatial environment, what we shall call *spacing*. Chapter 9 applies the process of *spacing* (together with perceiving, valuing, and deciding) to the physical environment of the family. The impact of household and residential crowding, mobility, and housing conditions on the family will be assessed in the light of what a transactional approach can teach. Emphasis will also be placed on the construction and design of settings as reflections of spacing needs.

BODY-IMAGE BOUNDARIES

The first and most basic form of spacing is the development of body boundaries.* You will recall that in Chapter 2 the individual was described as a relatively open system exchanging information with its environment through selectively permeable boundaries. This means that the individual sees himself or herself as distinct from the surrounding world, yet involved with it in important ways.

The sense of distinct self is one that evolves in infancy and early childhood from an initial lack of differentiation. In interaction with others, the child gradually experiences himself or herself as separate from objects and others. As an infant's cries bring nourishment and cuddling, a sense of successfully acting *on* the environment is nurtured. The child's self-image is first closely related to

---

* I am indebted to Norma H. Compton for much of the material in this section.

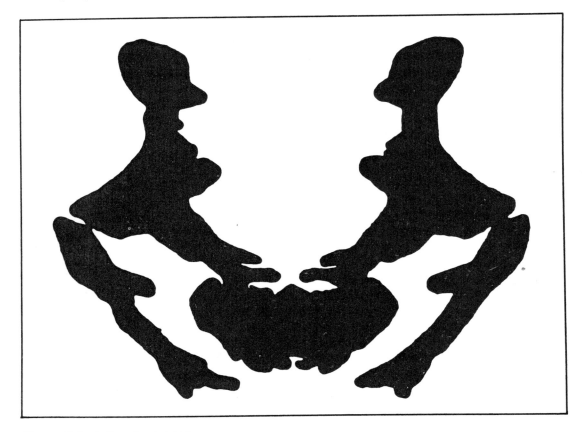

Figure 5.1. A Rorschach inkblot.

the body and its sensations. A *body concept,* or *body image,* is developed as the body is seen as having definite limits or boundaries that separate it from the outside world.

The *psychological self* is at first anchored in the sense of one's physical body as distinct from the environment. With development, however, significant objects and people with whom the child interacts becomes *internalized* or made part of the self. Physical settings are also internalized elements of self-identity. "My room," "my house," "my street" are elements by which the child identifies himself or herself.

Although this process of *psychological differentiation,* or the formation of a sense of self, is nearly universal—only the most pathological lack it completely—individuals vary in the definiteness and flexibility of their body-image boundaries. At one extreme, emotionally disturbed children seem unable to differentiate themselves from the social and physical environment. Sometimes a schizophrenic child develops an intense liking or dislike for a light, surface texture, or object. One study attempted to strengthen the diffuse body-image boundaries of a group of disturbed adolescent girls (Proshansky, 1971). When each girl was provided with a mirror near her bed, significant changes in appearance and behavior resulted. The mirror, it was thought, helped to strengthen the disturbed girls' sense of self and separate it from the surrounding environment.

Fisher and Cleveland (1956, 1957, 1958) have used the projective Rorschach inkblot test to measure the definiteness of a person's body boundary (Figure 5.1). A projective technique presents a relatively ambiguous unstructured stimulus or task. In responding to the task, such as interpreting a picture or supplying a story ending, the subject is assumed to reveal aspects of his or her personality that would be hidden under more direct questioning.

Fisher and Cleveland presented inkblots and asked subjects to describe what they saw. The responses were scored for the amount of boundary definiteness, as in responses like "cave with rocky walls" or "woman in fancy costume." This *barrier score,* as the final score was termed, was assumed to reflect the degree to which definite rather than ambiguous body boundaries existed.

The barrier score has been related to a variety of physiological and psychological measures. For example, an individual with strongly defined body boundaries tends also to be active, independent, interested in communicating with others, and self-oriented.

CLOTHING AND BODY-IMAGE

Clothing can be viewed as one way in which the body is marked off or differentiated from the outside world. It becomes an extension of the self, closely identified with the body and affecting body sensations. Women who have undergone surgery to remove a cancerous breast sometimes experience padded bras as an extension of themselves. In this way, their former body image may be restored.

Compton (1964) showed how clothing may compensate for weak body-image boundaries in some women. Using Fisher and Cleveland's Rorschach inkblot test, she measured the body-image boundaries of a group of female mental hospital patients. Those with weak body-image boundaries tended to choose brightly colored fabrics with strong contrast between design and background. It appeared that these women, many of whom were confused about the limits of their own bodies, used bright colors and strong contrasts to bolster their sense of identity. "Fashion therapy" programs in mental hospitals may be beneficial through their enhancement of weak body-image boundaries.

Clothing affects body boundaries in a variety of ways. Table 5.1 illustrates the relationship between clothing and both physiological and psychological body boundaries.

TERRITORIALITY IN ANIMALS

Interest in the human significance of space has stemmed from a number of sources. Research on the phenomenon of animal territoriality has emphasized the central importance of space regulation for the social life of many animal species, including our near relatives, the primates. Secondly, the population explosion, urban congestion, planned communities, and the possibility of extended living in small, artificially created spaces such as space capsules have all focussed interest on the significance of space for humans.

Let us consider first animal territoriality and the lessons it may hold for human spatial behavior. Ethologists, those who study the behavior of animals in their natural habitats, noted that in many species, the male establishes a geographical area as his own, reacting to intrusions by other species members with vigorous defense. Since securing a territory often preceded mating, territoriality appeared to serve the function of stabilizing the population along evolutionary lines. Those animals unable to defend a territory would be unable to mate and hence, the weakest of the species would be kept out of reproducing. Indeed, experimental studies of overpopulation in rat colonies illustrated that the breakdown of territoriality was accompanied by the disintegration of normal mating and childrearing patterns.

TABLE 5.1 RELATIONSHIPS BETWEEN SELECTED ASPECTS OF PHYSIOLOGICAL AND PSYCHOLOGICAL BODY BOUNDARIES AND CLOTHING

	Physiological Boundaries	Psychological Boundaries
Outline of boundary	Body membrane, skin hair	Me and not-me, indicated by feelings and thoughts
Function of boundary	To hold organs together and act as protective covering	Maintenance of self-image and self-esteem
Effects of clothing	May extend boundaries sensually May restrict boundaries (tight fit) May strengthen or weaken boundaries	May help define or change boundaries through bright colors and strong contrasts within fabric design

Printed with permission from Norma H. Compton

Territoriality also has been related to dominance in some animal groups. Among some primates, individuals may be ranked according to the privileges others accord them. These prerogatives of prior access to food, mating, and initial approaches to others are taken as evidence that the holder of these privileges is *dominant* or ranked above others. In many primate groups, a dominance hierarchy develops that is remarkably stable. Thus, continual conflict is avoided since members "know their place." Dominance and territoriality are often linked, since high-ranked animals appear to "own" more territory than more lowly ones and to be able to intrude upon the space of lower-ranked members with impunity.

In addition to dominance, territoriality appears to regulate many functions of animal social life, including nest-building, mating, role relations, and rearing of the young. Furthermore, territoriality is also applied to the animal group as a whole and not just to relations among individuals within the group. Thus, a group of chimpanzees may stake out a geographical area as their own and defend it against intrusions from other groups or stray individuals.

Before assessing the role of territoriality in humans, let's attempt to define the concept more rigorously. When existing definitions are reviewed, animal territoriality is seen to consist of the following components: (1) a place or geographical area in which an animal behaves for a relatively enduring period of time; (2) behavior within this area fulfills important functions, such as nest-building and mating; (3) intrusion into the territory by those defined as outsiders is met with vigorous defense. Often the territory is preventively marked to warn potential intruders, as in the example of dog urination. So territoriality may be thought of in terms of events that trigger its manifestation (e.g., intrusion), important needs of the animal or group (e.g., mating), and characteristic behaviors linked to geographical place (e.g., defense, use).

HUMAN TERRITORIALITY

Keeping these three components in mind, let us search now for glimpses of territoriality in humans. The central importance of territoriality as observed among our closest relatives in the animal kingdom has led many to believe that territoriality also pervasively regulates human social groups as well. This conviction has resulted in unfortunate generalizations in which territory is seen as part of man's genetic heritage necessary for the unleashing of aggressive impulses (Ardrey, 1966). At first glance, evidence of territorial behavior abounds in the human scene. Witness the home court advantage of sports teams. Consider the strong identification many individuals have with spaces—Dad's chair, Mom's kitchen. Note the fierce national loyalties that spring up to defend the "motherland" or "fatherland" from threat. Many are suggesting that territoriality is a central fact of human behavior. It is often difficult, however, to distinguish true territoriality from behaviors that only superficially resemble animal spacing patterns. Moreover, the same behavior in humans and other primates may serve very different functions. Finally, the great role of symbolic behavior in human life implies that territoriality may be elaborated and extended among humans in ways impossible for other species.

More systematic understanding of the way in which human territoriality works comes from experimental observations of social behavior under conditions of either extreme social isolation or crowding. For example, in one study (Altman and Haythorn, 1967), two individuals lived in a small room for ten days with no outside contact, while a matched group had outside contacts. The isolated pairs of men gradually developed territorial behavior. At first each laid claim to an area of the room and a bed; later more mobile and less personal objects fell victim to territorial behavior as well. Those with access to others did not exhibit such possessiveness, however. Furthermore, when the isolated individuals had incongruent personalities as in a pair of dominant individuals, stronger territorial behavior resulted compared with more complementary pairs such as a dominant-submissive combination.

Another study of isolated pairs confirmed these findings and added some interesting detail (Altman, 1970). In this experiment, strong preferences for objects and places again developed. Additionally, those pairs unable to complete the isolation experience (as long as twenty days) appeared to have imbalanced territorial patterns, with one man having several preferred places while the other had none.

Human territorial behavior has been observed under high-density conditions as well. When density was increased in a play setting for children (Hutt and Vaizey, 1966), increased aggressive behavior was observed, indicating a parallel between human and animal responses to "invasion." In another investigation of young children adjusting to a new nursery school, territorial preferences were observed. Although the children played in a large open-space setting, many used only 10 percent of the available space. Moreover, when within his or her preferred area, the child exhibited more self-confidence and ability to interact than when outside the territory.

It should be emphasized that this exploratory study observed children only during the first week of school. Thus, this analogue of territoriality may surface only during periods of adjustment to new environments. Moreover, other aspects of territoriality found among nonhuman primates—aggressive defense against intruders, for example—were entirely absent.

In general, the greater flexibility and complexity of human interactions mean that territorial behavior will not always occur when expected on the basis of animal studies and may occur when unexpected. For example, Freedman's density studies (1975) show that territorial responses do not necessarily occur even in conditions of extreme crowding. For one thing, sex of those crowded

A newspaper on an empty seat can be a "marker" of territory. (Photo by Natalie Leimkuhler.)

together appears to be important. A group of women or a mixed-sex group were unaffected by extremely high densities, while groups of men responded negatively and aggressively to the perceived "intrusions" of others.

Thus, while territorial behavior in humans has been repeatedly observed, it is by no means the same phenomenon as that seen in animal studies. First, because of the human propensity for symbolic behavior, possessiveness about people, objects, and ideas may be just as important or more important than staked out geographical areas. Secondly, despite some arguments that territoriality is instinctive in humans (Ardry, 1966), recent research, such as the Freedman density studies, compels us to emphasize the modifiability of such behavior. More attention appears to be paid by humans to preventive "markers" of territory than to defense against intrusion. We tell people not to disturb us, lock doors, glare at unwanted company, place books and coats on empty seats around us. Since such preventive actions are usually successful, there is little need for overt defense like that observed among many animal species. Indeed, few studies find human defense against intrusion, but many find a sense of ownership, preferred use, and preventive warning as the hallmarks of human territoriality. This idea of territoriality as preferred occupation and use of an area without the role of defense against intrusion has been defined as "home range" (Stea, 1970).

It has been argued that human territoriality should be thought of primarily in terms of discontinuous "home ranges"—one for work, one for recreation, one for family life—around which social life is organized (Stea, 1970).

In one analysis, four types of human territories were distinguished: *public, home, interactional,* and *body* territories (Lyman and Scott, 1967). *Public* territories such as courtyards and parks provide the citizen with freedom of access, but not necessarily of action. *Home* territories are public ones taken over by groups or individuals, as when a particular park area becomes a street gang's turf or when an elderly park stroller habitually claims "his own bench." *Interactional* territories are those where social gatherings occur, with marked boundaries and rules of access. The home is an example of an interactional territory. Finally, territories encompassing the body, what we have referred to in our discussion of body-image boundaries and what will appear below in the concept of personal space constitute *body* territories.

PERSONAL SPACE

A good illustration of the complexity of human spatial behavior is provided by a look at the concept of personal space and its antecedents. We may define *personal space* as that component of territorial behavior which refers to preferred distance from others. While defense against intruders does not necessarily occur, in practice personal space is thought to imply a moveable territory to which an individual lays claim and which he or she will attempt to "defend" against intruders.

On the cognitive level, personal space may be viewed as a *schema* defining preferred interpersonal involvement. A *schema* here refers to a mental representation or concept whose existence is inferred from behavioral clues. The notion of a schema helps one to understand how behavior is organized rather than random and allows one to predict certain behaviors consonant with the schema an individual is thought to have. The personal space schema has been likened to a continually shifting invisible bubble around the individual. When others intrude within the bubble, the individual feels threatened, perhaps hostile, and tries to reestablish the preferred distance. For example, a series of naturalistic studies was conducted at study tables in university libraries. The experimenter sat close to females studying alone and observed responses to such intrusion. Quickest flight was triggered when the experimenter sat next to the subject and moved her chair even closer. Over 70 percent of those intruded upon in this manner took flight within thirty minutes!

These studies showed that a variety of offensive and defensive moves were employed to keep a territory secure: for example, "territorial markers," books and papers strewn about, or asking someone to save your place—"the good neighbor" (Sommer, 1969). Since the personal-space construct refers not just to space but to interpersonal involvement generally, however, psychological distance may be recreated by averting one's gaze, turning the body aside, in general attempting to restrict any involvement cues. There are many situations in which personal space bubbles are violated and only these indirect means of "repairing the damage" are available. Consider behavior in a crowded elevator, during rush hour on the subway, or in a dentist's chair. In each case, the body is kept very still to attempt to minimize body contact, and the eyes are carefully averted. Conversation is superficial or avoided. Those little squiggles on the ceiling suddenly appear intensely fascinating.

Such strong reactions to invasion of the personal space bubble indicate that perception and use of space form an important component of an individual's involvement with an environment. Space is not perceived as neutral, but as charged with meaning and affect; certain spaces between individuals and nonhuman objects are felt to be optimal for communicating some feelings, but not others; maintaining some relationships, but not others. We often realize the meanings attached to space use only when the unwritten rules governing it are violated. As noted earlier, meetings between representatives of differing cultures may be characterized by discomfort from conflicting personal space norms. The distance we tolerate, indeed encourage in intimate relationships, are clearly viewed as inappropriate with acquaintances. Such intruders are resented as pushy for getting too close too soon. Clearly, part of individual development consists of thousands of daily learning experiences about the meaning of interpersonal distances and about the value of spaces in people's lives. Thus, interesting recent research (Guardo, 1969; Guardo and Meisels, 1971) has traced the development in children of personal-space concepts and preferences.

FACTORS INFLUENCING PERSONAL SPACE

Now that the ubiquity and importance of personal space have been demonstrated, let us consider the constantly changing nature of the personal-space bubble. What factors cause the bubble to change shape? There are many, and most factors operate simultaneously in real-life encounters; thus, predicting and understanding spatial behavior is really quite complicated. Several factors have been discussed already. For one, cultural background affects the size of the bubble.

Culture. In Chapter 4, discussion of cultural differences in receptor use and emphasis led to the conclusion that some cultures may encourage close interpersonal involvement, while others may be defined as noncontact. Similarly, a culture may emphasize the use of one sensory channel over others. For example, stress on the use of the visual channel creates a cultural valuation of visual space rather than auditory space, as seen in the traditional Japanese home with its aesthetically arranged visual spaces within paper-thin walls through which outside noises easily permeate. These observations of cultural contrast in the management of space imply that personal space will differ by culture. That is, in contact cultures, preferred interpersonal distance is on the average smaller than in noncontact cultures. This has been a difficult hypothesis to prove, however, since so many other factors simultaneously influence the nature of the personal-space bubble.

Level of acquaintance. One of these is the level of acquaintance. It is obvious that no matter what the culture, *close* friends are permitted to get closer than *distant* acquaintances, as our use of this spatial vocabulary illustrates. Hall (1966) distinguished four basic zones of personal space on level of acquaintanceship: public, social, personal, and intimate (Figure 5.2). He further divided each zone into a near and far subdivision. He argued that we quite instinctively assess the nature of our relationship with another (How well do I know X? How comfortable do I feel with him?) and the nature of the setting (Am I meeting X in a formal public setting or in my home?) and adjust the personal-space bubble accordingly.

Sex. In addition to culture and level of acquaintanceship, sex of interactants has been repeatedly identified as an important influence on personal space for both children and adults. It is well known that in American culture (and many others) women are seen as more "approachable," less psychologically distant than men. They are more willing to show emotion openly; observe the behavior of the sexes at a tear-jerker movie. The women are happily dabbing their eyes with handkerchiefs while the men affected by the movie claim to be getting irritants out of their eyes. Women are not only encouraged to be more emotionally open than men, but they also allow more interpersonal involvement. Women engage in more eye contact with an interviewer (Exline, 1963)

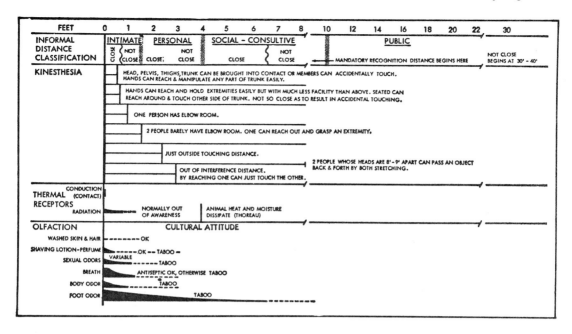

Figure 5.2. Interplay of the distant and immediate receptors in proxemic perception. (From *The Hidden Dimension* by Edward T. Hall. Copyright 1966 by Edward T. Hall. Reproduced by permission of Doubleday & Company, Inc., and the author, Edward T. Hall.)

and allow themselves to be touched more frequently by both sexes (Jourard, 1966). This sex difference begins very early. One observational study found that preschool children approached closer to a little girl than to a little boy (Lomranz et al., 1975). It is likely that these sex differences are the product of socialization rather than any inborn preferences, although the role of biological differences predisposing toward sociability and nurturance cannot be ruled out.

How are these personal space differences socialized? There is evidence that almost from birth the sex of the child is an important cue in determining distance, physical handling, and eye contact. For example, during the first six months of life, mothers are more likely to talk while looking at baby girls as compared with boys (Moss, 1967). The first tentative steps in independence striving are literally steps increasing distance from the caretaker, and these are likely to be more encouraged if a boy, rather than a girl, is making them. Later in school, teachers tend to engage in more nurturant physical contact with girls, while the pattern of interaction with boys consists of discussion at a distance about how to achieve instrumental goals.

Thus, typical teacher-girl interactions might look like this: Amy brings her work up to the teacher's desk. The teacher leans over the work with Amy, perhaps putting her arm around the girl as she softly talks. The teacher is apt to tell Amy how she feels about her work, that it pleases her, or that she needs to improve. By contrast, a typical teacher-boy interaction observed had the following characteristics: From her desk, the teacher is telling John at the back of the room how he might set up his science experiment. She gives several suggestions of strategies that might work. Of course, in doing so, she must raise her voice so that the instructions will carry to the back of the room. Interestingly, most of the teachers in this study reported that boys tended to be louder and noisier than girls without realizing how their own management of interpersonal distances had strengthened such a difference.

These examples illustrate differences in behavior toward the sexes which help to strengthen later sex differences in personal space. In addition, there are sex-role expectations that girls and women will be more nurturant, socially responsive, and approachable than will boys and men. These expectations cause girls to hone their awareness of others' unspoken social cues. Since the management of interpersonal space is just such a set of social cues, it is perhaps not surprising that even six-year-old girls are better able to discriminate between different interpersonal distances than are boys of the same age (Post and Hetherington, 1974).

Status. Status appears to be another important determinant of the personal-space bubble. Reminiscent of animal territorial behavior, humans will keep greater distances from others of higher status, as compared with those of equal or lower rank. Moreover, the higher ups are seen as having the initiative in increasing or decreasing distance. Theodore White, in his *Making of the President, 1960,* illustrates this point. When the Democratic party nominee John F. Kennedy emerged to greet his campaign workers shortly after the nomination had been secured, a space of about thirty feet was spontaneously made around him. Only when his brother and campaign manager, Robert F. Kennedy, motioned to the group, did they approach the man who had suddenly been transformed into a potential president.

Topic or task. In addition to culture, sex, acquaintance, and status, topic of conversation affects personal space. For example, pleasant topics are associated with closer distances than neutral or unpleasant ones (Little, 1968). In one study (Leipold, 1963), students anticipated speaking with a professor under three conditions—stress ("Your grade is poor, and you have not done your best"), praise ("You are doing very well, and Mr. Leipold wants to talk with you further"), and neutral ("Mr. Leipold is interested in your feelings about the course"). Those in the stress condition positioned their chairs at the greatest distance, while those in the praise condition sat closest to the experimenter.

Feelings. These studies of effects of praise and stress on personal space indicate that space conveys feelings about the interaction. Indeed, attitudinal factors are among the most important determinants of the personal-space bubble. For both children (Melson, 1976) and adults (Kleck, 1969), distance is strongly associated with the friendly-unfriendly dimension (Figure 5.3). In general, the closer the distance, the more friendly the pair, although since all the other factors mentioned above are operating, this general statement is often qualified. For example, when school-age children are asked to place figures at desired interpersonal distances, girls place friends closer than boys do. Similarly, under negative affect conditions, girls are more likely to increase desired distance and boys to decrease it (Guardo, 1969).

In addition to positive-negative affect, approval seeking may lead to closer approach. For example, female college students in one study sat approximately 57 inches from an interviewer from whom they were seeking approval, but over 90 inches from one from whom they were avoiding approval (Rosenfeld, 1965). When physical distance was fixed, women seeking approval sought to decrease psychological distance by smiling and gesturing more often.

Personality. Not only the motivation of the moment, but more enduring personality characteristics affect personal space. It is reasonable to hypothesize that extroverts, as more people-oriented, might approach and be approached more than introverts. People differ in their preference for orienting toward people versus orienting toward things. This *social* versus *object* orientation has been observed as a stable pattern in children as young as three years of age (Jennings,

Friendly children play at school

Unfriendly (angry) children at school

Figure 5.3. Representative responses of preschool-age children to hypothetical friendly and unfriendly encounters. (Original drawing based on research reported in Melson, G.F. Determinants of personal space in young children. *Perceptual and Motor Skills* 43 (1976): 1O7-114.)

1975). Support for such a relation between this personality variable and preferred seating position at a table was found (Cook, 1970). More extroverts chose positions close to others than did introverts.

PROBLEMS IN MEASURING PERSONAL SPACE

It is important to realize that while many studies indicate the diversity of factors affecting the personal-space bubble, this evidence comes from distinct, not easily reconciled methods. In some studies, the actual approach distance is observed and recorded, as in Leipold's study of approach under praise, stress, and neutral conditions. In others, however, subjects are asked to respond to paper-and-pencil hypothetical situations by indicating on a graph, feltboard, or picture where they would prefer to place themselves (Keuthe, 1964; Melson, 1976). Do these indirect measures predict the ways individuals are likely to respond in real-life encounters? Not necessarily. In one study comparing several methods of assessing personal space (Dosey and Meisels, 1969), no relation was found among observational and paper-and-pencil responses. Therefore, caution must be used in interpreting results of personal-space research. At present, perhaps the most one can say is that personal-space studies show that the bubble is extremely sensitive to personality, motivational, and situational cues, but that the resulting real-life behavior cannot always be inferred from responses to hypothetical situations.

The research on personal space cited thus far focuses only on preferred distance between people. Yet, spacing, broadly defined, includes distance from *objects* as well as people. Some people seem happiest in cluttered environments filled with objects, while others seek out a sense of barrenness and empty space. For some people, their sense of self extends to include many things. Objects are significant reflections of such persons' history and personality.

The personal pronoun "my" in the sense of "my room," "my desk," "my chair at the table," "my sheet," "my file," "my papers," etc., implies more than legal or normative ownership. These objects, spaces, and places are extensions of the individual's self, and in this sense, he and only he can determine who besides himself—if anyone at all—will use them, change them, or even view them (Proshansky, 1971, p. 18).

The importance of objects, as well as their arrangement and organization in space, has been studied relatively little. One might hypothesize that personality characteristics such as social versus object orientation would be related to the tendency to value and collect certain objects. Here is an area where additional research is needed.

SIGNIFICANCE OF THE PERSONAL-SPACE CONCEPT

The operation of the personal-space schema in individuals means that the effects of space upon people cannot be predicted from knowledge of the physical environment alone. It is impossible to specify what effects high-density situations will have on people without knowing what meanings differing spatial settings have for them. As the previous discussion of research showed, these meanings depend on characteristics of the situation, immediate feelings and motivations, and more enduring personality dispositions. What is unbearably crowded for one cocktail partygoer is pleasantly convivial to the next. More relevant, the tenement housing of one family may provide important social supports in terms of companionship, child care, and supplementary resources, while for another family it represents a situation threatening their integrity as a unit. The personal-space construct illustrates how the perception and needs of the perceiver must be taken into account in attempts to pinpoint environmental effects upon families. The complex determinants of personal space reviewed here provide a filtering lens through which the physical environment is viewed.

Personal space is an important factor in understanding people's responses to environments. Warnings about the effects of overcrowding on the mental and physical health of urban dwellers neglect the important dimensions of their psychological attitudes toward space. Similarly, indictments of particular housing or landscapes forms as "sterile" or "inhuman" must be checked against the perceptions and spacing needs of the users of such settings.

Personal space is also a construct describing active manipulation of the environment to fulfill spacing needs. The important settings of people's lives—home, work place, and playground—reflect the personal space constructs of their creators and users. Architectural design may be viewed as an expression of personal-space schemata. When Hall wrote his classic work, *The Hidden Dimension,* on cultural differences in proxemics, he noted striking differences between the design of homes in Japan and Germany. These differences, he argued, arose as expressions of each culture's desired level of personal space as well as the method by which it is achieved. Japanese screens achieve visual privacy, but their paper thinness permits noise to intrude, while the thick walls and doors of homes in Germany underscore the importance of personal space achieved through control of auditory stimulation. One writer put it like this: "Architecture is one way in which a culture makes its collective unconscious visible" (Thompson, 1978).

TERRITORIALITY AND PERSONAL SPACE IN THE FAMILY

The related concepts of personal space and territoriality may be applied to family transactions with their environment. Moving from the individual level to that of the small group of the family, the existence of personal-space concepts within each individual means that one task of the family is to work out an accommodation among distinct ways of perceiving and using space. In the words of one approach to family study, the family has the task of balancing tendencies toward separateness and connectedness (Hess and Handel, 1974). Each family member has particular needs for physical and emotional closeness with others. At other times, the same individual may require greater autonomy and privacy. These individual needs change not only with a particular situation or mood, but with broad developmental changes as well. The young child requires more emotional support and physical presence by caretakers than the adolescent who is likely to assert new-found independence.

Such shifting needs for separateness and connectedness make *distance regulation,* broadly defined to include emotional as well as physical distance, a central task of family interaction (Kantor and Lehr, 1975).

When family members come from the same cultural background and class, as they usually do, they are apt to have developed many similarities in personal-space concepts. However, since personal space is a function also of motivation, attitude, and situation, on the group level differences in feelings among family members will make this tendency toward separateness and connectedness a dynamically changing thing. Hence, personal space poses problems for family interaction because, as in any small group, individual needs must be balanced against concerns for group cohesion and functioning.

In addition, the notion of personal space may be applied to the family unit as a whole. We may say that each family develops a sense of its collective preferred distance, both psychologically and geographically, from others. These others include more distant kin, friends, local community members, and members of the larger society. Although the uniqueness of each family's life is an axiom, nevertheless the historical moment and cultural context are reflected in this group sense of personal space. To see this, one may contrast the social values and organization of medieval family life with that of the modern family and note that in each case the organization of family space supported differing conceptions of the family and its closeness or distance from others. As Breughel's *Country Wedding* indicates, medieval social life involved the entire community—all ages, all types jostling each other in what sometimes looks to our modern eyes like a chaos of revelry. If we make an imaginative effort to put ourselves back in that time, we find ourselves living in an environment organized primarily around the community, not the nuclear family. Privacy was nonexistent and nonvalued, age segregation was minimal, and households reflected this social organization by consisting of a series of large rooms, perhaps arranged around a courtyard. None of the rooms were specialized for particular functions (e.g., bedrooms for sleeping, dining rooms for eating). Instead, when the people were hungry, servants would carry in a table and chairs.

Medieval social life made little distinction between family and community as depicted in Breughel's "A Country Wedding," ca 1566. (Reproduced with permission of Kunsthistorisches Museum, Vienna.)

When people became sleepy, those of high rank got portable bedding set up by servants, while those of lower distinction found themselves a cozy or not-so-cozy corner.

The local community intruded into every aspect of family life, its subtle pressures compelling the forms of courtship, marriage, childrearing, indeed every aspect of social interaction. Consequently, a sense of family as important did not exist.

One historian argues (Aries, 1962) that only gradually did the idea of the family as distinct from the community develop, initially by the privileged classes as a means of separating and safeguarding the development of their children. Gradually, this new ethos of the family permeated the working classes in the cities and the peasantry as well, but not, in the view of another historian (Shorter, 1975), until the nineteenth century. Thus, the family as psychologically and physically distinct from the wider community may be a relatively recent social creation, the "modern" as distinct from the "traditional" family.

This changing relationship between family and community was reflected in parallel changes in the organization of space. The family withdrew itself both psychologically and physically from its intense community involvement. The notion of privacy as desirable was born, and the importance of a setting in which to nurture the family was emphasized. Indeed, contemporary organization of family life in America and most of Europe constitutes an extreme contrast to the brief sketch presented here of family life several hundred years ago. The family unit safeguards its contacts with the outside world and increasingly views the family as a needed refuge from the stresses of modernity. The detached family dwelling is the ideal, and privacy is a basic human need.

HOME AS FAMILY PERSONAL SPACE

If the concept of personal space is applied not to the individual but to the family as a unit, we may say that the personal-space bubble of the average American family is its home. Despite or perhaps because of high geographical mobility, many American families highly value the privately owned, detached single-family dwelling as the hallmark of domestic life.

Moreover, a contemporary view of housing developed over the last century sees space as *activity-specific*. In marked contrast to the unspecified use of space in medieval buildings, most homes contain spaces shaped to meet the demands of specific functions, so that family activities involve regular progression through spaces—a kitchen for eating, a bedroom for sleeping, a playroom for children's play. A historical and cross-cultural perspective is an invaluable antidote to generalizations based on biological needs for particular environments, showing that needs are largely a product of development within a culture. Although biological needs cannot be ruled out, we have no way of separating their effects from those of the environment, since all behavior exists within an environmental context. With respect to privacy, Margaret Mead (1966) thinks that this is the most variable of all human needs. She reports that in some societies there is no word for privacy and when the concept is explained, it is viewed with disgust.

Even though privacy needs and separate activity spaces vary by culture, families living in a culture emphasizing them may experience stress when these culturally defined space needs are not fulfilled. The author, together with M. Inman, investigated the space needs and actual use of space in a group of married-student families living in university-constructed married-student housing units. Those families who had to use the same area for multiple activities—living room for studying, viewing television, playing with the baby—were most prone to report feelings of stress. They were also most likely to define their family as one with a high level of conflict (Melson, Inman, and Kemp, 1978).

Hence, the detached single-family dwelling, as both ideal and growing reality, as well as the emphasis on individual and family privacy, reflects dominant personal-space values of American society. These values indicate the degree of interpersonal involvement family members seek with others and with each other. Arguments concerning the effects of high-density conditions, whatever their merits, are based upon a value system stressing maximal distance between family units and substantial individual requirements of personal space within the family. High-density settings may have destructive consequences for some people under some conditions, but to sound the general alarm reflects one's assumptions about optimal environments, not hard evidence concerning people's needs. In fact, a government-commissioned analysis of land use arrangements, published as *The Costs of Sprawl,* concluded that a planned mix of clustered and high-density areas was considerably more energy efficient and more environmentally sound than low-density, single-family dwelling patterns (Hoben, 1976).

Nevertheless, the single, detached dwelling is overwhelmingly the preferred image of home to Americans, despite skyrocketing costs of real estate and energy. In a recent survey, 85 percent of the respondents said they preferred single-family dwellings. This did not reflect preferences for existing living conditions only, since two-thirds of those living in multiple dwellings expressed the same preferences (Michelson, 1970). One professor of design (Cooper, 1976) suggests that the apartment is rejected by Americans because it threatens a self-image as a separate and unique individual, standing alone and independent. The results of survey data, however, show that the typical motivations for single-family dwellings are wide ranging. Those interviewed gave these reasons for single-home preference: privacy, best for raising children, easiest to do the things you want, best outside design, and best contact with neighbors (Michelson, 1966).

Some social critics have viewed detached family dwellings as a reflection, if not a cause, of family isolation, with each family unit on its own plot of land sealed in its own "little box," as depicted in Malvina Reynolds's song, "Little Boxes, Little Boxes." The results of empirical investigations, however, tend to show a quite different pattern. In the same survey cited above, families with private open spaces and single-family detached dwellings reported *more* socializing with neighbors than did those in multiple dwellings with shared open spaces. The director of the survey interpreted this finding thus: ownership of outdoor space frees the family to use that space at will without worrying about territorial needs of others. Thus, they are more likely to be outside and hence, run into the neighbors. Furthermore, home ownership itself represents a felt stake in the community, and activities like home repair and mowing the lawn often breed social contact.

Because of the historical trends outlined earlier, the nuclear family has become closely associated with a territory, known as its home. The idea of a home is a deep sense of permanence and continuity, a place where one's roots are, where one is safe from the outside world. Small wonder that in our national pastime we race for "home" plate, that "a man's home is his castle," and "there's no place like home." The myth of "home" dies hard in mobile, often rootless Americans who, as in Thomas Wolfe's novel, find "you can't go home again." In addition, the dramatic increase of connectedness through mass communication and transportation, the information explosion with which individuals are bombarded, has led to the feeling that home is the place to retreat from the stresses of the modern world. There we lick our wounds, gathering new strength to meet the onslaughts of an overwhelming, often hostile, outside world.

Just as the self and nonself represent the basic divisions of psychic space, the house represents the basic division of geographic space, the space of one's own versus the space outside. Thus, the home becomes a basic symbol of self as well as of family. In the process of becoming a home, a house becomes part of us and is felt to express our identity. In one study (Werthman, 1968), housing choices of California suburbanites were examined: those in business were more likely to choose ostentatious "display" houses, while those in helping professions preferred more restrained, inward-looking designs. Here it appeared to the observer that the home reflected the dominant occupational values of the male head of the household.

PRIVACY AND THE FAMILY

The gradual disengagement of family from community and the new importance placed on the home as a setting for family relations indicate that privacy is a crucial concept for the family. An exploration of this notion and its application to family-environment transactions is now in order.

First, a *definition of privacy*. Like territoriality and personal space, it will soon be evident that privacy is not one, but many things. The concept has been used by psychologists, sociologists, political scientists, anthropologists, and every other "-ologist," not to mention the proverbial "man (and woman) on the street." Sometimes the notion of privacy emphasizes "seclusion, withdrawal and avoidance of interaction, where the goal is to remove contact with others" (Altman, 1975). Other definitions stress "control over access to the self or to one's group" (Altman, 1975). This latter definition focusses not so much on withdrawal as on control over the flow of information outward to others from the person or group as well as inward from the environment. It permits us to see privacy as a transaction, involving inputs from the environment as well as outputs from the self or group *to* the environment. Privacy is not always a retreat into solitude; it may also mean the achievement of a desired level of interaction. Hence, in this discussion, we will follow the definition offered by Altman in his conceptual analysis of privacy: *"Privacy is the selective control over access to the self or to one's group."*

This definition of privacy as the control of the flow of information from self to environment and environment to self means that the voluntary nature of privacy is important to any understanding of the concept. When privacy is enforced against one's will, it may be termed *isolation.* Several analysts of privacy (Laufer, Proshansky, and Wolfe, 1975) have pointed out that if development is positive, aloneness is transformed from an enforced state in infancy to one freely chosen. The young child may fear aloneness because the ability to function autonomously is in doubt. Only when functioning alone becomes possible does the child see privacy as an expression and enhancement of the self. Privacy serves the function of safeguarding personal autonomy, making possible a sense of self-identity and self-worth. Time away from others, freely chosen, is time available for self-evaluation, integration of past experience, and planning for future action.

In addition to its volitional nature, another important dimension of the concept of privacy is its *interactional* quality (Laufer, Proshansky, and Wolfe, 1975). Privacy implies a relationship between at least two persons in which rules regulate the amount and flow of information about each other. When one party fails to understand or acknowledge these rules, we may say that the privacy of the other has been invaded. Thus, it has been pointed out that another important function of privacy, in addition to enhancement of the self, is release from the demands of constant interaction with others. Such aloneness may also provide time to "rehearse" upcoming social encounters. One sees this function most graphically in young children who often use time alone for monologues practicing language and for fantasies practicing newly acquired social roles. Among adults, Goffman (1959) has stressed what he calls the "backstage" use of privacy to prepare for "onstage" social interactions, much as some women before a party retire to their bedrooms for elaborate rituals of dressing.

Furthermore, modern society has been repeatedly characterized as one in which each individual manages a multitude of roles. Mr. X is husband and father at home, dutiful son to his aging parents, colleague in the insurance firm, and buddy in the bowling league. Daily juggling of all these roles requires that only information about the self appropriate to the role be shared with others. Mr. X will likely not dwell on intimacies of married life while checking insurance forms with his office partner, nor will he review the company's fiscal structure on visits to his ailing parents. In some encounters Mr. X will reserve certain information as private which he may volunteer in others. Perhaps contemporary emphasis on privacy is due in part to the heavy demand for managing complex sets of role relationships. While privacy is often seen as a means of preparing for and differentiating role performances, it may also serve as an emotional release from the tensions of playing social roles, a time to let down the facade one presents to others.

Finally, and perhaps paradoxically, privacy may serve the function of increasing communication and information flow between self and others. Privacy from one group, let us say neighbors, creates a setting for unhampered communication among family members. Lovers, for example, are sometimes blind to the public eye. In general restricting the flow of communication permits more intensive involvement with the chosen few remaining. This is most obviously the case with sexual behavior among intimates.

This function is particularly pertinent to the evolution of the modern family discussed earlier. As the family withdrew from the larger community, notions of intimacy, romance, and nurture grew up *within* sheltered family confines. As communication flow from one group, the local community, was restricted, communication within the family increased.

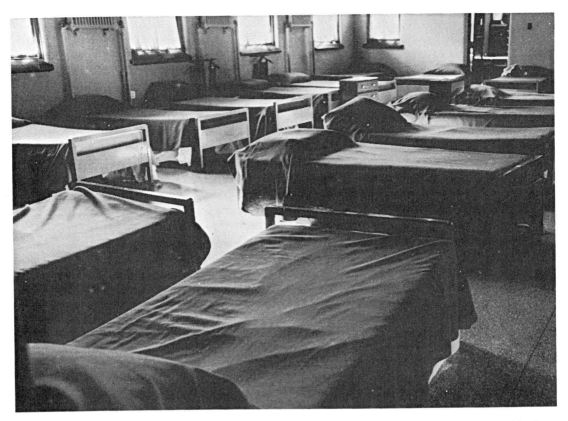

No sense of "mine" is possible in such an institutionalized setting. (Photo by Natalie Leimkuhler.)

To recapitulate, privacy, defined as selective control over access to the self, may serve any of the following functions: *enhancement of the self, regulation of social roles, release from role performance,* and *intensification of desired interactions* by sheltering them from others. In addition, one might mention certain behaviors, such as elimination of bodily wastes, which are culturally associated with exclusion of others.

In addition to its myriad functions, all of which may be understood through the central concept of *selective control,* privacy, like most everything else, is not static, but linked to a dynamically changing life cycle. Privacy needs vary with stages of the life cycle; the functions privacy serves also change. Young children develop a strong sense of mine (my toys, my family)— or in cultures emphasizing group upbringing, "our"—as a means of enhancing their fledging sense of self as distinct from others. Later, privacy provides an arena for rehearsing newly acquired roles. In adolescence, privacy is sought both to solidify an uncertain sense of adult identity and to begin the search for intimacy with others.

One of the few existing empirical studies of privacy illustrates the changing nature of the concept. In this study, interviews were conducted with 840 children aged four through nineteen, half from New York City and half from rural Wisconsin. From questions, the following picture of privacy emerged: (1) The youngest children had some idea of what privacy was; (2) privacy as "being alone" shifted gradually with age to privacy as being with desired others ("alone with my friends"); (3) privacy came to be seen as the ability to control access to self when wanted; and (4) privacy was most closely linked to the family, intrusion of family members, and management of family living space (Wolfe and Laufer, 1974; Laufer and Wolfe, 1973).

This study indicates that developmental changes in the meaning, function, and significance of privacy are a fruitful line of investigation. It is likely that certain levels of privacy are essential to healthy development. This possibility is strengthened by a study of privacy among emotionally disturbed children residing in a large state hospital. Studies of adults have shown that hospitals as total institutions deny patients control over access to themselves and others. Doctors and nurses feel free to intrude upon the patient at will, both physically and psychologically, while denying the same privilege. No sense of "mine" in terms of clothing, objects, or space is possible in the institutionalized setting. Even functions such as elimination and bathing, strongly governed by privacy rules in the outside world, often are carried out communally inside the institution.

Similar invasions of privacy are reported in this study of emotionally disturbed children. As a result, many of these children developed ideas that privacy was associated with negative feelings, since their only opportunity for aloneness came when they were put in the "seclusion room" as punishment for disruptive behavior. Not surprisingly, the investigators reported that the children often purposefully misbehaved in order to secure the only available opportunity for privacy. Thus, a Catch 22 situation developed. The children failed to improve because the therapeutic situation designed to cure them actually retarded their progress by denying them minimal privacy requirements.

While evidence concerning the importance of privacy for healthy development is indirect and incomplete, still less is known about adult conceptions of privacy. A glimpse into the complexities of privacy for adults is provided by one study of middle-management executives (Golan and Justa, 1976). In addition to conducting interviews, their on-the-job behavior was systematically observed. It soon became clear to the investigators that these men, all supervisors of others, saw their principal function as being "constantly available to others." Hence, individual privacy, even when necessary to complete reports, for example, was viewed as basically incompatible with other job requirements. Hence, these businessmen were constantly engaged in a delicate balancing act, juggling tasks conflicting in privacy demands.

This study suggests that adults who function in many different role settings have a highly sophisticated and variable conception of appropriate privacy behavior. Sometimes they must try to reconcile task demands with conflicting privacy requirements.

In addition, for adults, privacy may reflect the need for release from burdensome and sometimes conflicting role demands. The mother of young children often finds she is not at the helm when it comes to regulating communication with others. She is constantly "on call," ministering to the needs of her family. At the same time mothers at home all day with young children often feel that communication with others—the "outside," grown-up world—is too infrequent. Finally, as the aged experience loss of intimates, privacy needs may shift toward desire for more interaction and contact with others. If privacy needs are viewed in the perspective of the life cycle, one sees that a desired optimal level of interaction with others is the goal. Too little interaction, too much privacy, is as discomforting as too much interaction or too little privacy. Here the notion of level of adaptation, shifting with life cycle, situational and personality needs reappears. *Privacy is nothing more than the management of the boundary between self and environment to achieve a desired adaptation level for stimulation.* Altman (n.d.) has captured the same notion by contrasting "underachieved privacy" (too much stimulation) with "overachieved privacy" (feelings of isolation).

If privacy is the management of stimulation flowing in and out from the self, how is this management achieved? Verbally, Garbo's famous "I vant to be alone" is the most direct technique, but more indirect verbal mechanisms are perhaps more common. To exclude others and intensify contact with a chosen few, intimates may speak in a language unknown to the excluded, as when immigrant parents exchange secrets in their native tongue to "keep it from the children." Changes in speech rate, vocabulary, emphasis, and tone can all convey special meaning denied to outside eavesdroppers. Nonverbal mechanisms for ensuring privacy also abound. As mentioned earlier, invasion of personal space may be countered with glares, stares, body aversions, or diminished eye contact as well as physical flight.

A third major mechanism for regulating interaction is the management of the physical environment, the use of space and objects to let in and keep out. Some physical settings permit individuals to exercise freedom of choice about entering, participating, and leaving the setting. Many, particularly public settings such as hospitals and schools, do not. For example, an observational study of behavior in a psychiatric ward (Ittelson, Proshansky, and Rivlin, 1970) compared one-, two-, and three-bedroom rooms with larger dormitory wards. In the smaller rooms, a wider range of activities occurred, with social activity more frequent than isolated passive behavior. The authors concluded from their results that in the smaller settings, the patient perceived a wider range of activity open to him and felt free to choose desired activities. The smaller rooms provided more freedom of choice and hence privacy than the larger wards.

Environmental management may take on more subtle and elaborate forms. Anthropologists have furnished us with some graphic examples of such subtle space engineering. In one study of family life in a village in Southern France, spatial segregation of the sexes was emphasized (Reiter, 1975). Women "owned" interior spaces associated with the family, while men "owned" all public outdoor spaces, such as the cafes, public buildings, and the village square. Invisible walls were everywhere in the village; no self-respecting woman would enter a cafe, while no man who wished to avoid ridicule would remain at home longer than the bare minimum necessitated by his role as husband and father. Behavior in this village was regulated by its link to "owned" spaces and the sexes led parallel, but largely autonomous, existences.

In another study of the Armenian quarter, a walled city of 2,000 residents within the Old City of Jerusalem, "invisible walls" separating groups of residents, for example, the clergy from the laymen, were observed to regulate social exchanges (Azaria, 1977).

Moreover, in settings less exotic to American readers, environmental regulation of privacy is a well-established mechanism. One study of large families (Bossard and Boll, 1970) described family rituals such as bathroom policies, which ordered the flow of communication. The present author has conducted a series of studies of space use among married students with at least one child. All families lived in apartments with identical floor plans though, of course, each placed its own imprint upon the setting through decorating and personal possessions. When husband and wife were questioned concerning their identification with particular home spaces, it appeared that most couples developed a division of space as well as a division of labor. Although the apartments were perceived by the residents as quite small, most wives felt that they "owned" the kitchen, while most husbands had no sense of "owned" interior space, more often saying they went out of the apartment when they wanted more privacy. Direct observations of space use among these families confirmed a highly elaborated patterns of space regulation. These results echo that of the French village in which within-home spaces were strongly associated with women but not men.

What these diverse accounts share is the use of territoriality as a means of controlling access to the self or family group. Thus, territoriality is a basic mechanism for the regulation of privacy. Having one's own space allows at least the option of controlling interaction within it.

Not only does environmental management regulate interaction among the sexes within the family, but also that between family and community. As mentioned earlier, the shift from "traditional" to "modern" family was accompanied by physical changes in family setting, with the family's living quarters being more sharply distinguished from the outside by walls, passageways, doors, and rooms marked for specific family functions. No matter what the desired technique, Altman (n.d.) has suggested that mechanisms for regulating access to self and group are universal.

Concern with access of outside-family sources to the family itself is also expressed in political and social efforts to limit what is viewed as the intrusion of society into the family. Many social welfare programs have been opposed on that ground. Expansion of comprehensive day-care facilities has been seen by some as threatening the autonomy of the family as prime childrearing institution. Sex education and discussion of morals in the schools have been opposed as intrusion into the family's domain of value instruction. These kinds of controversies indicate a strongly held view that the family is under attack by societal institutions, and its cherished privacy, itself a recent historical development as we have seen, is threatened.

SUMMARY

Spacing has been discussed around three interrelated concepts: territoriality, personal space, and privacy. All three involve: (1) regulation of stimulation flowing out from the self to others and in from the environment to the self; (2) voluntary control; and (3) an optimal level of stimulation. All three may be viewed both from the vantage point of the individual and the perspective of the family as a unit. For example, we have shown that territoriality, privacy, and personal space function to structure distance between individuals as a means of regulating environmental stimulation. Similarly, such regulation is part of the interaction of family members with each other. Furthermore, the family as a unit regulates its distance, both physically and psychologically, from the "outside" environment. The historical development of the idea of family as distinct and private from its larger setting was briefly traced. The contemporary significance of the home as symbol and embodiment of this spacing of the family from others was emphasized.

Finally, the notion of privacy provided another perspective from which to view the spacing process among individuals and family units. Privacy is seen as a developmentally dynamic psychological need whose essence is regulation of stimulation. The management of privacy constitutes on the family level an important group task, balancing individual needs with group concerns. Finally, the privacy of the family from intrusion by the "outside" environment is a contemporary issue whose very existence highlights the importance of spacing as a means for regulating environmental stimulation in the family.

REFERENCES

Altman, I. Territorial behavior in humans: An analysis of the concept. In L. Pastalan and D. Carson, eds., *Spatial Behavior of Older People*. Ann Arbor: University of Michigan, 1970.

Altman, I. *Environment and Social Behavior: Privacy, Personal Space, Territory and Crowding.* Monterey, Calif. Brooks/Cole, 1975.

————. Privacy, a conceptual analysis. Unpublished paper. n.d.

Altman, I., and Haythorn, W. W. The ecology of isolated groups. *Behavioral Science* 12(1967): 169-82.

Ardrey, R. *The Territorial Imperative*. New York: Atheneum Press, 1966.

Aries, P. *Centuries of Childhood: A Social History of Family Life*. New York: Vintage Books, 1962.

Azaria, V. Personal communication, 1977.

Bossard, H. S., and Boll, E. S. *Ritual in Family Living*. Philadelphia: University of Pennsylvania Press, 1970.

Compton, N. H. Body-image boundaries in relation to clothing fabric and design preferences of a group of hospitalized psychotic women. *Journal of Home Economics* 56(1964): 40-45.

Cook, M. Experiments in orientation and proxemics. *Human Relations* 23(1970): 61-76.

Cooper, C. The house as symbol. In C. S. Wedin and L. G. Nygren, eds., *Housing Perspectives: Individuals and Families*. Minneapolis: Burgess, 1976.

Dosey, M., and Meisels, M. Personal space and self-protection. *Journal of Personality and Social Psychology* 11(1969): 93-97.

Exline, R. V. Explorations in the process of personal perception: Visual interaction in relation to competition, sex, and non-affiliation. *Journal of Personality* 31(1963): 1-20.

Fisher, S., and Cleveland, S. E. An approach to physiological reactivity in terms of a body image schema. *Psychological Review* 64(1957): 26-37.

Fisher, S. and Cleveland, S. E. Body image boundaries and sexual behavior. *Journal of Psychology* 45(1958): 207-211.

―――. Body-image boundaries and style of play. *Journal of Abnormal and Social Psychology* 52(1956): 373-379.

Freedman, J. L. *Crowding and Behavior*. San Francisco: W. H. Freeman, 1975.

Goffman, E. *The Presentation of Self in Everyday Life*. Garden City, N.Y.: Doubleday, 1959.

Golan, M. B., and Justa, F. C. The meaning of privacy for supervisors in office environments. Paper presented at the Environmental Design Research Conference (EDRA 7), May 1976.

Guardo, C. Personal space in children. *Child Development* 40(1969): 145-151.

Guardo, C., and Meisels, M. Factor structure of children's personal space schemata. *Child Development* 42(1971): 1307-1312.

Hall, E. *The Hidden Dimension*. Garden City, N.Y.: Doubleday, 1966.

Hess, R., and Handel, G. *Family Worlds: A Psychosocial Approach to Family Life*. Chicago: University of Chicago Press, 1974.

Hoben, J. E. The costs of sprawl. In C. S. Wedin and L. G. Nygren, eds., *Housing Perspectives: Individuals and Families*. Minneapolis: Burgess, 1976.

Hutt, C., and Vaizey, M. J. Differential effects of group density on social behavior. *Nature* 209(1966): 1371-1372.

Ittelson, W. H., Proshansky, H. M., and Rivlin, L. G. The environmental psychology of the psychiatric ward. In H. M. Proshansky, W. H. Ittelson, and L. G. Rivlin, eds., *Environmental Psychology: Man and His Physical Setting*. New York: Holt, Rinehart & Winston, 1970.

Jennings, K. D. People versus object orientation, social behavior, and intellectual abilities in preschool children. *Developmental Psychology* 11(1975): 511-519.

Jourard, S. M. An exploratory study of body-accessibility. *British Journal of Social and Clinical Psychology* 5(1966): 221-231.

Kantor, D., and Lehr, W. *Inside the Family*. San Francisco: Jossey-Bass, 1975.

Keuthe, J. L. The pervasive influence of social schemata. *Journal of Abnormal and Social Psychology* 68(1964): 248-254.

King, M. G. Interpersonal relations in preschool children and average approach distance. *Journal of Genetic Psychology* 109(1966): 109-116.

Kleck, R. Physical stigma and task oriented interaction. *Human Relations* 22(1969): 51-60.

Laufer, R. S., Proshansky, M. H., and Wolfe, M. Some analytic dimensions of privacy. Paper presented at the Third International Architectural Psychology Conference, Lund, Sweden, 1975.

Laufer, R. S., and Wolfe, M. Privacy as an age-related concept. Paper presented to the American Psychological Association meetings, Montreal, August 1973.

Leipold, W. E. *Psychological distance in a dyadic interview.* Doctoral dissertation, University of North Dakota, 1963.

Little, K. B. Cultural variations in social schemata. *Journal of Personality and Social Psychology* 10(1968): 1-7.

Lomranz, J., Shapiro, A., Choresh, N., and Gilat, Y. Children's personal space as a function of age and sex. *Developmental Psychology* 11(1975): 541-545.

Lyman, S. M., and Scott, M. B. Territoriality: A neglected sociological dimension. *Social Problems* 15(1967): 236-249.

Mead, M. Neighborhoods and human needs. *Ekistics* 21(1966), No. 123.

Melson, G. F. Determinants of personal space in young children: Perception of distance cues. *Perceptual and Motor Skills* 43(1976): 107-114.

Melson, G. F., Inman, M., and Kemp, P. Perceived environmental stress and family functioning in married student families. In S. Weidemann and J. Anderson, eds., *Priorities for Environmental Design Research,* EDRA, 1978.

Michelson, W. An empirical analysis of urban environmental preferences. *Journal of the American Institute of Planners* 32(1966): 355-360.

Michelson, W. Most people don't want what architects want. *Transaction,* July/August 1968.

Michelson, W. Analytic sampling for design information: A survey of housing experience. In H. Sanoff and S. Cohn, eds., *Proceedings of the First Environmental Design Research Association Conference,* 1970.

Montgomery, J. E. The importance of the house. In C. S. Wedin and L. G. Nygren, eds., *Housing Perspectives: Individuals and Families.* Minneapolis: Burgess, 1976.

Moss, H. A. Sex, age and state as determinants of mother-infant interaction. *Merrill-Palmer Quarterly* 13(1967): 19-36.

Post, B. and Hetherington, E. M. Sex differences in the use of proximity and eye contact in judgments of affiliation in preschool children. *Developmental Psychology* 10(1974): 881-889.

Proshansky, H. Visual and spatial aspects of social interaction and group process. Paper presented to Society for Human Factors, October 1971.

Reiter, R. R. Men and women in the south of France: Public and private domains. In R. R. Reiter, ed., *Toward an Anthropology of Women.* New York: Monthly Review Press, 1975, pp. 252-282.

Rosenfeld, H. Effect of approval-seeking induction on interpersonal proximity. *Psychological Reports* 17(1965): 120-122.

Shorter, E. *The Making of the Modern Family.* New York: Basic Books, 1975.

Sommer, R. *Personal Space: The Behavioral Basis of Design.* Englewood Cliffs, N.J.: Prentice-Hall, 1969.

Stea, D. Home range and use of space. In L. Pastalan and D. Carson, eds., *Spatial Behavior of Older People.* Ann Arbor: University of Michigan, 1970.

Stea, D., and Blaut, J. M. Notes toward a developmental theory of spatial learning. In J. Archea and C. Eastman, eds., *EDRA 2: Proceedings of the Second Annual Environmental Design Research Association Conference.* Pittsburgh: Carnegie Press, 1970.

Thompson, W. I. *Darkness and Scattered Light.* Garden City, N.Y.: Doubleday, 1978.

Tiger, L., and Shepher, J. *Women in the Kibbutz.* New York: Harcourt Brace Jovanovich, 1975.

Werthman, C. *The social meaning of the physical environment.* Unpublished doctoral dissertation, University of California at Berkeley, 1968.

Westin, A. *Privacy and Freedom.* New York: Atheneum Press, 1970.

Wolfe, M., and Laufer, R. The concept of privacy in childhood and adolescence. In D. H. Carson, ed., *Man-Environment Interactions.* Environmental Design Research Association Proceedings (V), Part 6, Milwaukee, Wis., 1974.

Valuing

6

Thus far, we have seen how the processes of perceiving and spacing structure a system's interactions with environments. The perspective may be that of the individual system and the family environment, the individual within a physical setting, or the family system in relation to its environments. In each case, perceiving and spacing determine what information and energy, basic system resources, will be made available to a system from the environment.

Valuing is the process by which this information and energy are rank-ordered or assigned priority in terms of importance in reaching desired goals. This may be illustrated by examining the resource of time. Individuals have limited time to engage in all the activities that interest or compel them, and the family as a unit has limited time to allocate to its activities as a group. Thus, how families allocate time for different activities provides an illustration of the management of a scarce resource. One family, the Maxwells, appears to allocate quite a bit of time to family activities. They make sure to have most meals together, weekends are reserved for family outings, and a structured family discussion is held once a week. Vacations are always family affairs, usually spent with relatives. The Wellborns, by contrast, seem to allocate most time to the pursuit of individual concerns. Each member eats at his or her convenience, since each has a different schedule of activities and responsibilities. Each reserves leisure time for nonfamily friends—Dad with his bowling league, Mom with the bridge club, Sis with her high school friends, and Junior with his Little League buddies. These two fictitious families, the Maxwells and the Wellborns, illustrate contrasting styles of managing the same scarce resource, time.

What underlies these styles? Both families are dealing simultaneously with two potentially conflicting values—the value of individual privacy and autonomy on the one hand, and the value of connectedness on the other. In every family, indeed in every group, there exists an inevitable dynamic tension between these two values, since the family is both a set of autonomous individuals and a mutually bound group. In the Maxwells' case, the value of family connectedness takes precedence over the value of individual autonomy, while with the Wellborns the reverse is true.

As in the above illustration, understanding the rank order of values in a family, the *value hierarchy,* helps to clarify how perceived resources will be used in decision making. When we speak of families, however, the notion of a value hierarchy is not a simple one. First, it may be difficult to speak of a single rank-ordering of values within a family. Often, substantial disagreement exists among family members. In the Wellborn family, for example, it may be that one member of the family, Junior, yearns for more time "all together as a family" and feels dissatisfied with the individualistic tone of the family. Understanding differences in value hierarchies may help to illumine family conflict.

Secondly, the notion of a rank order assumes a rather clear perception that A is more important than B, which is more important than C, and so on. In reality, people often hold values that are incompatible with one another, or fail to clearly rank one above the other, feeling all are important, or their rank order fluctuates with the situation and their own changing development as persons. Despite these complexities, values in the family can be studied. A major goal of such investigations is to answer the following question: What family characteristics help explain value conflicts and value change? What determines a family's value hierarchy? How are values used in allocating resources, making decisions, and carrying them out? Before dealing with these questions, let us consider the nature of values.

WHAT ARE VALUES?

A recent investigation of values (Rokeach, 1973) formally defined a value as "an enduring belief that a specific mode of conduct or end-state of existence is personally or socially preferable to an opposite or converse mode of conduct or end-state of existence" (p. 5). Note that two different types of values are described, "modes of conduct" and "end-states of existence." The former are *instrumental* values, means by which end-states or *terminal* values are achieved. Secondly, the definition refers to "personal or social preference." Values have an "ought" character that guides personal actions, provides standards for reaching decisions and resolving conflicts, justifies behavior, and maintains self-esteem. Moreover, values are standards by which the actions of others are judged. When held by a group or culture or institution, values act like a cement, drawing together group members. Similarly, if the group perceives a member as failing to live up to the values of the group, this perception may be enough to loosen the bonds between the group and individual.

Values may be understood most clearly by examining one's own value system. Table 6.1 lists eighteen terminal and eighteen instrumental values. Rokeach's well-known technique for assessing values invites the reader to rank-order each set of values separately in terms of personal importance.

Having gotten a sense of your own values, let us look at some other characteristics of values. Terminal values may be divided into two types, *personal* and *social*. Values such as "inner harmony," "pleasure," "mature love," and "social recognition" refer to end-states desired by the individual for him or herself, while values like "a world at peace," "a world of beauty," and "national security" are social in nature. Similarly, instrumental values seem to fall into two categories. Some refer to *moral* behavior ("honest," "forgiving," "loving") while others center on areas of *competence* ("ambitious," "intellectual," "imaginative") (Rokeach, 1973). Finally, it can be seen that some values emphasize *adjustment to others* ("obedient," "polite"), while other values concern *self-actualization,* or the development of one's full potential as a unique individual ("wisdom," "sense of accomplishment") (Rokeach, 1973).

The term *value-orientation* has also been used to refer to values as linked to a set of beliefs and attitudes to form a system by which much of experience is explained. These terms, *values* and *value-orientation,* may be applied at many levels, to the individual, small group, family, and culture. On the cultural level, dominant values are often described.

Having ranked your own personal value system, you may be curious to know how a representative sample of Americans ranked theirs in 1971 (Tables 6.2 and 6.3). Here one sees that as far as terminal values are concerned, both men and women ranked as first "a world at peace," second "family security," and third "freedom." Among instrumental values, "honest" emerges as first and "responsible" as third, but men and women disagree on the second most important values ("ambitious" for men; "forgiving" for women).

TABLE 6.1 TEST-RETEST RELIABILITIES OF 18 TERMINAL AND 18 INSTRUMENTAL VALUES. FORM D (N = 250)

Terminal Value	r	Instrumental Value	r
A comfortable life (a prosperous life)	.70	Ambitious (hard-working, aspiring)	.70
An exciting life (a stimulating, active life)	.73	Broadminded (open-minded)	.57
A sense of accomplishment (lasting contribution)	.51	Capable (competent, effective)	.51
A world at peace (free of war and conflict)	.67	Cheerful (lighthearted, joyful)	.65
A world of beauty (beauty of nature and the arts)	.66	Clean (neat, tidy)	.66
Equality (brotherhood, equal opportunity for all)	.71	Courageous (standing up for your beliefs)	.52
Family security (taking care of loved ones)	.64	Forgiving (willing to pardon others)	.62
Freedom (independence, free choice)	.61	Helpful (working for the welfare of others)	.66
Happiness (contentedness)	.62	Honest (sincere, truthful)	.62
Inner harmony (freedom from inner conflict)	.65	Imaginative (daring, creative)	.69
Mature love (sexual and spiritual intimacy)	.68	Independent (self-reliant, self-sufficient)	.60
National security (protection from attack)	.67	Intellectual (intelligent, reflective)	.67
Pleasure (an enjoyable, leisurely life)	.57	Logical (consistent, rational)	.57
Salvation (saved, eternal life)	.88	Loving (affectionate, tender)	.65
Self-respect (self-esteem)	.58	Obedient (dutiful, respectful)	.53
Social recognition (respect, admiration)	.65	Polite (courteous, well-mannered)	.53
True friendship (close companionship)	.59	Responsible (dependable, reliable)	.45
Wisdom (a mature understanding of life)	.60	Self-controlled (restrained, self-disciplined)	.52

Reprinted with permission from Rokeach, *The Nature of Human Values* (1973), and from Holgren Tests, Sunnyvale, Calif.

TABLE 6.2 TERMINAL VALUE MEDIANS AND COMPOSITE RANK ORDERS FOR AMERICAN MEN AND WOMEN

	Male	Female	
N =	665	744	p
A comfortable life	7.8(4)	10.0(13)	.001
An exciting life	14.6(18)	15.8(18)	.001
A sense of accomplishment	8.3(7)	9.4(10)	.01
A world at peace	3.8(1)	3.0(1)	.001
A world of beauty	13.6(15)	13.5(15)	—
Equality	8.9(9)	8.3(8)	—
Family security	3.8(2)	3.8(2)	—
Freedom	4.9(3)	6.1(3)	.01
Happiness	7.9(5)	7.4(5)	.05
Inner harmony	11.1(13)	9.8(12)	.001
Mature love	12.6(14)	12.3(14)	—
National security	9.2(10)	9.8(11)	—
Pleasure	14.1(17)	15.0(16)	.01
Salvation	9.9(12)	7.3(4)	.001
Self-respect	8.2(6)	7.4(6)	.01
Social recognition	13.8(16)	15.0(17)	.001
True friendship	9.6(11)	9.1(9)	—
Wisdom	8.5(8)	7.7(7)	.05

Reprinted with permission from Rokeach, *The Nature of Human Values* (1973).

Figures shown are median rankings and, in parentheses, composite rank orders.

Other, more descriptive accounts have characterized American values as emphasizing individualism, achievement, rationalism, and competition. However, these values are obviously not shared equally by all Americans. Other value-orientations, called *second-order* ones (Kluckhohn, 1951) remain as acceptable though not dominant. For example, while individualism may be dominant, many areas of American life place high value on cooperative task performance. The football team, the governmental committee, the parent cooperative, all reflect this second-order orientation of cooperation for the common good. Americans, of course, differ in important respects, particularly in social class, age, religion, race, and ethnic origin. Such differences are reflected in differences of rank ordering of both terminal and instrumental values. The same national sample described in overall terms in Table 6.2 revealed differences in value systems when subgroups were compared. The most important distinction proved to be social class. The poor and poorly educated ranked "clean," "a comfortable life," "salvation," "cheerful," "forgiving," "obedient," "helpful," and "polite" higher than did the more affluent. These more valued behaviors are generally *adjustment oriented* rather than directed toward *self-actualization.*

While social class is related to pervasive differences in value system, blacks and whites (social class controlled) differ only in the priority they attach to "equality," with blacks not surprisingly

TABLE 6.3 INSTRUMENTAL VALUE MEDIANS AND COMPOSITE RANK ORDERS FOR AMERICAN MEN AND WOMEN

	Male N = 665	Female 744	p
Ambitious	5.6(2)	7.4(4)	.001
Broadminded	7.2(4)	7.7(5)	—
Capable	8.9(8)	10.1(12)	.001
Cheerful	10.4(12)	9.4(10)	.05
Clean	9.4(9)	8.1 8)	.01
Courageous	7.5(5)	8.1(6)	—
Forgiving	8.2(6)	6.4(2)	.001
Helpful	8.3(7)	8.1(7)	—
Honest	3.4(1)	3.2(1)	—
Imaginative	14.3(18)	16.1(18)	.001
Independent	10.2(11)	10.7(14)	—
Intellectual	12.8(15)	13.2(16)	—
Logical	13.5(16)	14.7(17)	.001
Loving	10.9(14)	8.6(9)	.001
Obedient	13.5(17)	13.1(15)	—
Polite	10.9(13)	10.7(13)	—
Responsible	6.6(3)	6.8(3)	—
Self-controlled	9.7(10)	9.5(11)	—

Reprinted with permission from Rokeach, *The Nature of Human Values* (1973).

Figures shown are median rankings and, in parentheses, composite rank orders.

valuing "equality" more strongly. Religious differences, similarly, are limited to the relative importance attached to "salvation" and "forgivingness," characteristically Christian values which nonbelievers and Jews rank rather low. Finally, age comparisons reveal a complex pattern of change in values from adolescence through old age (Rokeach, 1973).

If one places the value rankings of Americans in a broader cross-cultural perspective, then differences of cultural emphasis on certain values become apparent.

VALUE-ORIENTATIONS

In a different formulation of values focussing on cultural values in the family, five basic value-orientations—activity, relational, time, man-nature, and human nature—were described (Kluckhohn, 1951). They provide a useful framework for understanding basic value-orientations around which the family is organized in differing cultures (Papajohn and Spiegel, 1975).

The activity orientation answers questions about the nature of human behavior. The answers indicating cultural preferences may be either being, being-in-becoming, or doing. Being expresses a preference for activity as a spontaneous expression of personality, encouraging impulse expression within cultural limits. The concern is with what the human being *is,* not with what he does. The doing orientation, by contrast, emphasizes accomplishment, not being. Most valued are activities that result in accomplishments evaluated by standards of excellence. In between is the being-in-becoming orientation, a concern with activity that enhances the development of the whole personality. Contemporary American culture is clearly one whose dominant value-orientation in terms of activity is doing, yet in some spheres of life, for example, at holidays and in sports, the being orientation prevails, while for some Americans, particularly artists and intellectuals, the activity orientation is predominantly being-in-becoming.

Related to this activity orientation is the distinction Erich Fromm (1976) makes between societies emphasizing *having* versus those stressing *being*. To him, the acquisitive society is the basis for the having mode: "To acquire, own, and make a profit are the sacred and inalienable rights of the individual in the industrial society." Persons become things; interpersonal relations take on the character of ownership. Cultures emphasizing a having orientation may ignore deep-seated needs to be, to express human faculties, and to be related to others. Moreover, as the global ecosystem's perilous ecological balance is threatened by the having mode, new interest in a being orientation surfaces in the midst of acquisitive societies such as the United States. Gurus, transcendental meditation, sensitivity training, biofeedback, and assertiveness training are all expressions of the need to enhance being.

The second orientation, called the *relational,* has three preferences: the lineal, the collateral, and the individualistic. The lineal refers to an emphasis on interpersonal relations based on age, generational differences, and tradition. This is reflected in the belief that when there is a problem to be solved, the oldest male member of the clan is to take charge. The collateral preference refers to a group emphasis on problem solving. If a problem arises, the family as a group, perhaps including extended kin, is involved in reaching a common solution. If a leader is needed, it is likely to be the one viewed as most qualified through expertise, not age or tradition.

The third preference, the individualistic, emphasizes the problem-solving ability of the individual standing alone. Again, although American culture strongly values the individualistic solution, collateral emphases are there too in the stress on team spirit and collaboration at work. Similarly, the lineal emphasis on age, generational linkages, and tradition is stronger among upper-class American families than middle- or lower-class families. Moreover, since America is itself a multi-racial, multi-ethnic country, a smorgasbord rather than a melting pot, it is not surprising that emphasis on lineal-collateral-individual value orientation has been found to vary with ethnic group.

In the Mexican-American family, for example, the kin of one's extended family remain a powerful force for family loyalty and identification. All the individual's actions reflect upon the family, and above all one must not cast shame upon it. Patriarchal authority is strong; men are more powerful than women, and age carries with it the weight of authority. This lineal emphasis extends beyond the nuclear unit. Grandparents, uncles, and aunts are given deference and obedience. Indeed, the lineal emphasis includes even those bound by nongenetic, social bonds through the institution of *compadrazgo,* or coparenthood, by which close friends who sponsor an infant at baptism assume familial ties and responsibilities. Such *compadres* will care for the child in the event of the parents' deaths (Forbes, 1966; Madsen, 1964).

For the poor Mexican-American especially, this lineal emphasis provides sanctuary in an often hostile world. Humiliation from Anglos at school may be cushioned by the protection of love at home (Madsen, 1964). Thus, discussion of the relational dimension of values illustrates the variation among families within the same culture, subcultural differences, and the existence of second-order preferences.

The time orientation reflects preferences for present, past, or future. Traditional Chinese culture is considered an example of a past-time emphasis, with its veneration of ancestors and strong family traditions. Mexican-American culture has been viewed as one placing stress on present time; the future is seen as vague, unpredictable, and resistant to successful planning, while the past holds equally little value. The dominant Anglo-American culture is thought of as strongly future-time oriented, always planning for a better tomorrow, dissatisfied with the present, and viewing the past as an outmoded idea ripe for change.

A fourth orientation deals with the question of man's relation to nature. Are the forces of nature more powerful than human striving (subjugation-to-nature preference), or susceptible to human mastery and control (mastery over nature)? A third preference, harmony with nature, views no real distinction between humans and nature. Both are needed, existing in harmony. This is the value preference associated with environmentalists of the current ecology movement. Again, in general Americans are seen as strongly preferring mastery-over-nature solutions. We look to the challenges of an unruly environment, conquering the moon and Mars, as believers in the triumph of ultimate technology over natural disasters and limited natural resources.

Finally, a fifth orientation wrestles with man's true nature. This orientation may be thought of as the traditional domain of religious thought. Preferences may be that human nature is basically evil, basically good, or a mixture of good and evil. In addition, one may believe that human nature is susceptible or resistant to change. Table 6.4 summarizes these five value-orientations and their possible solutions.

TABLE 6.4 VALUE-ORIENTATIONS

Orientations	Preferences		
Activity	Being	Being-in-becoming	Doing
Relational	Lineal	Collateral	Individualist
Time	Past	Present	Future
Man-nature	Subjugation-to-nature	Harmony-with-nature	Mastery-over-nature
Human nature	Evil	Good-and-evil	Good

Reprinted with permission from Papajohn and Spiegel, 1975, p. 22.

VALUE CHANGE

Immigrant families often feel pressured to modify cultural values in adopting the dominant American values of doing, future orientation, and mastery over nature. Not all family members may react to this cultural demand similarly; some may resist the new value system wholeheartedly, others may rush to adopt it, still others may feel torn between the old and the new.

In periods of rapid change, dominant cultural values themselves undergo change and no longer are transmitted clearly to family members. The youth movement of the sixties challenged doing and future-time orientations in arguing that the joys of the present moment (being orientation) were lost by those who emphasized delayed gratification. In addition, they claimed that a doing orientation prevented the development of the whole person, encouraged cutthroat competition, and prevented true intimacy among people. The youth movement also challenged the strong individualistic orientation of American life with claims that it eroded a sense of community and sharing. Although only a minority of the nation's young raised these challenges, the effects, amplified through the media, reverberated throughout much larger segments of society with reactions of both sympathy and outrage.

Similarly, the women's movement has called attention to the fact that these dominant value-orientations are reserved primarily for only half the American population—men. Although the doing orientation is most highly valued and rewarded, women are still expected to structure their activity as support for the doing orientation of their husbands. Childrearing and homemaking, still the most prominent activity areas for women, are not included as part of the doing orientation but are seen as group-maintenance activities. Similarly, the women's movement has pointed out that an individualistic orientation is primarily reserved for men, while women are expected to retain a collateral or group orientation. Thus, the value-orientations most valued by American culture are set aside for men, and hence women are relegated to secondary status in terms of the values structuring their behavior.

Thus, in an open society, while dominant value-orientations can be identified, they are never static, and counter-values are always well represented among the population, always offering alternative value expressions to the dissatisfied.

Similarly, in discussion of race relations, Myrdal (1944) called attention to the discrepancy between the "American creed" of freedom, democracy, and justice, and actual behavior toward blacks and native Americans. Ideology and behavior send conflicting value messages.

DEVELOPING VALUES

How does the individual acquire value-orientations? It is thought that the child acquires values primarily within the family. Cultural values are transmitted to the child through his parents and other representatives of that culture.

Freud viewed the father particularly as the one who symbolizes the authority of society. Father transmits the culture's prohibitions and rules and urges his children to incorporate them. The father must wean the children away from the mother's greater protectiveness and nurturance. In a different formulation, Talcott Parsons (1955) distinguished two major roles within the family—the "instrumental" and the "expressive." The instrumental role is the one that relates the family to the wider society, while the expressive role concentrates on ensuring that the emotional needs of the family group are being met. It was Parsons's view that to be effective, a group needed to have both "instrumental" and "expressive" specialists. The same individual could not adequately perform both roles.

In most cultures, the instrumental role is played by the father or other males in the family and the expressive role by the mother. One survey of many societies (Zelditch, 1955) found forty-eight with such a division and eight exceptions. Thus, it is usually the father as the instrumental leader who links the family with the outside community. He interprets societal expectations to his children and represents the family in the wider world. Thus, both Freud and Parsons in different formulations concurred in the central importance of the father as the interpreter of societal values.

Recently this view has been challenged. Some who work with families experiencing conflict (Rausch et al., 1974) are convinced that all family members need highly developed expressive skills. Since communication is a give-and-take process, it is bound to be impaired when only one family member, the mother, has heightened interpersonal skills. Others have compared families with high and low role specialization. Following Parsons's view, the family highly specialized into instrumental and expressive roles should function more smoothly and express greater satisfaction. The results

Children absorb a great deal through observational learning. (Photo by Natalie Leimkuhler.)

have been mixed. Some studies have found the predicted difference, but it is not known whether wives in high specialization marriages were really happier than those in low specialization marriages or whether they were less ready to admit unhappiness. Jessie Bernard (1974) has argued from census data that the full-time housewife role is associated with increased mental and emotional sickness.

Amid the debate about the functionality of instrumental-expressive specialization comes the question about the extent to which it really reflects a dominant American pattern. Here too the evidence is mixed. In interviews about childrearing views, fathers do tend to stress explicit values and goals and to approve of punishment and control more than do mothers (Lynn, 1974). However, mothers appear more responsive to outside advice on childrearing, gleaning information from the media, friends and relatives, teachers, and clinics (Lynn, 1974). In other research, fathers did not see their role as a specialized instrumental one. Far from being just the breadwinner, they saw childrearing as an integral part of their role, highly valuing companionship with their children (Tasch, 1972).

If parents are not clearly differentiated into instrumental and expressive roles, do their children see this? Sometimes children have more stereotyped views of their parents' roles than do the parents themselves. Some of the trends outlined in Chapter 3 would be expected to erode this distinction. For example, increased involvement by the wife-mother in outside-home employment clearly involves her in instrumental behavior and tends to make the husband-father more expressive. The declining birth rate means that the family group no longer challenges expressive skills as would a larger family. It requires less time and effort to keep three people functioning smoothly as a group than six or eight.

Thus it's probably better to think of both father and mother as transmitters of cultural values, exhibiting *both* instrumental and expressive behaviors, rather than as specialists in these roles. Hence, both parents are functioning as agents of the outside culture to their children. Recent research supports this view. In comparing mothers' with fathers' influence on the child's religious and political values, it was found that the mother consistently appeared more important, even in such areas as attitudes about maintaining the *status quo*, work ethic, and militarism in society (Acock and Bengston, 1976). In an extensive review of moral development in children (Hoffman, 1970) more associations between mothers' than fathers' childrearing practices and children's moral behavior were obtained.

REINFORCEMENT AND MODELLING

The transmission of values operates primarily through two mechanisms: reinforcement and modelling. With the first mechanism, reinforcement, the child is rewarded for behavior reflecting desired values, and punished or simply not rewarded for behavior contradicting approved values. For example, in some families, emphasis on achievement is brought home to the child as his parents react with delight or dismay at the report card, visible evidence of academic achievement. The very importance of the report card to children, school, and family reflects and communicates the strong achievement value-orientation.

Perhaps even more important than the reinforcement is modelling to the child. Parents and other socializing agents such as teachers communicate by their own behavior what is desired and expected of the child. "Do as I say, not as I do" has never been an effective teaching device, since children absorb a great deal through *observational learning*. Many studies (Bandura, 1965; Bandura and Walters, 1963) have confirmed the finding that without reward and punishment children learn behaviors merely by observing others engaged in them. The message of parents who emphasize caring for others but whose behavior continually says "Me first" is not lost on their children. It is important to keep in mind the distinction between *learning* and *performance*. While children may learn a behavior through observation alone, they may not necessarily give evidence of such learning through performance. For example, if they also observe that the model is punished for his behavior, this punishment may inhibit performance. Similarly, when children observe a model being rewarded, but are not rewarded themselves, this *vicarious reinforcement* will prompt their performance of what they have observed. Moreoever what has been learned through observation at one time may not affect behavior until much later. Because for many years, parents are the only close-up example a child has of an intimate heterosexual relationship, observations of this relationship will color later adult capacity to sustain such close relationships. Basic views concerning the nature of the environment—friendly or threatening—are absorbed as children watch their parents react to stressful events with passive resignation, anger, or resourceful coping (Rutter and Madge, 1976). Thus, we cannot always know just what children have learned through observation merely by observing their performance.

SOURCES OF VALUES

This notion of observational learning implies the importance of sources outside the family for the transmission of values. As we noted earlier, in Chapter 3, many feel the American family has lost its role as the prime source of values. With the rise of preschool education, children begin school early and are surrounded by peers and teachers as models just a few years after birth. Second only to television is school as a consumer of the child's time. During elementary school years, the child spends an average of thirty hours weekly in school. Moreover, the schools have the power to compel attendance and attention in a manner quite different from the family (Jackson, 1968). Potentially far more important, however, than school or peers is the competing model within the home—television. According to one estimate, the average male American child watches 34.5 hours of television per week (38 percent of all time awake) (Stein and Friedrich, 1975). In fact, children spend more time watching television than engaging in any other single activity besides sleep. Heavy television viewing continues in later years, with sixth graders watching an average of 31 hours per week and tenth graders an average of 28 hours per week (Lyle and Hoffman, 1972). The principles of observational learning suggest that television may be the major source of values for both children and adults.

What are these television-transmitted values? "Sesame Street" and "Roots" illustrate that children may be stimulated cognitively and prodded to think critically about social issues by high-quality programming. Indeed, other media could not hope to reach such mass audiences. The potential of educational television is hardly tapped. For example, television can acquaint people with more diverse personalities, roles, and activities than those they might encounter in real life. With proper adult support, it can also encourage children to imitate positive behaviors such as cooperation and helpfulness (Stein and Friedrich, 1975). The bulk of television programming, however, is not educationally sound. Moreover, most reputable scholars think that the steady diet of violence and commercialism that television dishes out is potentially harmful, although dissenting voices are still heard (Noble, 1975). While some argue that televised violence may have a cathartic effect, helping viewers to get violence "out of their system" (Noble, 1975), most studies of the effects of televised violence on children support the conclusion of a link, under certain conditions, between viewed mayhem and children's subsequent aggression. Even if such a link had not been found, critics of televised violence could argue that it teaches children antisocial behavior, since as previously mentioned, observational learning studies distinguish between behaviors *learned* through observation and the conditions under which these behaviors are subsequently *performed*.

Observational learning of violence is only one part of the problem. Long hours of television watching are hours *not spent* doing other things, particularly interacting with others. Young children normally progress from self-centered play to a gradual ability to truly interact with others. While there is no proof that television watching per se hampers this process, educators are concerned that passive, solitary viewing may prevent the complete development of interpersonal skills.

Television not only communicates high levels of violence and passivity, but it also tells the viewer that no problem is too difficult to solve within thirty minutes, or at most an hour. It breeds an insistence on constant novelty. The intercutting of violence, pathos, and human suffering with commercials for toothpaste designed to "get your teeth whiter than white" and cars that will make you a swinger promotes confusion, and perhaps callousness. When commercials are interposed between scenes of destructive motives, violence, and negative consequences of aggression, it is difficult for young children to integrate these scenes. Such separation of scenes has been related to increased preference for aggressive response by third graders but not sixth or tenth graders (Collins, 1972). Those who have studied the effects of indiscriminate television viewing upon children are convinced that one of the most damaging is the erosion of moral sensibility.

There is also evidence that heavy viewers of television may develop a distorted picture of the real world, seeing it as more hostile and crime-ridden than in fact it is. Television also portrays a distorted picture of family roles. Sexism is rampant on television (Busby, 1975). Despite the climbing proportion of employed mothers in America, the employed mother is rarely portrayed. While some efforts to change such portrayals have begun, most commercials still depict a smiling housewife dancing with a broom across gleaming floors and anxiously awaiting her family's approval of dessert. When a woman *is* shown in an occupational role, it is usually a low-status, low-paid one (Downing, 1974).

Commercials themselves constitute a form of value training. Among those products pitched specifically at children, 70 percent are peddling food for "sugar junkies"—sugar-coated cereals, candy, and chewing gum. Many of the so-called breakfast foods on these commercials actually contain more sugar than candy bars. Toys that are dangerous, or at best shoddy constructions that disintegrate after a few weeks, are made irresistibly appealing on television. Children shift from innocent gullibility to the realization that these smiling adults and children on television are, quite simply, lying to them. There is concern among educators that commercials are selling to children along with cereal and toys the conviction that the adult world is riddled with hypocrisy and bad faith, antisocial behavior, passivity, sexism, callousness, impatience, and cynicism (Figure 6.1). If these are the values transmitted by television, and if television is competing with parents for prime spot as value instiller, what then is to be done?

Since television potently affects attitudes and values, it can enhance positive behaviors. Educational programs and others emphasizing helping and sharing can, in the context of follow-up activities, lead to better grades (Gadberry, 1977), more sophisticated reasoning skills (Schultz, 1977), and more frequent positive social interaction (Stein and Friedrich, 1975). Hence, quality of programming is the key.

Secondly, research emphasizes that adult guidance and monitoring of television is essential to minimize harmful messages and maximize beneficial ones. High levels of adult television viewing provide a model of indiscriminate watching. Average adult viewing has been estimated at forty-four

Figure 6.1. (Reprinted with permission from *Who was that dog I saw you with, Charlie Brown?* by Charles M. Schulz. © 1967 United Feature Syndicate, Inc.)

hours per week. It is no secret that television is used as a babysitter by many parents. Studies indicate that an average of two hours of the day are spent in mother-child interaction while the remaining time is filled with the tasks of housework—cooking, cleaning, shopping, and other activities. The young child at home must be kept amused or at the least out of harm's way. The television is often irresistible as an instant activity guaranteed to keep children quiet. Hence, the impact of television on children is part of the larger question: How are the burdens of home-making, child care, and employment distributed in the family?

This description of the acquisition of values must also emphasize the fact that the child is never merely the passive receiver of values through reinforcement and modelling. As the previous discussion of perceptual and cognitive styles emphasized, the child actively selects from his environment those messages to which he or she will attend. Thus, aggressive children are affected differently by televised violence than are nonagressive children. Children ages ten to twelve are more affected by occupational and national stereotypes portrayed on television and in other mass media than teenagers with more developed critical faculties. Middle-class children may react with greater anxiety than lower-class children to realistic scenes of violences, such as those on TV news. Social isolates or children with inadequate family relationships may be drawn to family situation dramas on television as sources of normal, satisfying social relationships (Noble, 1975).

Moreover, the developing child's changing cognitive capacities lead him or her to process television messages in ways quite different from adults. For example, younger children recall more "incidental" as opposed to "central" incidents (by adult definition) in a program than do older children (Stein and Wright, 1977). The four year old, eight year old, and twelve year old may see entirely different programs when they sit together to watch the same show. The child attempts to integrate the diversity of sometimes conflicting value communications so that they fit together as a whole, fit with his or her psychological needs and unique history, and fit the changing circumstances of his or her own development.

DIVERSITY IN FAMILY VALUES

The general statement that the family reflects and transmits cultural values to the child must be further qualified. Not all families adhere with equal strength to dominant cultural values. Class differences in value-orientations have been identified. For example, upper-class families place greater stress on kin ties and ancestry than do middle-class families, who more strongly emphasize individualism and achievement. Similarly, lower-class families place stronger emphasis on extended family ties as a framework for economic and emotional support than do middle-class families. Using the typology presented in Table 6.1, we would say that lower-class families emphasize the *collateral* rather than *individual* relational value-orientation.

The three class divisions—upper, middle, and lower—are further divided by many into nine separate classes (upper-upper, middle-upper, lower-upper, etc.) with corresponding differences in value orientations. For example, if the lower-upper class is considered the *nouveau riche* (literally, "new rich"), this group with self-made and newly acquired wealth has weaker kinship ties and less emphasis on ancestry and traditionalism than does the "old money" part of the upper class.

Such class differences in value emphasis may be understood in terms of group difference in the availability of resources. The foundation of all resources lies in energy transformations from the natural environment. Light energy converted into food is consumed by the family and provides caloric energy for all other activities. Thus, the resources of income and education are ultimately rooted in the availability of food resources. If a family is poor, lacking in the resources of food, education, and income, it is natural that they might turn for help to their relatives.

These extended kin therefore become important individuals in their lives and maintaining close and cordial relationships with them becomes a more important value than individual development. At the same time, economic deprivation cuts down the likelihood that individuals will be able to move away and up the social ladder, leaving the rest of their family contacts behind. Thus, studies of poor, urban, female-headed black families (Heiss, 1975) find the use of an extended network of relatives and close friends to offset financial hardship and to provide emotional support. It is important to point out that such family structures characterize only a minority of black families, most of whom are two-parent household units with stable marriages (U.S. Census).

Middle-class families lack accumulated wealth but are usually high in the resources of education and have at least adequate to comfortable incomes. Since such parents cannot usually bequeath to their children resources that will ensure them affluence, they must count upon their children's own efforts. To this end middle-class parents not surprisingly emphasize individual achievement, doing rather than being, and a future rather than a past orientation.

Upper-class families of established wealth have concentrated economic resources that they wish to pass intact to their children. Hence, responsibility to the family—a linear rather than individual orientation—conserves this resource within the family. For families of any class, differences in value-orientation reflect the need to make the most of available resources for both present and future generations.

Class position is a shorthand way of expressing differences in environment. Hence, it is not surprising that class differences in values reflect the family's perception of its environment and their position in it (Kohn, 1969). For example, lower-class families have been found to choose conformity as a central value. They, more often than middle-class families, see the world as a potentially threatening place over which they can exert little control. Events happen *to* them, rather than *by* them. Recall that earlier we defined such a feeling as an *external* locus of control as contrasted to an *internal* locus of control, a feeling of mastery and control over events. The greater external locus of control expressed by lower-class families means that authorities—"them"—are seen as invested with power over the family; hence, conformity is important to avoid antagonizing the powers that be. In summary, four organizing value-orientations have been identified for lower-class families: fatalism, concreteness, authoritarianism, and orientation to the present (Irelan and Besner, 1966). Because most parents envision the same sort of future for their children, they tend to encourage for their children the same values which fit their own present life circumstance. Thus, one investigation (Franklin and Scott, 1970) showed that well-educated parents were more likely to emphasize self-control than parents with less education.

This discussion of class differences in value-orientations, however, can give the misleading impression that socio-economic classes represent solid blocs of distinctive value systems and life styles. *Class* is a term of convenience, lumping together diverse families who nevertheless share similar levels of education and income, but what they share is less than what makes them distinctive from one another. Families from the same socio-economic class belong to different ethnic groups and religions, and come from differing geographical regions. Their life histories differ. Some of the families are cohesive, strong in their sense of unity and identity. Others are fragmented and dissatisfied. They are in all stages of the family life cycle, some newly formed, some rearing children, others with children full grown. They include childless couples, the divorced and remarried; in short, all varieties of family structure.

For example, highly cohesive poor families are more likely to emphasize achievement goals for their children than less cohesive poor families (Firebaugh, Woodward, and Daly, 1975). High achievement among teenagers of all classes appears to be related to a close family atmosphere in which activities and confidences are shared (Morrow and Wilson, 1961). In a large-scale study of lower-class family values (Firebaugh, Woodward, and Daly, 1975), geographical region was important as well. Urban poor and those in Texas had a more fatalistic orientation toward education and jobs, feeling that it would be all right to drop out of school to help the family in a difficult financial situation, than did those from rural areas and other states.

Finally, there is evidence that the age of family members and their stage of the family life cycle are important. Younger family members from the same class are more often optimistic, less alienated, less authoritarian, and less dependent than their elders (Youmans, 1973). On the other hand, young adults, while more optimistic, are likely to also be more dissatisfied with their present situation than older people (Campbell, Converse, and Rodgers, 1976). They are more impatient to better themselves, more aware of other worlds where people live differently, less reconciled to their present position than older people. In the large-scale study of poor families' values cited above, older people felt that they had less control over their lives than younger people, especially when it came to improvement through education. It seems that the wisdom of accumulating years is most often reflected in the replacement of idealism with a more resigned view of life's possibilities.

As already noted, ethnic differences in value orientations are an important source of value diversity. Studies of immigrant families over several generations show that European, Mexican, and Asian immigrants often come with value-orientations that contrast sharply to dominant American ones. The process of *acculturation* means gradually modifying original value-orientations so that they are consistent with American emphases (Tharp et al., 1968).

Earlier we described the *lineal* emphasis of Mexican-American families as a contrasting value-orientation to the individualistic emphasis of the dominant Anglo-American culture. While many Mexican-Americans are concerned to preserve their distinct heritage, some acculturation has been observed. For example, when Mexican-American wives speak English as a native language, their marriages are more likely to be egalitarian than the unions of Spanish-speaking wives (Tharp et al., 1968). Since acculturation is fast in some families, slow in others, and uneven within a single family, immigrant families represent an amalgam of cultural values.

Religious differences in value-orientation have also persisted. For example, in studies comparing the three major religious groups—Catholic, Protestant, and Jewish—stronger kinship ties with corresponding emphasis on cooperation and mutual help were found among Jewish families than in either of the other two religious affiliations. Regional differences in emphasis on tradition and individualism are evident when California and New England are compared.

Thus, the old image of melting pot America with a set of dominant values must be discarded in favor of a smorgasbord image depicting the diversity of value-orientations, each on the same table but distinct in flavor, appearance, and essence.

THE FAMILY THEME

In addition to the differences reflected in culture, religion, regionalism, and sex roles, the family as a collection of individuals must be seen as ultimately reflecting its own family value-orientation. Families choose from the range of cultural values the particular value-orientations that best fulfill their own needs as individuals and as an interacting small group. Finally, the family value-orientation must be expected to change as the family itself changes and develops. The honeymoon couple, for example, may organize around the values of romantic love and emotional expression, while the retired man and his wife may come to appreciate claims to privacy and to accept each other as flawed but caring human beings. Thus, the discussion of family values is really a discussion of two complex types of values, both changing—cultural values and family value-orientation, or theme. Both types of values must be understood to appreciate how family values act to modify family resources, decision making and action. Finally, these two types of values color the feedback process as well.

Moos (1976) calls the family value-orientation *the family environment*. He has developed a scale to measure how family members perceive their family environment or value-orientation. This scale consists of three major dimensions: *relationship*, *personal-growth*, and *system-maintenance* dimensions. Each dimension can be further divided into components. For example, the relationship dimension consists of cohesion, expressiveness, and conflict. A family would get a high score on cohesiveness if all members strongly agreed with the statement "Family members really help and support one another." Table 6.5 lists the three dimensions and their subscales of the family environment according to Moos.

When a variety of families fills out the Family Environment Scale, different value-orientations emerge as expected. For example, some families are strongly *expression oriented*. They emphasize open expression of emotions including conflict, but score low on systems maintenance or personal growth. In other words, structuring of family activities and clarity of rules and responsibilities in the family take second place to expressiveness. By contrast, other families emerge as *structure oriented*. They emphasize moral-religious values and inhibit open expressions of conflict or anger. Such a family is clear about its rules and activities (Table 6.5). Similarly, independence, achievement, moral-religious, and conflict-oriented families have all been identified based on their Family Environment Scale scores. Interestingly, when Moos investigated the drinking habits of these families, he discovered that most high-drinking families came from conflict-oriented family environments (Moos and Moos, 1976).

In a related approach to family values, the family value-orientation has been called the *family theme* (Hess and Handel, 1974). The family theme may be summed up in the phrase "what we are all about." The theme reflects basic issues around which the family is organized, fundamental concerns to which it returns. The theme is born out of both the individual psychological needs of family members and their interdependence as a group. Often the theme is not consciously present to the family and must be inferred by a sensitive observer.

In their book, *Family Worlds*, Hess and Handel draw five family portraits based on extensive interviewing and testing with each family member to illustrate family themes. For example, the Clarks (the names are fictitious), Henry and Thelma, both grew up in broken, unstable homes. Their still vivid memories of poverty, social isolation, and insecurity make them determined to avoid such dangers in the future. Now age thirty-five, the Clarks live with their two children in Gary, Indiana, where Henry is an office manager. Thelma expends considerable energy in running the household, keeping everything neat and well organized. Household routine is predictable and

TABLE 6.5 FAMILY ENVIRONMENT SCALE SUBSCALE DESCRIPTIONS

Relationship Dimensions

1. Cohesion — The extent to which family members are concerned and committed to the family and the degree to which they are helpful and supportive to each other.
(Family members really help and support one another.)

2. Expressiveness — The extent to which family members are allowed and encouraged to act openly and to express their feelings directly.
(There are a lot of spontaneous discussions in our family.)

3. Conflict — The extent to which the open expression of anger and aggression and generally conflictual interactions are characteristic of the family.
(Family members often criticize each other.)

Personal-Growth Dimensions

4. Independence — The extent to which family members are encouraged to be assertive, self-sufficient, to make their own decisions and to think things out for themselves.
(In our family, we are strongly encouraged to be independent.)

5. Achievement Orientation — The extent to which different types of activities (e.g., school and work) are cast into an achievement-oriented or competitive framework.
(Getting ahead in life is very important in our family.)

6. Intellectual-Cultural Orientation — The extent to which the family is concerned about political, social, intellectual and cultural activities.
(We often talk about political and social problems.)

7. Active-Recreational — The extent to which the family participates actively in various recreational and sporting activities.
(We often go to movies, sports events, camping, etc.)

8. Moral-Religious Emphasis — The entent to which the family actively discusses and emphasizes ethical and religious issues and values.
(Family members attend church, synagogue, or Sunday School fairly often.)

System-Maintenance Dimensions

9. Organization — The extent to which order and organization are important in the family in terms of structuring of family activities, financial planning, and the explicitness and clarity of rules and responsibilities.
(Activities in our family are pretty carefully planned.)

10. Control — The extent to which the family is organized in a hierarchical manner, the rigidity of rules and procedures, and the extent to which family members order each other around.
(There are very few rules to follow in our family.)

Reprinted with permission from Moos and Moos, 1976, p. 360.

emphasizes a firm schedule. Proper conduct, "doing the right things," and strong religious convictions are also a part of the family theme. Both Mr. and Mrs. Clark are firm disciplinarians, considering an important goal of childrearing that the children "know their place." Yet their control is not harsh or inconsistent, but follows both their own ideology of order and their strong religious convictions. Experimentation, adventure, and autonomy are all expected to be restrained. This stress on control of unacceptable feelings has led to a family sense that they are somehow not emotionally close enough. In summing up the Clarks' family theme, Hess and Handel term it "flight from insecurity."

Its elements are an amalgam of cultural, religious, regional, and role-based values stamped with individual histories and affected by the family as an interacting unit.

While values themselves have been portrayed as changing and complex, they nonetheless act as modifiers in family-environment transactions. This section will indicate briefly how values may affect the gathering of information about the environment, decision making, and family action.

VALUES AS MODIFIERS OF INFORMATION

Much as perceptual and cognitive styles, values may act as selective mechanisms in filtering information concerning the environment. For example, in 1950 Riesman described a change he observed in the American value-orientation, from "inner- to outer-directed." Formerly, Americans as predominantly inner-directed individuals listened to their inner voices of conscience and followed their own value systems in making choices. Now, Riesman argued, Americans are increasingly attuned to others, and less attentive to the still small voice inside. They are following the pack, unable to take an unpopular position, conformists. Thus, Riesman's emphasis on the shift from inner- to outer-directed value-orientations is similar to the discussion in Chapter 3 of field independence-dependence perceptual style. Both emphasize the difference between reliance on internal cues residing within the individual versus external cues from the outside environment in selecting information. Since the dominant American value-orientation is individualistic, it is little wonder that Riesman and others who draw this distinction find fault with outer-directed, field-dependent tendencies.

Value-orientations not only predispose the family to select information of a certain kind, but they also give greater weight and importance to information which fits the value-orientation.

Case Study: The Mitchells

Marina Mitchell is a divorced mother with three children. In the six years since the divorce she has gone back to school while continuing to work, and she just recently feels that the years of struggle are beginning to show positive results. Her new job as manager of a boutique—the first job in fifteen years—excites her. Marina is herself the youngest of six children in a close family. Her return to school and now work wouldn't have been possible, she's convinced, without the help of her older sister Anne or her mother, both of whom live close by. Marina's children seem as attached to Aunt Anne and Grandma as they do to Marina herself. In Marina's new job, for the first time in six years, she is meeting men and being asked out. For the first time, too, Marina is confronted with her sister's disapproval and her mother's occasional outbursts against Marina's "airs." Now, to make matters more complicated, Antony, Marina's seven year old, has started to stutter. Can it be possible that her yearning for a "normal" life is responsible, as Anne hints? Although she doesn't want to, Marina can't help feeling guilty.

In this family, the reader will recognize a *collateral* value-orientation with respect to family relations, although Marina's return to school and work has prompted her growing *individualist* orientation (see Table 6.1). This family is also an example of the use of relatives for economic and emotional support when resource levels are low. The Mitchells are attempting to understand the problem behavior of one family member, namely the son Antony's stuttering. Such problems are not uncommon in school-age children, but they cause parents and other involved adults great concern nonetheless. Such a problem is also one without clear-cut causes. Dealing with it requires a search for information from the environment. Because of this family's strong collateral value-orientation, information supporting such a value receives most support. Antony's problem is "explained" by his mother's failure to respect family obligations, by her individualism, which is reckless in her relatives' eyes.

Marina, however, is experiencing many changes. Her new life, made possible through kin supports, is now pulling her away from a collateral value-orientation to a more individualistic one. This has caused both internal and family conflict.

In summary, this case study illustrates that while family value-orientations affect the information-gathering process, change in family circumstances and in different individuals intensifies the impact of value-orientations on information seeking.

VALUES AS MODIFIERS OF DECISION MAKING

Values are a way of structuring the decision-making process as well. If each decision were "made from scratch" without benefit of experience and without the guidelines set down by a common value-orientation, family members would be unable to carry out even the simplest tasks. In reality, many decisions are made quickly and automatically, thanks to the guiding properties of value orientations. The important decision concerning who will decide different matters may be answered by the division of responsibility and tasks prescribed by the sex-role value-orientation. In the "traditional" family, matters dealing with the outside world of work may be largely decided by the husband, while matters internal to the family, like child care and discipline, for example, are seen as the wife's province.

In addition to answering the question "Who will decide?" values provide a framework for assigning priorities to decisions and making certain outcomes more likely than others. For example, in a study of consumer decision making (Hill, 1970), it was found that those families who had a "family policy" were most successful in making consumer decisions, carrying them out and being fairly satisfied with the results. This "family policy" might be a set of priority decisions or simply an understanding made in advance to guide future decision making, such as "We will save to buy durable, high-quality goods as investments for the future." It is clear that the family policy concept in turn reflects the family's value orientations in terms of the five basic categories outlined earlier such as time (present, past, future) and activity (doing, being, being-in-becoming). The *family policy* might also be considered a reflection of the family theme, in Hess and Handel's terms, or *family environment* in Moos' scheme.

VALUES AS MODIFIERS OF ACTIONS

How family members carry out decisions and in general act, since many actions do not flow from prior decisions, will also reflect underlying value-orientations. For example, beliefs about appropriate tasks for men and women will underlie family division of labor. As Blood and Wolfe pointed out, flexible decision making is often accompanied by high specialization in the carrying out of decisions taken. These beliefs about appropriate sex-role behavior are deeply rooted and stubbornly persisting.

An illustration of their tenacity is provided by the social experiment of the Israeli *kibbutz*, or collective settlement briefly sketched in Chapter 3. Founded on principles of sexual equality, the kibbutz ideology emphasized the interchangeability of men and women in tasks to a far greater extent than anywhere else. Despite this, over the past fifty years, the *kibbutz* has become an overwhelmingly sex-segregated setting as far as division of labor is concerned, with women almost exclusively engaged in childrearing and service areas, such as food preparation and laundry, and severely under-represented in industry and agricultural production, despite lessened emphasis in the latter on physical strength. In a recent analysis of this trend (Tiger and Shepher, 1973), the authors concluded that such sex specialization was based not on exclusion of women or prejudice, but on the positive needs of men and women to do different but complementary things. While there is no proof of this, the kibbutz example does illustrate the strong impetus underlying a division of labor based on sex role. It must be considered a basic and persisting value system for regularizing family behavior.

As with values concerning proper sex-role behavior, so views about time itself affect family behavior. A *being* orientation allows family members more spontaneity than one emphasizing weighing present action for its possible future consequences.

Values concerning one's orientation to nature would be expected to affect behavior, especially that showing environmental concern. Table 6.4 distinguished among three attitudes toward nature: subjugation-to-nature, harmony-with-nature, and mastery-over-nature. Behaviors that show concern for the physical environment appear to stem from the second view of nature, harmony, along with a view that one's ethics should guide behavior (Borden and Francis, 1977).

Recall that different value orientations toward human nature were distinguished in Table 6.4. Human nature may be viewed as basically evil, basically good, or a mixture of both. Families who see human nature as basically evil would be unlikely to react to stressful life circumstances with positive coping behaviors. In their view, resourcefulness would probably not succeed anyway. On the other hand, a view that people are basically good or a mixture of good and evil holds out hope that one's actions can improve conditions.

Just as value orientations affect family behavior, they also help determine how the family will evaluate information or feedback concerning the effect of family decisions and actions. Feelings of present-time orientation and helplessness concerning the future make a family unlikely to seek out feedback for use in planning future action. Strong future orientation, by contrast, emphasizes the gathering of information with an eye to future action, sometimes at the expense of a savoring of present experience.

SUMMARY

This discussion of valuing in the family covered five basic value-orientations—activity, relational, time, man-nature, and human nature—and described how the family may be characterized as having differing preferences or stances on each one. These value-orientations have been applied to the family on three levels: cultural, individual, and familial. The family as transmitter of cultural value-orientations was described within the context of cultural-value diversity and change. On the individual level, the process of developing values within the family was briefly described, with the mechanisms of reinforcement and modelling through observational learning being highlighted. The importance of observational learning implied that sources outside the family, particularly the mass media, are critical and perhaps competing molders of values. Finally, the chapter discussed valuing from the point of view of the family as a distinctive unit. The *family environment* and *family theme* were different but related ways of describing the way individual value-orientations and cultural influences combine to form a particular set of concerns unique to the family as a group. Finally, the chapter examined the way family environment or theme affects how information is gathered and evaluated, how decisions are taken, and how actions are carried out.

REFERENCES

Acock, A., and Bengtson, V. On the relative influence of mothers or fathers: A covariance analysis of political and religious socialization. Paper presented at the American Sociological Association Meeting, 1976.

Bandura, A. Vicarious processes: A case of nontrial learning. In L. Berkowitz, ed., *Advances in Social Psychology*. Vol. II. New York: Academic Press, 1965.

Bandura, A., and Walters, R. H. *Social Learning and Personality Development*. New York: Holt, Rinehart and Winston, 1963.

Bernard, J. *The Future of Motherhood*. Chicago: Aldine, 1974.

Blood, R. O., and Wolfe, D. M. *Husbands and Wives: The Dynamics of Married Living*. New York: Free Press, 1960.

Borden, R. J., and Francis, J. L. Who cares about ecology? Personality and sex differences in environmental concern. Paper presented to Midwestern Psychologcial Association, Chicago, 1977.

Busby, L. Sex-role research on the mass media. *Journal of Communication* 25(1975): 107-131.

Campbell, A., Converse, P. E., and Rodgers, W. L. *The Quality of American Life: Perceptions, Evaluations, and Satisfactions*. New York: Russell Sage Foundation, 1976.

Collins, W. A. Temporal integration and inferences about televised social behavior. Paper presented at the biennial meeting of the Society for Research in Child Development, New Orleans, 1977.

Downing, M. Heroine of the daytime serial. *Journal of Communication* 24(1974): 130-137.

Firebaugh, F., Woodward, J., and Daly, R. Homemakers' value orientations to education and jobs. *Home Economics Research Journal* 4(1975): 90-102.

Forbes, J. D. *Mexican-Americans: A handbook for educators*. Far West Laboratory for Educational Research and Development, 1966.

Franklin, J. L., and Scott, J. E. Parental values: An inquiry into occupational setting. *Journal of Marriage and Family*. 32(1970): 406-409.

Fromm, E. *To Have or to Be?* New York: Harper and Row, 1976.

Gadberry, S. Television viewing and school grades: A cross-lagged longitudinal study. Paper presented at the biennial meeting, Society for Research in Child Development, New Orleans, 1977.

Hartley, R. W. Children's concepts of male and female roles. *Merrill-Palmer Quarterly* 6(1966): 83-91.

Heiss, J. *The Case of the Black Family: A Social Inquiry*. New York: Columbia University Press, 1975.

Hess, R., and Handel, G. *Family Worlds: A Psychosocial Approach to Family Life*. Chicago: University of Chicago Press, 1974.

Hill, R. *Family Development in Three Generations*. Cambridge, Mass.: Schenkman, 1970.

Hoffman, L. W. Social change, the family, and sex differences. Address to the National Council on Family Relations, October 1976.

Hoffman, M. L. Moral development. In P. H. Mussen, ed., *Carmichael's Manual of Child Development*. 3rd ed. Vol. 2. New York: Wiley, 1970.

Irelan, L. W., and Besner, A. Low-income outlook on life. In L. M. Irelan, ed., *Low-Income Life Styles*. U.S. Department of HEW Publication No. 14. Washington, D.C.: U.S. Government Printing Office, 1966.

Jackson, P. *Life in Classrooms*. New York: Holt, Rinehart and Winston, 1968.

Kluckhohn, C. Values and value orientations. In T. Parsons, ed., *Toward a General Theory of Action*. Cambridge: Harvard University Press, 1951.

Kohn, M. L. *Class and Conformity: A Study in Values*. Homewood, Ill.: Dorsey Press, 1969.

Lyle, J., and Hoffman, H. The effects of television on children. In J. Murray et al., eds., *Television and Social Behavior*. Vol. 2: *TV and Social Learning*. Washington: HEW, 1972.

Lynn, D. *The Father: His Role in Child Development*. Monterey, Calif.: Brooks/Cole, 1974.

Madsen, W. *The Mexican-American of South Texas*. New York: Holt, Rinehart and Winston, 1964.

Miller, D., and Swanson, G. *The Changing American Parent: A Study in the Detroit Area*. New York: Wiley, 1958.

Moos, R. H., and Moos, B. S. A typology of family social environments. *Family Process* 15(1976): 357-371.

Morrow, W. R., and Wilson, R. C. Family relations of bright high-achieving and under-achieving high school boys. *Child Development* 32(1961): 501-510.

Myrdal, G. *An American Dilemma*. New York: Harper and Row, 1944.

Noble, G. *Children in Front of the Small Screen*. Beverly Hills, Calif.: Sage Publications, 1975.

Papajohn, J., and Spiegel, J. *Transactions in Families*. San Francisco: Jossey-Bass, 1975.

Parsons, T., and Bales, R. *Family, Socialization, and Interaction Process*. Glencoe, Ill.: Free Press, 1955.

Rausch, H., Barry, W., Heryel, R., and Swain, M. *Communication, Conflict, and Marriage*. San Francisco: Jossey Bass, 1974.

Reisman, D. *The Lonely Crowd*. New Haven: Yale University Press, 1950.

Rokeach, M. *The Nature of Human Values*. New York: Free Press, 1973.

Rutter, M., and Madge, N. *Cycles of Disadvantage*. London: Heinemann, 1976.

Schultz, T. Does television facilitate the child's understanding of behavior? Paper presented at the biennial meeting, Society for Research in Child Development, New Orleans, 1977.

Stein, A., and Friedrich, L. Televised content and young children's programs. In J. Murray, E. Rubenstein, and G. Comstock, eds., *TV and Social Learning*. Washington: HEW, 1972.

————. The impact of television on children and youth. In E. M. Hetherington, J. W. Hagen, R. Kron, and A. H. Stein, eds., *Review of Child Development Research*. Vol. 5. Chicago: University of Chicago Press, 1975, pp. 183-256.

Stein, A. H., and Wright, J. C. Modeling the medium: Effects of formal properties of children's television programs. Paper presented to biennial meeting Society for Research in Child Development, New Orleans, 1977.

Stolz, L. Old and new diretions in child development. *Merrill-Palmer Quarterly* 12(1966): 221-232.

Tasch, R. J. The role of the father in the family. *Journal of Experimental Education* 20(1972): 319-361.

Tharp, R. G., Meadow, A., Leunhoff, S. G., and Satterfield, D. Changes in marriage roles accompanying the acculturation of the Mexican-American wife. *Journal of Marriage and the Family* 30(1968): 404-412.

Tiger, L., and Shepher, J. *Women in the Kibbutz*. New York: Harcourt Brace Jovanovich, 1975.

U.S. Bureau of the Census. The social and economic status of the Black population in the United States: 1974, current population reports. Special Studies Series, No. 54, p. 23. Washington, D.C.: U.S. Department of Commerce.

Youmans, E. G. Age stratification and value orientations. *International Journal of Aging and Human Development* 1(1973): 53-66.

Zelditch, M. Role differentiation in the nuclear family: A comparative study. In T. Parsons and R. Bales, eds., *Family, Socialization, and Interaction Processes*. Glencoe, Ill.: Free Press, 1955.

Deciding

7

Nancy and George Hawkins and their three children have been thinking about Christmas vacation for months. Tim, the oldest and a would-be ski bum, worked all summer to outfit himself with new skis, boots, and jacket. He can hardly wait to make his spectacular appearance on the slopes. Esther, at fourteen, has fallen hopelessly in love with a check-out clerk at the supermarket. She is determined to stay home and continue dropping in at the store for forgotten milk and bread all during the holidays. Nobody seems to listen to her though, so she broods resentfully. Jimmy, the spoiled baby of the family (or so Esther thinks), talks only about the trip to Disneyland he thinks he was promised last year. Only nobody remembers. As for the parents, Nancy feels obligated to spend the holidays with Grandma and Grandpa, her own parents, who have broadly hinted how hurt they will be if the Hawkinses go off on their own. George, for his part, doesn't see how they can afford to go anywhere. Besides, when else will he have the time to paint the boys' room, something he's been promising since the summer?

The Hawkins family is faced with the limited resources of time, money, and energy, and desired actions that are potentially in conflict. They cannot both go skiing and go to Disneyland. A trip to the grandparents, several hundred miles away, will take Esther from her supermarket crush and George from the badly needed paint job. The Hawkins family is faced with a set of decision problems centered on the question: What shall we do on the Christmas vacation?

How such a decision gets made is the subject of the present chapter. It is evident, in this five-person family, that the decision-making process will involve interaction and communication among all family members. It will grow out of their complex relationships. The decisions that the Hawkinses face may seem to just happen without the family realizing how they had resolved their problem. Or, the decision-making process may be a deliberate weighing of alternatives. Decision making arises, furthermore, because certain desired actions are seen as potentially in conflict because of limited resources and differing views about their allocation. When there is no choice among competing alternatives, then by definition no decisions need be made. Thus, the notion of conflict is built into the decision-making process, which may be thought of as a *conflict-management process*. The conflict may be within the individual, as when a homemaker decides which meal among several different possibilities to prepare. Or, as in the Hawkins family, the conflict may be among family members with different desired decision outcomes. In both cases, understanding the decision-making process is the same as understanding how families manage conflict.

This process reflects both individual needs—to see aging parents, to have adventure, to take care of family obligations—and family values. Family values will rule out certain solutions and make others more likely. For example, Nancy *could* journey alone to her parents to spend

Christmas, while George stayed home and painted the boys' room, but the Hawkinses share the value that holidays should be family occasions. This shared value excludes any separate vacation plan.

Our picture of the Hawkins family also illustrates how perceptions color the decision-making process. Each family member perceives his or her own role as central or peripheral, as influential or relatively powerless, as an important voice to be heard or a dim whisper. Each family member has a vision of the way things get done in the family. George and Nancy have always believed in giving the children a voice in family activities and often congratulate themselves on the democratic atmosphere they have created. Yet lately it seems to Tim and Esther that although they have their say, things seem to go pretty much the way Mom and Dad want it, in the end. "It's just a farce," Esther thinks in some of her angry moments. George, for his part, sees himself as a clear-headed, straightforward thinker, speaking his mind and setting out the pros and cons of a problem. But Nancy sometimes senses his hidden resentment that so much free time is spent with her parents, emotions George never expresses. The decision-making process often brings such perceptual differences to light and part of the conflict to be managed is to reconcile differing perceptions.

The dilemma of the Hawkins family also illustrates that decision making reflects authority and power relationships within the family. While the children have influence, they, especially Esther, feel it is very limited and often summed up in the sentence "I never get my way." Are some members of the family more likely to be decision makers than others? Does this happen only when certain problems arise, or may a general pattern be distinguished? If so, why are they in that position? Is it expertise? Because George has been doing the bills in recent months, he feels that he knows better than Nancy and surely more than the children about what they can realistically afford to do. Is it resources contributed to the family? Since Nancy started employment when Jimmy began school, some of the added income has been put aside in a travel fund. Nancy sometimes reminds George that after all, if it wasn't for her, they probably couldn't even think about holiday trips. She used to feel uncomfortable about urging outings when she wasn't bringing in any money, but not any more. In the Hawkins family the resource of external employment enhances Nancy's ability to act as a decision maker when it comes to allocating funds. Her power in the decision-making process has increased.

The decision-making process is also extended in time and has no clear beginning or end. While Nancy and George believe in discussing problems like this and reaching a common agreement, Nancy can't help reminding George that "We did what you wanted last summer—that fishing trip." What she doesn't say but feels is "Now it's my turn." Past decisions influence present ones, which in turn set the stage for future actions.

This fictitious case study also shows that people outside the immediate family influence the decision-making process often as strongly as family members themselves. Nancy feels the expectations of her own elderly parents as guilt feelings within her. Tim's enthusiasm for skiing can be traced to his recent friendship with a boy whose family are devoted skiers. Jimmy caught the Disneyland bug from television commercials promising trips to Disneyland as prizes. The decision-making process thus involves the wider social and physical environment of the family.

As the Christmas vacation approaches, how will the Hawkinses deal with this set of decision-problems? Does the family have a *decision-making style*, a characteristic approach to decision making that can help one to predict the process by which they will arrive at a solution? The term *set* is important here. In reality, no one decision, but a whole set of interrelated decisions must be made. If the Hawkinses do make a family trip, George must figure out what to do about painting the boys' room. Should they hire painters? If this proves too expensive, as George is sure it will,

will he spend next weekend home painting instead of working on the car? If they don't go skiing now, how can they plan for Tim, who worked so hard for ski equipment, to do so perhaps later with his friend? One decision makes a number of other related ones necessary. This kind of linkage among decisions has been termed "central-satellite" because one central decision—here, what to do over vacation—is tied to a number of other, lesser decisions (Plonk, 1968).

Another type of linkage among decisions may also be identified. Once the Hawkinses come to some kind of answer about what they will do during Christmas, a series of sequential decisions, or steps, leading from that decision are entailed. For example, if they decide to go skiing, they must decide exactly where, what means of transportation to take there, where to stay, how long to stay, whether to buy or rent additional equipment, and whether to take lessons (Paolucci, Hall, and Axinn, 1977). In sum, decision making may be thought of as a *web* of linked decisions and the decision-making process as part of the ongoing interaction and communication network of the family, without clear beginning or end, tied to past experiences, built on expectations for the future, influenced by outside relationships and environments, and colored by the perceptions, needs, and values of the family members.

Information about the environment is transformed or made available to family members for use in their behavior. This transformation of information, affected by the perceptions, needs, and values of individual family members and the family as a unit, constitutes the process by which the family acts on its environments and is affected by them. Since decision making is an ongoing process, it also includes the gathering of information about the family's past decisions and actions. This feedback allows evaluation to guide future decision making. The Hawkinses stayed home last Christmas vacation to give everyone "a chance to relax and catch up on things." Looking back on it (feedback), however, they realized that Esther was unbearably bored, all Tim's friends went away, and George couldn't get anything done with all the kids underfoot.

Not all families use feedback. Some families seem doomed to repeat past mistakes. In general, models of decision making that emphasize rational weighing of alternatives, assessing possible risks and benefits, canvassing all relevant information, and monitoring the consequences of past decisions rarely fit real-life decision situations, particularly those reflecting family values. Janis and Mann (1977) view decision making as an inherently stressful activity that people often try to avoid. The decision maker is typically beset by conflicts and doubts, torn by conflicting loyalties and longings, procrastinating, rationalizing, and denying responsibility. Keeping this in mind, it is nonetheless helpful to have an ideal rational model of the decision-making process to understand in what ways and under what circumstances families will inevitably depart from it.

For example, in the chapter on values, we emphasized differences in time orientation. Families with a strong present-time orientation may be expected to pay scant attention to evaluating past decisions in the light of their future consequences. The Hawkinses, however, are strongly future oriented. The adults, at least, are very conscious of how past decisions influence future ones. By contrast, Tim and Esther seem caught up in the present; in her new enthusiasm, Esther has forgotten all about last year's boredom. Here one sees that just as with perceptions, needs, and values, family members may be at variance in their use of feedback from past decisions and actions.

In summary, our examination of the Hawkinses before Christmas vacation has led to the following important characteristics of decision making:

1.   It involves conflict management.
2.   It reflects family members' perceptions, needs, and values.
3.   It reflects family interaction patterns, including authority and power relationships.

4. Decision-making styles may be identified.
5. It is a process linked to past and future decisions.
6. It is a process tying central to satellite decisions.
7. Decision making involves information processing.

These seven characteristics provide a framework by which the decision-making process may be examined in greater detail. First, however, a few definitions are in order.

The terms *decision making*, *power*, and *authority* need to be distinguished. *Power* refers to potential ability to influence other family member's behavior (Blood and Wolfe, 1960). *Authority* refers to beliefs concerning the proper exercise of power within the family. Statements like "Father is head of the household" identify an authority pattern that may or may not reflect actual power relations within the home. *Authority* here refers to attitudinal statements, while *power* identifies actual influence. Thus, in the Hawkins family, the belief is shared that each member including the children has an equal voice in influencing behavior. For this family, authority is strictly *egalitarian*. However, the teenagers see themselves as really very limited in their ability to determine family events. Hence, they see their *power* as considerably less than their authority.

Decision making constitutes only one set of behaviors that may reflect power relations within the family. Unfortunately, many studies equate decision-making patterns with family power or authority. Power, however, may be exercised in many other ways—by immobilizing the family through negative behavior, by monopolizing or disrupting family communication, by focussing all family concern on one's weakness and vulnerability, by granting and withdrawing expressions of love. In this chapter the terms *power* and *authority* will be distinguished from the more specific *decision making*.

It is also important to distinguish between decision making and *action taking*. One pattern may exist within the family to determine who makes decisions and how decisions are reached. Another pattern may be involved in the implementation of those decisions. For example, decisions may be reached by group consensus but carried out by individual family members who have interest or expertise in an area. For example, when the MacCleans make a trip, all the arrangements are handled by Mrs. MacClean, who works part-time for a travel agency. However, the decisions about where, when, and how to go are reached jointly by all family members. Mrs. MacClean's superior expertise makes it natural for the family to delegate to her the carrying out of their travel decisions. Or, decisions may be reached by individual fiat but executed in the spirit of group cooperation, as when one family member plans a meal that several help prepare.

DECISION MAKING AS CONFLICT MANAGEMENT

The presence of a decision or set of decisions to be made implies a conflict between at least two alternative outcomes. On the individual level, the shopper may ask herself, "Should I buy this pair of shoes or that?" On the interactional level, family members have to decide among far-reaching alternatives, such as: "Shall we have a child or not?" "Shall we buy house X, stay in our present apartment, or rent house Y?" Conflict among possible choices abounds in the details of everyday family life: "Shall we repair the broken washing machine or get a new one?" "Should I help Mary with her homework or let her work it out herself?" "How should John be punished for staying out late with the car?" "How do we deal with the kids' endless fights?" "What shall we have for dinner tonight?"

Sometimes, the conflict is among a small number of clearly stated alternatives, as in the decision of the shoe shopper above. But often, decision making involves choice from among an

Decision making in a family involves conflict. (Photo by Natalie Leimkuhler.)

unknown number of poorly understood options. Thus, in dealing with the question "How should we deal with the kids' endless fighting?" it is not clear to the parents just what alternatives there are, what their likelihood of success is, and how to put them into practice. Should fighting be punished and if so, how? Should they attempt to assign blame? Should they ignore the fights, try to divert attention from fighting by interesting the children in other activities, plan events that separate the children, or channel their aggression into competitive games?

Sometimes, as in the Hawkins family described earlier, the conflict among alternatives is also a conflict among different family members, each wishing a different, potentially incompatible outcome. Then decision making becomes a process of managing conflict among the clashing desires of family members.

Many studies of decision making in families make the mistake of treating this process as though it were a simple win-lose situation. The family member who gets his or her own way wins that decision and the other members lose. By this line of reasoning, the member who wins most of the time is thought to have power in that family as prime decision maker. Writers on the family such as Jetse Sprey (1972), however, have pointed out that although such a view may be suitable for sports events, it is not appropriate for the family, where relations are expected to be intimate and of long duration, where conflict and argument must be absorbed and not allowed to damage such relations.

It is unfortunate that so many studies of decision making focus solely on answering the question "Who wins?" As Bach and Wyden (1969) point out, in intimate relationships to win is often to lose and to lose may well be to win. This is because "victory" in a conflict of interests may alienate other family members and impair close relations with them. The effect of the whole decision-making process on the relationships among family members is far more important than simple outcomes in terms of wins and losses. No one can clearly "win" without ultimately losing the far more important relationship itself. In fact, few families actually think in terms of winning and losing, but rather in terms of the process of conflict management itself, in which the outcome is, they hope, satisfactory to all concerned. Conflict is a necessary and pervasive part of any close relationship between people. Indeed, some who work with families (Bach and Wyden) feel that constructive conflict, which focusses on the problem rather than personality and remains open to others' views, is a positive force in strengthening relationships. The so-called conflict-free relationship is one, they feel, in which bitterness is swallowed only to later poison communication.

Is conflict-filled communication harmful to children, both when they are directly involved and when they witness conflict between parents? Research evidence suggests that when conflict is constructive, it is not harmful and may even be beneficial. For example, one study concluded that when children were encouraged to participate in family decision-making discussions where conflicts of interest were inevitable, their level of moral judgment was enhanced (Holstein, 1970). Conflicts that permit an airing of moral issues appear to help the child move from immature views of morality—that moral behavior is that which wins approval and obeys authority—to more sophisticated understanding of morality as obeying the dictates of one's conscience according to universalistic principles (Kohlberg, 1963).

While conflict is a necessary part of a relationship and will often be a component of communication, it may be more likely in some situations rather than others. For example, when basic values and attitudes are shared, many areas of conflict do not arise. There is prior agreement about how many decisions should be reached and what their outcomes should be. This is one reason why homogamy (like marrying like) is related to lower divorce rates than cross-class, inter-ethnic or inter-religious marriages. Individuals from similar backgrounds tend to share a similar outlook on many matters of mutual importance.

Individuals who hold compatible views on how decisions should be reached and by whom are less likely to have conflicts. Families are not static, however. Agreements at one time have a way of dissolving at another. Changes in relationships over the life cycle will create conflicts where none had existed previously and demand restructuring of old decision-making habits. The birth of the first child is often a difficult transitional time for couples. A pattern of decision making that may have been based on both spouses' employment must now be revised. The new family member is most efficient at communicating demands (at any hour); a family with a single pair relationship suddenly contains three dyads: mother-father, mother-child, and father-child. Decision making tends to become more specialized at this time; the couple finds it must divide up responsibility and labor to work more efficiently. But this in turn cuts down on interaction. Couples discover they are able to do fewer things, including reaching decisions, together.

DECISION MAKING REFLECTS FAMILY PERCEPTIONS, NEEDS, AND VALUES

The earlier chapter on perceiving emphasized individual differences in processing information from the environment. Some individuals see a problem globally, others tend to break it down into its components. Some view problems in terms of their personal relationship to the problem, others can see the issue objectively, independent of themselves. Some tend to require greater environmental stimulation than others. Individual differences in temperament—in activity level, threshold for pain, distractibility, and attention span—were also noted. Taken together, these differences may be summarized as differences in optimal levels of stimulation or information from the environment.

Because of these differences, family members are not likely to perceive the decision-making process similarly. Hence, family conflict management is also a process of checking out differing perceptions and attempting to bring them into harmony, or at least peaceful coexistence. Such sharing has been termed *consensual validation* and takes place through family communication.

Both individual and family needs help determine decision making. Individual differences encompass not only perceptual styles, but also needs. For example, Ann was brought up in a large family of close, intense family contacts. Tempers flared easily and emotions were easily expressed. Only Ann—shy, quiet, and private—seemed uncomfortable in such a setting. Now as a wife and parent, Ann's strong needs for privacy and quiet in the home are often puzzling to her husband and children, who wonder why she is so "sensitive." Or take the case of Samuel, who fled war-torn Europe to begin a new life in America. Despite his current prosperity, he cannot shake feelings of fear and vulnerability. His children complain that he is overprotective, never letting them test their own independence.

Each individual's differing history marks not only perception of the environment, but also intensity of need. Despite such individual variation, however, each family has certain common needs that must be fulfilled through transactions with the environment and that thus guide decision making. Maslow (1954) in a well-known formulation has identified a need-hierarchy that all individuals and families share. By need-hierarchy is meant the fact that more basic needs must be satisfied before higher-order ones can be activated. Most basic, according to Maslow, are *physiological needs* such as hunger and thirst. The starving individual cannot begin to deal with other needs until nutrient requirements are met. Next in importance are *safety needs*. The self must be maintained against dangers from the environment. The family as a unit must be able to sustain itself as a unit relatively secure in its setting.

Once this is achieved, *belonging and loving needs* may be activated. These include the need for close and enduring relationships with others in which feelings of belonging and love are both received and given. In contemporary society this need is uniquely met by the family. Yet the ability to meet this need is undermined when more basic physiological and safety needs cannot be adequately satisfied. Thus, the poor family that struggles for daily bread within a hostile environment will have difficulty providing its members with a sense of closeness and caring. That many impoverished families manage to do so despite such difficulty is testimony both to the adaptability of families and to their strong drive for loving bonds.

The next set of needs Maslow posits are *self-esteem needs*. These include feelings of self-acceptance, self-worth, confidence, and strength. It is only when the family provides members with a sense of belonging and love that they can fulfill personal needs of well-being. Finally, *self-actualization needs* may be pursued when all other needs are adequately met. By this is meant the need to develop one's capacities, to discover one's unique contributions. This flowering of individual potentiality occurs only in a family context based on security, safety from danger, belonging, mutual love, and self-esteem.

How exactly do these needs influence the decision-making process? Do self-actualizing people go about deciding things differently from those stuck at the stage of safety needs? Some exploratory research suggests that they do (Price, 1973). The members of forty families, each with a

Family communication patterns are an integral part of all decision making. (Photo by Natalie Leimkuhler.)

teenage child, were individually classified as either "self-actualizing," "normal," or "non-self-actualizing" by their responses to a questionnaire. The families were then observed in a decision-making simulation; that is, they were given a number of hypothetical problems to resolve and were asked to record both individual and joint decisions.

Analysis of the decision-making process indicated that self-actualizing people were willing to make a decision that carried a high risk of negative outcome, while the others preferred to play it safe. In addition, when the conversations of these families were classified as either "social/emotional" or "task," self-actualizers were found to devote nearly half of their communication to the former, while the other two groups spent only quarter of their time in social/emotional communication. Thus, self-actualizers appeared to be more attuned to the needs and feelings of others, while "normals" and "non-self-actualizers" concentrated on getting the task done. The individual's needs, as described by Maslow, influenced the character of the decision-making process.

In addition to the influence of needs, values guide the decision-making process at every stage. Values determine what environmental information will be selected and how it will be weighted. Values affect communication patterns. "Children should be seen and not heard" and "Everything should be discussed democratically and put to a vote" lead to very different styles of decision making. Values may rule out certain possible decisions and make others more likely. For example, a family emphasizing education and individual striving for advancement is likely to place greater weight on the quality of the school system in considering a residential move than a family that more strongly values close ties with friends and relatives.

Shared values give structure to the decision-making process. It is not surprising that married couples tend to bring many more shared values than pairs of strangers to a decision problem (Winter, Ferreira, and Bowers, 1973). Moreover, the absence of such shared values characterizes families defined as disturbed by family therapists (Ferreira and Winter, 1965). Because of such shared values, married couples who are functioning well are able to reach mutually satisfying decisions relatively quickly (Winter, Ferreira, and Bowers, 1973).

Shared values may also be thought of as shared assumptions about the way the world should be, the way each family member should behave, and what each family member is really like. While these shared assumptions allow for smooth, efficient decision making, if too rigid they may impede the free flow of information among family members. If, for example, one sibling sees the other as spoiled and grasping for parental attention, these expectations will act as a filter through which all the sibling's actions are understood. Rigid expectations lock in family members to fixed images of each other (Boyd et al., 1974). In summary, shared values provide a framework for the decision-making process. This framework may vary in flexibility from relatively open to rigidly fixed. Families experiencing interpersonal troubles and communication difficulties are often characterized by overly rigid assumptions.

DECISION MAKING REFLECTS INTERACTION PATTERNS

Decisions that are called for or potentially desired in the family are, above all, group decisions. Even when an individual family member makes a spontaneous, autonomous decision, as when the mother buys a dress on the spur of the moment, it is always with *reference* to others, particularly the family. Does the budget allow for the purchase? What will be other family members' reactions? Will my sister-in-law think I'm trying to prove something? These thoughts may come after the decision is taken, but they are there nonetheless.

This group nature of decision making, visible even in acts of individual spontaneity, is most evident in the bulk of family decisions, which clearly require communication among family members. Communication itself might be best defined as the flow of information from one individual (sender) to another (receiver) that affects the receiver in some way (Rausch et al., 1974). This communication may be overt and highly structured as in a family conference around the dinner table. Despite the pervasiveness of this type of communication for decision making on television family dramas, it is unlikely that most families make extensive use of it. For one thing, family members are often pulled by pressing demands on their time and attention, demands from work, volunteer and social activities, school, sports, and clubs. One family was highlighted in a national magazine some years ago because of their novel solution to this pull of individual concerns. They had instituted family dinner at *six a.m.*, the only time when all family members could reliably be counted on to appear!

Most decision making in the family is based on patterns of communication, built up from thousands of daily interactions among family members. These patterns comprise felt attitudes and values, a sense of what family members and in some ways the family wants. The sources of this sense, this feeling cannot always be consciously articulated. Nevertheless, its base is in the verbal and nonverbal messages exchanged in the flow of interaction within the family.

If family communication is an integral part of all decision making (and failure to make decisions), then the nature of the family as a communicating small group is of utmost importance.

How do family resources affect communication? How does the structure of the family influence its intra-familial communication? What is the relationship between the family's near environment and its communication patterns?

When we speak of the decision-making process in the family, we imply that the heart of this process is communication among family members. The decision to watch a particular television program at eight p.m. is likely to be the final product of statements of different desires, influence attempts, bargaining, threats, and appeals. Mr. Jones has planned to watch a football game, but his wife has been waiting to catch that musical comedy on the other station for weeks, while the children are sure that they will die without the "Brady Bunch" special. But only one outcome is possible.

How family members communicate (or fail to do so) will determine whether each one's wishes are made known to the others, the importance placed on those wishes, and the slight attention given to some communications while emphasizing others. In short, the decision-making process *is* a process of communication. This does not mean that interchanges always will be democratic, mutually satisfying, or conflict-free. On the contrary, communication among intimates is likely to be far more complex than these terms suggest. For example, Mr. Jones may mishear his wife's request. She may escalate the conflict of interests into one that involves basic values and attitudes ("It's always like you to think of yourself and no one else"). The parents may retreat in the face of a barrage of whining demands. Nonetheless, each of these patterns of communication may be described and indicates the processes that led up to the decision to watch program X.

Emphasis on communication patterns illustrates that the decision-making process is considerably more complex than its final outcome. Family members interact and attempt to influence one another. Influence attempts may be so subtle that the person in authority to make the decision may be unaware that he or she has been quietly brought around. A well-worn plot of situation television comedies involves the ploys of the heroine to get her way, while the bumbling hero is convinced the decision (that the heroine had wanted all along) was his own idea. Some research confirms this pattern. In a study of Detroit families (Safilios-Rothschild, 1969a), in three-fourths of those identified as husband-dominated in decision making, the wife used verbal and nonverbal influence attempts and a similar pattern existed in wife-dominated decision making.

As family members cajole, persuade, threaten, bribe, wheedle, plead, and rationally discuss the pros and cons, all the complexities of their relationships are involved.

Some families experience severe difficulties in communicating with one another. As mentioned earlier, family members may hold such rigid assumptions about one another that they fail to hear messages that challenge their beliefs. They simply tune out information that doesn't fit preconceived notions. It has also been suggested that family members with a history of child abuse or neglect may have failed to learn positive communication skills. For example, one observational study of such families found that abusive parents tended to interact with other family members much less than matched "controls." Interestingly, they also seemed to avoid physical communication, both positive (a hug), negative (hitting), and neutral (tapping on the shoulder to get attention). The observers concluded that the abusive parent, unskilled in the use of physical contacts, uses them inappropriately (Burgess and Conger, 1977). The same study found that both abusive and neglectful families were less reciprocal and equitable in their communication than controls. Other work with families displaying deviant behavior confirms that they tend to be more silent, talk less equally, be more negative, and less active than normal families (Winter and Ferreira, 1969).

Such disruptions in communication are severe enough to gain the attention of legal authorities or impel the family to seek professional help. It is important, however, to emphasize that so-called normal families are not characterized by eternally flexible assumptions, open communication, and perfect reciprocity. The disturbed communication of the deviant family occurs much less severely and less frequently, but nevertheless *occurs* in most families and forms a part of the decision-making process.

POWER AND AUTHORITY

Keeping in mind the distinction between *power* and *authority*, some researchers have suggested that patterns of decision making reveal who has decision-making *power* in the family. In the early years of marriage, decision making may be spontaneous, but as similar decisions need to be made repeatedly, a pattern soon develops. Although these patterns may and probably do exist in endless variety, some basic types have been distinguished. In addition to the husband-dominated family, in which most important decisions are made or at least sanctioned by the male "head-of-household," the wife-dominated, conflict-ridden, and egalitarian or "colleague" families have been identified (Miller and Swanson, 1958; Strauss, 1964).

Most studies of decision making ask one or more family members who has the final say in a variety of areas (for example, housing, allocation of money, child care, household tasks) and sums the number of responses in favor of husband or wife. If most of the answers favor the husband, the decision-making pattern is identified as husband-dominated; if they favor the wife, it is seen as wife-dominated. When decisions are identified as shared and arrived at jointly, this egalitarian pattern is considered syncratic and when roughly equal numbers of decisions are made by husband and wife it is identified as "autonomous."

While such studies have their value in describing perceptions of decision making, they are inherently limited. First, by summing up decisions to arrive at a single decision-making "score," equal weight is given to each decision. But it is obvious that decisions vary both in importance and frequency (Safilios-Rothschild, 1971). Child care, housekeeping, and budget management involve daily decisions, while major purchases such as home and car occur infrequently. Household tasks may be viewed by the family as much less important than the decision to move to a new home or take different employment. Some decisions are frequent, others rare.

Important, infrequent, policy decisions have been termed *orchestration decisions,* while frequent decisions involving tactics and administration have been called *instrumentation* decisions (Levin, Kelley, and Riordan, 1976). Orchestration decisions might include buying a car, how many children, if any, to have, changing jobs, or moving to another city. Examples of instrumentation decisions are buying clothes, punishing children, choosing a doctor, deciding what to cook.

More important, studies that try to decide who has more decision-making power—husband or wife—in this manner ignore the *process* nature of decision making emphasized in our discussion of the Hawkins family. They also slight the involvement of children, relatives, friends, and other environmental factors.

Another problem with studies of decision-making power is the level of analysis at which patterns are identified. Is the primary decision-maker the one who decides how to allocate the budget or is it the one who has decided that that person should decide? For every pattern of decision making we can ask who has decided that such a pattern should exist. For example, the wife may decide how much to spend for food each week, but this power may have been delegated to her by her husband, who has charge over the budget as a whole.

Finally, a most important problem with the study of decision making stems from the method of inquiry. Questionnaires and interviews are limited means for studying decision making in the family because of the disparity between what people say they do and what they actually do. One extensive study of over two hundred families concluded that family behavior when directly observed was unrelated to questionnaire responses.

For example, families attributed almost no decision making power to children on the questionnaire, but when observed, children were found to have considerable influence (Turk and Bell, 1972). Questionnaire responses often reveal adherence to democratic ideals of decision making that may not reflect reality. Or responses may as readily indicate a reluctance to admit maternal power in the culture of machismo. The gap between reality and appearance, however, remains even when families are observed making decisions in the home or laboratory. There they are aware that what they do is public and desire to put on a good face. Observations cannot capture the subtleties of influence techniques which may involve private behavior such as sexual relations. Furthermore, one decision cannot be isolated from another in reality. A spouse may be allowed to "win" on one decision in order to ensure the other a later victory (Safilios-Rothschild, 1971).

Thus, family members may present to the outside, observing world an inaccurate picture of their actual behavior, often exaggerating the amount of democractic participation in decision making (Herbst, 1954). But this may not stem solely from a desire to look good but also from real misperceptions about each other. For example, Heer (1962) found that both husbands and wives tend to exaggerate the power of their spouses, husbands seeing wives as more powerful than they really are, and wives seeing husbands as wielding more power than they really do.

Finally, most studies of decision making and action taking are open to criticism because they seldom interview or observe all family members (Herbst, 1954). In most cases, the wife is seen as a reliable informant for the entire family. She is most accessible to the researcher and hence, what is known about family decision-making is largely what the wife tells him or her. This is a serious shortcoming in view of the inevitable misperceptions and misunderstandings of power and authority relations within the family. Indeed studies in which both spouses are asked about decision making find considerable disagreement. In some cases, more than one-half the answers are discrepant (Safilios-Rothschild, 1969a).

In summary, most studies of decision-making power have the following shortcomings:
1. They consider all decisions of equal importance.
2. They consider only the case of husband-wife conflict.
3. They view each decision in isolation rather than as process.
4. They fail, in most cases, to get *both* husband's and wife's perceptions.
5. They rely on questionnaire, interview, or laboratory observation.

Keeping in mind these limitations, what does investigation of decision-making power reveal about the American family? Are the categories of traditional, husband-dominated, wife-dominated, conflict-ridden, and egalitarian applicable? What couples are likely to fall into each category?

While traditional expectations remain important, decision making in the contemporary American family does not neatly follow traditional lines. Most decisions involve some sort of group decision-making process and the importance, at least in theory, of democratic ideals is often mentioned. Therefore, traditionalism is an insufficient explanation for patterns of decision making. There is considerable evidence that traditional patriarchal notions of authority are losing ground in determining actual power relations in American families. In fact, a spate of books, particularly during the 1950s and 1960s, decried the weak position of the American husband as a Caspar Milquetoast henpecked by "momism."

It seems closer to the truth to state that the American family is neither completely male- or certainly female-dominated. During the twentieth century, we have witnessed increased participation of women in employment outside the home, increased education, and increased availability of options to make choices out of what had been life's necessities—in everything from birth control to marriage itself. All this has transformed the American family from one essentially patriarchal in values and generally in practice to a system espousing democratic decision making and attempting to carry it out. Even groups like Mexican-American families, with the reputation for machismo-based authority patterns, show highly egalitarian decision-making patterns (Hawkes and Taylor, 1975).

In one classic study of decision making among Detroit families in the late 1950s (Blood and Wolfe, 1960), eight important decisions affecting the family were studied:*

1. What job the husband should take
2. What car to get
3. Whether or not to buy life insurance
4. Where to take a vacation
5. What house or apartment to take
6. Whether or not the wife should go to work or quit work
7. What doctor to have when someone is sick
8. How much money to spend each week on food

The only decisions clearly the husband's province were job and car, while the wife had discretion only over food expenditures. Even the wife's employment status was seen as a joint decision.

Blood and Wolfe argued that this was because the wife's employment was seen as supplemental to her husband's and that her work was likely to disrupt family functioning, requiring the husband to change his routine. By contrast, the husband's involvement with his job as part of his central breadwinner role was unquestioned by the family and any disruptions caused by it were perceived as legitimate. For example, in one study (Lopata, 1965) 64 percent of the women interviewed identified economic support as the primary male role, ranked above the roles of husband and father.

Since the Blood and Wolfe study almost twenty years have passed, and during that time increased employment for women, as well as new sensitivity to the creation of options for both men and women, has somewhat changed this view of husband and wife employment. Thus, it is likely that should the Detroit study be repeated today, all eight decisions might now be seen as joint ones (note that child care questions were not asked in this study so that childless couples could also be studied). The husband's concentration on his role as exclusive or at least primary breadwinner is still high, but increasingly his work is seen as *part* of the total package of resources that enhance family quality of life. Therefore, if his job interferes with important opportunities for his wife or time with the children, the family may be more likely to have its say in the matter. For the same reasons, one would predict that the wife's employment would remain a matter of joint concern.

Another force undermining the centrality of the husband's breadwinner role for the family is the rise of the modern welfare state (Benson, 1968). Public expenditures for education, social programs, and supplemental funds in times of crisis are all direct or indirect payments to the family independent of the husband's adequacy as a breadwinner. No longer is his behavior a do-or-die matter, and this must contribute to its lessened importance.

* Reprinted with permission from Blood and Wolfe, *Husbands and Wives: The Dynamics of Family Living*. New York: Macmillan, 1960.

If tradition is no longer the answer, how otherwise may decision-making power be explained? One view, the resources theory (Blood and Wolfe, 1960) holds that decision-making power in the family is a function of resources, such as relative earning power or education. Thus, if one spouse is much better educated than the other, the resource theory would predict that the more learned would wield more power. The resource theory helps explain why middle- and upper-class men have been found to have greater family decision-making power than lower-class men. It also would lead to predictions that a wife's decision-making power would increase if she were employed or obtained further education.

This prediction is supported in studies of dual-income families who tend to be less traditional and more evenhanded than one-income families. In the area of important decisions involving major financial expenditure, the employed wife is accorded more of a role in saying how and where the money should be spent (Nye and Hoffman, 1963). Just as the wife's employment draws her into decisions concerning major financial expenditures, it draws the husband into decisions about housekeeping and child care, domains more exclusively the wife's when she is not working. The demands of outside employment leave many household tasks to be filled and greater husband participation in them. This appears to be leading to greater convergence in the decision-making powers of both husband and wife. This does not mean that decision making becomes an entirely fifty-fifty thing. Resistance to the sharing of all concerns remains, particularly in the area of housekeeping and cleaning (Dyer and Urban, 1958).

In cases where the wife earns more than the husband, her power may rise so high that marital conflict ensues, since this arrangement too grossly violates assumptions about the superior bread-winning ability of the husband. Among lower-class families, it is more likely that the working wife will earn as much as, perhaps more than her husband. Marital problems are also more widespread among this group. It has been suggested (Odom, Seeman, and Newbrough, 1971) that one of the factors responsible for such marital discord is the wife's superior decision-making power through superior earnings, but there is no proof of anything more than an association.

When wives are not employed, this does not immediately mean that they are relatively powerless in the family decision-making process. While the resources of earning power may be low or nonexistent, other resources may function as a source of power. The definition of resources in the theory is sufficiently broad to include such attributes as attractiveness, charm, and homemaking skill. In the absence of employment or education, these are often alternative sources of familial power for women. The very broadness of the definition of resources is a difficulty, however. It becomes difficult to disprove the resources theory when every decision-making pattern may be "matched" to a set of superior resources, if the latter are defined loosely enough. Thus, examples of wife-dominated decision making where the wife has inferior education and no earning power may be "explained" by reference to her greater homemaking skill or child care expertise or communication skills, all "resources" that are hard to verify independently. And indeed, some evidence finds that wife's education or employment has no effect on her decision-making power, contrary to the predictions of the resources theory (Safilios-Rothschild, 1969b).

How can one reconcile resources theory with numerous examples, particularly in cross-cultural research, that decision-making power is sometimes strongest just where one would least expect it—among those low in obvious resources of education, income, and the like? One way to do so is to argue that resources theory does not apply in all cases. It holds only for societies that are not strongly tradition-bound. In these egalitarian cultures, decision-making power is not rigidly set and thus is sensitive to fluctuations in resources (Richmond, 1976; Rollins and Bahr, 1976).

A second view, which may be called the *interest theory* (Heer, 1962) states that the family member most interested in an area will exert most decision-making power there. Thus, wives who have most concern with housekeeping are also dominant when it comes to making decisions in this sphere. Benson (1968) has criticized this theory as being too limited, since it does not tell us anything about the majority of family decisions, in which both members have a stake. Interest theory does not illuminate the decision-making power when *conflict* of interest exists.

Interest and resource theory have been combined by stating that both resources and their use in the service of attaining a desired goal are important. Therefore, maximum decision-making power will be achieved when high resources are combined with high interest in applying those resources to reach a desired end.

Another modification of resources theory is the "exchange-value" theory (Heer, 1962). Here decision-making power is thought of as a function of the family member's resources *relative* to those resources available in alternative arrangements. Thus, a kind of mental, usually unconscious arithmetic takes place by which present resources are weighed against expected outcomes should the marriage be dissolved or somehow restructured. This weighing of alternatives clearly indicates that marriage is no longer thought of as immutable. People expect to stay in an arrangement only as long as it pays off in terms of maximizing their power.

Thus, the resource theory, with its refinements and modifications, is an attempt to account for patterns of decision-making power. Even though couples may not—and probably are not—aware of their resources and their exchange value, the student of family life may use this information to predict the pattern of decision-making power most likely to develop. However, one must emphasize once again the limits of this approach. Within these limits, theories explaining patterns of decision-making power may be useful.

DECISION-MAKING STYLES

While family communication is constantly changing, it is not random. Regularities can be observed in the way individuals and groups reach decisions. For example, in one three-year study of newlyweds, consistent differences among couples in discussing conflicts of interests were observed (Rausch et al., 1974). Some pairs were "discordant," chronically given to bickering and anger, while others were "harmonious." Among the latter, some achieved this harmony by avoiding conflict, others by confronting the issues that divided the pair and trying to learn from them. During the three years of the study and in a variety of hypothetical conflict-situations, couples tended to be consistent in their preference for a particular decision-making style. While communication patterns were not static, they were relatively stable.

Based on her observations of three-person families (parents plus one teenager), Price (1973) identified two decision-making styles. Decision Style I was largely task oriented. The family gathered information from many sources, including those outside the family, and concentrated on finding the "best" solution to the decision problem. Family members were guided by the "good of the group" rather than individual preferences. Such decision makers scored fairly low on self-actualization, high on task orientation, and high on outer- rather than inner-directedness.

In contrast, Decision Style II focussed less on the task and more on the social and emotional needs of the family. Members emphasized the unique nature of the problem, its underlying values, its long-term implications, and its personal nature. Information was sought only within the group. Individual preferences were not subordinated to the good of the group. When wishes conflicted, the family recognized these differences and did not attempt to force a group solution. Such decision makers scored higher on self-actualization and social/emotional orientation than did those using Decision Style I. Finally, Decision Style II was more likely to be used when the educational level of husband and wife were high and the wife was employed outside the home on a professional level.

Different decision-making styles also assign differing roles to children. For example, the "socio-oriented" style is one in which children are expected to defer to parents in initiating and ending conversation—the "children are to be seen but not heard" school. By contrast, the "idea-oriented" style is characterized by free expression of ideas and emotions, including those that differ from the parents' (McLeod, Chaffee, and Eswara, 1966). The "socio-oriented" style is one of high parental control while the "idea-oriented" style is one of lower control.

Do these differences in decision-making style have any broader implications for child or parent? It appears that they do. When high- versus low-adjustment children were compared, the former engaged in more direct, open communication with their parents on a joint decision-making task observed by researchers (Odom, Seeman, and Newbrough, 1971). One cannot conclude from this that idea-oriented decision-making *causes* good adjustment in children, but only that the two are found to be associated. Similarly, high school students given a substantial voice in family decision making exhibit greater self-reliance, confidence, and satisfaction with home life than those more shut out from the decision making process (Kandel and Lesser, 1969; McPartland and Epstein, 1975).

A second dimension of parent-child communication that has received repeated emphasis is that of warmth-rejection. Parents communicate varying levels of acceptance and caring in their communications (both verbal and nonverbal). It appears that a parental style combining warmth and moderate firmness is optimal for the young child's moral and cognitive growth and for his strong attachment to and identification with parents.

An example of this may be illustrated in the following study conducted by Witkin et al. (1962), a major investigator of perceptual-cognitive styles discussed in Chapter 4. He was interested in the kind of parent-child communication related to the development of analytic thinking in children. He selected a group of ten year olds and their parents for study and measured the children's tendency to think analytically rather than globally. He then interviewed the mothers and asked the children for their views of their parents as well. Results from both mother and child interviews indicated that boys with analytic thinking skills had supportive, involved fathers. By contrast, boys with a more global approach tended to have psychologically absent fathers who, when they did spend time with their sons, tended to share passive activities such as television watching. Other research (Corah, 1965) suggests that girls are similarly affected by their mothers.

Just as intellectual abilities appear to prosper when parents are warm and involved with their children, so does social and moral behavior. A study of generosity in children illustrates this (Rutherford and Mussen, 1968). Four-year-old boys were given candy and two extra bags in which they might place candy for their two best friends. In a separate doll-play session, the children were encouraged to verbalize their feelings about their parents. The more generous boys in sharing candy also perceived their fathers as more nurturant, affectionate, and comforting than did the boys who shared little. Note that this study relied on the children for evidence about their parents. Thus, it could be that generous children *perceive* their fathers more positively than they really are. In another study in which parents were directly interviewed, however, the father's involvement in caring for the child during infancy was related to the child's altruism in elementary school (Lynn, 1974; Speece, 1968).

One must not conclude that decision-making styles, once identified in families, are static. After all, the changing developmental needs of individuals are bound to bend and alter the style.

Changes in family decision making are triggered by the physical changes of puberty. (Photo by Natalie Leimkuhler.)

For example, as children reach adolescence they may begin to make new demands. Their parents, however, may react to this new insistence with acceptance, mixed feelings, or annoyance. Steinberg and Hill (1977) examined such changes by comparing the decision-making styles of families with boys eleven to fourteen years old. Based on their physical appearance, some boys were classified as "prepuberal" (without any overt sign of puberty), "apex puberal" (at the height of puberal changes), or "late puberal" (with puberal changes apprently completed). Their intellectual level, particularly their ability to reason formally, was also assessed.

When decision-making styles were examined in each family, the researchers concluded that with physical maturation, male adolescents become more assertive toward their parents. The parents, in turn, generally react to this by increased attempts at control. Interestingly, this change in the decision-making process is triggered not by increasing age or by improved ability to reason formally, but only by the visible signs of physical maturation. By the time the adolescent completes puberty, parental control has dropped down to its former prepuberal level.

The Steinberg and Hill study illustrates how family decision-making styles may change with changing individual needs. Changes in the structure of the family group may have a similar effect. When the family grows or diminishes in size, new demands are made on members.

The resources of time and personal energy are limited. As family size increases, parents must divide up their available time and energy among more individuals. Hence it is likely that any single family member will get less attention in a large family than in a smaller one. Research on family size confirms that in large families the amount of interaction time per child is considerably less than in smaller families. In addition, some cross-cultural research reports that mothers of large broods are seen as less warm toward their children (Blood, 1972). With more fragmentation and less time and attention invested in each child, it is not surprising that large families have been found to exert less control over their children. Because adolescent children from small families spend more time with their parents, these children are more likely to turn for advice to parents rather than peers (Douvan and Adelson, 1966). The parents, for their part, are more likely to be informed about their children's activities and feelings.

In contrast to the large family, the only child generally receives most communication time and concentrated attention from his parents. Indeed, only children tend to be high achievers, leaders, more self-assertive, and more successful in their careers than others (Thompson, 1974). They also perceive their relationship with their parents as significantly more positive than do first-born children. The former report more warmth and respect from both their parents than do the latter. Singleton adolescents also state that their parents enjoy being with them more than do first-born (Kidwell, 1977). In short, research on only children doesn't support the widespread belief that the singleton status is bad for the child.

In summary, just as studies of decision-making power emphasized the *outcome* of a conflict of interest, research on decision-making styles highlights the *quality* of the communication process through which decisions are reached. Decision making is in reality a process rather than an isolated event, and this quality is most important, since it permeates the family's interaction. Secondly, decision-making style is a dynamic rather than a static concept. Changes in individual needs are reflected as changes in group process. Similarly, changes in the structural characteristics of the family impel adaptations in decision-making style.

DECISION MAKING AS A PROCESS LINKING PAST AND FUTURE DECISIONS

This and the remaining two characteristics of decision making to be discussed here emphasize its process nature. Because processes are far more complex than outcomes, relatively little research has been conducted on this aspect of decision making. Just how do past decisions influence future ones? How does the knowledge that the family is bound up together for the long term influence its handling of present conflicts?

Clearly, orientation toward time itself affects the linkage among past, present, and future decisions. Such family differences have been identified and discussed under values. In addition, commitment to family relationships themselves is important. Perhaps when family members are certain that they are together for better or for worse, then present conflicts are likely to be resolved with an eye to future harmony or at least coexistence. Earlier, in discussing marital power studies, the exchange value theory was briefly described.

According to this theory, the marital partner who sees attractive alternatives outside the relationship is able to wield more power since he or she has more options. As divorce, separation, and termination of relationships become more common and acceptable, partners may be less motivated to overlook or live with present conflicts in the hope of future improvement. One could also argue, however, that precisely because partners feel freer to leave or change a relationship than previously, they must be more attuned to each other's future needs. When partners are bound together no matter what, consideration of the linkage between past and future decisions may be unnecessary. After all, resentment against overbearing decision-making power at time X won't be likely to lead to breakup at a later time. Of course couples can find many ways of expressing resentment and making each other's lives miserable, but on balance, it is likely that the lure of outside alternatives makes each partner more sensitive to the mental arithmetic of the other. Such sensitivity pressures the couple to an increasingly egalitarian communication pattern in which the statement "You got your way before; now it's my turn" is often implicit.

Indeed, there is an association between cultures with strict controls on the dissolution of marriages and traditional, husband-dominated or patriarchal decision-making patterns. That is, when marriages are immutable and made in heaven, there does seem to be less attention paid to the mutual needs of both husband and wife to take part in the decision-making process and less recognition that present decisions taken by the husband may lead to later resentment by the wife.

While one automatically thinks of commitment to family relationships in terms of the marital bond, it should be emphasized that commitment to children by parents and vice versa also varies and would be expected to influence the linkage among past, present, and future decisions. As discussed earlier, the historical evolution of the modern family is characterized by increased valuation of children. We suggest that as commitment to children as members of the family increased, so did recognition that present decisions affecting them must be made with an eye toward their future concerns.

Regardless of the role of commitment, the linkage between past, present, and future decisions often means that some decisions, once taken, close off certain future options. For example, occupational choices are particularly difficult for many young people because of the feeling that preparing for one particular career will prevent later exploration of other attractive possibilities. To a certain extent this is of course true. Time invested in preparing for a career in medicine is time taken away from training in other fields. Yet many college students are perhaps unaware of the large numbers of successful professionals who change careers at midlife.

Thus, the sense that present decisions close off later possibilities is also influenced by one's *feelings* about how much one is determined by one's past actions. The old argument about free will versus determinism in guiding human actions is relevant here. The determining power of past decisions is usually greatest when people are convinced that despite their wishes, their past decisions have set them on a narrow predetermined path. When family members believe they can change course, reevaluate their past decisions, and to some extent break free from them, then in fact, past decisions less tightly constrain their future ones.

CENTRAL AND SATELLITE DECISIONS

Decisions are linked, not only in time, but in webs of interrelationship. Once a central decision is taken, many other decisions linked to it must be resolved. The decision to have a child, to move to a new home, to separate, are all such central decisions. Earlier, we termed them orchestration decisions. The importance of such central decisions is not always fully appreciated by the family. For example, couples are often unaware of how radically the decision to have a child will affect their lives. It may be linked to the wife's decision to withdraw from outside employment, to alterations in the division of household responsibility, to subtle changes in marital power (LaRossa, 1978). Take Joe's feelings of increased power:

Joe: I'm sort of proud and happy now that my wife's pregnant and we're going to have a child, and it was the motivating force in terms of me thinking about being the breadwinner, assuming a specific role. She's going to be staying home. Before I was just another person going out and working and now I'm going to be the breadwinner. . . . When you have responsibilities you end up being in charge.

Or Debby's new-found assertiveness toward her husband Daryl:

Debby: I just have a feeling that I can say anything I feel like saying, and nobody
          dares do anything about it! Isn't that awful?
Interviewer: Do you think that's related to the pregnancy?
Debby: Yes. Who is going to say anything to me now? They have no "weight."
Daryl: I never noticed that.
Debby: Just keep on *not* noticing it, and we'll get along fine.*

In these examples, the central decision to have a child and the ensuing pregnancy was much like a stone thrown into a still pond, causing ripples to spread in widening circles. Similarly, a central decision affects many aspects of family functioning.

DECISION MAKING AND INFORMATION PROCESSING

Central to the decision-making process is the use of information extracted from the environment, information about what alternatives are available, what benefits and risks are associated with possible outcomes, and how important others feel about these alternatives. In an ideal situation, each family member would carefully weigh each possible alternative, assess its cost-benefit ratio, determine through flexible, open communication the feelings of others about each of these alternatives, and democratically reach a decision satisfying to all. In reality, few of these conditions can be met even when family members understand and desire them. In the helter-skelter of real life, it is often unclear just what alternatives exist, and information about their possible risks and benefits is lacking. For example, the important decisions of family planning—whether to have children, how many and their spacing—may be taken without inadequate information concerning birth control, the real feelings of other family members, or the attitudes of society. A family may erroneously believe that "everyone has three children, each two years apart." A wife may be convinced that her husband really doesn't want children since he appears short-tempered with the neighborhood kids. In the absence of more open communciation, she will remain unaware of his strong positive feelings. Moreover, the benefits and costs to the family of a particular family size and spacing cannot be clearly predicted.

Many transactions with the environment are unguided because of inadequate information, as in the case of family planning. Many others are equally unplanned because of too much information. Research on information processing concludes that the human brain can hold about seven items of information in the absence of organizing principles or general rules. When families are bombarded by information about their decisions as consumers, for example, much of this information will be unusable. Too much choice may be tantamount to no choice at all. Any parent who has tried to select a breakfast cereal based on knowledgeable comparison of the contents of each brand on the grocery shelves knows the futility of such a task. Habits quickly develop to thread the maze of information.

Part of the information used in making decisions is knowledge stored concerning relevant past decisions and their outcomes. Central or orchestration decisions are difficult in part because of their infrequent character. Family planning, family residence, and family employment are generally stable; hence, changes in these areas cannot draw on a wealth of previous relevant decisions.

---

* These excerpts are reprinted from *Conflict and Power in Marriage: Expecting the First Child*, Sage Library of Social Research, Volume 50, by Ralph LaRossa, © 1978, p. 48 by permission of the publisher, Sage Publications, Inc. (Beverly Hills/London).

Feedback plays a greater role in peripheral or instrumentation decisions, which occur with greater frequency. Meal preparation and planning is an obvious example of this. Decisions about what to have for dinner are constantly being affected by feedback from family members about the success or failure of previous meals.

Information gathering in general and feedback from past decisions in particular vary considerably in families. As mentioned earlier, families experiencing interpersonal troubles often have rigid mental sets excluding new information. Other families are oriented to the present and hence, do not take past decisions into account.

Poor families are less likely than more affluent ones to have access to information concerning alternatives. One comparative study of 150 low-income and 150 middle- to high-income families concluded that poor families (1) were slower to recognize problems, (2) could not extensively search for information, (3) were unable to evaluate possible choices, (4) engaged in more irregular consumer behavior, and (5) expressed more regret over their choices (Verhallen, 1975).

Families experiencing very high levels of environmental stimulation and change may be unable to cope with the onslaught of information and decisions to be made. For example, consider the events which have occurred to the Miller family during the past year: John, the father, has quit his job and is attempting to set himself up in business. Beth, the mother, has gone back to work as a nurse after fifteen years. Sally, the oldest girl, has recently announced her plans to leave high school and get married. Beth's mother has died after a long illness. The family dog was run over and killed. John's sister Ann is divorcing after twenty-five years of marriage. Against this background of change, it will be difficult for the Millers to use the lessons of past decisions in making new ones. Thus, when the prospect of moving arises—John's fledgling business and Beth's work at the hospital are both across town—the entire family feels overwhelmed and unable to consider clearly the alternatives open to them.

How can families be aided to extract information, make use of available information, and cut overload down to size? One experimental scheme has been developed to help people think through their decisions about whether to have a (another) child (Beach et al., 1976). A list of values that children can fulfill for parents is prepared. This list is then used by a couple to break down their birth decisions into manageable chunks. The couple then considers whether each chunk of values would be attained personally for them if they decided to have a child.

SUMMARY

We have considered seven general characteristics of the decision-making process in families. In doing so, we have emphasized its *process* nature rather than its outcome, viewing decision making as one part of family communication in all its complexity. These seven characteristics are:

1. Decision making involves conflict management.
2. Decision making reflects family members' perceptions, needs, and values.
3. Decision making reflects family interaction patterns, including authority and power relationships.
4. Decision making styles may be identified.
5. Decision making is a process linked to past and future decisions.
6. Decision making is a process tying central to satellite decisions.
7. Decision making involves information processing.

REFERENCES

Bach, G., and Wyden, P. *The Intimate Enemy: How to Fight Fair in Love and Marriage.* New York: Morrow, 1969.

Beach, L. R., Townes, B. D., Campbell, F. L., and Keating, G. W. Developing and testing a decision aid for birth planning decisions. *Organizational Behavior and Human Performance* 15(1976): 99-116.

Benson, L. *Fatherhood: A Sociological Perspective.* New York: Random House, 1968.

Blau, P., and Duncan, O. *The American Occupational Structure.* New York: Wiley, 1967.

Blood, R. *The Family.* New York: The Free Press, 1972.

Blood, R., and Wolfe, D. *Husbands and Wives: The Dynamics of Married Living.* New York: The Free Press, 1960.

Boyd, E., Clark, J., Kempler, H., Johannet, P., Leonard, B., and McPherson, P. Teaching interpersonal communication to troubled families. *Family Process* 13(1974): 317-336.

Burgess, R. L., and Conger, R. D. Family interaction in abusive, neglectful and normal families. Paper presented to the biennial meeting of the Society for Research in Child Development, New Orleans, 1977.

Corah, N. L. Differentiation in children and their parents. *Journal of Personality* 33(1965): 300-308.

Douvan, E., and Adelson, J. *The Adolescent Experience.* New York: Wiley, 1966.

Dyer, E., and Urban, D. The institutionalism of equalitarian family norms. *Marriage and Family Living* 20(1958): 53-58.

Ferreira, A. J., and Winter, W. D. Family interaction and decision-making. *Archives of General Psychiatry* 13(1965): 214-223.

Hawkes, G., and Taylor, M. Power structure in Mexican and Mexican-American farm labor families. *Journal of Marriage and the Family* 37(1975): 807-811.

Heer, D. Husband and wife perceptions of family power structure. *Marriage and Family Living* 24(1962): 65-67.

Herbst, P. G. Conceptual framework for studying the family. In O. A. Oeser and S. B. Hammond, eds., *Social Structure and Personality in a City.* New York: Macmillan, 1954.

Holstein, C. Parental consensus and interaction in relation to the child's moral judgment. *Dissertation Abstracts International* 30(1970): 1888-1889.

Janis, I. L., and Mann, L. *Decision-making.* New York: The Free Press, 1977.

Kandel, D., and Lesser, G. Parent-adolescent relationships and adolescent independence in the United States and Denmark. *Journal of Marriage and the Family* 31(1969): 348-358.

Kidwell, J. Raising an only child: Should it be avoided? Paper presented at the annual meeting of the Indiana Council on Family Relations, 1977.

Kohlberg, L. The development of children's orientations toward a moral order: I. Sequence in the development of moral thought. *Vita Humana* 6(1963): 11-33.

LaRossa, R. *Conflict and Power in Marriage: Expecting the First Child.* Beverly Hills, Calif.: Sage Publications, 1978.

Levin, E. L., Kelley, J. D., and Riordan, R. J. The marital power structure. Paper presented to the National Council of Family Relations, 1976.

Lopata, H. The secondary features of a primary relationship. *Human Organization* 24(1965): 116-123.

Lynn, D. *The Father: His Role in Child Development.* Monterey, Calif.: Brooks/Cole, 1974.

McLeod, J., Chaffee, S., and Eswara, H. Family communication patterns and communication research. Paper presented at Association for Education in Journalism, Iowa City, 1966.

McPartland, J. M., and Epstein, J. L. An investigation of the interaction of family and school factors in open-school effects on students. Center for Social Organization of Schools Reports, no. 192. Johns Hopkins University, 1975.

Maslow, A. H. *Motivation and Personality.* New York: Harper, 1954.

Miller, G., and Swanson, G. *The Changing American Parent.* New York: Wiley, 1958.

Nye, I. Maternal employment and marital interaction: Some contingent conditions. *Social Forces* 40(1961): 113-119.

Nye, I., and Hoffman, L. W. *The Employed Mother in America.* Chicago: Rand McNally, 1963.

Odom, L., Seeman, J., and Newbrough, J. R. A study of family communication patterns and personality integration in children. *Child Psychiatry and Human Development* 1(1971): 275-285.

Paolucci, B., Hall, O. A., and Axinn, N. *Family Decision-making: An Ecosystem Approach.* New York: Wiley, 1977.

Plonk, M. A. Exploring interrelationships in a central-satellite decision complex. *Journal of Home Economics* 60(1968): 789-792.

Price, D. Relationship of decision styles and self-actualization. *Home Economics Research Journal* 2(1973): 12-20.

Rausch, H., Barry, W., Hertel, R., and Swain, M. *Communication, Conflict, and Marriage.* San Francisco: Jossey-Bass, 1974.

Richmond, M. Beyond resource theory: Another look at factors enabling women to affect family interaction. *Journal of Marriage and the Family* 38(1976): 257-266.

Rollins, B., and Bahr, S. A theory of power relationships in marriage. *Journal of Marriage and the Family* 38(1976): 619-628.

Rutherford, E., and Mussen, P. Generosity in nursery school boys. *Child Development* 39(1968): 757-765.

Safilios-Rothschild, C. Patterns of familial power and influence. *Sociological Focus* 2(1969): 7-19. (a)

———. Family sociology or wives' family sociology? A cross-cultural examination of decision-making. *Journal of Marriage and the Family* 31(1969): 290-301. (b)

———. The study of family power structure: A review 1960-69. In C. Broderick, ed., *A Decade of Family Research and Action.* Minneapolis: Minnesota, NCFR, 1971.

Speece, B. A. Altruism in the elementary school. *Dissertation Abstracts* 28(1968): 3519.

Sprey, J. Family power structure: A critical comment. *Journal of Marriage and the Family* 34(1972): 235-238.

Steinberg, L. D., and Hill, J. P. Family interaction in early adolescence. Paper presented to the biennial meeting of the Society for Research in Child Development, New Orleans, 1977.

Steinmann, A. Lack of communication between husbands and wives. *Marriage and Family Living* 20(1958): 350-352.

Straus, M. Power and support structure of the family in relation to socialization. *Journal of Marriage and the Family* 26(1964): 318-326.

Thompson, V. Family size: Implicit policies and assumed psychological outcomes. *Journal of Social Issues* 30(1974): 93-125.

Turk, J. L., and Bell, N. W. Measuring power in families. *Journal of Marriage and the Family* 34(1972): 215-222.

Verhallen, T. M. The decision process among low income families. *Tijdschrift voor Psychologie* 3(1975): 362-383 (English abstract).

Winter, W. D., and Ferreira, A. J. Talking time as an index of intra-familial similarity in normal and abnormal families. *Journal of Abnormal Psychology* 74(1969): 575-57 .

Winter, W. D., Ferreira, A. J., and Bowers, N. Decision-making in married and unrelated couples. *Family Process* 12(1973): 83-94.

Witkin, H. A., Dyk, R. B., Faterson, H. F., Goodenough, D. R., and Karp, S. A. *Psychological Differentiation.* New York: Wiley, 1962.

Nutrition: The Internal Environment

8

Nutrition may be defined as the *process by which an individual takes in and utilizes food.* For the individual system, nutrition is the most fundamental process of extracting energy from the environment and transforming it to fuel the system's activity. Although it is customary to think of nutrition as an individual activity, an ecosystem framework stresses how food consumption depends upon family functioning, which, in turn, is inseparably linked to the surrounding physical and social environments.

Starting with the widest ecological context, the planet Earth, we may identify forces that affect the family's nutrition. As Table 8.1 shows, climate, population, soil conditions, and energy supply will determine what crops are grown. At the global level of analysis, these factors are important:

1. Rate of growth of world population
2. Composition of diet of the affluent (high consumption of meat places high demand on a finite supply of world grain)
3. Distribution of limited global resources, such as fertilizer
4. Distribution of productive agricultural practices and technology. Much of the world's population is dependent upon food exports from North America
5. Readiness of the affluent nations to advance the principle that an adequate diet is a basic right of each individual (Newberger, Newberger, and Harper, 1976)

The availability of food resources has been a great force determining world history. Populations have migrated from famine to the promise of lush green fields. In this way, the Irish potato famine brought millions to America. Wars have been fought for possession of rich farming lands or the waterways along which their produce could be transported and traded.

International political and economic forces will influence the way each society is organized for food production, distribution, and consumption. In America, the trend has been toward large, heavily mechanized agriculture. Millions of small farmers have joined the urban or rural wage-earning population. The nutritional status of those made landless or jobless in the process of improving agricultural efficiency often suffers. As Newberger and colleagues point out (1976, p. 169), whenever food is allocated according to purchasing power, hunger and malnutrition will inevitably be concentrated among the poor.

At the level of the family unit, many family characteristics affect what the family eats and how it is eaten. Not only family size and patterning of interaction, but values and folkways are important. An individual family's style of functioning affects the physical, social, cognitive, and psychological development of the child and every other family member. Finally, at the level of the individual system, its functioning will determine how available food will be used to fulfill system

TABLE 8.1 A FRAMEWORK FOR AN ECOLOGICAL ANALYSIS OF NUTRITION

Level of Analysis	Given Context	Relevant Forces	Nutritional Variable
I	The planet Earth	Reality of climate, population and soil; supply of energy and fertilizer; politics and balance of trade	International availability of nutritional resources
II	The international economic and political order	Social, economic, and political order in a given country	Availability of food to family units
III	Social, political, and economic order in a given country	Family functioning: stresses, distribution patterns, food beliefs, parental maturity, family size	Family ability to get food to its members
IV	A given family's way of functioning	Physical, social, cognitive, and psychological characteristics of each family member; health of each family member	Family member's ability to use what is available

Adapted with permission from Newberger, Newberger, and Harper, 1976, p. 161.

demands for nutrient energy. For example, central nervous system disease affects appetite; fever, infections, or malignancy increase metabolic requirements. Emotional functioning is as important as physical. A disease like *anorexia nervosa*, occurring most frequently among adolescent girls, involves a self-induced undernutrition of such proportions that starvation may occur. Among young children, a syndrome of infantile "nonorganic" malnutrition, called *failure to thrive*, has been observed. Such children fail to gain expected weight and height in the absence of any demonstrated organic causes. Failure to thrive, like *anorexia nervosa*, may have its roots in the child's social relationship with other family members. The young child must feel that social relationships are mutually satisfying in order to develop a sense of *basic trust* in the environment. Without this feeling, he or she may withdraw from nurturance and nutrition, as if giving up on the world.

THE SYMBOLIC SIGNIFICANCE OF FOOD

Religious taboos prevent the ingestion of certain foods, as in the Hindu prohibition against the eating of meat, Catholic dietary restrictions during Lent, or Jewish dietary laws of *kashrut*, which prohibit mixing milk with meat.

These taboos mean that certain foods must be eaten in certain prescribed ways. Hence, they structure social interactions with the family and between the family and outsiders. Cultural folkways have the same effect. In some societies, women prepare and serve food for men, eating later with the children. This pattern reinforces segregation by sex and communicates differences in power and prestige within the family. Religious prohibitions against consuming certain foods tend to prevent contact between the believer and the nonbeliever. One function of food taboos is to maintain the cohesiveness of the religious or cultural group.

The breaking of bread and the convivial glass of wine share emotions, not just calories. Thanksgiving dinner is a vivid picture of how symbolic significance is served up with the turkey.

Food is a vehicle for the many rituals around which family life is organized. (Photo by Natalie Leimkuhler.)

Food, like the birthday cake or wedding feast, is an important part of the many rituals around which family life is organized. Food may be used to express and confer status, as when an expensive wine is ordered. The preparation of food may express creativity and, in some cases, be elevated to an art. Small wonder that food habits remain among those customs most resistant to change.

NUTRITIONAL REQUIREMENTS

Today, in what many Americans think of as a postindustrial era, much of the world's population goes to bed hungry. For them, the struggle for one's daily bread is still life's central preoccupation. Periodic mass starvations flicker briefly to our attention over the evening news. In our own country, the extent of undernutrition and malnutrition is gradually coming to public attention. The Ten State Nutrition Survey identified borderline malnutrition in vulnerable groups like the urban poor, Mexican-American children living along the Rio Grande, and pregnant and lactating women.

Overnutrition is also a serious health problem. It is estimated that three million adults are obese and that 30 to 40 percent of them have diabetes and heart disease (Senate, 1973).

There are forty-four nutritional requirements for humans. They include water, glucose, cellulose, eighteen minerals, eight amino acids, ammonium acetate, one fatty acid, and thirteen vitamins. Can these requirements be translated into an optimum diet which, if followed, would prevent both malnutrition and overnutrition, as well as enhance health and the feeling of well-being? In an effort to address this question, U.S. Dietary Goals have been published (Table 8.2).

Carrying out these goals would involve increased consumption of fruits, vegetables, vegetable oils, and cereals, decreased consumption of red meat, eggs, table sugar, and whole milk, and

TABLE 8.2 REVISED U.S. DIETARY GOALS (1978)

1. To avoid overweight, consume only as much energy (calories) as is expended; if overweight, decrease energy intake and increase energy expenditure.
2. Increase the consumption of complex carbohydrates and ''naturally occurring'' sugars from about 28 percent of energy intake to about 48 percent of energy intake.
3. Reduce the consumption of refined and processed sugars by about 45 percent to account for about 10 percent of total energy intake.
4. Reduce overall fat consumption from approximately 40 percent to about 30 percent of energy intake.
5. Reduce saturated fat consumption to account for about 10 percent of total energy intake; and balance that with poly-unsaturated and mono-unsaturated fats, which should account for about 10 percent of energy intake each.
6. Reduce cholesterol consumption to about 300 mg/day.
7. Limit the intake of sodium by reducing the intake of salt to about five grams a day.

Reprinted with permission from Olson, 1978.

elimination of table salt. However, dietary practices over the last fifty years show no indication that Americans are moving in this direction. Since 1955, consumption of dairy products has declined 21 percent, that of vegetables 23 percent, and that of fruits 25 percent. In contrast, consumption of soft drinks has increased by 80 percent, pies, cookies, and cakes 70 percent, and potato chips and other snacks by 85 percent. The percentage of people eating what the Department of Agriculture defines as a "poor" diet has increased over the last twenty years from 25 to 29 percent (Westerberg, 1978). Moreover, the "optimum diet" that would result from following U.S. Dietary Goals has been the focus of considerable controversy. The American Medical Association has refused to endorse the dietary goals, cautioning that conclusive proof of their value has not yet been shown. Others have questioned whether a single set of recommendations can be suitable for diverse groups, such as infants, pregnant women, and the elderly, each with different nutritional needs (Olson, 1978).

The question of an optimum diet for overall health is not the only subject of heated debate. Diseases vary in the degree to which nutritional intervention can be effective (Figure 8.1). At one end of the continuum are genetic diseases such as sickle cell anemia, which are nutrition-resistant. At the other end are diseases such as scurvy, caused by specific vitamin deficiencies. In the middle are chronic degenerative diseases such as cancer. Here, the degree to which nutritional changes can affect the progress of the disease is unknown. Do optimum diets exist for the prevention of such diseases as cancer, diabetes, heart disease, stroke, and cirrhosis of the liver? Debate over the exact role of cholesterol in the incidence of heart disease continues. Traditionally, medicine has not concerned itself with nutrition as a fundamental component of internal medicine. Internes often do not know the exact composition of the hospital diets they prescribe. In fact, one study (Butterworth and Blackburn, 1975) found that malnutrition was more likely inside a hospital than outside!

With scientific knowledge in such a state of disarray, it is not surprising that families with the economic means to be adequately nourished feel too confused to know how to go about it.

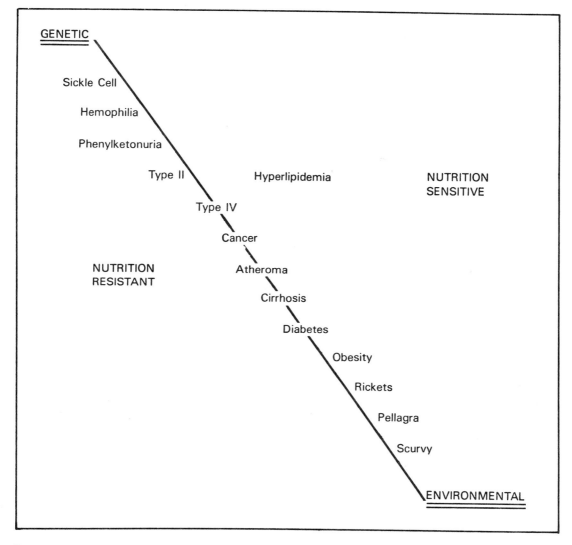

Figure 8.1 The reciprocal genetic and environmental determinants of thirteen diseases as shown on a linear scale. The extent to which nutritional intervention can modify the disease is indicated by the degree of displacement of each bar to the right of the line. (Reproduced with permission from Olson, 1978, p. 26.)

Expenditures for food represent a major budget item, and shopping itself has become a central aspect of consumer decision making and behavior, involving the entire family. Nutritional specialists, food experts, and faddists, not to mention product manufacturers, all bombard the public through media campaigns designed to influence food purchases and consumption. Government, primarily through the Food and Drug Administration, also participates in monitoring food quality and ensuring accurate package labelling and advertising. Finally, consumer groups such as Action for Children's Television (ACT) have become concerned about the advertising of "empty-calorie," high-sugar food products such as sugar-coated cereals. They are arguing that not only the accuracy of labelling, but also the quality of nutritional products, be considered as appropriate criteria for evaluating advertising.

With increased awareness of nutritional quality and greater demands for more nutritional information come a new concern. Do individuals have the ability to sort through all this information? Will the lines of tiny print on the side of each package detailing the nutritional quality of the contents be read and understood by anyone but a professional biochemist with the eyesight of the Six Million Dollar Man? Consumer studies are finding that too much environmental information may result in *information overload* (see Chapter 4).

If more education about nutrition is needed, particularly for children whose food habits tend to persevere into adulthood, what exactly should be taught, by whom, and in what manner? The educational system is drawn into concern with nutrition.

In fact, everyone is in on the food game. For family members, the food that comes to the table to be eaten, in a literal sense, provides their only source of energy, making all other behavior possible. Moreover, the social and symbolic significance of food means that much family interaction will be organized around its purchase, preparation, and consumption. In its reactive role, the family is affected by nutritional supply and consumption in many ways. Their functioning, both as individuals and as a family unit, may be impaired by malnutrition. More subtly, however, the nutritional quality of "adequate" diets and the style of their consumption reflect and help to mold family interaction.

Family nutrition will depend, not only upon objective levels of available resources, but also upon values concerning food and information about food—its characteristics, availability, and significance. Family organization will affect patterns of food consumption. In turn, the availability of food and the style in which it is consumed will affect family processes such as perceiving, valuing, spacing, and deciding. Nutrition is inextricably tied up in the whole fabric of a culture. In what has been termed an *adaptive cycle* (Adams, 1968), cultural context affects nutrition, which, in turn, modifies and forms part of the culture.

DEFINING TERMS

There is often confusion among the terms *starvation, undernutrition, hunger,* and *malnutrition. Starvation* is a life-threatening deprivation of nutrients. *Undernutrition* refers to a deficiency in the total number of calories needed to sustain body weight and well-being. This would occur if the amounts of food in a well-balanced adequate diet were simply cut in half. *Hunger* is the affective state associated with undernutrition, but since hunger is psychological, it does not always reflect undernutrition. Some people react to boredom or tension by feeling hunger and then overeating.

Primary and *secondary malnutrition* have been distinguished. Primary malnutrition refers to the unavailability of certain nutrients. In some cases, nutrients may not be utilized by the body because of certain inborn errors of metabolism. In other cases, the malnutrition may be limited to certain specific deficits, as when a diet is low in foods containing vitamin C. Malnutrition may also stem from deficiencies in certain types of foods, such as those containing high-quality protein. Such malnutrition often exists alongside undernutrition, in a diet deficient in certain nutrients and also too low in calories. When the adverse effects of malnutrition are discussed, it is usually such *protein-calorie malnutrition* that is in mind. Although in developing countries protein malnutrition and undernutrition are in practice often found together, it is important to keep the distinction clear between them, since research has shown the effects of undernutrition and malnutrition upon the body and the emotions may be different.

Secondary malnutrition may exist in the midst of plenty; it refers to inadequate intake and usage of nutrients due to social and psychological factors. Almost all instances of malnutrition involve both primary and secondary types. This is because the individual is embedded in a nested series of environments. Malnutrition occurs as a breakdown of energy exchanges, in this case in the form of food, within and between systems (Sims, 1972). Malnutrition involves breakdowns in the system of food production, distribution, and consumption—through natural disasters such as drought, through inadequate distribution patterns, through folkways that prohibit some from receiving proper nutrition and label certain foods as taboo. The study of nutrition illustrates the way in which physical, social, and economic forces interact as a complex environmental setting within which families function as participants (Suchman, 1968).

MALNUTRITION IN ANIMALS

Much has been learned concerning the effects of malnutrition by studying animal behavior. With animal subjects, it is possible to control dietary intake accurately, to determine exactly the onset, duration, and severity of malnutrition, and to observe systematically its effects on learning, emotion, and other behaviors. However, to what degree can the results of such animal experimentation be readily applied to humans, for whom social, cultural, and economic factors are so intertwined?

The results of malnutrition in experimental animals are dramatic and unpleasant. For example, pigs offered unlimited amounts of low-protein diet are thin, undersized creatures with scaly, cracked, and wrinkled skin. They stumble about with a stiff-legged gait. Some collapse and suddenly die (Stewart and Platt, 1968). The physical growth of the brain is stunted, particularly if malnutrition occurs during the vulnerable fetal and newborn period of greatest brain-cell growth (Dobbing, 1968). Malnourished rats and dogs show similar symptoms.

These effects are more severe when animals are malnourished rather than undernourished. In addition, the age at which the deficient diet is begun is significant. For example, pigs who were malnourished from the fourteenth day of life were more severely affected than those who were malnourished from the nineteenth day. These animals, in turn, were more severely affected than pigs given deficient diets beginning on the twenty-sixth day of life (Stewart and Platt, 1968).

The earliest possible time at which malnutrition can occur is during the period of fetal growth. However, the fetus is much less vulnerable than the infant to the effects of malnutrition, because of its ability to gain nourishment at the expense of the mother. If an infant born to a malnourished mother receives adequate nourishment immediately after birth from a well-nourished foster mother, growth and development will be normal. If, however, the newborn continues to be malnourished after birth, the effects of previous fetal malnutrition will then be felt. The offspring of nutritionally deficient mothers are born with smaller stores of important nutrients and, hence, are more vulnerable to the effects of dietary deficiencies after birth. Thus, the earlier the onset of malnutrition, the more severe and lasting its effects. Very early and severe animal malnutrition may result in permanent impairment that later feeding cannot reverse.

Early malnutrition affects the adult animal's feeding patterns. For example, increased hoarding of food as well as increased rates of food consumption have been observed in animals with a history of earlier food restriction. Animal malnutrition also affects emotionality. Monkeys, normally very curious and social creatures, when malnourished exhibit fear and withdrawal when confronted with novel objects. They do not play with their peers but spend time alone in self-stimulation. Their behavior resembles that of monkeys raised without mothers.

This lack of interest in the environment and retarded social development can be produced in monkeys by feeding them a diet containing the same number of calories as adequately nourished monkeys, but one-fourth of the protein. Since this is precisely the type of malnutrition most prevalent among young children in poor countries, the implications of this research for humans are important (Kerr and Waisman, 1968).

In general, the effects of environmental isolation and protein-calorie malnutrition on experimental animals are strikingly similar. In both cases, early deprivation results in later emotionality and impaired learning in novel situations. In both cases, experiences during early development have long-term behavioral effects lasting into maturity. It appears that early environmental stimulation equips animals to deal more flexibly and effectively with later novel experiences. Students of animal behavior hypothesize that early malnutrition may in some way block this ability (Levitsky and Barnes, 1973).

Animal studies show wide-ranging and severe effects of experimental undernutrition and malnutrition. For obvious ethical reasons, evidence concerning the effects of undernutrition and malnutrition on humans has come from studies of naturally occurring disasters, such as famines, and the chronic nutritional disaster conditions pervading much of the world.

Of particular concern is possible damage to intellectual ability caused by undernutrition and malnutrition in the early years. The precise role of nutritional status in this matter is hotly debated, because of the impossibility of separating genetic from environmental influences. Among environmental influences themselves, nutrition is but one of many interrelated factors, as Figure 8.2 illustrates.

Can the negative consequences of poor nutrition to physical and mental well-being be aced directly to undernutrition and malnutrition, or are they part of a complex picture including poor sanitation, susceptibility to disease, crowded housing conditions, and low income? Keeping in mind that a clear answer to this question cannot now be given, we will examine first research on the effects of human undernutrition, then of protein malnutrition on both physical and mental well-being.

EFFECTS OF UNDERNUTRITION ON HUMANS

Unless near-starvation conditions occur, undernutrition does not adversely affect the ability to bear children. In some cities in Holland during the Second World War, starvation conditions resulted in irregular menstruation among half the women of child-bearing age and a subsequent drop in the rate of conception occurred. However, some of the poorest and most poorly nourished parts of the world have the highest birth rates.

Stillbirths, premature births, malformations and infant death have all been associated with undernutrition, although it is not possible to pinpoint undernutrition as the *cause*. Babies born to undernourished mothers tend to have lower birth weights than those born to adequately nourished mothers. The low-birth-weight baby is a vulnerable baby. When follow-up observation of a group

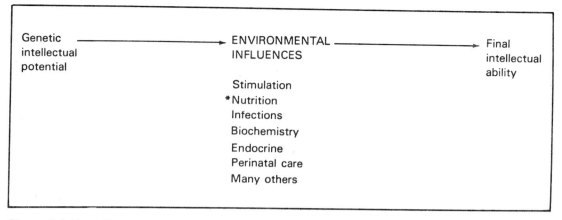

Figure 8.2 Many "internal" and "external" influences occur with undernutrition that can influence brain development and intellectual testing. (Reproduced with permission from Chase, 1976.)

of such babies was made at school age, 24 percent were observed to be suffering major physical defects, as compared to 2 to 3 percent of those who had normal birth weights (Robinson and Robinson, 1965).

The undernourished child is susceptible to infection. Diarrhea, the leading cause of infant mortality in developing countries, rises precipitously at time of weaning. Diarrhea aggravates further the severity of undernutrition, since food passes more quickly through the body and fewer nutrients are retained (Lowenberg et al., 1968).

As with animal studies, evidence collected on humans emphasizes the importance of *timing, severity,* and *duration* of undernutrition. The earlier its onset, the more severe the consequences.

Undernutrition among adults has wide-ranging consequences as well. In a rare experimental study, thirty-two healthy, well-nourished Americans voluntarily underwent a period of severe undernutrition (Keys et al., 1950). They subsisted on a diet of 1570 calories over a period of twenty-four weeks. As expected, substantial weight loss occurred. The men felt physically weak and unable to do even simple things like ascending a flight of stairs without resting. The emotional effects were also dramatic. They became preoccupied with food. They were often depressed, with mood swings affected by the weather. Their personal appearance deteriorated, as did their ability to get along with one another. They became suspicious of strangers. While their intellectual ability did not suffer, they found it hard to concentrate on problem-solving tasks. Thoughts of food constantly got in the way. During their rehabilitation period, the effects of this semistarvation persisted for several weeks.

Much of the world's population in developing countries is undernourished. Despite negative consequences to physical and mental well-being, humans are able to adapt to such stresses on their systems. Body movements are lessened and basal metabolism is reduced so that the total energy expenditure is decreased and fewer total calories are needed. In this way, life may be maintained for long periods on greatly reduced food intake (Lowenberg et al., 1968). For example, if 20 percent is lost from previously normal body weight, then a diet of 50 percent of the previous total caloric intake will be enough to maintain the body at its reduced weight level. Thus, decreased environmental supply is met by decreased system demand to maintain adaptation.

MALNUTRITION IN HUMANS

It is estimated that 70 percent of all preschool children in developing countries are malnourished. Chronic protein deficiency affects more than 360 million children (Keppel, 1968). Such estimates are very rough, since many areas lack vital statistics or medical personnel who might keep records. No matter what the exact number, it is evident that malnutrition, particularly among children, is perhaps the world's number one health problem.

Based on food consumption, Americans are the best fed population on earth. However, segments of the childbearing population have diets deficient in high-quality foods. Pregnant teenagers, among whom the birth rate is sharply increasing, are more likely than other groups to have inadequate diets, buying a six pack of Coke rather than a carton of milk. Peer pressure, persistence of poor childhood eating habits, lack of education about nutrition, all contribute to a diet high enough, perhaps too high, in calories, but poorly balanced and lacking high-quality protein (Hepner, 1958.)

As with other animals, the human fetus is able to withdraw nutrients from the mother, so that malnutrition during pregnancy has less severe consequences than malnutrition soon after birth. A vicious circle exists, however, of low socio-economic status, poor nutrition, small birth weight, and greater infant vulnerability. As the discussion of undernutrition showed, poorer women, when compared with those from more advantaged classes, have less nutritious diets, more complications of pregnancy, and babies with lower birth weights, more malformations or disease, and lower probability of surviving. Studies that have used vitamin and protein supplements to eliminate the diet differences among the classes, while not affecting any other presumed life stresses, have, nevertheless, produced dramatic results. Babies born to lower-class mothers given diet supplements during pregnancy were significantly healthier than those born to women on unsupplemented diets (Ebbs et al., 1942).

Despite the dramatic success of such short-term intervention, the long-range importance of good nutrition has been emphasized repeatedly. One longitudinal study, following 200 women for twenty years, concluded that nutrition not only during pregnancy, but also when the mother *herself* was a child, was important (Kirkwood, 1955). A closer look at some other research illustrates how nutritional status may affect several generations. In one study, infants' birth weights were positively related to their mothers' heights, which in turn were related, not to the present, but their childhood socio-economic status. Thus, the social-class standing of a young girl predicted well the ultimate birth weight of her infants (Knobloch, 1956). It has been suggested (Walter, 1955) that inadequate nutrition may prevent not only full potential maternal height, but also full growth of the pelvis, thereby making a less than optimally hospitable environment for the fetus.

In summary, the quality of maternal nutrition affects the fetus in both short- and long-term ways. During pregnancy, poor nutrition is associated with low birth weight and other at-risk factors. Moreover, a woman's nutritional habits from girlhood will help determine the extent to which she will realize her full potential growth. Since this affects pelvic size, a girl's early nutrition has a "sleeper effect" helping to determine the quality of the fetal environment.

In addition to the fetal period, improper nutrition during early childhood may have long-range negative consequences. The causes of malnutrition in early childhood are considerably more complex than the quality and quantity of food ingested. Aspects of health and disease, particularly infection, may indirectly affect nutritional status. As with undernutrition, a host of interrelated social factors play an important role. In technologically underdeveloped countries, low purchasing power may require the provider of food to devote most available time to securing food and other necessities, making the accumulation of reserves of food unlikely. The need for working hands to maintain even a minimum of food supply means that individuals cannot have the luxury of staying in school. Leaving school early is encouraged by necessity. In turn, illiteracy and ignorance of proper nutrition and health persist. Hence, susceptibility of the young child to disease is heightened.

In addition, custom often prevents high-protein food from being distributed in greatest amounts to the young child. Father gets the best; women and children, the leftovers (Cravioto, 1968). Religious beliefs and taboos are important also. In certain rural areas of Nigeria, for example, pregnant women are not allowed to eat fruits and vegetables. Children must not drink coconut milk, or they will become morons. They should not eat eggs, lest they become liars and thieves (Collis and Janes, 1968).

Just as the causes of malnutrition are wide-ranging and complex, so, too, are the effects. Fewer children now die of severe protein malnutrition. In 1952, 30 percent of severely malnourished children died, while during 1963–1964, only 5 percent did so (Gomez, 1956). Mere survival, however, does not mean that serious negative consequences have been avoided. Some of these effects concern physical growth patterns. Children recovered from severe malnutrition are on the average shorter and more retarded in general skeletal development in comparison with similar individuals who escaped malnutrition. Other effects center upon possible delay or permanent impairment of mental development in children malnourished as infants. The severely malnourished child is not a pretty picture. In its extreme form the disorders resulting from protein-calorie malnutrition, often called in one of its African names "kwashiorkor," look something like this:

> The children affected are nearly always not only small for their age, with hair and skin of a pale color, but also exhibit feet and legs swollen from an accumulation of excess fluid; their appetites are capricious, and they are easily liable to digestive upsets. Those more severely ill may have hair of any color to greyish-white, very pale skins, and swellings of the legs, thighs, hands and face. In the most advanced state the hair is so loosely embedded that it can be pulled out in tufts without causing pain; the eyes may be closed with swelling, which occurs in nearly every part of the body, and the skin may break down as though it had been burnt. At this stage the child appears to be desperately unhappy or sunk in apathy. He will not stand or walk and will not willingly move his head except to pull the covers over his head. He resists any interference, even feeding (*Malnutrition and Disease,* 1963).

Longitudinal studies of children suffering from severe malnutrition are very sparse and do not answer the question of effects conclusively. For one thing, malnutrition is difficult to diagnose early. Infants who are breast-fed will continue to grow at normal rates, and even those who later develop kwashiorkor, a degenerative disease that means literally "occurs when displaced from the breast by another child," grow well during the first months of life. Moreover, the measurement of intellectual capacity during the early years (Bayley, 1958) bears little relation to intelligence tests administered in later childhood and adulthood. Despite the problems in measurement, there is some evidence, by no means conclusive, that very early severe malnutrition, occurring before six months of age, may have long-term effects on mental performance. In one study (Cravioto, 1968) of children hospitalized for treatment of malnutrition, physical and mental well-being improved with each day of care *with the exception of* those infants hospitalized under six months. For them alone, the initial deficit remained constant even after six months in some cases. Another study of malnourished Yugoslavian children followed them up seven to fourteen years after discharge from the hospital and found that among those hospitalized between four and twenty-four months of age, none had an IQ over 110 and 17 percent had IQ's under 70. This is in marked contrast to a similar group of well-nourished Yugoslav children, only 2 percent of whom had IQ's under 70 (Cabak and Najdanvic, 1965). The number of cases studied is small, and it is impossible to say that the only difference between malnourished children and their well-nourished controls is quality of nutrition.

Cravioto (1968b) compared the intersensory integration of children whose height-for-age was subnormal with normal controls. He reasoned that once genetic factors are taken into account, shortened stature is a good indication of malnutrition. Intersensory integration is the ability to match an auditory pattern to a visual one. This is an important intellectual skill underlying the process of learning to read. Visual patterns, printed words, must be matched to auditory patterns, spoken words. He found that short children between nine and twelve years of age scored poorly on intersensory integration tests.

Cravioto believes that while the generally poor social environment of these short children contributed to their impaired intellectual performance, malnutrition is the principal culprit. He found no association between intersensory integration and such factors as father's education, father's financial status, personal cleanliness, or housing conditions. An association was found only between mother's education and intersensory integration ability. Cravioto interpreted this finding to show that the better-educated mother was able to provide better nutrition to her child which, in turn, positively affected intellectual performance.

Well-nourished children usually are reared in an environment generally more conducive to good intellectual and social development than are malnourished children. Since nutrition is an inextricable part of the quality of the child's early setting (Richardson, 1976), it is difficult to link malnutrition alone directly to impairment of mental abilities. When the background histories of malnourished and well-nourished young children are compared, a host of ecological factors are significant. Table 8.3 lists some family and environmental characteristics that one study identified as important in determining the conditions under which malnutrition would be linked to impairment of mental performance.

Poor nutrition means loss of learning time. The child is less able to attend and respond to stimuli in the environment. He is more vulnerable to disease and more likely to miss school. Secondly, recent evidence of early adult-infant interactions has underscored the importance of the child's role in initiating and maintaining interaction (Bell, 1971). The apathetic, withdrawn child cannot emit as many social responses as can the well-nourished child; hence, the caretaker of an apathetic child, in turn, becomes withdrawn and the level of interaction and mutual stimulation decreases. Since early social interactions are also the setting for much cognitive learning, the apathy of the malnourished child puts him or her at a disadvantage. It appears that episodes of malnutrition within the first two years of life need not lead to later intellectual impairment if the child is in a generally positive family environment. However, if early malnutrition occurs within an unfavorable environment, then later intellectual deficiency is likely (Richardson, 1976).

The timing of malnutrition appears critical. Brain growth is complete by the end of the second year of life. The brain grows most rapidly, through protein synthesis, during the first few months after birth. Approximately 25 percent of the adult number of total brain cells are present at birth, 66 percent by age six months, and 90 to 95 percent by one year of age. Some believe that severe malnutrition during this period may result in irreversible mental impairment (Monckeberg, 1968). Furthermore, Caldwell (1962) and Scott (1963) feel that there exist "critical periods" for learning. Rather than viewing the process of learning as slow and cumulative, it is seen as occurring in bursts during periods of maximum susceptibility to stimulation. Since a critical period for learning

TABLE 8.3 ECOLOGICAL FACTORS RELATED TO INTELLECTUAL DEVELOPMENT

Child's Biologic Mother
Reproductive history
Health history

Mother's or Caretaker's Capabilities and Activities
Verbal ability
Values
Exposure to ideas
Activities and affiliations
Human resources
Training and upbringing of the child
Aspirations for the child
Mother as teacher of the child

Father or Adult Male
Presence of adult male role model in the household
Existence of affectionate ongoing relationship with the child
Joint activities of husband and wife with the child
Degree of conflict or cooperation between husband and wife in
    childrearing

Family
Composition
Stability
Extended family
Social relations between family, friends, and neighbors
Alternative caretakers available for the child

Physical and Economic Resources of the Family
Income in cash and kind
Type and size of dwelling
Water supply
Availability of electricity
Appliances
Type of fuel used
Transportation

Area of Residence
Spectrum ranging from isolated rural location to
    large urban center

Child's Background History
Pregnancy number and ordinal position
Birth weight and general health history (other
    than malnutrition)
Feeding during the first two years of life
Continuity in prime caretaker
Continuity in composition of family
Relationships with adults
Relationships with other children
Exposure to ideas and language
Activities and experiences outside the home
School history

Reprinted with permission from Richardson, 1976, p. 261.

is felt to exist from approximately six months to two years, the consequences of malnutrition during this period are viewed as serious indeed.

In summary, it is likely that malnutrition acts directly to produce organic damage only during the vulnerable period of brain-cell growth; thereafter, poor nutrition combined with other social factors provides a less than optimal environment for attentiveness to stimulation.

To what extent can the adverse consequences of fetal malnutrition continuing through early childhood be arrested and even reversed? Can environmental enrichment programs be used to counteract the vicious cycle of which poor nutrition is a part? A study by Zeskind and Ramey (1978) helps to provide some answers to these questions. They placed a group of infants who had been fetally malnourished in a day-care enrichment program that included medical, social, and nutritional services. A matched group of infants remained at home, but social services were also provided to them. At three months of age, the malnourished infants scored significantly lower on a test of infant mental capacities, the Bayley Mental Development Index, as compared with well-nourished peers. Environmental enrichment, begun shortly before this, did not appear to make any difference. When tested at eighteen months and again at two years of age, however, the malnourished infants in the enriched day-care program had made significant gains and now scored as high as normal infants. This was not so for those malnourished infants who had remained at home. Their scores continued to drop, and the gap between their functioning and those of well-nourished babies continued to widen.

One reason for the deteriorating functioning of the malnourished infants cared for at home lay in their mothers' responsiveness toward them. By eighteen months of age, malnourished infants at home were getting significantly less attention and interest from their mothers as compared with those infants in the special enrichment daycare experience.

The Zeskind and Ramey study provides hopeful evidence that intervention programs can reverse the negative effects of fetal and infant malnutrition, even when such programs do not directly change food consumption.

In addition to early childhood, another significant, possibly critical period during which nutrition affects development is adolescence. The growth spurt of puberty is well known. It is characterized by an increase in body size at a rate matched only by the developing fetus and infant in the first year of life. The precise role played by nutrition during this period is not clear. It is likely, however, that the growth spurt is sensitive to nutritional intake. Survey data from countries with high rates of malnutrition in children indicate little or no adolescent growth spurt (McKigney and Munroe, 1975). Furthermore, during the Second World War, growth rates for Japanese adolescents dropped below prewar levels. With increased postwar prosperity, the growth spurt reappeared and currently exceeds prewar levels (McKigney and Munroe, 1975).

Exact nutrient requirements during the growth spurt have not been determined. Surveys of adolescent nutrition, however, indicate that some segments of the American adolescent population, particularly pregnant adolescents and those involved in sports, are receiving inadequate intakes of certain nutrients.

As with the undernutrition with which it is often associated, malnutrition in adulthood has been related to lack of energy, susceptibility to infection, and psychiatric disorder. A study of psychiatric disorders in Nigeria noted that improved nutrition was often accompanied by improved psychological functioning (Collis and Janes, 1968).

While research on undernutrition and malnutrition provides the most dramatic evidence that nutrition has wide-ranging effects on all aspects of behavior, it is well to keep in mind the importance of nutrition for adequately nourished families.

FOOD AS SOCIALIZER

Food is a powerful reinforcer. From the earliest days of infancy, satisfaction of the hunger drive is a powerful motivator of behavior. Freud (1949) saw oral ingestion as the archetype of all psychological functioning. Others (Brody, 1956) have viewed the act of feeding as central to the mother-infant interaction. How the mother feeds her child is most representative of all other caretaking behaviors such as cleaning or cuddling.

Because of the significance of early feeding, anything associated with satisfaction of oral needs acquires reward characteristics. Moreover, the act of feeding itself is a social situation that teaches the child many things about the patterning of relationships within the family.

Much learning occurs through the interaction patterns organized around mealtimes. The child absorbs through the sharing of food, the "breaking of bread," the society's values and the family's relationships. Often meals provide the only regular opportunity for communication with all family members. If the food supply is inadequate, the family meal organization is likely to break down, and this important source of learning is lost. Moreover, the family, in the absence of alternative modes of communication, will suffer in its ability to function as a cohesive unit. The family functions as the system within which the child not only receives food, but also social support and cognitive stimulation. The child's nutritional status (and that of other family members) must be viewed not merely as a function of food availability, but as a result of the way in which the family, as the system managing environmental sources, provides these to the child.

Sims, Paolucci, and Morris (1972) suggest the following conceptual scheme for depicting the relations among food resources, family as intervening system, and child's nutritional status.

As Figure 8.3 illustrates, the family functions as a system processing environmental resources in such a way as to provide nutrients to the child. The child, too, functions as an ecosystem, utilizing nutrient supply from the family together with the emotional climate in which it is given to produce outcomes of physical and emotional growth and nutritional status. This view of the family as manager of nutritional information and energy for the child implies that the flow of information within the family will be most important for the understanding of nutritional status.

Chapter 7 discussed the use of information and energy within the family system in the form of decisions, emphasizing the importance of communication among family members as the process by which decisions are reached. Sims and Morris (1974) have argued that nutritional status of family members may be best understood by considering the communication network through which flow energy and information concerning food. Particularly in the case of childhood nutrition, they suggest that the wheel network is most appropriate model of communication flow. The mother is at the center of the wheel with other family members as the spokes. She occupies this central position by virtue of her role as the one responsible for food purchase, preparation, and distribution. Thus, she acts as the "gatekeeper" controlling the flow of food into the family system and its distribution within the system. Her attitudes, values, and personality will affect the nutritional status of all family members, particularly her children.

In one investigation (Steidl, 1972), about two hundred wives rated the complexity of housekeeping tasks. Tasks involving food preparation, purchase, and distribution were rated as most complex and challenging. They were more likely to involve attention, judgment, and planning than any other area of homemaking, including child care. In addition, complex tasks were most often rated as most enjoyable (Steidl, 1975). Thus, the study indicated that women with central responsibility for the family's food often take this responsibility quite seriously and see it as one of the more challenging and rewarding of their tasks.

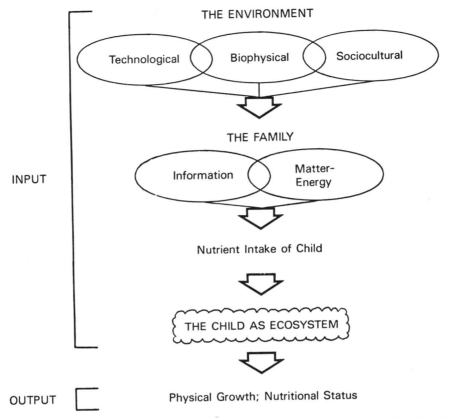

Figure 8.3 A conceptual model for the study of nutritional status of children. (Reprinted with permission from Sims, Paolucci, and Morris, 1972.)

In addition, the management of food resources as with other tasks within the home may be supported or undermined by the quality of the immediate physical environment. The above study asked what factors made household tasks more difficult or more easy (Figure 8.4). Both inhibiting and facilitating factors were seen as primarily rooted in the near physical environment, particularly in adequacy of equipment, space, and rooms. Actual work content, the family, community, or emotional considerations were secondary.

Food preparation offered an expressive outlet as well. The wives studied felt they could show the family how much they care by the way they planned and prepared food. The biological and symbolic importance of food makes it naturally the source of both satisfaction and conflict in the family.

This central importance of food tasks to the homemaker role implies that maternal characteristics will be related to patterns of children's nutritional intake. Such a relationship was confirmed in a study by Sims and Morris (1974). The nutritional status of 163 preschool children was examined in relation to their family environment, particularly the psychological attitudes of their mothers. Based on the patterns of results, two types of mothers were identified. Type I mothers were relatively affluent, had egalitarian attitudes toward childrearing, felt that nutrition was

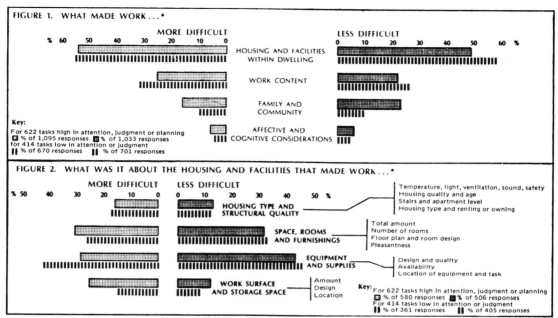

Figure 8.4 Factors making work hard or easy. (Reprinted with permission from Rose Steidl, Factors of functionality and difficulty in homemaking tasks, *Human Ecology Forum*, Cornell University, Autumn, 1972.)

important, and showed evidence of nutritional knowledge. Type II mothers, by contrast, came from poorer families, felt more powerless, had lower self-concepts, less nutritional knowledge, and more authoritarian feelings about raising children. Children of the more enlightened Type I mothers tended to have higher intakes of calcium and ascorbic acid (vitamin C), while children of Type II mothers had higher intakes of calories and carbohydrates. In addition, children of Type II mothers weighed somewhat more for their height than did those from the other group. The Sims and Morris study clearly showed a link between maternal characteristics and the child's nutrition. Support for Sims and Morris's conclusions comes from an earlier survey of homemakers (Young, Waldner, and Berresford, 1956). Nutritional knowledge was greatest among younger, better educated homemakers from upper-income groups. Even when nutrition was not specifically studied, number of years of formal education was strongly related to amount of nutritional knowledge.

The wife-mother's central position in the wheel of the family communication network is not inevitable, however. Chapter 3 emphasized contemporary changes in defining the homemaker role as well as the dual-role commitment of many employed homemakers. These changes in the wife-mother's definition of her role introduce changes in the reciprocal definitions of the roles of husband-father and child. To a certain extent, responsibility, decision making, and action taking concerning homemaking activities become shared with other family members. When this happens, we may predict less centrality for the mother in affecting the nutritional status of her family. Since she is able to "show that she cares" by supplementing family income, the employed wife-mother may see food tasks as just another job rather than an important symbolic expression of her concern for her family.

Furthermore, other trends outlined in Chapter 3 of climbing divorce rate, later marriage, and increase in singleness as a life style have resulted in a nationwide shift in eating habits, with many more Americans eating outside the home in fast-food restaurants, or bringing in ready-to-eat meals. Such changes in family structure appear to be linked to changes in family organization of food consumption.

CHANGING FOOD HABITS

This chapter has stressed the resistance of food habits to change. People living on a traditional low-protein diet may give a high-protein grain to their livestock as unfit for human consumption. Even when a group's overall economic and social position improve and educational level rises, nutrient intake may not change, as one investigation of Indian rural families discovered (Thimmayamma et al., 1976).

Within our own country, poor eating habits appear to be on the upsurge. Are these conditions modifiable by some form of education about nutrition? Within the developing world, efforts continue to improve nutritional status by providing acceptable low-cost, high-protein foods. *Incaparina* is one such new food. A vegetable protein mixture made from local ingredients, it contains the same amount of protein as milk. Tests on local populations in South America indicate that its taste and consistency are acceptable (Lowenberg et al., 1968).

Nutrition education is another avenue toward improving diets by making consumers better informed. However, accurate information alone does not seem to affect behavior. In one study, school children were given a four-week nutrition course with half-hour daily classes. At the end of the course, knowledge about proper nutrition did increase significantly. But when lunch selection and plate waste were examined at the school lunch cafeteria and parents were questioned about eating habits at home, it was evident that the course had no effect on behavior (Westerberg, 1978). Other studies of school children have confirmed these findings (Bell and Lamb, 1973). Adults fare no better. When the effects of a college-level nutrition course were evaluated, food knowledge scores increased significantly, but food behavior was unchanged (Westerberg, 1978). In the rare cases in which courses in nutrition do modify behavior, the gains are short-lived. Soon after the course is over, the students revert to their old eating habits (Westerberg, 1978).

Variations in teaching techniques do not substantially alter this general picture of increased knowledge without changed behavior. This is true even when instruction is designed to be culture-specific, as in a nutrition-education program for young Chinese-American children (Wang and Dwyer, 1975). Similarly, individualized instruction does not produce gains over more traditional methods (Westerberg, 1978). Even lively attention-getting television shows such as "Mulligan Stew," using puppets, cartoons, and music to ensure maximum audience involvement, improve knowledge but do not affect food behavior.

What then *is* effective in changing food behavior? Several generalizations can be made:

1. Change can be brought about by preparing and handling novel foods without necessarily increasing nutrition knowledge. In one study children prepared snacks using fruits, vegetables, and cottonseed flour. As a result, their acceptance of these foods later increased (Westerberg, 1975). Julia Child, the master chef, reminds us of the other messages imparted to children as they participate in food preparation:

> The small rituals, like the clean hands and clean apron before setting to work; the precision of gesture, like leveling off a cupful of flour; the charm of improvisation and making something new; the pride of mastery; and the gratification of offering something one has made—these have such value to a child (Child, 1978, p. 147).

2. The younger the child, the more successful the attempt to change food habits. Studies comparing the success of nutrition programs at various grade levels are consistent in finding most desired change at the youngest grades (Westerberg, 1978).

3. When information processing and decision making occur, changes in food behavior are more likely. The *group-decision* and *request* methods have been compared. In the group-decision method, a group decides whether it wants to change food habits and how much. In the request method, an outside request is made, perhaps from an educator, who also sets the goals for the group. When the two methods are compared, the group-decision approach is superior. This is because more individual involvement in the issues during group discussion occurs when the group must make its own decision. The individual sees how others feel, is able to clarify his or her own position, and experiences group pressure to conform. The majority can override and squash any opposition (Lowenberg et al., 1968).

The family as a small group is likely to change food habits only when information-processing, valuing, and deciding activities have a chance to run their course. Most nutritional education takes the form of request approaches in which outside experts present family members with desired changes.

SUMMARY

The family is a unit for extracting and transforming nutrient energy. The quality of nutrition has far-ranging effects, particularly on the developing individual. Both undernutrition and protein malnutrition pose serious health threats to much of the world's population. The process of extracting and transforming nutrients is tied up with all aspects of family interaction. It reflects and helps determine family perceptions and values, it involves the decision-making process, and it may be supported or undermined by the family's spatial environment. As such, these active processes determine the way in which nutrient resources will be transformed into energy to drive the family machine. Nutrition education that occurs at an early age and that allows the family to clarify its own values and arrive at its own decisions is more effective than merely transmitting nutritional information or requesting changes in food habits.

REFERENCES

Adams, R. N. Cultural aspects of infant malnutrition and mental development. In N. S. Scrimshaw and J. E. Gordon, eds., *Malnutrition, Learning and Behavior.* Cambridge, Mass.: MIT Press, 1968.

Bayley, N. Value and limitations of infant testing. *Children* 5(1958): 129-133.

Bell, R. Q. Stimulus control of parent or caretaker behavior by offspring. *Developmental Psychology* 4(1971): 63-72.

Bell, C. G., and Lamb, M. W. Nutrition education and dietary behavior of fifth graders. *Journal of Nutrition Education* 5(1973): 196-199.

Brody, S. *Patterns of Mothering.* New York: Hallmark Press, 1956.

Butterworth, C. E., and Blackburn, G. L. Hospital malnutrition. *Nutrition Today* 10(1975): 8-18.

Cabak, V., and Najdanvic, R. Effect of undernutrition in early life on physical and mental development. *Archives of Disturbed Children* 40(1965): 532-534.

Caldwell, B. The usefulness of the critical period hypothesis in the study of filiative behavior. *Merrill-Palmer Quarterly* 8(1962): 229-242.

Chase, H. P. Undernutrition and growth and development of the brain. In J. D. Lloyd-Stills, ed., *Malnutrition and Intellectual Development.* Littleton, Mass.: Publishing Sciences Group, 1976.

Child, J. *Julia Child and Company.* New York: Alfred A. Knopf, 1978.

Collis, W. R. F., and Janes, M. Multifactorial causation of malnutrition and retarded growth and development. In N. S. Scrimshaw and J. E. Gordon, eds., *Malnutrition, Learning and Behavior.* Cambridge, Mass.: MIT Press, 1968.

Cravioto, J. Nutritional deficiencies and mental performance in childhood. In D. Glass, ed., *Environmental Influences.* New York: Rockefeller University Press, 1968.

Cravioto, J., and Licardie, E. R. Intersensory development of school age children. In N. S. Scrimshaw and J. E. Gordon, eds., *Malnutrition, Learning and Behavior.* Cambridge, Mass.: MIT Press, 1968.

Dobbing, J. Effects of experimental undernutrition on development of the nervous system. In N. S. Scrimshaw and J. E. Gordon, eds., *Malnutrition, Learning and Behavior.* Cambridge, Mass.: MIT Press, 1968.

Ebbs, J. H., Brown, A., Tisdall, F. F., Moyle, W. J., and Bell, M. The influence of improved prenatal nutrition upon the infant. *Canadian Medical Association Journal* 46(1942): 6-8.

Freud, S. *Three Essays on the Theory of Infant Sexuality.* London: Imago, 1949.

Gomez, F., Ramox-Galvan, R., Frenk, S., Cravioto Munez, Jr., Chavex, R., and Vazquez, J. Mortality in second and third degree malnutrition. *Journal of Tropical Pediatrics* 2(1956): 77-83.

Hepner, R. Maternal nutrition and the fetus. *Journal of the American Medical Association* 168(1958): 1774-1777.

Keppel, F. Food for thought. In N. S. Scrimshaw and J. E. Gordon, eds., *Malnutrition, Learning and Behavior.* Cambridge, Mass.: MIT Press, 1968.

Kerr, G. R., and Waisman, H. A. A primate model for the quantitative study of malnutrition. In N. S. Scrimshaw and J. E. Gordon, eds., *Malnutrition, Learning and Behavior.* Cambridge, Mass.: MIT Press, 1968.

Keys, A., Brozek, J., Henschel, A., Mickelsen, O., and Taylor, H. L. *The Biology of Human Starvation.* Minneapolis: University of Minnesota Press, 1950.

Kirkwood, W. Aspects of fetal environment. In H. Wolff, ed., *Mechanisms of Congenital Malformation.* New York: Association for the Aid of Crippled Children, 1955.

Knobloch, H., Rider, R., Harper, P., and Pasamanick, B. Neuropsychiatric sequelae of prematurity: A longitudinal study. *Journal of the American Medical Association* 161(1956): 581-585.

Levitsky, D., and Barnes, R. Malnutrition and animal behavior. In D. J. Kallen, ed., *Nutrition, Development and Social Behavior.* Washington, DC: U.S. Department of Health, Education and Welfare, pub. no. (NIH) 73-242, 1973.

Lowenberg, M. E., Todhunter, E., Wilson, E. D., Feeney, M. C., and Savage, J. R. *Food and Man.* New York: Wiley, 1968.

McKigney, J. I., and Munroe, H. N., eds. *Nutrient Requirements in Adolescence.* Cambridge, Mass.: MIT Press, 1975.

Monckeberg, F. Effect of early marasmic malnutrition on subsequent physical and psychological development. In N. S. Scrimshaw and J. W. Gordon, eds., *Malnutrition, Learning and Behavior.* Cambridge, Mass.: MIT Press, 1975.

Malnutrition and Disease. WHO, 1963.

Newberger, C. M., Newberger, E. H., and Harper, G. P. The social ecology of malnutrition in childhood. In J. D. Lloyd-Stills, ed., *Malnutrition and Intellectual Development.* Littleton, Mass.: Publishing Sciences Group, 1976.

Olson, R. E. Clinical nutrition. *Nutrition Today* 13(1978): 18-28.

Richardson, S. A. The influence of severe malnutrition in infancy on the intelligence of children at school age: An ecological perspective. In R. N. Walsh and W. T. Greenough, eds., *Environments as Therapy for Brain Dysfunction.* New York: Plenum, 1976.

Robinson, N. M., and Robinson, H. B. A follow-up study of children of low birth weight and control children at school age. *Pediatrics* 35(1965): 425-433.

Scott, J. P. Theory of critical periods. *Monographs of Sociological Research in Child Development* 28(1963): 31-34.

Sims, L., and Morris, P. Nutritional status of preschoolers. *Journal of the American Dietetic Association* 64(1974): 492-499.

Sims, L., Paolucci, B., and Morris, P. A theoretical model for the study of nutritional status: An ecosystem approach. *Ecology of Food and Nutrition* 1(1972): 197-205.

Steidl, R. Difficulty factors in homemaking tasks. *Human Factors* 14(1972): 471-482. (a)

———. Factors of functionality and difficulty in homemaking tasks. *Human Ecology Forum* 3(1972): 10-11. (b)

———. Complexity of homemaking tasks. *Home Economics Research Journal* 3(1975): 223-240.

Stewart, R. J. C., and Platt, B. S. Nervous system damage in experimental protein-calorie deficiency. In N. S. Scrimshaw and J. E. Gordon, eds., *Malnutrition, Learning and Behavior.* Cambridge, Mass.: MIT Press, 1968.

Straus, M. B. Anemia of infancy from maternal iron deficiency in pregnancy. *Journal of Clinical Investigation* 12(1953): 345-353.

Suchman, E. A. Sociocultural factors in nutritional studies. In D. Glass, ed., *Environmental Influences.* New York: Rockefeller University Press, 1968.

Thimmayamma, V. S., Parvathi, R., Desai, V. K., and Jayaprakesh, B. N. A study of changes in socioeconomic conditions, dietary intake, and nutritional status of Indian rural families over a decade. *Ecology of Food and Nutrition* 5(1976): 235-243.

Walter, J. Aspects of fetal environment. In H. Wolff, ed., *Mechanisms of Congenital Malformation.* New York: Association for the Aid of Crippled Children, 1955.

Wang, M., and Dwyer, J. Reaching Chinese-American children with nutrition education. *Journal of Nutrition Education* 7(1975): 145-148.

Westerberg, L. H. Review of nutrition education research. Unpublished manuscript, 1978.

Young, C. M., Waldner, B. G., and Berresford, K. What the homemaker knows about nutrition. *Journal of American Dietetic Association* 32(1956): 214-222.

Zeskind, P. S., and Ramey, C. T. Fetal malnutrition: An experimental study of its consequences on infant development in two caregiving environments. *Child Development* 49(1978): 1155-1162.

Resource Management

9

The family transacts with its many environments by four processes. These processes—perceiving, spacing, valuing, and deciding—are viewed as the means by which the family extracts information, formulates goals, and acts in order to reach its ends. Family life is ultimately based on the ability to extract energy from the environment. Originally in the form of solar energy, it is transformed into nutrient energy which, in turn, provides the basis for all behavior and all other resources.

This continual process of extraction and transformation of energy within the family is not random. Both individual family members and the family as a unit have perceptual styles, patterns of preferred spacing, value-orientations, and decision-making styles. When these active processes are viewed as a whole, we may say that the family has a preferred *adaptation level* with respect to environmental stimulation. The process of extracting and transforming environmental energy for family use is geared to family needs, values and patterns of behaving. Families differ (and individuals within them differ) in preferred level and pace of stimulation, rate of change, and amount of uncertainty. These components of adaptational level become principles guiding environmental transactions, even though they may not be consciously formulated. The family not only extracts and transforms environmental energy, but it also attempts to manage resources to maintain a desired adaptation level. Resource availability and use, in turn, affect family processes. Changes in the amount of energy available may give rise to changes in values and prompt different decision outcomes (Cottrell, 1955).

It is to this environmental resource-management process that we now turn. In this chapter and the four following it, the active processes of perceiving, spacing, valuing, and deciding will be applied to the study of how the family transacts with basic environmental resources. First, we will consider fossil-fuel sources of energy, examining the reciprocal relationship between the family as a goal-directed system of interacting individuals and its environmental supports.

While the family ultimately depends upon its management of basic material resources, these are transformed into other, symbolic resources such as income and education, which take on importance of their own. Moreover, the family ecosystem is the primary creator of human energy in the form of developed abilities and skills. Material resources are used to "fuel" the family system, which in turn is the crucible in which vital human resources are created, maintained, and sometimes impaired.

In the process of transacting with its environments, the family brings resources of its own in varying levels of stability, openness to information, cohesiveness, flexibility and proneness to conflict. Such family resources are themselves dependent on the family's natural resources, which may limit or expand its ability as an environmental resource manager.

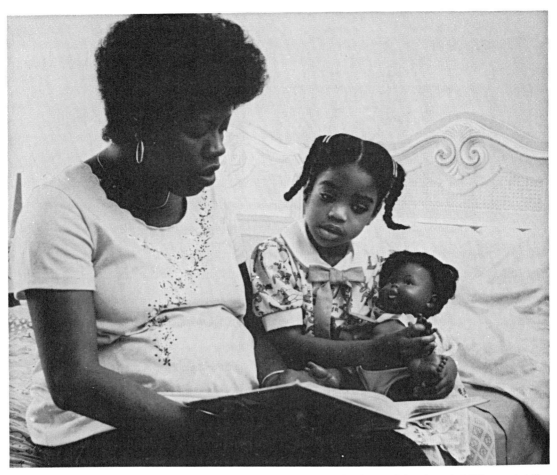

The family ecosystem is the primary creator of human energy in the form of developed abilities and skills. (Photo by Natalie Leimkuhler.)

While resources are rooted in energy extracted from the material environment, the human propensity for symbolic behavior and social life means that such resources are transformed and elaborated into symbolic ones. Humans have a great "propensity to symbolize everything that happens . . . and then react to the symbols as if they were the actual environmental stimuli" (Dubos, 1965, p. 7). Thus, material resources and their symbolic meaning for different cultures can never be separated.

While this chapter focusses on the family as the transformer of environmental energy, it is well to keep in mind that the family ecosystem does not exist in isolation. Families are linked, not only to other families through kin networks, but also to neighborhood and community. They are tied to the world of work and to the educational system. Through the mass media, they participate in a larger cultural milieu and are affected by business and advertising. As citizens, they are subject to the legal system. A host of service agencies, from health delivery-systems to social security, intersect with the family at various stages in the life cycle. Periods of family crisis often highlight the linkages between family and service agencies. The economic system affects the family as well, determining the availability of mortgages, the cost of living, the likelihood of job transfer and unemployment. It is common to refer to these systems—educational, occupational, legal, and economic—as "support systems" which connect with the family ecosystem. Yet this term implies that a supportive relationship always exists. As we have seen in earlier chapters, the occupational system may act destructively on family stability by encouraging frequent transfers or work schedules which threaten family interaction patterns. The regulations of some service agencies, such as welfare, may unintentionally weaken family cohesiveness. The legal system may discriminate against the family by, for example, granting lower taxes to an unmarried couple living together compared with a similar married couple. The educational system may devalue the immigrant or minority child's family culture.

On the other hand, these intersecting systems may truly support the family. Evaluation of their impact on the family will aid such systems to enhance rather than diminish the family's quality of life.

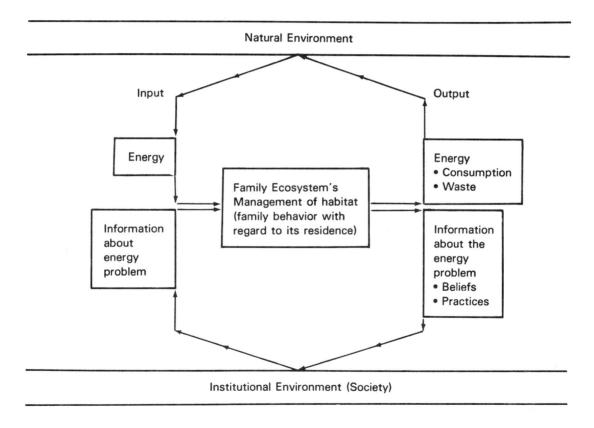

Figure 9.1. Interactions: the natural environment, society, and the family. (Reproduced with permission from Morrison and Gladhart, 1976, p. 16.)

Keeping in mind these linkages of family with other systems, this chapter focusses on the management of the material resources of fossil fuels as major sources of environmental energy. Attention is paid to the various ways in which families transform these resources into human symbolic ones. Resource management is viewed as the extraction and transformation of environmental energy through the active processes of perceiving, spacing, valuing, and deciding. These processes, taken together, may be viewed as the means by which the family seeks to maintain an adaptation level for environmental stimulation in order to achieve family goals. Figure 9.1 depicts the relationship between energy resources, information about energy, societal institutions, and family management of energy resources.

INTERLOCKING SYSTEMS OF ENVIRONMENTAL RESOURCES

All resources on the globe are inter-connected by reciprocal relationships of energy transformation. The natural environment of water, land, and fossil and nuclear energy materials makes possible the production of nutrient and other forms of energy, which in turn fuel production and consumption processes in agriculture, industry, and the family. Such production-consumption processes are linked, not only to their organic resource foundations, but also to man-made regulatory systems—legal, economic, political, and cultural. Such systems develop rules, some explicit, some implicit, about the "what" and "how" of resource use.

In Figure 9.2, note the appearance of the family as both a production-consumption unit and a regulatory unit. As noted earlier, the contemporary American family is primarily a *human* energy producer. In its socializing role, it creates individuals (and thus family units) who will make possible production in agricultural, industrial, and human services spheres. Moreover, the family is the primary unit of consumption, creating patterns of energy consumption that will affect all the interlocking levels of the global ecosystem. It is estimated (Hannon, 1975) that the household sector of the economy consumes two-thirds of all U. S. energy consumed. In direct energy use, families consume 37 percent through such items as heating-cooling systems and automobiles. If one adds as indirect energy consumption the energy required to manufacture and distribute such items, the major portion of U. S. energy is consumed by the family unit (Hogan and Paolucci, 1979).

Although most attention is directed toward high-cost items such as heating fuel, one must remember that *all family behavior carries an energy price tag*. For example, food may be evaluated not just in terms of its nutritional quality, but in terms of *energy cost per serving*. Over the last twenty-five years, Americans have been eating more foods requiring processing before consumption. The more processing required, the higher the energy cost in terms of fossil fuel (Holmes and Gladhart, 1976).

The active processes to which we have given so much attention in this volume determine how the family as both a collection of individuals and as a small group *regulates* such energy exchanges. Keeping in mind the complexities of these transactions, let us examine the family's role in the management of fossil fuel energy. The natural environment of the family must provide nutrient resources to be transformed into caloric energy, the basis for all activity. In addition, the natural environment must provide energy stored in fossil fuels to maintain constant body temperature (shelter), to aid in the transformation of nutrients (cooking) and for other uses. All families in all environments share this basic dependence.

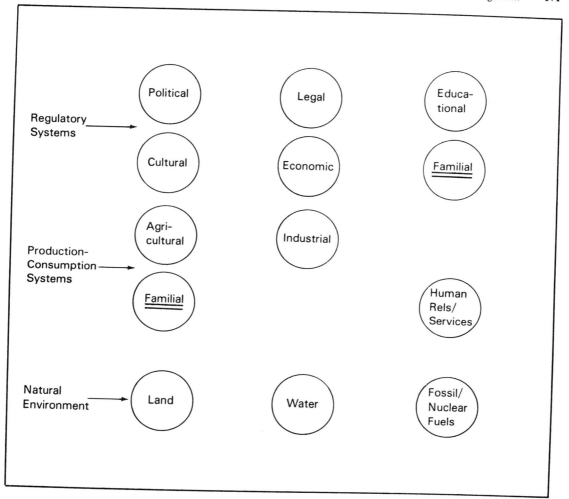

Figure 9.2. The family as production-consumption and regulation unit. (Adapted with permission from Paolucci, Hall, and Axinn, 1977, p. 28.)

> We passed the women and children, and shortly afterward we passed a second group....They were still sitting around the fires they had built to cook themselves a meal. Every woman, when moving camp, carries with her a burning ember wrapped heavily in fire-resistant leaves. None of these Pygmies knows how to make a fire. The first thing they do when they stop on the trail for a rest is to unwrap the ember and, putting some dry twigs around it, blow softly once or twice and transform it into a blazing fireball (Turnbull, 1961, p. 58).

Thus did one anthropologist depict the relationship of Pygmy family life in central Africa to its energy sources. Of course, in technological societies, dependence upon vast supplies of fossil fuels is far greater than in nontechnological ones and constantly growing. The resulting energy crisis has become a central concern of contemporary politics. Reexamination not only of public policy, but also of family habits in relation to fossil-fuel resources has been urged.

Energy conservation has been established as a pressing need. Yet, ultimately, changes in energy use within families cannot be brought about without understanding how the family manages such environmental resources. What family characteristics are associated with high energy use of environmental concern?

FAMILY CHARACTERISTICS AND ENERGY USE

As might be expected, income and family size affect energy consumption. Richer families tend to use more energy than poorer ones. Large families use more total energy, but expend less energy per person than small families. One study found that the average energy cost per person in a family of five or more persons was *less than half* the per-person cost in a two-person family (Gladhart, 1977). Yet, as Chapter 3 emphasized, current trends in family life style are toward even smaller units. Will rising energy prices provide economic incentives to check this and even encourage the recombining of small units into more energy-efficient groups (Gladhart, 1977)? Families rearing children generally use more energy than those without children or at later family life-cycle stages (Morrison and Gladhart, 1976). It is reasonable to assume that dual-employed couples might use more energy than couples with only one person employed, since the energy of appliances could substitute for less available human energy. Yet, the Michigan State University study of family energy practices found that families in which homemakers were employed full-time use 8 percent *less* residential energy than those with homemakers not employed.

Despite its importance as a public-policy issue, relatively little is known about the family's management of fossil-fuel energy sources, and hence, the likelihood that programs for change might succeed. Our earlier discussions of the family's active processes of perceiving, valuing, spacing, and deciding give rise to some hypotheses.

PERCEPTUAL STYLES

Energy sources and their environmental implications must first be brought to awareness before the process of management can take place. Long periods of living in particular environments lead to adaptation, even when such environments may cause actual physiological harm. Thus, one study of Detroit students showed that they perceive brown-gray to be the *normal* color of the sky, while rural Colorado students immediately identify such conditions as unacceptably polluted (Swan, 1974). Advocates of environmental education urge that exercises in increasing sensory awareness be included in such curricula so that people can come to perceive the links between energy-use patterns and environmental quality.

Chapter 4 described family perceptual style in terms of the *extensity* of the family's horizons or boundaries. It is likely that families with broad perceptual horizons that include an awareness of global forces would be likely to view environmental resources as limited and interdependent. By contrast, families who see the needs of region, country, or globe as unconnected with their smaller world would have no reason to respond to appeals based on wider responsibilities.

One investigation assessed family members' sense of "human responsibility" defined as "the degree of personal responsibility that individuals feel for helping to solve the energy problem"

(Gladhart, Zuiches, and Morrison, 1978). Both lower energy consumption and greater acceptance of government policies like tax deductions for insulating older homes or driving small cars, designed to encourage conservation, were associated with a sense of larger family responsibilities.

Families also differ, as discussed earlier, in perceived locus of control. A largely external locus perceives little family power to affect events, while an internal locus of control recognizes greater ability to determine one's own destiny. It is likely that notions of environmental responsibility and planning for efficient energy use would be held by families with an internal locus of control.

The earlier chapter on perceiving likened perceptual style to preferred means of extracting information from the environment. Energy-resource management may be considered as a problem of gathering relevant information to guide decision making and action taking. In general, knowledge about energy matters and their links to environmental quality is poor. A 1971 survey on this topic by CBS News found that 54 percent of those responding could answer only half or fewer of the questions asked. Meaningful information about energy systems and their relationship to family life style is unlikely to come from lists of facts. Families need experiences, incentives, and community support to help them perceive options which they might otherwise not know about. Currently those who do actively seek out information on energy sources and their environmental implications are usually those *already concerned* with environmental issues (Lingwood, 1974). Thus, values, as we shall discuss shortly, underlie the information-extraction process.

It is important to point out that the perception of energy resources is limited, not only by family perceptual style, sensory awareness, information seeking and the like, but also by the family's links to the other environmental systems within which it is embedded—the legal, economic, educational, and political systems. Families in economic duress cannot afford the luxury of managing energy resources with environmental quality in mind if this means higher expenditure. Poor education also limits information-seeking ability. It is interesting to note in this regard that the most powerful predictor of environmental concern is education (Lingwood, 1974). Advertising often urges wasteful and environment-damaging behavior upon families. Political pressures now encourage, now discourage, differing patterns of energy resource management. The educated citizen not only has access to information, but also possesses the analytic tools to sort through often contradictory messages.

VALUES AND ECO-CONSCIOUSNESS

The five value orientations discussed in Chapter 6 have implications for attitudes toward energy use. Present-time orientation is likely to be associated with low concern for projected energy needs, while future-oriented individuals and families would be more likely to show concern for ensuring adequate energy supplies to following generations. Attitudes toward nature itself are perhaps most directly related to energy resource use. In Chapter 6 three contrasting attitudes toward nature were identified: subjugation to nature, harmony with nature, and mastery over nature. Rapoport has defined these differing stances, under other names, as shown in Table 9.1.

Rapoport points out that in many traditional peasant societies, human life is seen as part of nature, not counterposed against it. This attitude affects the way material resources are used to create and sustain family life. For example, "the pueblo looks like a land form because the close relation of house form and landscape reflects the harmony of man and nature. The whole landscape is sacred, as is the house, and the whole environment influences all of Pueblo life. In fact, Pueblo Indians beg forgiveness every time they fell a tree or kill a jack rabbit" (Rapoport, 1969, p. 76).

TABLE 9.1 ATTITUDES TOWARD NATURE

Text	Rapoport	Definition
Subjugation to nature	Religious and cosmological	The environment is dominant; man is less than nature.
Harmony with nature	Symbiotic	Man and nature are in a state of balance, and man regards himself as responsible to God for nature and the earth and as a custodian of nature.
Mastery over nature	Exploitative	Man is the completer and modifier of nature, then creator, and finally destroyer of the environment.

Adapted from Amos Rapoport, HOUSE FORM AND CULTURE, © 1969, p. 750. Reprinted by permission of Prentice-Hall, Inc., Englewood Cliffs, N.J.

Western industrial society is largely a "mastery-over-nature" or "exploitative" culture, one in which ideas of ecosystem relatedness and energy conservation are new. Moreover, within a particular culture, those who see nature as a wild force to be tamed and put to human use are likely to be less environmentally concerned than those with a harmony-with-nature outlook. Again, we can draw on some recent research within an ecosystem framework to bolster claims that value orientations underlie energy-resource management.

In a study conducted by Borden and Francis (1977), high- and low-environmentally concerned undergraduates were identified on the basis of their responses to a questionnaire. Personality tests given these two groups revealed that environmentally concerned individuals placed greater emphasis on values in general, were more person-oriented, and were more ethically conscientious than low-environmentally concerned individuals. Interesting sex differences were also found. High-environmentally concerned women were more likely to be extroverted "leader-types" than low-concerned women, but the opposite pattern was true for men.

Interpretation of the sex differences is difficult. It may be that environmental concern is perceived as an aspect of male sensitivity or of female assertiveness. If this is so, traditional sex-role stereotypes emphasizing masculine aggressiveness and feminine dependence may reinforce low environmental consciousness. To the extent that such stereotypes are being challenged, a more fertile ground for environmental advocacy may be laid. An alternative explanation is also possible. Assertive women and introspective men may be more likely to show environmental concern because of some third variable, such as education. Further research is needed to explore the meaning of these sex differences.

The general conclusions of this study confirm that value orientations affect attitudes toward environmental resources, including energy. However, it is important to note that individuals outside their family contexts were investigated and hence, the role of the family system is unclear. Yet to a large extent, the family is the unit of energy consumption in America. Work by Paolucci and her colleagues takes a more appropriate family perspective (Hogan and Paolucci, 1979). Four family values—eco-consciousness, self-esteem, social responsiveness, and familism (the value placed on family life)—were measured, and a family score measuring household energy conservation practices was developed. The value "eco-consciousness" in this study is similar to "environmental concern" in the investigation of Borden and Francis. The results indicated that only eco-consciousness was significantly related to adoption of household energy-conservation practices. In addition, higher levels of education for both husband and wife and husband's occupation were associated with higher commitment to eco-consciousness. This study supports the conclusion that a value orientation of harmony with nature, one more likely to be nurtured with higher education, underlies a conservation-minded attitude (and practice) toward energy use within the home.

DWELLING CHARACTERISTICS

It is obvious that the size, layout, and design of the family home directly affect energy consumption. Single-family homes use 35 percent more energy than multi-family dwelling units or mobile homes (Gladhart, 1977). Moreover, multi-unit structures, by concentrating population in clusters, are better suited to energy-efficient mass transit than are thinly spread out single-family homes. One study found that rural families living more than twenty miles from an urban center used 42 percent more gasoline to fuel their automobiles than did their urban counterparts (Gladhart, 1977).

Many aspects of the home affect energy consumption. The more windows, exterior doors, and rooms in a house, the more energy will be used. For example, one investigation determined that each outside door increased energy use by almost 7 percent (Gladhart, 1977). The placement of a house affects its exposure to wind and sun. Surrounding trees may alter the heating and cooling of a home. The thermal properties of construction materials affect the rate of heat exchange between the interior and exterior (Gladhart, 1977). In most cases these aspects of a dwelling—type of heating/cooling system, exposure to sun, construction materials—are determined by someone other than the family presently occupying the structure.

Less obvious than materials and layout is the way in which patterns of spatial interaction in the family affect energy use. The privately owned, single-family dwelling has emerged as a kind of family "personal space" in much of the United States. Within the home, large amounts of space per person, relative to other cultures, are deemed necessary. Such spatial organization supports and is tied to family interaction patterns. These norms obviously place relatively high demands on energy consumption.

DECISION MAKING AND ENERGY MANAGEMENT

The concept of *management* of resources is linked to decision making. Environmental-resource management may be thought of as a subset of continuing decisions that all families must make. However, it may be idealizing family decision making to characterize its use of fossil-fuel energy as *management*. For a major interdisciplinary study of family energy use has concluded that energy consumption is largely determined by the *nondecisions* of families (Morrison and Gladhart, 1976). That is, families decide where they want to live or travel, and the amount of energy needed for these activities is then a *consequence* of the family's life style. A family is more likely to choose a home for privacy, investment, neighborhood, or attractiveness over its energy efficiency (Gladhart, 1977). Some feel that as more Americans become aware of limited energy resources, decision making will be directed at energy use. However, when families' responses to the 1973-1974 energy crisis were studied, about 50 percent of those queried did not believe it was an immediate problem, and among those who *did* believe in the reality of the crisis, the amount of energy consumed in the household did not diminish in any meaningful way (Morrison, 1975).

As the energy crunch bears down on more families, it may force the rising cost of energy to become a direct part of the family's decision-making process. Morrison and Gladhart (1976) have warned: "When circumstances force families to cope with external reality through decisions viewed as necessary but foreign to the family's value systems, the result may be alienation and social disintegration" (p. 18).

Hence, it is important to consider the family's process of decision making with regard to energy resources. All the components of the decision-making process, communication patterns, decision-making power, linkages among decisions, conflict management, and the relation between decision making and later behavior are important.

One investigation (Sullivan et al., 1977) illustrates how the type of energy-management decisions that a family makes will influence its later behavior. Several groups of families were asked to participate in a project on energy conservation. One group was told that the results would be published in a newspaper article (public commitment), another group expected only a private interview and examination of utility records (private commitment), and a third group received no interview. The results showed that public commitment alone significantly reduced energy consumption. A follow-up study one year later investigated the durability of such increased energy conservation as a result of public commitment. Consistently lower rates of natural gas consumption in the publicly committed families as compared with those privately committed or the controls were found throughout the twelve-month period.

It appears that if one feels that a decision is "for the record," it is more likely to govern behavior than decisions not subject to the scrutiny of others. Perhaps such decisions are more carefully made at the outset. It may also be that the desire to appear consistent and thus to maintain one's social reputation underlies the force of such public decisions. Since this study did not examine the *process* of decision making, but only the product, it is impossible to examine what factors were responsible for the results.

In addition to public commitment, certain types of feedback to families concerning their energy use are effective in promoting energy conservation. In a study by Cook (1977), some families received either usage or *comparison* feedback. Usage feedback informed the family of their electricity meter readings and approximate cost, while *comparison* feedback included information about their present increase, how that compared to the average increases of a control group, and how much of a savings or cost that represented. Families given comparison feedback information conserved more energy throughout a three-month summer period than those given only usage feedback.

Comparison feedback emphasized the savings or additional cost of each month's energy use. Thus, families had the feeling of reward (savings) or punishment (additional cost) following their energy usage. Since positive reinforcement or reward tends to increase the behaviors preceding it, energy conservation went up. The comparison-feedback technique also informed families how their behavior measured up to that of a group of other families (the control group). In this way the social context of public opinion was made salient. Whether by "going public" as in the study by Sullivan or by having one's behavior compared to that of a group of other families, such techniques seem to be effective in linking the family's decisions to those of other families. When the larger social milieu supports and expects certain behavior, it is more likely to be maintained.

In addition, although supporting evidence here is meager, it is likely that communication patterns *within* the family, as well as between the family and others, would affect fossil-fuel energy management. For example, a family in which such decisions are centralized in one decison maker might be able to implement changes in energy-resource management more easily than a family in which such decision making is shared. Suggestive evidence in support of this was obtained in the above follow-up study of families publicly versus privately committed to energy conservation. Publicly committed families with central air conditioning were successful in reducing energy usage levels over a one-year period, while those with window air conditioners were not. The effect of public commitment in the latter group wore off more quickly. Why? As the investigators suggest, energy use is more easily monitored with the thermostat-controlled central air conditioning. In addition, however, those with window air conditioners are likely to make decisions about energy use and act on them in a less centralized manner than those in centrally air conditioned dwellings. In such a context, more family members are likely to be involved, and differences in the perception and valuation of energy conservation are more likely to arise.

In summary, the processes of perceiving, valuing, spacing, and decision making color the family's management of fossil-fuel resources. Understanding them makes possible better assessment of the chances that energy-conservation programs aimed at the family will be successful.

In the management of fossil-fuel resources, as in all other things, the family is interlocked, not only with the natural ecosystem, but also with man-made technological and social control systems. Families are linked through communication and transportation networks that demand a certain level of energy use. In highly industrialized societies, this level is very high. Sectors of the economy, such as the automobile industry, may be geared toward encouraging even higher levels of energy use. The legal and political systems through their regulatory practices may encourage or discourage waste, particularly by large industrial energy-users. Thus, the family's management of fuel-energy resources reflects the interplay of multiple, often conflicting forces, products of its involvement in other systems. Because of this, the family may be too weak to affect anything but personal changes in energy consumption.

ENERGY RESOURCES INTO SYMBOLIC RESOURCES

As mentioned earlier, energy in the form of nutrients and fossil fuels is transformed within the family into symbolic resources. What are such resources? We may think of them as *transactions* between the family and its energy inputs; that is, family members bring characteristics to their encounters with the material environment that help determine how resources will be extracted and transformed. Family differences in cohesiveness, communication patterns, stability, conflict proneness, value orientations, and perceptual styles imply, as we have seen, differences in the management of material resources. At the same time such differences themselves are, to a certain degree, dependent on the family's material resource base. For example, in Maslow's need hierarchy, survival needs are prerequisites to the satisfaction of all other needs. Thus, adequate nutrition to ensure survival and eliminate fear of future want is essential if the family is to attempt to nurture its members and give them room to develop as full individuals. Thus, in Maslow's view, a family cannot hope to provide a loving, supportive atmosphere if inadequately nourished and sheltered.

Moreover, anthropologists have alerted us to the way in which a culture's relationship to its food and energy sources helps determine what resources are considered important. For example, in hunter-gatherer cultures, where skill in these ways of providing food is paramount, little emphasis is placed on the symbolic resources of income or education geared for entry into a world of monetary exchanges. High value must be placed on the resources of inter-family cooperation and conflict resolution, since the hunt requires that a band of families coordinate their efforts and divide the fruits of their labors.

By contrast, in industrial societies, material energy resources are usually available to the family as a *result* of their expertise in the symbolic economy of monetary exchanges. Therefore, stress is placed on preparing individual family members, largely through education, to function in such an economy. Individual competence, supported by the family, is of paramount importance, not cooperation among family units. Thus, each culture's relationship to its energy base helps determine what family characteristics will be valued and what kinds of human resources will be viewed as most important. Differences within cultures, such as class distinctions, have similar effects. For example, within American culture, lower-class families tend to make somewhat greater use of social support among kin and quasi-kin than do more affluent families. Similarly, middle-class families cannot ensure that present high levels of income will be passed on to the next generation, which must achieve anew for itself. Hence, education and achievement motivation as resources are most important, while upper-class families secure in monetary reserves are primarily concerned with maintaining family solidarity. In each case, varying levels of monetary resources lead to different emphases on family cohesiveness and individual development.

Family organization and functioning also affect the degree of success families will enjoy in securing and transforming energy resources. It is a truism that a stable, happy family does better in securing resources, whatever they may be, than a conflict-prone, unhappy one. Many studies illustrate this. For example, in cultures where individual competence is the prime valued resource, supportive family structures are enhancing. Exceptionally competent young children—independent, achieving, socially responsible, and self-reliant—tend to have parents who effectively combine firm control with positive encouragement of the child's autonomy (Baumrind, 1971). Treatment of alcoholic patients is more likely to be successful if the patient enjoys a stable marital relationship (Bromet, 1977). Similarly, family members are likely to be in generally better health when in supportive family networks (Pratt, 1972). Thus, the structure and quality of family interactions, themselves dependent upon the family's relationship to energy resources, in turn affect the family's ability to extract such resources. In this sense, the family can most properly be considered to be in a *transactional* relationship to energy-resource management.

THE MANAGEMENT OF TIME

How families manage the limited resource of time also illustrates the active processes by which they seek to adapt to their environment. The use of time, like that of fossil-fuel energy, reflects values emphasizing present-, past-, or future-time orientation. Other values influence the way family members assign priorities to certain activities. This means that behavior is *sequenced* in time: "We will do X, then we will do Y, and then, if we have time, we'll do Z."

Perceptual styles, particularly those aspects which determine tempo, affect the pace of this sequencing process. Performance in roles outside the home affects time left to perform those most closely related to the family. This has been illustrated by research on employed and nonemployed homemakers. In general, increased time spent working outside the home is not matched by decreased work within it. On the average, employed homemakers used only two hours a day more for household work than did nonemployed homemakers (Larsen, 1978). Many employed wives and mothers carry a double workload with an average work week of seventy hours. They may also lower performance standards (Sponcil, 1975), which, in turn, may lower feelings of satisfaction.

Apparently, despite increased rhetoric about male participation in homemaking, studies of dual-employed couples show that the wife's commitment outside the home does not significantly affect the amount of help received from husbands. While decision making tends to be shared, implementation of those decisions remains specialized and fairly traditional. Nevertheless, when current rates of male participation in household labor are compared to those of a generation ago, a relative increase over the patterns of the past is evident. Rates of participation in homemaking among cohabitating couples are not significantly different from those among their married counterparts. An idea of how time is allocated may be gleaned from a survey of families conducted by Walker (1971). Physical maintenance tasks increased for women, even when working, from 9.1 hours for one child to 10.7 hours per day for two children. This increased to 11.4 hours with three children and 12.6 hours per day for families with four to six children. As children grow older, time devoted to their physical care declines.

The relationship between fossil-fuel and time allocation is an interesting one. It was assumed that the use of fossil-fuel energy and "labor-saving" appliances would significantly reduce the amount of time spent in homemaking activities. Yet, studies conclude that while time is saved on individual activities, it is merely allocated to others, so that the total amount of time remains constant.*

SUMMARY

The family has been viewed in this chapter as an energy-extracting and information-processing unit. Basic environmental resources of nutrients and fossil fuels are utilized by the family as the foundation upon which other energy transformations are built. The family may be likened to a machine driven by such energy sources. The family is part of a set of interlocking systems characterized by reciprocal relationships of energy transformations.

When family management of fossil-fuel resources is examined, it becomes clear that the process of energy extraction and transformation is colored by the family's perception of energy sources and their environmental implications. Families with broad perceptual horizons, internal focus of control, and active information-seeking abilities are most likely to be well informed, efficient, and ecologically concerned.

Similarly, values, particularly those concerned with man's relationship to nature, have been seen to underlie energy-resource management. The way families decide on patterns of energy usage appears to be influenced by such factors as public commitment to energy conservation, feedback about the consequences of decisions taken, and perhaps patterns of communication within the family. While the processes of perceiving, valuing, and deciding are given central importance, constraints upon the family stemming from their involvement in the larger society are emphasized. In particular, economic well-being has a pervasive effect upon the ability to gather information about resources, the level of resources themselves, and flexibility in energy resource use.

While all sources of energy are ultimately rooted in fossil-fuel and nutrient sources, which in turn are based upon solar energy, the family is the arena in which such energy resources are transformed into others, most importantly into human resources. Fossil-fuel management and time management influence the family's ability to rear children to be effective adults. In turn, family organization and family characteristics help determine how these very resources will be extracted. Thus, the concept of *transactions* between family and its resource bases is most appropriate.

---

*Personal communication from Beatrice Paolucci, November 9, 1978.

REFERENCES

Baumrind, D. Child care practices anteceding three patterns of preschool behavior. *Genetic Psychological Monographs* 75 (1967): 43-88.

Bordon, R. J., and Francis, J. E. Who cares about ecology? Personality and sex differences in environmental concern. Paper presented to the Midwestern Psychological Association meeting, 1977.

Bromet, E., and Moos, R. Environmental resources and the post-treatment functioning of alcholic patients. *Journal of Health and Social Behavior* 18 (1977): 326-338.

Cook, D. A., Sullivan, J. J., and Pallak, M. S. The effect of self-monitoring and feedback on energy conservation. Paper presented to the Midwestern Psychological Association meeting, 1977.

Cottrell, F. *Energy and Society*. Westport, Conn.: Greenwood Press, 1955.

Dubos, R. *Man Adapting*. New Haven: Yale University Press, 1965.

Gladhart, P. M. Energy conservation and lifestyles: An integrative approach to family decision-making. *Journal of Consumer Studies and Home Economics* 1 (1977): 265-277.

Gladhart, P. M., Zuiches, J. J., and Morrison, B. M. Impact of rising prices upon residential energy consumption, attitudes, and conservation policy acceptance. In S. Warkov, ed., *Energy Policy in the United States: Social and Behavioral Dimensions*. New York: Praeger, 1978.

Hannon, B. Energy conservation and the consumer. *Science* 189 (1975): 95-102.

HEW News. Washington, D.C.: Department of Health, Education and Welfare, October 1975.

Hogan, M. J., and Paolucci, B. Energy conservation: Family values, household practices and contextual variables. *Home Ecnomics Research Journal* 7 (1979): 210-218.

Holmes, C. L., and Gladhart, P. M. The energy cost of food: The family can now make informed decisions. Occasional paper no. 5, Family Energy Project, 1976.

Larsen, L. Review of resource management research. Unpublished paper, 1978.

Lingwood, D. Environmental information-seeking through a teach-in. In J. Swan and W. Stapp, eds., *Environmental Education*. New York: Sage Publications, 1974.

Morrison, B. M. *Socio-physical factors affecting energy consumption in single family dwellings: An empirical test of human ecosystems model*. Unpublished doctoral dissertation, Michigan State University, 1975.

Morrison, B. M., and Gladhart, P. M. Energy and families: The crisis and the response. *Journal of Home Economics*, 1976, pp. 15-18.

Paolucci, B., Hall, O.A., and Axinn, N. *Family Decision-Making: An Ecosystem Approach*. New York: Wiley, 1977.

Pratt, L. Conjugal organization and health. *Journal of Marriage and the Family* 34 (1972): 85-95.

Rapoport, A. *House Form and Culture*. Englewood Cliffs, N.J.: Prentice-Hall, 1969.

Sullivan, J. J., Pallack, M. S., Cook, D. A., and Cummings, W. The long-term effects of commitment on voluntary energy conservation. Paper presented to the Midwestern Psychological Association, 1977.

Swan, J. The environmental crisis: Why now. In J. Swan and W. Stapp, eds., *Environmental Education*. New York: Sage Publications, 1974.

Turnbull, C. *The Forest People*. New York: Simon and Schuster, 1961.

Walker, K. E. Time used for household work. Washington, DC: U.S. Department of Agriculture Research Service, ARS Summary Report, June 15, 1971.

10

The Family as Consumer

Contemporary American life has often been described as the age of the consumer. A highly technological society such as our own offers a dizzying array of goods and services from which to choose. How to choose becomes a central family task. The lines between what one needs, might like, ought to have, and can only dream about become hazy. Since we may define consumer behavior as those *activities by which products and services are sought out, secured, used, and evaluated*, it is evident that it is an all-pervasive feature of individual and family life. Most consumer behavior takes place with reference to and in the context of family life. Many products, such as a home, are purchased by the family unit or by individuals on behalf of or with reference to the family. Despite the increase of singles, the delay and decline of childbearing, and the increased longevity of widowed elderly, the family remains the primary consumption unit.

Another way to view the contemporary American family's role in extracting and transforming environmental energy is to consider its consumption role. The family is the prime agent for the recycling of energy products. With increased public awareness that such resources are limited comes the need for new understanding of the crucial role the family plays in molding attitudes toward consumption, in developing enduring habits, and in acting as agent for change. The family is the arena in which consumer attitudes are developed in childhood, attitudes that form predispositions for adult behavior.

Within this emphasis on family consumer behavior, it is important to recognize the different kinds of consumer activities in which the same individual may be engaged. As a family member, one may be involved in family consumer behavior, such as the decision about where to live or what car to buy. Other aspects of consumer activities will be more individual. Personal tastes in clothing, food, or other products may override the interests of other family members. Then, too, individuals with weak, conflictive, or disorganized family ties may have little interest or ability in coordinating their consumer activity with others.

Whether consumer behavior is an individual or family-based activity, many have emphasized the difficulties inherent in it. Adults today confront a multiplicity of decisions. Often through the sheer overload of information, individuals are unaware of the options potentially available to them. Once aware, selecting and carrying out strategies for maximizing values may be difficult. National surveys indicate that adult consumer behavior is often ineffective. Many consumers lack the fundamental math skills required to deal with everyday economic problems (Reys, 1976). Another survey examined the ability to use basic skills to deal with job hunting, shopping, and understanding insurance. Only one-third of the adult population was proficient in such routine consumer transactions as managing the family budget (*HEW News*, 1975).

The same analysis applied to the management of fossil-fuel resources (an important set of consumer products) can also be applied to the family as a consuming agent. Perceiving, valuing, spacing, and decision making all affect consumer behavior. Moreover, these processes dynamically influence family members, creating consumer attitudes in children or making changes in consumer habits more likely.

THE PROCESS OF CONSUMPTION ACTIVITY

Liston (1965) has identified seven stages of consumption activity. These stages are linked together in an interactive circle so that no real beginning or end point exists. However, we may arbitrarily begin with a particular stage for convenience.

Stage 1. *Allocating* available resources to satisfy family needs. This involves considering what values and goals are to be reached and their relative importance, determining what resources are available and comparing alternative patterns of allocation. The family must establish priorities shaped by values for the allocation of resources.

Stage 2. *Earning.* This is defined as "the exchange of family resources (human, financial, and material) for money income from the market economy" (Liston, 1965, p. 97). With regard to this stage, the family must decide who will earn money, at what kinds of jobs, and in what locality. It must also deal with the related question of training for earning power.

Stage 3. *Spending* involves the use of resources to make choices concerning specific purchases. This stage is the one most often referred to as "consumer" behavior or "consumership," the development of attitudes and skills that facilitate the best purchase for the most reasonable expenditure of time, money, and effort. The ability to gain reliable consumer information and to develop critical attitudes toward advertising are important here. Liston (1965) suggests that an increasingly important family role is that of *spending agent*. This role is an exceedingly complex one for several reasons. First, the proliferation of products and advertising techniques means that the spending agent will be barraged with information about a product, such as an automobile. Assimilating all the potentially relevant information concerning makes, models, options, construction, resale value, etc., seems virtually impossible. Winnowing reliable reports in publications such as *Consumer Reports* from the chaff of rhapsodic singing commercials requires a rational, planned approach to spending. Finally, the spending agent must keep in mind the relation between resource expenditure and family satisfaction as outcome. How will a particular purchase affect the family in terms of its goals and values? Often unintended consequences follow a spending decision. For one family, the move from a cramped apartment in the city to the suburbs was intended to provide fresh air, space, and privacy, but the family had not realized that their life style based on strolls through city streets and visits to theatres and museums would be drastically altered.

Stage 4. *Participating* and *supporting* government and community organizations affect consumer behavior. Liston emphasizes the intersection between the family as consumer and the political and economic system. In the fifteen years since her article, government involvement in consumer behavior has grown still further and consumer understanding that political activism is a necessary part of consumership has also increased.

Stage 5. *Saving* or adding to durable goods and assets will affect later patterns of consumption.

Stage 6. *Converting* consumer goods and services for use in the home. This is the stage most often referred to as "housework" in which products are maintained, kept clean, prepared (e.g., food), and made available to family members.

Stage 7. *Socialization for consumer roles* has been identified. How do children acquire attitudes and values concerning the consumption process and their roles as consumers? A substantial part of the advertising market is already geared to children and teenagers as specialized consumer markets. As mentioned earlier in discussing television as a value-formation agent, children shift from early naivete to cynical appraisal of advertising promises. The effect of this cynicism upon attitudes toward other societal institutions that also make promises, such as political parties, is unknown. It is disconcerting however, that distrust and withdrawal from the political process have grown apace with the increasing importance of the consumer role.

Furthermore, preadolescence has been defined by Erik Erikson as the period of "industry" in which children need to feel productive and competent, makers, not consumers of things. In a society in which meaningful production is often less important than consumer savvy, the child's need to be efficacious and industrious may be thwarted.

In sum, seven stages of consumer process within the family have been identified. They may be viewed also as an interlocking set of roles which family members play. Six consumption-related roles which family members fill have been identified (from Schiffman and Kanuk, 1978, p. 238):

1. *Influencers*—family members who provide information and advice concerning the selection of a product or service.
2. *Gatekeepers*—family members who control the flow of information or the use of a product or service into the family.
3. *Deciders*—family members who have power to determine whether or not to purchase a product or service.
4. *Buyers*—family members who actually make the purchase.
5. *Preparers*—family members who transform the product into a form in which it will be used or consumed.
6. *Users*—family members who use the product or service.

In some families the roles may be relatively specialized, with the father in the earning stage (Liston's Stage 2), the mother in the converting or preparer one (Liston's Stage 6). Such a division of the consumer process among family members, however, is fast disappearing as the norm. Which consumer roles family members fulfill depends upon the particular product or service. The more important a purchase and the higher the potential risks it may entail, the more will family members fulfill many consumer roles, rather than specialize. Whether specialized or shared, the consumer process involves a complex meshing of information, resources, decisions concerning allocation and saving, articulation of values and goals, and socialization of both children and adults for consumer roles.

CONSUMER SOCIALIZATION

The development of consumer attitudes and behavior begins in early childhood and never ends.* Multiple influences—school, peers, mass media—converge on the child. However, it is likely that the family is the most important of these influences, particularly during early childhood. Within the family, consumer training may not take place in a formal context, but it is intensive nonetheless. When children accompany parents on shopping trips, they are receiving field training in the art of being a consumer. Such training takes place largely in the context of *observational learning* rather than reinforcement (Ward and Wackman, 1972). Thus, as children copy consumer behaviors, they often include the mannerisms, voice inflections and attitudes that their parents

---

* The author is indebted to Patricia Pingel for much of the material on which this selection is based.

never directly attempted to teach. Over time, these "training" sessions leave enduring effects. Studies of college students reporting brand loyalty and store preferences find marked similarity between student and parental views.

How precisely does family consumer-socialization progress? McNeal (1965) conducted an interesting study of five, seven and nine year olds focussing on changes in the following areas: consumer attitudes, participation in shopping with parents, and independent shopping. While five year olds did not view money as a purchasing tool, by age nine the child was a fairly sophisticated consumer with money from allowances and odd jobs and the desire to do some independent shopping. These changes were reflected, furthermore, in changed parental behavior. Over half of the mothers of older children in the study sought their children's advice on the purchase of certain items, while very few of those with five year olds did so.

As we have seen in other areas of research, this study, too, found sex differences. Parents sought their daughters' opinions about products more often than their sons', and when refusing girls tended to give explanations rather than flat denial. Boys' requests were brushed off more abruptly. By age nine, twice as many girls as boys were observed conversing with store personnel about purchasing. These results are linked to others discussed earlier which emphasize greater feminine sociability and verbal skill. Moreover, it seems to indicate a view that the consumer, often acting on behalf of the family, is a more integral part of the adult female than adult male role.

While parents are an important force in socializing children, children are also busy training parents to purchase their wants, often learned from other sources of consumer socialization, such as advertising. A common sight in any grocery store is a little tyke pulling his mother toward a brightly colored box and pleading, "Mommy, Mommy, buy me." The results of a 1966 survey showed that parents identified their children over television, store displays, catalogues, newspapers, and other adults as their most frequent source of toy ideas (Newspaper Publishers Bureau, 1967). Interestingly, it has been found (Berry and Pollay, 1968) that more child-centered mothers tended *not* to yield to such purchase suggestions, while less child-centered mothers were more permissive. The child-centered mother critically evaluated products with the child's welfare, not wants, in mind. The results may be related to an earlier one in Chapter 8, namely the findings of the Sims study, which linked maternal characteristics to the child's nutrition. Recall that Sims found better nourished children had what she termed Type I mothers—those with high nutritional knowledge, egalitarian attitudes toward childrearing, and high valuation of good nutrition. It is likely that such Type I mothers are also more child-centered and, hence, more discriminating consumers in general.

Other research (Ward and Wackman, 1972) found that as children grow older, their attempts to influence consumer purchases of their parents *decrease*, while their mothers' *yielding* to the requests they do make tends to *increase*. It may be that children become more discriminating in their requests; at the same time, mothers appear to take their consumer requests more seriously as they mature.

While emphasizing the importance of familial influences on consumer socialization, we must also take cognizance of the important roles peers and media play. McNeal's study, previously mentioned, found that from age six, peers begin gradually to replace parents as sources of consumer attitudes and behavior. The importance of television as a source of values has been widely noted.

Young children frequently describe television as an accurate portrayal of reality (Greenberg and Dervin, 1970). Television pervades, some might argue even dominates, their experience. Ninety-eight percent of all families in the United States have at least one television set and half of that number have two (*Insights Into Consumer Issues*, 1979). Children typically begin watching television regularly at age two (Lyle and Hoffman, 1972). By age three they have developed definite tastes in television programming (Greenberg and Dervin, 1970; Lyle, 1972), and are spending an average of twenty-eight hours a week in front of the small screen. The television children watch is largely devoid of parental influence. In one sample of nursery school children, 40 percent said they made their own program selections (Lyle and Hoffman, 1972).

The consumer choices that television advertising depicts are learned by the child according to the principles of observational learning. For example, studies of learning from models have found that *perceived similarity* to the model is an important factor in directing attention to the model's behavior. Thus, if a child watches another child much like himself or herself engage in a destructive act, do something charitable, or ogle a candy bar, these behaviors are more likely to be absorbed than if a dissimilar model is observed. Advertising uses this finding that peers are influential as models to good effect. Many products that children tend to buy for themselves (e.g., candy) or whose purchase they are likely to influence by their requests (e.g., breakfast cereals) are sold through ads featuring peer models.

Susceptibility to advertising is, not surprisingly, greater when the child is very young. Many children feel commercials *always* tell the truth. With increased age, children pay less attention to commercials and are better able to discriminate reality from fantasy. Children of kindergarten age, by contrast, have trouble discriminating between commercials and the products themselves. Young children have no way of evaluating the validity of advertising claims. The development of such evaluation appears to take the following course:

Kindergarten age — no understanding of purpose; no basis for judgment
Second grade age — distrust of "bad" products
Fourth grade age — recall of specific commercials distrusted, but no generalized mistrust
Sixth grade age — all commercials are bad

In general, the amount of television viewing is greater for children who are nonwhite, of lower socio-economic status and who have lower IQs and achievement motivation (Greenberg and Dervin, 1970; Lyle and Hoffman, 1972). Thus, children who are least able to critically evaluate advertising and most likely to be frustrated by the inability to purchase enticing items are exposed to higher commercial doses. While children gradually develop the ability to critically evaluate the truth of commercial claims, their attention continues to be drawn and held to television advertising. Commercials are often the most perceptually salient aspect of a show, quicker in tempo, outfitted with a catchy tune and spiced with humor. It is perhaps not surprising that with repeated exposure to such messages, many young children learn verbatim the contents of commercials and then use them as elements in their play, acting out commercial messages themselves, incorporating them into their humor, and relating to the characters they depict, such as Ronald MacDonald.

We will now consider how consumer behavior is affected by perceiving, valuing, spacing, and deciding—the processes by which individual and family transact with the environment.

PERCEPTION AND CONSUMER BEHAVIOR

Individual and family perceptual style will affect consumer behavior. In general, perceiving involves the unconscious selection of relevant aspects. In this way, what has been termed "the buzzing, blooming madness" of stimulation impinging on the senses is reduced to a coherent order. The process of perceiving is an important element of consumer behavior because it determines where attention will be drawn. In essence, what is not perceived is not potentially available for selection and use.

The selectivity of perception of consumer products and services is affected by many factors. First, people tend to perceive according to their *expectations*, or *set*. If friends have complained that a certain car model is a "lemon," it is likely to influence one's perception, which is then "set" to notice negative characteristics of that product.

Perceptual selectivity is also governed by one's *needs* or *motives*. Attention will be drawn to descriptions of products for which one is searching. Attention will be deflected from information that contradicts one's needs. Heavy smokers may avoid exposure to messages warning them about the health hazards of their habits. Once exposed, they may subconsciously fail to perceive such warnings.

The sheer amount of pace and stimulation affect perceptual selectivity. It is likely that if the amount of information about consumer products and services to which one is exposed is far above one's accustomed level of stimulation, the response may be to tune out the excess. For example, when the number of ads to which individuals are exposed rises too high, they are likely to screen out many of them (Bauer and Greyser, 1969). Exposure and perception are not the same thing.

Finally, perceptual selectivity is affected by principles of *perceptual organization*. This refers to the fact that stimuli are perceived not as isolated elements, but as organized wholes, according to principles of perceptual organization first identified by the *Gestalt* school of psychologists. For example, the principle of *figure and ground* refers to the fact that we organize our perceptions in terms of stimuli that stand out as figure from a background. This ensures that certain elements from an array of stimuli will get more attention than others. Elements perceived as figure literally seem to stand out from those seen as background. Background also subtly influences how figure stimuli will be perceived. A picture of a smiling child against a background of ominous clouds and "who-dun-it" music suggests sinister implications, while the same picture against a background of sunshine, balloons, and circus music sets quite a different mood. Advertisers skillfully use figure-ground organization to ensure that their products will capture the attention of the consumer and that the desired mood will be set.

Perceptual *grouping* refers to the fact that information is processed in chunks or groups. Stimuli are stored and remembered more easily when organized into meaningful wholes rather than discrete bits. *Closure* refers to the need of a perceiver to fill in incomplete stimuli so that they are perceived as complete. A slightly broken circle is likely to be seen as a closed one, particularly if surrounded by other closed circles. Both grouping and closure organize the consumer's perceptions of products and both are used by advertisers to direct attention to their products. For example, grouping a car, a sexy girl, and an idyllic vacation spot sets up associations of pleasures other than driving when the consumer contemplates the ad.

While all humans select and organize their perceptions, considerable individual and family variation exist in the degree to which selectivity is employed. Such variations have been termed *perceptual style*. Differences in perceptual style reflect differing predispositions to fit new perceptions into old expectations, to be influenced by background, and to distort perceptions that threaten one's needs. Openness to information, information-processing style, preferred level and pace of stimulation, all affect consumer behavior. Consumer acts may be analyzed in terms of sets of concrete situations which, according to one formulation (Belk, 1975) are made up of the following components:

1. *Physical surroundings*—including geographical location, decor, sounds, aromas, and lighting.
2. *Social surroundings*—other persons, their characteristics, roles, and interactions.

3. *Temporal perspective*—specification of time of consumer situation and its temporal relation to other consumer situations.
4. *Task definition*—intent to select, shop for, or obtain information about a purchase.
5. *Antecedent states*—momentary moods or conditions, such as anxiety, hostility, pleasure, fatigue, or illness, rather than enduring traits.

Thus, the many dimensions of the perceiving process both on the individual and family level will determine how each component of the consumer situation will be perceived. This largely determines what the *perceived* consumer situation will be. For example, products are displayed in physical settings designed for maximum appeal. Individual differences in responsiveness to certain spatial arrangements or sound levels will mean differences in attention to and appeal of the product. Perceptual styles tap differences in orientation toward other people as well. The field-dependent person is more socially oriented than the field-independent person. In evaluating perception of the social surroundings of the consumer situation, such perceptual style differences will be important. The socially oriented consumer is likely to be swayed by product appeals associated with respected persons or featuring a social context and implying social acceptance. Socially oriented consumers, also termed "other-directed," also have been found to prefer more traditional products and services. The more innovative the product, the less likely they are to adopt it (Donnelly, 1970).

Active processes of perceiving also have a temporal dimension. Individuals and families differ in their preferred pace of stimulation and information extraction. These tempo differences will subtly affect the readiness of the consumer to tune in or tune out fast-paced information about products. If the amount of advertising or other information about products exceeds the consumer's level of tolerance, it is likely that excessive stimulation will be perceptually blocked. Recent survey information concerning Americans' exposure to commercial advertising and their recall of the ads to which they have been exposed tends to support this. It has been estimated that Americans are exposed to about three hundred ads daily, yet one large-scale investigation found that only about thirty to forty of those ads could be recalled (Bauer and Greyser, 1969).

VALUES AND CONSUMER BEHAVIOR

Just as values have been linked to family energy-consumption, so have value and attitude linkages been established with many other aspects of family consumer behavior. In general, consumers who critically evaluate products with "quality of life" in mind have been termed "socially conscious consumers" (Webster, 1975). They are nonjudgmental of others, resist conventional demands, and tend to evaluate products in terms of both their own and social betterment. Such descriptive labels closely correspond to Maslow's *self-actualizer*. Indeed, one study (Brooker, 1976) confirmed that people rated as self-actualizers in terms of values were observed to selectively buy ecology-minded products such as phosphate-free detergent more often than non-self-actualizers.

Dogmatism has been defined as the amount of rigidity a person displays toward the unfamiliar and toward information contrary to established beliefs (Rokeach, 1960). A highly dogmatic person approaches the novel and unfamiliar with distrust and suspicion, while the individual low on dogmatism is responsive to new and challenging information. It might be expected that dogmatic individuals would avoid innovative products and services, and this has been supported by research (Jacoby, 1971; Coney, 1972). For example, when self-service gasoline stations were first

Product information may exceed the consumer's ability to process it. (Courtesy of Cereal Institute, Inc., Schaumburg, IL.)

introduced, their customers were found to be significantly less dogmatic than those who continued to patronize the traditional full-service facilities (McClurg and Andrews, 1974). Persons low in dogmatism are also more responsive than dogmatic individuals to product appeals which stress factual differences in quality and performance.

There are occasions on which dogmatic individuals are *more* responsive to new products than open-minded persons. When product appeals are made by authoritative persons or "experts," highly dogmatic consumers are likely to respond favorably (Blake, Perloff, and Heslin, 1970).

Values appear to underlie even apparently trivial preferences for particular brand products. For example, college students were asked to indicate their preferences for three similarly priced automobiles: Chevrolet, Ford, and Plymouth. College men preferring Chevrolets valued quality significantly more than men preferring the other two makes, while college women preferring Plymouths ranked "respect from others" and "politeness" significantly higher than women preferring Fords or Chevrolets (Rokeach, 1973). Similarly, interviews with housewives concerning detergent preferences indicated that Ivory users emphasized salvation, cleanliness, equality, and broad-mindedness more than did users of All or Wisk (Rokeach, 1973). Seemingly, the advertising images that various products convey tap underlying differences in values.

Market analysts use this fact to aid their advertising campaigns. They develop inventories of the psychological characteristics of consumers of various products. The resulting profiles help identify existing and potential markets. This approach, called *psychographic research*, may be illustrated in a study which contrasted the profiles of "heavy" moviegoers (more than nine times during the preceding year) with nonmoviegoers. The portrait of the heavy moviegoer which emerged included such characteristics as: more socially oriented, more active, more ambitious, more "contemporary" in values, more inclined toward new possessions and "swinging" interests (Homan, Cecil, and Wells, 1975).

It is important to point out that despite the roles perceiving and valuing play, there are constraints on the family's consumer behavior. These constraints come about because of the family's linkages to regulatory systems—legal, economic, educational, and political. Obviously poor families cannot afford to buy a more expensive, but perhaps more durable, product. In general, poor families are unlikely to be able to afford the luxuries of product discrimination and "swinging" interests. They have impaired access to consumer information and a more limited array of consumer choices to begin with than the more affluent.

DECISION MAKING AND CONSUMER BEHAVIOR

We have seen that the contemporary family is to a large extent a consuming unit. Historically, its production functions have become less important as its consuming role has grown in significance. Indeed, media images often depict the family as little more than a compulsive consumer, as this satirical reminiscence illustrates:

> My mother was a wonderful cook. I remember the tantalizing smells in the kitchen when I came home from school. Mama turned out every kind of cake imaginable. I remember the roseate hues in the rows of boxes on her pantry shelf. I remember Pillsbury, Duncan Hines, Dromedary. But most of all I remember Betty Crocker.

> The high point of my youth was my birthday dinner. There wasn't another woman on earth who could defrost Mrs. Paul's Frozen Fried Eggplant Sticks the way Mama did, or who could drop the yummy plastic bag filled with Stouffer's Frozen Creamed Spinach into a pot of boiling water with such *elan*. To make my favorite salad, Mama would snip open a bag of greens and gaily toss with Porky Manero's Gorgonzola Salad Dressing. The birthday cake was always a Betty Crocker, accompanied by a gurgling glass of freshly mixed Starlac for the children and a steaming cup of Instant Sanka with Pream for Mama and Papa (*Saturday Review*, May 18, 1963, p. 8).

In a more serious vein, a great deal of decision making centers on consumer behavior. This decision-making process is a complex one, involving articulating family goals, assigning priorities, determining the timing and character of consumer purchases, as well as deciding about specific items. One author (Blum, 1977) has distinguished seven steps in the purchase process alone:

1. Initiation of the idea
2. Exploration and investigation
3. General shopping
4. Decision to buy
5. Specific shopping
6. Purchase
7. Post mortems (e.g., feedback)

Families must deal with dilemmas like, "Shall we spend more money for an item that may last longer or less money for one which may require earlier replacement?" "What are luxuries; what are needs?" "What consumer items are most important to us?" "How do we go about deciding which among several consumer needs will be satisfied, since we can only afford to satisfy one?" "How will we finance consumer spending?" "How much debt is acceptable for us?"

Some families may have thought through some of these dilemmas and worked out patterns of dealing with them. In the phrase of one analyst of family consumer behavior, Reuben Hill (1970), such families may be said to have a "family policy" which guides the decision-making process. For example, one family may say, "The Nortons don't believe in getting into debt. If we don't have the money, we do without." Having a policy of some kind appears to give families a greater sense of satisfaction, a stronger feeling of having done the right thing when they evaluate the consequences of past decisions.

Deciding about consumer products also involves an assessment of potential risks and benefits. Some individuals tend to respond to high-risk decisions by trying to eliminate errors, even if some potentially satisfying or positive outcomes might also thereby be eliminated. They prefer the safe course. Other people have been found to be more tolerant of error in the hope of maximizing postive outcomes. Error-tolerant consumers have been characterized as *broad categorizers*, while consumers with low tolerance for error have been termed *narrow categorizers*. The distinction between these two types might be illustrated by their choices when faced with two television models of the same cost: (a) a familiar model of adequate but not exceptional quality versus (b) a new model which promises improved performance but with an uncertain repair record. Research evidence (Popielarz, 1967; Donnelly, Etzel, and Roeth, 1973) suggests that consumers who are broad categorizers are more willing to try new products than are other consumers.

Deciding about consumer behavior is, to a large extent, information gathering and processing. In a society that heavily emphasizes competition through advertising for the consumer choices of its citizens, this information-processing role is by no means a simple one. Consumer education becomes a major challenge. Not only does the consumer need to become aware of the objective attributes of product X as compared with Y and Z, but he or she must also develop sophistication about the advertising techniques that often obscure such an objective evaluation. It should not be surprising to learn that relatively poor and uneducated family members are able to acquire little useful information about the merits of consumer products. They are often unaware of manipulative advertising techniques. Finally, the more restricted one's financial resources, the more constricted is the range of consumer items from which to choose. Thus, the family's access to environmental resources broadly defined helps determine its competence as consumers.

Access to enviromental resources also affects motivations and attitudes concerning consumption. To be poor in a land the media depict as a land of never-ending plenty is particularly frustrating. The concept of *relative deprivation* states that those who are able to compare their situation to similar others who yet are better off will feel more deprived than people who perceive all others like them as equally poor. In other words, misery loves company. The plight of the aged is especially difficult in this respect since aging often brings about downward mobility, or a drop in economic status. The senior citizen not only feels relatively deprived when compared to other segments of the population, but deprived, too, when present conditions are compared to the purchasing power of years past.

While economic deprivation handicaps one's consumer behavior, affluence predictably enhances it. A particular type of affluent family has been identified as influential in affecting others' consumption patterns. Liston (1965) terms such families "the tastemaker elite," early adopters of new products. By watching their behavior, it is often possible to predict what most consumers will be buying in the near future. Who are these tastemakers? Researchers identified them as highly mobile families. Their definition of mobility included, in addition to geographical mobility, occupational, economic, educational, intellectual, and social mobility. The tastemakers were likely to change jobs, income, reach for more intellectual experiences, and associate with a wider range of people than other families. When these types of mobility were combined, 63 percent of the highly mobile were tastemakers, while only 21 percent of the low-mobility families could be so defined (Liston, 1965). This relationship between mobility and consumption indicates that families oriented toward change in one area of their lives tend to be so oriented in other areas.

After a consumer purchase has been made, *post-purchase evaluation* usually occurs. As a means of helping to live with the decision once made, the consumer tries to bolster the feeling of having done the right thing and to dispel any lingering doubts. The psychological term given to such doubts is *cognitive dissonance*, and the post-decision mechanisms used to dispel them, *dissonance reduction*. Examples of dissonance reduction strategies are: (1) selectively paying attention to information and ads about the product chosen, (2) seeking out others who have made similar purchases, (3) trying to persuade others who may be making similar choices to purchase the product one chooses. Dissonance reduction is more likely when the decision has been a central one, involving extensive problem solving.

The use of dissonance reduction does not mean that the consumers are incapable of recognizing poor performance in a product for which they had initially high hopes. Part of the post-purchase evaluation process is the assessment of product performance. While individuals are undoubtedly predisposed to feel that their decisions, particularly important decisions, have been justified, information challenging this assumption will gradually cause reevaluation. When a product does not live up to expectations, this feedback will influence future decisions. The consumer will be likely to look for other alternatives when in a similar situation.

CONSUMER EDUCATION

The poor record of Americans as effective consumers has stimulated many to call for consumer education programs. In cases where consumers lack the skills to evaluate critically advertising claims, one strategy might be to concentrate on the development of such skills. Yet, as with nutrition education programs, their success is mixed at best. A review of such consumer-education efforts (Tanny, 1978) concluded that, while some show increased consumer awareness, virtually no evidence exists that consumer *behavior* changes. Another, the *regulation* strategy, focusses on stiffer standards for advertisers themselves to eliminate deceptive claims, provide adequate information, and minimize appeals to emotional, irrational elements of the consumer's personality. When advertising is directed to children, the regulation strategy is most appropriate since young children are developmentally incapable of using adult evaluation skills. It is estimated that children view over 21,000 ads per year. Thus, national organizations such as Action for Children's Television, the Council of Children's Media and Merchandising, and the Children's Advertising Review Unit have been formed to monitor advertising practices aimed at children and lobby for stricter standards. Currently underway is a movement to ban all advertising on television programming aimed specifically at children on the grounds that persuasive techniques which take advantage of individuals incapable of evaluating them violate their constitutional liberties. Those opposed to this move point out that children spend only about 16 percent of their viewing time watching "children's programming" (*Insights Into Consumer Issues,* 1979). Thus, even if the ban were approved, it would not affect 84 percent of the average child's television viewing.

SUMMARY

Consumer behavior, an increasingly important function of the family, has been described in terms of seven stages—allocating, earning, spending, participating and supporting, saving, converting, and socializing. Family members fulfill consumption-related roles such as influencer, gatekeeper, decider, buyer, preparer, and user. The role of the family as socializing agent for the development of consumer attitudes and behaviors in children has received particular attention. While parents are important, the impact of media and of peers increases as the child grows older. Young children watch a great deal of television and receive a steady, high-level dose of commercial advertising. Their cognitive limitations make them incapable of discriminating commercials from products themselves, deceptive from truthful claims. The perceptual characteristics of television ads—short, fast-paced, highly stimulating—are optimal for securing the child's attention and facilitating his or her learning the behavior demonstrated by the televised model.

The processes of perceiving, valuing, and deciding are illustrated in the way they influence consumer behavior. The perceptual characteristics of most successful advertising are designed to be maximally attention-getting and stimulating to the public. The consumer's own perceptual style affects what messages will be selected and how they will be retained. It is likely that the consumer's adaptational level for stimulation operates to help screen out excessive perception of advertising under conditions of extremely frequent exposure.

Values are important in directing individuals and families to particular products and to particular styles of consumer behavior. The environmentally conscious consumer appears to have values resembling the self-actualizer, in Maslow's terminology. Values also appear to underlie specific product choices whose advertising associates them with cleanliness, salvation, equality, and other values.

Consumer decision making follows the course of other decision-making processes in the family. It involves information seeking, comparisons of alternatives, assessment of risks and benefits associated with each alternative, exploration and investigation, deciding to buy, and post-purchase evaluation. In some families the process is facilitated by certain family policies that guide consumer behavior. Family members may specialize in aspects of the decision-making process or may make joint decisions. The more important and complex the consumer decision, the less likely that specialization or autonomous decision will take place.

The decision-making process is constrained by the family's material resources. Social class and educational background affect the family's accessibility to information about products and their ability to evaluate conflicting claims. Higher levels of income broaden the range of alternatives that can be considered. Interactional resources of the family—communication skills, cohesiveness, conflict-handling mechanisms—affect how they will be able to use information gathered in making decisions that will bring them closer to their goals. After purchase, family members are disposed to dispel their doubts about the decision through dissonance reduction, but they also engage in critical evaluation of the product to some degree. If such evaluation is overwhelmingly negative, further purchases of the product are unlikely.

REFERENCES

Bauer, R., and Greyser, S. *What Americans Think of Advertising.* New York: Dow-Jones-Irwin, 1969.

Belk, R. Situational variables and consumer behavior. *Journal of Consumer Research* 2(1975): 157-164.

Berry, L. A., and Pollay, R. W. The influencing role of the child in family decision making. *Journal of Marketing Research* 5(1968): 70-72.

Blake, B., Perloff, R., and Heslin, R. Dogmatism and acceptance of new products. *Journal of Marketing Research* 7(1970): 483-486.

Blum, M. *Psychology and Consumer Affairs.* New York: Harper & Row, 1977.

Brooker, G. The self-actualizing socially conscious consumer. *Journal of Consumer Research* 3(1976): 107-112.

Coney, K. A. Dogmatism and innovation: A replication. *Journal of Marketing Research* 9(1972): 453-455.

Donnelly, J. H., Jr., Social character and acceptance of new products. *Journal of Marketing Research* 7(1970): 111-113.

Donnelly, J. H., Jr., Etzel, M. H., and Roeth, S. The relationship between consumers' category width and trial of new products. *Journal of Applied Psychology* 57(1973): 335-338.

Greenberg, B. S., and Dervin, B. *Use of the Mass Media by the Urban Poor.* New York: Praeger, 1970.

HEW News. Washington, D.C.: Department of Health, Education and Welfare, October 1975.

Hill, R. *Family Development in Three Generations.* Cambridge, Mass.: Schenkman, 1970.

Homan, G., Cecil, R., and Wells, W. An analysis of moviegoers by life style segments. In M. Schlinger, ed., *Advances in Consumer Research, 2.* Association for Consumer Research, 1975, p. 219.

Insights Into Consumer Issues. New York: J. C. Penney, 1979.

Jacoby, J. Personality and innovation proneness. *Journal of Marketing Research* 8(1971): 244-247.

Liston, M. I. Dynamics of consumption. In *Family Mobility in Our Dynamic Society.* Ames, Iowa: Iowa University Press, 1965.

Lyle, J. Television in daily life: Patterns of use (overview). In E. A. Rubinstein, G. A. Comstock, and J. P. Murray, eds., *Television and Social Behavior.* Vol. 4: *Television in Daily Life: Patterns of Use.* Washington, D.C.: U.S. Government Printing Office. 1972, 1-32.

Lyle, J., and Hoffman, H. R. Explorations in patterns of television viewing by preschool-age children. In E. A. Rubinstein, G. A. Comstock, and J. P. Murray, eds., *Television and Social Behavior.* Vol. 4: *Television in Daily Life: Patterns of Use.* Washington, D.C.: U.S. Government Printing Office, 1972, 257-273.

McClurg, J. M., and Andrews, I. R. A consumer profile analysis of the self-service gasoline customer. *Journal of Applied Psychology* 59(1974): 119-121.

McNeal, J. U. An exploratory study of the consumer behavior of children. In *Dimensions of Behavior.* New York: Meredith, 1965.

Paolucci, B., Hall, O. A., and Axinn, N. *Family Decision Making: An Eco-system Approach.* New York: Wiley, 1977.

Popielarz, D. T. An exploration of perceived risk and willingness to try new products. *Journal of Marketing Research* 4(1967): 368-372.

Pratt, L. Conjugal organization and health. *Journal of Marriage and the Family* 34(1972): 85-95.

Reys, R. E. Consumer math: Just how knowledgeable are U.S. young adults? *Phi Delta Kappan* 19(1974): 65-66.

Rokeach, M. *The Open and Closed Mind.* New York: Basic Books, 1960.

———. *The Nature of Human Values.* New York: Free Press, 1973.

Schiffman, L. G., and Kanuk, L. L. *Consumer Behavior.* Englewood Cliffs, N.J.: Prentice-Hall, 1978.

Tanny, L. Review of consumer education. Unpublished paper, 1978.

Tussing, D. Poverty and education and the dual economy. *Journal of Consumer Affairs* 4(1970): 93-102.

Ward, S., and Wackman, D. Purchase influence attempts and parental yielding. *Journal of Marketing Research* 9(1972): 316-319. (a)

———. Television advertising and intra-family influence: Children's purchase influence attempts and parental yielding. In E. A. Rubinstein, G. A. Comstock, and J. P. Murray, eds., *Television and Social Behavior*, Vol. 4. Washington, D.C.: U.S. Department of Health, Education and Welfare, 1972. (b)

Webster, F. E. Determining the characteristics of the socially conscious consumer. *Journal of Consumer Research* 2(1975): 188-196.

Housing

11

This chapter analyzes the impact of the spatial environment on family relations, both among individual family members and between the family as a unit and its "outside" environment. The discussion illustrates how the processes of acting in the environment—perceiving, spacing, valuing, and deciding—may be applied to understand family transactions with the spatial environment. Two related types of questions will be asked. First, what is the impact of particular spatial environments on families? How is family functioning, particularly the active processes of perceiving, spacing, valuing, and deciding, affected by such dimensions as crowding, housing density, and spatial design? The second set of questions addresses how families *transact* with their spatial environment. When and why do families move? How do they assess their spatial environment? How do they act on it to bring about change? How do they fashion a distinctive environment? These two types of questions suggest that the spatial environment of the family, particularly housing, is a significant factor in understanding the way families live.

Much of a family's life centers on its dwelling. Poor housing is associated with social disadvantages and personal troubles (Rutter and Madge, 1976). Less noticeable but equally important is the impact of the spatial environment on families in adequate housing. For all families, their interactions take place in a specific spatial context that gives form to them. The family spatial environment both *reflects* and *affects* the active processes of perceiving, spacing, valuing, and deciding that constitute the tools of transactions with the environment.

As Maslow's need-hierarchy states, shelter is a basic human need, which must be satisfied before higher-order needs can be met. When human needs are viewed in the perspective of other animal species on the planet, the basic functions which shelter performs can be listed (Fabun, 1971):

1. The support of homeostasis through limiting solar radiation as expressed through temperature
2. Protection against discomforts from changes in weather
3. Protection against predators
4. Privacy for biological activities
5. Symbolic communication

This last function of symbolic communication illustrates the important point that the spatial environment not only protects its inhabitants from harm, but also expresses attitudes, values, and yearnings. A dwelling and its location quickly acquire symbolic meaning. Families may see their status in the community reflected there. Others' responses to a family are partially determined by

Housing needs exist because people believe that particular spatial patterns can meet their values and life style successfully. (Photo by Natalie Leimkuhler.)

their evaluation of housing quality. When housing is viewed as socially undesirable, it may have adverse effects upon the family and upon the self-image of family members.

Housing is also seen by families as fulfilling or failing to fulfill their needs. A family may feel they need a single-family detached dwelling with a large lot in the suburbs in order to provide their children with what they feel is adequate play space. These housing needs exist because people believe that particular spatial patterns can successfully meet their values and particular life style. Even when experts provide proof to the contrary, families may hold firm to the conviction that certain housing arrangements are essential to ensure their desired style of family functioning.

In this chapter we will first examine selected aspects of housing in terms of their impact on family functioning. Consistent with a process, transactional approach, the importance of taking family characteristics into account in understanding housing impact will be emphasized. Not all characteristics of the housing environment will be reviewed; rather, we will concentrate on those attributes that most directly affect the *amount* and *quality of stimulation* family members receive from one another and from the environment external to the family unit. Thus, attention will be focussed on the concepts of *housing density* and *crowding* because they refer to the likelihood that family members will be in close, often nonvoluntary, contact with one another. The concept of *residential propinquity*, which refers to the distance between family dwellings, will be examined because distance between dwellings affects the likelihood that family units will come into contact with one another. This is one of the reasons why so many Americans place emphasis on the neighborhood in their evaluation of housing.

THE IMPACT OF SPATIAL ENVIRONMENTS ON FAMILIES

Housing Density and Crowding

The census defines a household as overcrowded if the number of persons exceeds the number of rooms. The 1970 census reported 5.2 million overcrowded households. Of these, 1.4 million were living at densities of 1.5 persons or more per room. If age, sex, and relationship of household members is taken into account in evaluating density, then by the census definition, overcrowding is more than nine times the current estimate (Greenfield and Lewis, 1973). Central-city poverty areas contain more than half of all such dwellings, most of them occupied by nonwhites. The poor spend more of their available income on housing than any other class, although they are less likely to receive value for their money.

Now that the extent of crowding and its concentration among the poor has been briefly documented, let us critically evaluate the common wisdom that one of the major adverse influences of the physical environment stems from crowding or overcrowding. The very term conjures up dreary tenements with forlorn souls crammed together. Interactions among adults are impaired; intimate exchanges like lovemaking cannot be carried out in private, and children are traumatized by early exposure to sexuality. Infectious diseases are easily spread, while accidents rise since people are literally tripping over one another. Most important, humans, meant to live in small groups, cannot carry on positive social interactions under crowded conditions; they become aggressive, antisocial criminals. Hence, the argument goes, crowding becomes synonymous with crime, or at the very least criminal tendencies. Crowding becomes viewed as an ever-increasing by-product of overpopulation, which will erode the quality of life, destroy the natural environment, make it impossible to satisfy human longings for quiet, privacy, and independence, and make a world in which personal freedom becomes a rare commodity. As one writer, alarmed at population growth, put it: "If men allow themselves to continue breeding like rabbits, their fate will inevitably be to live like rabbits, a precarious and limited existence" (Dubos, 1965, p. 317).

How much truth does this gloomy assessment contain? Some studies have documented a host of negative behaviors statistically associated with crowded conditions. For example, doubled-up families in high rises tended to develop higher levels of emotional illness and hostility than those not sharing their family dwelling (Mitchell, 1971). Family members were more apt to spend time outside the home, children less likely to be supervised adequately. Crowding has been associated, too, with respiratory diseases, skin problems, and accident rates. The Kerner Commission found that in those metropolitan areas affected by the 1967 rioting, 24 percent of all nonwhite households were overcrowded, while only 8.8 percent of white households were.

It has been argued that overcrowding, combined with inadequate sanitation and other characteristics of substandard housing, produces feelings of poor self-esteem, a sense that one cannot control the environment and provide even a modicum of shelter and safety to one's family. One large study of rehoused slum dwellers reported increases in feelings of self-worth, better family relations, particularly in maternal handling of discipline, more pride in one's neighborhood, and more assistance to neighbors (Wilner et al., 1962). Yet, other evidence contends that some of those relocated from slums to new housing are more dissatisfied as a result of the change, that they "grieve" for a lost home and that family relations are impaired, not improved. Moreover, the statistical association between crowding and negative physical and social outcomes does not always appear. Some of the most crowded spots on the globe, such as Holland, have remarkably low crime, mental illness, and physical illness rates.

Yet, the view that crowding must lead to a breakdown in family relations persists. Two major sources of this view may be identified. First, an abundance of animal studies has shown that when population builds up within a limited space, abnormalities of behavior, physical symptoms, and even widespread death ensue. The most famous example of this is the lemmings' "march to the sea." When the lemming population reaches extremely high densities, every three to four years, it appears to be gripped by an irresistible suicidal urge and the lemmings plunge, en masse, into the fjords. Similar abrupt population "crashes" have been observed in several other species. These curiosities of nature have been reproduced experimentally in many species (Dubos, 1965).

Some of the most dramatic of these experiments were conducted by John Calhoun on wild Norway rats (Calhoun, 1962a, 1962b). In four adjoining experimental pens, Calhoun allowed the wild rat population to build up to about eighty rats. Observations of these rats in their natural setting had indicated that when the group totaled forty, fighting and other forms of social stress began to occur with increasing frequency. When the population reached eighty, Calhoun began to observe gross distortions of normal mating, nest building, and child-care behaviors, which he termed a "behavioral sink."

Specifically, many male rats would try mounting any rat, male or female, young or old. Other male rats withdrew from all social interactions. Nest building activity often failed to be completed; a female would be observed carrying material and then inexplicably drop it and wander off. Mothers appeared forgetful and unprotective of their young rat pups, often dropping them in easy reach of rapacious, hyperactive males who would promptly devour them. Calhoun concluded that the behavioral distortions of the "sink" were the direct result of overcrowding, and not decreased availability of food and water, which continued in plentiful supply despite population increase.

Similar dramatic consequences flowing from crowding appear when other species are studied. Christian (1963) and Christian and Davis (1964) investigated the seemingly bizarre mass deaths of deer on a small island in Chesapeake Bay. A few years after a population build-up to about one deer per acre, large numbers of deer appeared to die off spontaneously, amid adequate food supply and protection from predators. Examination of the dead deer showed them in the peak of condition with shining coats and well-formed muscles. Only one thing seemed unusual. Many of the dead deer had severely enlarged adrenal glands. Since the adrenals enlarge in response to frequent and prolonged stress, Christian concluded that the deer had literally died of shock. Overcrowding had disrupted social relations, and constant mobilization of energy to meet these encounters had finally caused the deer to collapse.

Another ubiquitous animal phenomenon related to these crowding effects is *territoriality*. The existence of territoriality implies certain minimal distances between species members and makes crowding synonymous with social breakdown. Hence, experimental studies with rats, observations of naturally occurring population build-up among deer, and the widespread phenomenon of territoriality have led many to the conclusion that similar adverse effects of crowding must be operable in humans.

The process of industrialization during the nineteenth century gave some support to this view. As society shifted from agriculture to industry, millions were crammed into city tenements by night and factories by day. Tremendous increases in mortality and morbidity resulted, malnutrition was endemic, infectious diseases rampaged, and social organization broke down. Again, crowding was singled out as the villain and the term *crowd diseases* was coined to describe the easy spread of microbal agents under high-density conditions (Dubos, 1965).

Where humans are concerned, one must distinguish between *density* and *crowding* (Stokols, 1976). *Density* is an objective measure of the number of people per unit-space and may be increased by adding more people, while keeping area constant ("social density") or by decreasing space while keeping the population constant ("spatial density"). *Crowding*, on the other hand, is a subjective term that depends upon the perception of the individual in a situation of given density. It is a feeling of discomfort that may be due only in part to the actual density level. Also of importance will be the situation and how it is defined. A successful cocktail party involves rubbing shoulders with a goodly number of people in fairly small rooms, but a study hall does not. Crucial, too, will be the needs and goals of participants and the degree to which the density level interferes with their goal-directed behavior. If it is impossible to do what you need to do, then the situation begins to feel intolerably crowded. When density is accompanied by low levels of resources, this situation is likely to engender competition for scarce goods, feelings of thwartedness, and hence, perception of crowding. To evaluate an environment as crowded, one must *perceive* it as thwarting *values*.

Since crowding is an individual or group evaluation, one would expect that personal differences would influence this appraisal. Past experience with different density conditions may lead to adaptation to certain density levels. The zestful living that the native city dweller experiences may be an oppressive push of humanity to the life-long resident of a small community. In addition, personality characteristics, such as introversion-extroversion, might dispose some to close and frequent social contact, others to valued solitude.

Cultural differences in personal space also affect perception of crowding. In contact cultures valuing a high degree of close interpersonal involvement, high-density conditions are less likely to be perceived as crowded than in noncontact cultures. Within a given culture, an optimal level of social contact exists. When housing conditions result in *social overload* (too much contact) or *social underload* (too little contact), negative consequences for family functioning can be predicted. Some research confirms this prediction. Tenants in fourteen-story apartment buildings were compared with those in three-story walk-ups within the same low-income housing project. Those in the high-rise residence were brought into contact with so many people they experienced social overload and felt crowded as a result. These feelings of crowdedness made the high-rise residents feel powerless to affect their environment, alienated, withdrawn, and unfriendly (McCarthy and Saegert, 1978).

Sex differences in personal space have implications for the perception of crowded housing conditions as well. Some experimental studies of reactions to high density (Freedman, 1975) indicate that women are less likely to experience discomfort while men are more likely to feel angry and aggressive.

Thus, there is no simple connection between density level and the evaluative experience of crowding. This does not mean, however, that crowding is a purely psychological state independent of environmental conditions. Crowding appears to be a complex interaction between the ability to process stimulation and the degree of complexity of a particular situation (Chandler, Koch, and Paget, 1977). Being crowded means operating in a social context the complexity of which exceeds one's processing capabilities. We cannot define crowdedness in terms of situation alone, nor personality alone, but as a consequence of their *interaction*.

Concern with the nature of crowding may blind us to the fact that human nature is gregarious. The forces which prompt close association among humans, both in pursuit of common goals and *for its own sake*, are often overlooked. As more of America (and indeed much of the world) becomes urban, we increasingly adapt to life in areas of population concentration. Some (Dubos, 1965) have suggested long-range negative consequences of such adaptation. But others (Freedman, 1975) argue that socializing in groups is our natural proclivity, and that isolation produces the most damaging effects. The question remains: What is the optimal ratio of people to space? And it's likely that no simple answer to that question is possible, for such an answer depends upon a host of simultaneously occurring factors, such as past history, culture, personality, definition of the situation, and resources. Further, these factors are integrated into a judgment (often unconscious) about the discomfort or crowdedness of the situation.

Substandard Housing

It has been the belief underlying urban renewal that slum living was the cause of mental and physical disorders as well as crime, and that changing the physical environment alone would bring about improvements in these aspects of the quality of life. This belief grew out of crusading investigations of slum conditions from the nineteenth century on. The public gradually became aware that a relation between overcrowding, poor sanitation, dirt, and unsafe buildings on the one hand, and infectious disease and mortality on the other did indeed exist. Much thinking about the impact of housing stems from this tradition. However, it is now seen that altering the physical setting *alone* without affecting the social context brings about little real change. Families may be miserable in new housing erected to replace slums or relatively cohesive and satisfied in the objectively defined substandard housing of the slum itself. Housing exists within a neighborhood, a way of life that is part of what residents call "home" (Hartman, 1963). Housing cannot be considered in isolation from the fabric of life into which it is woven.

In part, the traditional belief that social problems could be cured through urban design stemmed from studies showing the adverse effects of extreme environments, particularly on developing children. For example, institutionalized children were observed in some cases (Spitz and Wolfe, 1946; Dennis and Najarian, 1957) to be markedly retarded in motor and social skills, some unable to walk or sit up at two years of age. Further research indicated that these children suffered from an environment affording minimal social and physical stimulation. The setting was boring, monotonous, unmarked by changes in routine or social encounters except to fulfill basic physical needs. In a similar emphasis on physical-setting effects, Kagan et al. (1974) have suggested that the so-called disadvantaged lower-class child suffers not so much from inadequate stimulation, but from lack of *distinctive* stimulation. So much noise and activity is constantly swirling around the child that the distinctive messages from parents are often lost. Kagan is suggesting that, just as too little stimulation has been shown to produce adverse effects on the development of children, so does too much stimulation. In the latter case, the child is likely to feel bombarded and tune out. This is another example of the importance of an adaptation range, or optimal range of stimulation, within which the individual can most effectively function.

There is some support for this overstimulation hypothesis of poor housing. One study (Cohen, Glass, and Singer, 1973) related the effects of noise to children's auditory discrimination (their ability to distinguish sounds) and reading achievement. By examining children living on different floors of an apartment building built over a particularly noisy expressway, they found that the closer a child lived to the source of noise, the more impaired was auditory discrimination. Thus, children living on the lower floors of the building scored significantly lower than children living further up. Reading achievement was also affected, but less dramatically.

Another investigation (Wachs, Uzgiris, and Hunt, 1971) also supported the conclusion that overstimulation, both in level of noise and amount of social stimulation, had adverse effects on cognitive functioning. Studies conducted by Wachs and his associates underscored the importance of a room to which the young child could "retreat" to be alone. This finding indicates the link between overstimulation and the importance of privacy. In addition to directly affecting their abilities to discriminate, overstimulation may be detrimental to family members by denying them privacy or control over level of stimulation. To the extent that housing deprives family members of this control, it may impair cognitive and emotional functioning, particularly in children.

Poor housing may not only provide too stimulating an atmosphere, but pose a threat to family health through inadequate heating, cooling, greater likelihood of accidents in poorly maintained structures, and greater likelihood of infection from inadequate sanitation. In addition, the negative self-image the status of such housing communicates to its occupants would be likely to affect psychological functioning.

When housing surveys found correlations between slum living and social morbidity, these results were viewed as confirmation of the causal relation between inadequate housing and social ills. In a review of forty studies of housing and health adjustment (Wilner and Walkley, 1963), twenty-six showed a positive association between housing and health or housing and social adjustment, eleven showed no relationship, and three indicated a negative relationship. Thus in most studies, good housing does appear to be associated with good health and good social adjustment. But, as every beginning student of statistics is reminded, correlations do not imply cause and effect relationships; they merely indicate the associations between two variables. One might as easily explain a correlation between slum dwellings and social morbidity in the following way: people prone to social problems gravitate to slum areas where their preoccupation with their own problems leads them to ignore maintenance of their environment, thereby causing the increase in substandard housing. Of course, this explanation is not seriously advanced. It is no more (or less) plausible than the explanation that slums *cause* social problems. Moreover, housing is related to many other characteristics that might influence both health and adjustment, such as education, income, cultural background, and use of medical facilities. As with nutrition, how is it possible to pinpoint housing per se as the culprit? That it is sometimes undeservedly accused may be illustrated in one study (Lander, 1954), which found a strong association between housing adequacy and juvenile delinquency. When other related nonhousing factors were controlled, however, the connection between housing and juvenile delinquency approached zero.

It should not be concluded, however, that housing quality bears *no* relationship whatsoever to health and adjustment. In one carefully conducted study, the Johns Hopkins longitudinal study (Wilner and Walkley, 1963), 300 test families selected for study had moved from a slum area to public housing projects. They were matched with 300 "controls" who remained in the slum. One "before" and ten "after" interviews were conducted over a period of three years. The results indicated that, particularly among those under age twenty, illness, disability, and accident rates were significantly lower in the test sample as compared to the controls. In fact, among children whose families had moved to the housing project, the accident rate was one-third lower! Similar, but less drastic, differences favoring the test sample were found among those over twenty years of age. Interestingly, babies born to test-sample mothers tended to have higher birth weights than infants of mothers remaining in the slum. Since the low-birth-weight baby is an at-risk baby, this finding implies that housing can have effects extending beyond the present generation.

Is housing quality also related to social and personal adjustment? Those who indict slum living see this environment as discouraging neighborliness, hampering family relations, dampening morale, lowering positive self-concepts, and blocking individual aspirations. Hence, the Johns Hopkins longitudinal study tested this hypothesis through interviews (mother only) and examination of school records. Few of their findings, however, were statistically significant. That is, differences were found between the two groups of families, and most of the differences were in the predicted direction. Nevertheless, these differences could have been due to chance and were not necessarily the result of the one difference of interest, namely, housing quality.

The study did find that children remaining in the slum were more likely to be held back a grade or two than those children who had moved. Upon further examination, this promotion difference was related to differences in school attendance. The lowered illness and accident rates meant that children had to miss school less, and hence school attendance made it more likely that the child would be able to advance normally in grade level. No differences in achievement or IQ scores, however, were obtained between slum and project children.

In summary, while most evidence for an association between housing quality and health is based on inadequately designed studies, a carefully controlled comparison between movers and nonmovers out of slums did find significant differences in health, but not in social adjustment factors.

While this study carefully compared movers and nonmovers out of a slum, it did not critically examine its assumption that the slum constituted "bad" housing and the public housing project "good" or at least "better" housing. The public housing project did provide improved space, structural safety, better heating and plumbing, and more modern facilities. However, it did not improve the social environment of the new residents, provide a more convenient location, or give them a sense of greater control over their setting.

In fact, public housing projects have been criticized for worsening the social problems of their inhabitants. In a study of the Pruitt-Igoe project in St. Louis (Yancey, 1971), families were observed to retreat into their apartments. In the absence of safe, semi-private spaces where they might establish social contacts, families lacked the sense of security and social support they had maintained in their previous slum neighborhoods. Newman (1972) has argued that the most important characteristic of urban public housing is its provision of *defensible spaces*. By this he meant that residents must feel a sense of control, ownership, and territoriality about their residential setting. Otherwise, their position will become somewhat like birds in spatially adequate cages, vulnerable to crime and vandalism, feeling like victims.

Housing Design and Family Functioning

Most housing studies are like the Johns Hopkins study, although perhaps not as extensive or well designed; they focus on the impact of substandard housing and public housing projects designed to replace these slums. Far less attention has been devoted to other types of dwellings; apartment complexes of the middle-income bracket, private homes of varying sizes and designs, particularly those dwellings chosen and inhabited by choice.

Since housing and families are potentially, at least, infinitely variable, it is important to ask how *dimensions* of the housing environment are related to *dimensions* of the family. Dimensions of the housing environment might include size, materials, number and layout of rooms, number and organization of objects, amount of closed versus open space, ratio of glass to nonglass materials, color, convenience to shopping and schools, quality of neighborhood, relationship to landscape outside, or proximity to other dwellings. Dimensions of the family would include the following among others: size, stage of life cycle, social class, religion, communication style, division of labor,

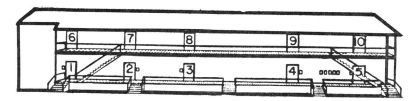

Figure 11.1. Schematic diagram of a Westgate West building. (Reproduced from *Social Pressures in Informal Groups* by Leon Festinger, Stanley Schacter, and Kurt Back, with the permission of the publishers, Stanford University Press. © 1950 by the Board of Trustees of the Leland Stanford Junior University.)

decision-making patterns, and value orientation. By looking at the relationships between these two sets of dimensions, a number of interesting questions emerge, such as: (1) How do housing dimensions such as size, layout of rooms or distance from neighbors affect family interaction? (2) How does the spatial environment change, if it does, with changes in the family's life cycle or size? Can such changes be predicted?

It is important to note that these questions concern not only the *impact* of the housing environment on the family, but also include the *action* of the family in modifying its housing environment.

Residential Propinquity

Just as housing density and crowding indicate the degree to which family members receive stimulation from each other, the concept of residential propinquity reflects the degree to which family units come into contact with one another. How does residential propinquity affect social interaction between families? In simpler terms, this question asks what impact living near others has on a family. Are neighbors ignored, the source of conflict, or likely to become friends? Since all three outcomes are common, is it possible to predict which is most likely for Family X in dwelling Y?

This question was first addressed in a comprehensive manner by a now classic study by Festinger, Schacter, and Back (1950). They studied an apartment complex for married student families of veterans returning to school after World War II. Families were assigned apartments randomly so that the authors were sure that friends did not arrange to move in near each other. In the process of examining the adjustment of these veterans to university life, the authors were startled to discover that they could, after a period of time, predict exactly who were friends by looking at only one bit of information, "functional distance," defined as *residential design features that promote interaction*. For example, as Figure 11.1 illustrates, apartments 1 and 5 are the only first-floor apartments adjacent to the staircases. Families in these two dwellings had more "upper story" friends than any other families on the first floor. Dwellers in adjacent apartments tended to become friends more readily than those living a greater distance from each other. The placement of mailboxes also affected interaction. Note that apartment 5 is adjacent to the stairs and mailbox. The family there tended to make more friends with second-story apartment dwellers, particularly those in apartments 9 and 10, than other first-floor families. This is not surprising when traffic patterns are examined. Second-floor residents pass by apartment 5 more often than other first-floor apartments and so happen to run into the family living there. From such encounters, acquaintance and then friendship tend to develop.

The authors concluded that *housing design largely determined traffic patterns which, in turn, predicted who would run into whom.* People who saw each other often were more likely to make friends than people who saw each other rarely.

These conclusions appear to have far-reaching practical significance. Perhaps problems of ethnic and racial antagonism could be solved by placing families close together in integrated housing. The design of the apartment complex or neighborhood could "engineer" social interaction. Potentially hostile families would see each other as human beings, prejudice would break down, and perhaps real friendship develop.

Such a happy outcome, however, has not generally been the fruit of such experiments in integrated housing. The bitter resistance of whites to housing integration is well known. Less well known is the persistence of geographically distinct ethnic neighborhoods in most of America's cities. Chicago's Poles would rather not live with Chicago's Italians, but "among their own." The Festinger, Schacter, and Back study does not really contradict these findings. In their study, the returning veterans who occupied the apartment complex were from similar class backgrounds. They were a relatively homogeneous populuation and did not include potentially hostile groups. The implication might be stated thusly: If families are basically similar, then placing them in housing which "throws them together" will stimulate friendship formation. It will not, however, "wash away" differences that residents feel are important. The study illustrates that, while the housing of families can be demonstrated to be significant in affecting their behavior, it is a complex relationship, not a simple cause-and-effect one. The characteristics and past histories of families are important.

For example, other research has shown that what families do to encourage or discourage the friendship formation-process is important. They can leave their apartment door ajar most of the day or keep it firmly closed, thereby communicating to others their desired rate of social contact.

Interior Design

Housing characterisics within the individual dwelling may be related to aspects of family functioning. For example, the size and layout of rooms relative to the number of inhabitants would be expected to affect their frequency of interaction. When siblings share a bedroom they would be expected to be in more frequent contact than siblings with separate rooms. This, however, may not be the case. Families show considerable creativity in how they use available space to express their own individuality. In one family, sisters who share a room may spend much time in each other's company, while in another family, separateness may be accentuated by using the room at different times or establishing patterns of territoriality ("my half" versus "your half").

Other examples of "impact" research on the relationship between housing design and family relations indicate the importance of considering family characteristics. The effect of high-rise versus low-rise apartment living on *intrafamilial* relations has been explored. High-rise living may be detrimental to families with small children whose outside play cannot be properly supervised from ten floors up, but has no adverse effects on other families (Rutter and Madge, 1976).

Housing design particularly affects the elderly whose capacity to cope with environmental stress may be impaired. For example, elderly people, particularly those in poor health, need common spaces, like apartment lobbies, where they can sit and observe the social scene (Lawton, 1970). Basic safety features, important in any dwelling, are particularly important for the elderly.

Electrical outlets waist high, grab bars in the bathroom, and excellent indoor and outdoor illumination are essential (Lawton, 1975). In general, housing design needs to reflect the capacities, goals, and values of those who will use it. To do this, social research on families needs to link up with architectural design (Brolin and Zeisel, 1968).

Again and again, housing-impact research reveals how characteristics of the spatial environment *interact* with family characteristics to produce effects. Hence, the term *transactions*, indicating mutual influence, is more accurate than *effects* for describing the relation between family and spatial environment.

FAMILY TRANSACTIONS WITH THE SPATIAL ENVIRONMENT

As seen above, asking questions about the impact of the spatial environment on families has led to consideration of family characteristics in the answer. This importance of the nature of the family in determining environmental impact underscores the significance of family perceiving, spacing, valuing, and deciding—active processes—in family transactions with the environment.

Perceiving and Evaluating the Spatial Environment

Residential satisfaction. If we could interview a representative sample of Americans and ask them to evaluate their residential environment, what would we find? How would home, neighborhood, and community be related? How would different ages, educational levels, sexes, and races differ in their evaluations? How important, finally, is residential satisfaction for an overall sense of well-being?

Just such questions were posed as part of a larger inquiry into "The Quality of American Life" by Campbell, Converse, and Rodgers (1976). This important survey interviewed 2,164 adults in 1971. The sample was drawn to reflect faithfully the age, sex, race, and general educational differences current in the U.S.A. at that time.

Their findings, with respect to residential satisfaction, may be summarized as follows:

1. Most Americans are satisfied with where and how they live, describing their homes in largely positive terms.

2. Evaluations of home, community, and neighborhood are closely related. Not surprisingly, people often choose a home because it is situated in an attractive neighborhood and is part of a safe community. The authors conclude that home, neighborhood, and community are "nested environments" which mutually influence one another.

3. Although as we too have emphasized, individuals bring to bear their personal histories and personalities in evaluating housing conditions, the survey results also indicated that most Americans accurately perceive objective housing conditions. When interviewers' ratings of housing conditions were compared with reports of respondents, a close match was obtained. Furthermore, in evaluating the quality of housing and in assessing satisfaction, most people accurately assessed objective conditions and judged them against their own standards of comparison.

4. Despite this general sensitivity to objective conditions, some initially surprising results were obtained. For example, older people were more likely to be satisfied with their residential environment (and their lives as a whole) than younger people, although America's senior citizens are more apt to live in substandard housing and unsafe neighborhoods than younger families or singles. Similarly, the better educated the respondent, the less satisfied he or she was with the residential environment, despite the likelihood that it was objectively better than the housing of a less educated counterpart. Why, then, were young, well-educated people more dissatisfied, though

living better than older, less educated people? The authors explain this finding in terms of differences in *standards of comparison.* Satisfaction is an evaluation, based on what one has done in the past and on sights set for the future. Satisfaction, they maintain, is also based on comparison of one's fortunes with those of one's friends and neighbors. As people acquire more education, their horizons are broadened and they become aware of still better and more interesting ways to live. Thus, relatively, their level of satisfaction drops. Similarly, as one ages, one may become reconciled to one's fate, ceasing to strive for things which now seem unattainable.

Perceiving and evaluating are colored by the resources families bring to these processes. Families with many resources perceive many alternatives and apply high standards of comparison. Thus, being objectively well off can be associated with increased dissatisfaction.

A study by Lansing, Marans, and Zehner (1970) further illustrates the role of perceiving in determining residential satisfaction. They found that perceiving that neighbors are similar to oneself and that they are friendly was associated with neighborhood satisfaction. *Actual* homogeneity in terms of age, education, income, and race, however, was not related to the perception of either similarity or friendliness. This surprising result indicates that people may perceive neighborhood characteristics inaccurately. Their satisfaction will depend on their perceptions and not on actual conditions. An important question that further research must answer is: Why are perceptions of the housing environment in some cases accurate (the Campbell study) and in other cases, inaccurate (the Lansing study)?

While perceived similarity and friendliness are determinants of residential satisfaction, other aspects of the housing environment are also important. In the Lansing study, less satisfied people were those who heard their neighbors often, felt the neighborhood was noisy, had no privacy in the yard, and considered their outdoor play space inadequate. A number of studies have reported other factors: crime rate, sense of safety, quality of schools. While dwelling satisfaction is influenced by the perception of the neighborhood, it is also affected by perceived characteristics of the dwelling itself. An important source of dissatisfaction here is amount of space, particularly number of bedrooms (Yockey, 1976). Studies that the present author has carried out with her associates (Melson, Inman, and Kemp, 1978; Inman and Melson, 1978) also underscore the importance of the fulfillment of spatial needs as underlying housing satisfaction. In a sample of young married student families, lack of adequate indoor space, particularly space to ensure privacy, was strongly related to feelings of residential dissatisfaction as well as environmental stress and to difficulties in family functioning.

Interior design. Perception and evaluation are important processes in understanding not only families' feelings about their home and neighborhood, but also their feelings and actions about *interior spaces* of the home. Even the most modest home contains small touches to personalize the environment. For many, the design of the home is a reflection of its renters' or owners' personalities. As an example, consider the interplay of family characteristics and interior design in this description:

> Being in the Lanson home for a short time, one gains a feeling that here life is tranquil and subdued. No forceful sounds to be heard, no visible assertions arrest the eye. Care and containment are suggested in the plastic coverings on the conventional furniture. People speak quietly in this house, with an evenness of tone that extends into the physical surroundings. Walls, carpet and furnishings are in pale neutral shades. . . . The modest but new five-room house is, in almost all respects, a suitable setting for family life as the

Lansons believe it should be: harmonious, quiescent, and unspectacular. For such a life, few paraphernalia are necessary, and few are immediately in evidence. The visitor in the living room sees no books, pictures or magazines—only yesterday's newspapers.*

Here, in the Lanson home, it is possible to experience visually the family theme as expressed by the home's decor. Of course, modification of the housing environment to express the family's perceptions and values is limited by resources and interest. Recall that we included in our discussion of *spacing* the idea of *orientation towards things* versus *people*. It is likely that families that invest a great deal of time and energy in attempting to create a distinctive home environment emphasize orientation to physical objects as arranged in space. But for every family, their dwelling reflects important family themes.

Deciding for Change

In a free society, many families live in a particular environment by choice and may change that setting if sufficiently dissatisfied. This fact, however, should not blind us to the millions of families who, by government estimates, are living in substandard housing and who are unable to make significant changes in their environment. In this section, however, we will focus on the active process by which families make decisions and carry them out concerning change in the spatial environment.

It has been said that "mobility has been written into the American character" (Gutman, 1963). We think of ourselves as a people on the move, on the go, on our way up (or down), oriented toward change in physical setting as well as everything else (Table 11.1). What has been the extent of geographical mobility and what has been its character? An analysis of census data (Wattenberg, 1976) indicates a dramatic increase in the suburban population and decreases in both central city and rural population. The flight to the suburbs represents a massive migration; more than 35 million additional suburbanites have been added during the past twenty years.

---

*Reprinted with permission from R. Hess and G. Handel, *Family Worlds: A Psychosocial Approach to Family Life.* Chicago: University of Chicago Press, 1974.

TABLE 11.1 PERCENTAGE OF AMERICANS LIVING IN CENTRAL CITY, SUBURBAN, AND NONMETROPOLITAN (INCLUDING RURAL) AREAS, 1950, 1960, 1970

	1950	1960	1970	Change 1950-1970
Suburban	27%	33%	37%	+11%
Central city	36%	33%	31%	− 5%
Nonmetropolitan (including rural)	38%	33%	31%	− 7%

Excerpted from *The Real America* by Ben Wattenberg. Copyright © 1974 by Ben J. Wattenberg. Reprinted by permission of Doubleday & Company, Inc.

1970 boundaries in all instances. Rounding of percentages yields totals that do not add to 100 percent.

It is said that mobility is written into the American character. (Photo by Natalie Leimkuhler.)

Families may regard a move as temporary, expecting another transfer soon, as in the case of Army personnel and corporation middle management. Perhaps the move is viewed as transient because the family sees it as a temporary way station in their search for a better locale—"just until we find something better." Others may regard the move as permanent. Despite the massive numbers of Americans who move, one should not exaggerate the disruptive effects of mobility. Most moves involve short distances and impose few changes in social relations (Burchinal and Bauder, 1965). A pattern of "nomadism" has also been identified. This refers to the fact that a large volume of moves are made by a small proportion of families who seem to move frequently for the sake of change or because of unstable family and occupational commitments (Goldstein, 1958).

Some mobility is a by-product of occupational change. Since 1940, new professions and new skills in old professions have been proliferating. Workers find themselves obsolete within a few years. Cutbacks in industries produce instant gluts in professions that a year earlier were much in demand. These dramatic and often traumatic shifts in job availability act as major prods to family mobility.

However, even if jobs were stable, mobility would probably remain high. After all, as Wattenberg points out, except for native Americans, the rest of us would not be here if an ancestor had not moved willingly or through force. American society is, in the anthropologist's term, *neolocal*. That is, new families are expected to take up a new residence away from both the wife's and husband's families. We are also a socially mobile society, with as many as 25 percent of our population moving up in social class and about 5 percent moving down. Social mobility has long been associated with geographical mobility. Moving up in the world is signalled by moving out of the old neighborhood to a more affluent one (Wattenberg, 1976).

Geographical mobility rates historically reflect high occupational instability, custom, and social mobility. From 1950 to 1965, approximately 20 percent of the population moved each year. In addition to job changes, mobility is likely when changes in the family make the nest a tight fit—the advent of another child often precipitates a move.

Obviously, not all those who are motivated to move actually do so. Among voluntary movers, a rather complex process intervenes between the first stirrings of a desire for change and the completion of an actual move. Morris and Winter (1975, 1978) have provided a conceptual framework for understanding the active processes by which the family attempts to match needs and values to a housing environment. According to them, the family continuously evaluates its housing relative to *family* and *cultural norms*. Cultural norms refer to a set of standards about what constitutes proper housing in a given culture. When a particular family's housing does not meet these norms, it feels a loss of self-respect and the withdrawal of respect from others. Morris and Winter point out the tremendous differences in housing characteristics and quality across cultures, from the Eskimo igloo to the hollow in the ground with a makeshift skin windbreak of the Tierra del Fuegans. Thus, family housing "needs" in America are really a set of cultural values about what constitutes proper housing conditions. These values specify relatively large amounts of space per family member, preference for home ownership, preference for single-family detached dwellings, and preference for "good" residential neighborhoods.

Just as we emphasized a family theme or value orientation apart from cultural value orientation, so do Morris and Winter stress a family set of housing norms that may or may not coincide with cultural norms. Other values are important factors in stimulating or discouraging moving discussions. The value of home or farm ownership, "familism" (the value placed on the family), "careerism" (the value placed on occupational success and upward mobility [Bell, 1958]), and the value placed on residential stability ("putting down roots") — all would affect the likelihood and seriousness of moving discussions. When a family feels its housing does not meet these two sets of norms, housing dissatisfaction occurs.

For families experiencing some of the above-mentioned changes and whose values would dispose them to want to move, moving discussions may begin. These discussions are a special case of the decision-making process outlined in Chapter 7. It is for many families more important a decision than almost any other, except perhaps for decisions concerning family size. The concepts of authority, power, communication, and decision-making *process*, however, apply equally to the decision to move as they do to more mundane matters such as which television program to watch.

During the decision-making process, information concerning family resources for the move, probable consequences of the change, and available options will be shared. This information gathering, review of alternatives, and allocation of resources is an example of the consumer process as well. As consumer decisions involve more resources, they are less likely to be specialized and more likely to be shared by both husband and wife. Since residential moves are clearly major decisions for any family, the decision-making process is likely to be a shared one in which no single family member lays claim to specialized ability. Sixty percent of the couples studied by Blood and Wolfe (1960) reported that husband and wife had approximately equal chances of making the final decision on which house or apartment to take. However, as stressed in Chapter 7, this emphasis on the final outcome rather than the process of decision making obscures its complexities. The communication process becomes of central importance in order to understand the outcome of moving discussions.

Such discussions will vary in rationality. The framework used in this book relies upon concepts such as information, resources, decision making, and feedback. At each point, families depart from a hypothetical model of pure rationality in weighing information against available resources in the light of values and making decisions which are then carried out in planned actions. Although families are purposeful and goal-directed, they are humans intimately interlocked and, hence, never purely rational. Therefore, the sources of rationality and irrationality will be important in moving discussions as in all other aspects of decision making. As Janis and Mann (1977) persuasively argue in their book *Decision-Making*, important real-life decisions are psychologically stressful events. Often, people will react to them with uncertainty and fear, seeking to avoid the necessity of deciding at all.

Not only do families differ in their ability to make decisions, to achieve consensus, and to act on decisions once taken, but economic, social, and political factors are important. Racial discrimination prevents full social mobility. Economic fluctuations shrink the housing market at times. Family action will involve a compromise between family dissatisfaction with their own housing situation relative to cultural and family norms and various economic and social constraints.

Resulting family action, according to Morris and Winter (1975), may take different forms: (1) residential mobility, e.g., moving to a new residence, (2) residential alterations and additions, e.g., remodeling current housing or moving the baby's crib, or (3) family adaptation, e.g., altering family composition to adjust to housing conditions. Examples of family adaptation include postponing childbearing or encouraging an aged parent to enter a nursing home.

While family members are usually not aware that such actions have any relationship to housing conditions, Morris and Winter (1978) suggest that they are, nonetheless, responses to dimly perceived pressures of crowding or excess space. Another kind of family adaptation is *organizational*, involving not alterations of family composition, but changes in patterns of interaction, power, and dominance, or other aspects of family functioning. Such changes may be subtle ones, out of the family's awareness. For example, in a study conducted by the author (Melson, 1976) couples who perceived their apartments as being crowded reported tendencies to resolve marital conflicts by retreat or withdrawal. One person would usually leave the house. The same families were also aware of specific organizational changes. Some attempted to enforce cleanliness standards more strictly to make the place seem larger; others reported that their lovemaking became more inhibited by proximity to their neighbors through "paper thin" walls (Melson, Inman, and Kemp, 1978). Still others took to going out and socializing with neighbors more often.

Another response to discrepancy between family norms and existing housing might be to change norms rather than do anything about housing. A family could decide that after all, it's not so important for the kids to have their own bedrooms or that living in an apartment seems more friendly and desirable than a privately owned home. As the chapter on valuing (Chapter 6) emphasized, values are changing, not static. When perceived conditions don't fit family values, the response may to be adjust one's values rather than act to change conditions.

The changing nature of values may also result in the *creation* of housing dissatisfaction. A family may raise its standards of acceptability, deciding that it now needs a larger, more luxurious or differently designed home, although no changes in family composition or housing conditions have occurred. This is likely to happen during periods of rising affluence for the family or the society as a whole (Morris and Winter, 1978).

Thus, changing the spatial environment is just one of a number of possible outcomes of the family's perceiving, spacing, valuing, and deciding processes. If mobility does occur, what are some of its consequences?

Consequences of Mobility

The term *mobility* covers the influx of poor southern blacks into major northern cities, the relocation of slum dwellers in the wake of urban renewal, the transfers of corporate executives and Army personnel, the wanderings of fruit pickers, and the move from inner city to suburb that represents a step up in social mobility. Clearly, geographical mobility has no general effects when applied to such diverse populations with correspondingly disparate motives, resources, and life circumstances. One must examine carefully the circumstances of the move, its voluntary or nonvoluntary nature, the motivations underlying the change, the resources of those moving, and characteristics of the environments themselves.

Toffler has suggested that one by-product of frequent geographical mobility is the unwillingness to make long-term commitments to others. "Here today, gone tomorrow" is often literally true. Hence, the transient comes to specialize in "hurry-up friendships," shallow relationships easily made and easily broken. There is some research support for this. In *The Organization Man*, Whyte (1956) reports the instant rush to neighborhood contacts when a new family moved into the housing development. In another study (Gutman, 1963) transients also reported "hurry-up" friendships, while those whose moves were considered permanent felt they had little social contact with neighbors during the early months.

How does a residential move affect social roles? Does the family find the same or similar schools, associations, and social organizations in its new setting? Many residential moves do not disrupt social roles markedly even though the family may be moving to a different community. Precisely because America is so mobile, uniformity of institutions helps cushion transitions for families. The familiar McDonald's golden arch is there, as is the local PTA, YMCA, Scouts, church, shopping mall, and supermarket chain. Daily patterns of activity can persist with only minor adjustment.

Adjustment to a move will be easier, of course, if the family has substantial material and psychological resources with which to ease their transition. Similarly, adjustment will be most difficult when the new setting requires new roles, as is the case with culturally different migrants, or throws up discriminative barriers as in the case of blacks, Mexican-American, and native American newcomers to northern urban centers.

Before considering in detail some examples of this adjustment process, difficulties in measuring adjustment should be mentioned. Research that asks new residents to recall the moving process they have recently gone through is suspect because people notoriously color their memories in the light of their present experience. Particularly if a move has been eagerly anticipated, few families are willing to admit that the change they had worked for so hard has turned out to be a bust.

Another research approach to adjustment involves comparing a group of new residents with another group of long-time residents. For example, one might compare urban residents who have recently come from rural communities with life-long city folk. This procedure is difficult, since it is virtually impossible to match two groups on all characteristics save length of residence. For example, life-long urban residents may have different educational and occupational opportunities and have developed attitudes that set them apart from rural migrants.

A third problem with research on adjustment to mobility concerns the types of measures taken. Most studies have focussed on individual adjustment, psychologically in terms of attitudes, goals, and aspirations, and sociologically in terms of changed educational and occupational roles. But little is known concerning changes in *family* behavior during the moving process.

Finally, measures of adjustment may be *objective* or *subjective*. In the first case, the investigator establishes a standard of adjustment and evaluates the behavior of the new resident; in the second, the mover is asked about his or her own perception and feelings. Objective indices of adjustment are sometimes misleading if the investigator and subject of investigation are using different standards for adjustment. The following example illustrates this:

> Much of the concern of the "plight" of the Mexican-Americans (in Racine, Wisconsin) revolved around the apparent lack of concern over their own sorry state of affairs evidenced by the Mexicans. This in itself was cause for great alarm on the part of middle-class persons. Knowledge of the environment from which the Mexicans came might have tempered local concern over the attitude of the Mexicans toward their present living conditions.*

In this example, the poor migrant, evaluating the present relative to his or her own past sees a substantial improvement, which the observer from an urban middle-class background might miss.

Forced Relocation

The experience of many families forcibly relocated from urban slums has been highly disruptive and disturbing. Their reactions have been likened to expressions of grief for the loss of a loved one—feelings of painful loss, general depressions, even helplessness, symptoms of physical and mental distress, expressions of anger, and tendencies to idealize the lost home (Fried, 1963). In one study of 250 women and 316 men from working-class backgrounds, 45 percent of the women and 38 percent of the men reported long-term (six months to two years) grief reactions after relocation. The severity and frequency of this grief reaction indicate how important the physical setting is for a sense of continuity and belonging. Individuals interviewed in the above study had been residents of the West End neighborhood of Boston, a highly cohesive community which was truly "home" to its members. The community placed high value on relationships and loyalty to the group, and thus, community residents developed a strong sense of group identity. Within this context, a geographical move also represented a wrenching away from extended family and friendship ties.

Such studies of forced relocation illustrate a more general principle, which has been called the *sense of spatial identity* (Fried, 1963). This refers to the fact that spatial conceptions serve to organize and make meaningful behavior. They provide a vantage point for locating the self in relation to others and for meaningfully organizing experiences in the environment. Some contend (Fried, 1963) that working-class families are more likely to have a strong sense of spatial identity than middle-class families. Indeed, there appears to be a relation between status and expressions of grief at relocation; the lower the status, the greater the grief. Why might this be so? Analysis of class differences in extended-family contacts indicates that working-class families are more tightly

---

*Reprinted with permission from L. Shannon, *Labor Mobility and Population in Agriculture*. Ames, Iowa: Iowa State University Press, 1961, p. 130.

enmeshed in a large family network than are middle-class families. The former visit each other more often, consult one another, lean on each other for help, and are generally more central figures than the latter. This working-class value emphasis on relationships rather than individual achievement and autonomy underscores the importance of the locality in which friends and family are encountered.

As one woman in the West End relocation study, Mrs. Figella, put it: "It's a wonderful place, the people are friendly" (Fried and Gleicher, 1961; Fried 1963). Their relocation did not produce any economic hardships; in fact, they were able to buy a house. While expressing satisfaction with the physical arrangements, the Figellas were unhappy about the social consequences. Their sense of isolation was summed up by Mr. Figella thusly: "I come home from work and that's it. I just plant myself in the house" (Fried, 1963).

Not all members of the West End study exhibited this sense of loss, however. The intensity of pre-relocation feelings of spatial identification were a good predictor of post-relocation reactions. For the Guilianos, life in the West End never held the charms that the Figellas perceived. "For me, it is too congested. I never did care for it . . . too many barrooms, on every corner, too many families in one building. . . . The sidewalks are too narrow and the kids can't play outside" (Fried, 1963, p. 163). Here, adjustment to relocation was good; the Guilianos, in fact, reported improvement in their marital relationship since Mr. Guiliano was now at home more. In an analysis of these case studies, the researchers point out that the Guilianos were upwardly mobile. They perceived themselves as moving up and out of the lower class. These aspirations made discontinuities in their life palatable if such changes appeared to foster their ambitions for a better life.

For still other families studied, despite strong commitments to the neighborhood, adjustment to a new environment proceeded remarkably smoothly. These families showed coping techniques that facilitated their adaptation to environmental change. In some families, the marital relationship was strengthened as husband and wife drew closer together. As one woman put it: "Home is where you hang your hat; it's up to you to make the adjustments" (Fried, 1963). Other families tried to minimize the impact of relocation by remaining as physically close to the old area as possible or moving in among other relatives.

What factors dispose one family to severe stress and another to successful adaptation? Unfortunately, we do not have definite answers. The strength of pre-relocation spatial identification, the robustness of the marital relationship, the number of new options available, have been cited as factors, but they do not tell the whole story.

The "forced" aspect of relocation plays a large part in determining grief reactions. Quite simply, those who move do not wish to do so, and thus have no reason to justify the move. Satisfaction with a physical setting has a lot to do with one's feelings of ownership, control, and volition. It appears that feelings of control are basic to a sense of ego mastery and provide a rock-bottom source of satisfaction. Furthermore, when decisions are made voluntarily, later information or events that conflict can be more easily ignored or reinterpreted to justify the original decision. For example, couples may do a lot of soul-searching and hand-wringing before deciding to purchase a particular automobile. Should they get the compact to save gas or the station wagon for convenience? Good reasons exist for both purchases, but only one is possible, and so the couple finally takes the plunge and buys the compact. Once the decision is made, discrepant or dissonant information tends to be ignored. The couple may spend some time congratulating themselves on having done the right thing, pointing out the deficiencies of the station wagons they pass. In this way they attempt to bolster their decision with supporting evidence and new arguments. This post-decision reaction has been termed "cognitive dissonance" (Festinger, 1962). It is important to note that the phenomenon is at work only when decisions have a voluntary aspect; its function is to help us live with our choices. Forced relocation fails to mobilize cognitive dissonance in the family; the decision is out of their hands, and they have no reason to live with it.

Mobility as Desired Change

Most changes of residence are voluntary. Approximately 20 percent of the population moves each year. While some moves are related to economic conditions, job transfer or the prospect of a new job, most stem from housing-related factors. Morris and Winter (1978) have distinguished between *residential mobility* (changing residence within a local area) and *migration* (intercommunity, intermetropolitan, or long-distance moving). This distinction is difficult to maintain in practice, however. A family may move to a different community, yet stay within the same school district and consider the change a local one. Because of this, we will use both mobility and migration interchangeably to refer to changes in the housing environment of the family.

Voluntary mobility may come about for a variety of reasons. The previous discussion on sources of residential satisfaction indicated that space deficits and safety deficits were two important reasons. Increases in family size, especially with the birth of the first child, may put a pinch on available space. Decreases in family size, when children are grown and have left home, may make the dwelling seem "too large." Thus, changes in family composition are related to space deficits which, in turn, form the basis for much voluntary mobility.

Childless couples are obviously less affected by changes in family composition. Yet their mobility rates are no lower than those of families with children and in some studies are higher (Goodman, 1974). Perhaps childless couples are less subject to the constraints that often tie families to one place (quality of school system, children's attachments to neighborhood friends). Childless couples may view a house as a sound investment in inflationary times and purchase a much larger house than space needs alone would justify. Despite the growing numbers of childless families and single-parent families, relatively little research on residential mobility has focussed on them.

Moving to the Suburbs

Families not only move because of specific dissatisfactions with where they are, but also because of the appeal of other places. Primary among such places have been suburbs. A wave of migration to suburbia has characterized much mobility during the last twenty years. The phenomenon of suburbia gave rise to largely negative views of its life style. Suburbia has been attacked as providing a boring, monotonous life with conformity the rule and keeping up with the Joneses the maxim. With the dawn men are seen leaving the nests in droves for long, exhausting commutes, while their families remain behind with only gossip and endless cups of coffee to fill the days. Thus, much as the slum dwelling has been implicated as the cause of crime and morbidity, so, too has suburbia been indicted as the source of psychological malaise.

How accurate is this picture? Not very. When studies of family moves from city to suburb are examined closely, they reveal few of the negative effects advanced by the suburbia myth (Berger, 1960; Gans, 1963; Wilmott and Young, 1960). In fact, for most people, the changes associated with the move to suburbia are positive. Moreover, among all the changes that do occur, few are causally connected to the suburbia move per se, but stem from factors prompting that move in the first place.

First of all, the extent of changes wrought in families by the move to suburbia has often been exaggerated. As one respondent expressed it: "I don't know how a new house changes your life. You have a pattern you go by and that stays the same no matter where you live" (Gans, 1963, p. 185). By and large, among those families studied, most experienced continuity rather than change in life style.

Of those changes reported by new suburban residents, most were positive; for example, satisfaction in home ownership, increased living space, better social life, more organizational participation.

All was not rosy, however. Among those negative changes reported was an increase in financial problems. That new house and increased living space had a hefty mortgage attached to it. Moreover, in new suburbs with growing families tax pressure to finance new schools and public services began to mount. Young families already strapped might easily be overwhelmed under such conditions. And a minority of new suburbanites experienced social isolation and adaptation problems. This minority consisted of two disparate groups, upper-middle class cosmopolites who missed the cultural opportunities of the city and the company of similar others, and working-class families, particularly wives who perceived their new middle-class milieu as different and alien.

Finally, another group of discontents had potential members within almost every family. The adolescent often perceived suburbia, with its absence of public transportation, cultural facilities, and just plain spaces to "hang out" as nowhere. The new community, already burdened with school and public service taxes was unreceptive to the creation of teenage facilities which, as some elders undoubtedly thought, would only fall victim to vandalism eventually. In most middle-class suburbs, however, the problem of teenage dissatisfaction was minimized by emphasis on school achievement and involvement in school activities.

Responses to Migrants

Thus far, we have considered the motivations of those who move. What are the responses of those into whose midst the new resident comes? One type of residential mobility has been the migration of people into larger American cities. Ethnic minorities who have been traditionally persecuted—southern blacks, Puerto Ricans, Mexican-Americans, native Americans, and rural white "hillbillies"—have made up much of this wave. In addition, less visible white farm-to-city migration of midwesterners has been taking place. It is well known that ethnic migrants to large cities such as Chicago meet with residential, economic, and social discrimination. They do not disperse throughout the city, but are concentrated in ghettos. Indeed, some inner cities, such as Chicago, are organized around relatively homogeneous, identifiable ethnic communities highly resistant to "invasion" by outsiders. By contrast, the nonethnic farm migrant from the Midwest meets with no discrimination and is more readily dispersible in the city where he or she can afford to live and work. However, precisely because of the banding of ethnic groups, nonethnic new residents appear to feel more lonely and isolated from their former network of family and friends (Choldin, 1965).

SUMMARY

In this chapter we have examined family transactions with their spatial environment from two complementary perspectives. First, the impact of housing conditions on families was assessed. Determining the adverse effects of crowding and other dimensions of substandard housing was seen to be complex and to involve an understanding of family characteristics. It was suggested that dimensions of the spatial environment, such as number of rooms, design, and proximity to other families, be related to dimensions of the family, such as size, stage of life cycle, type of communication pattern, and type of value orientation. To illustrate this approach, we looked at the relation between spatial propinquity of families (spatial-environment dimension) and interfamily contacts (family dimensions) as an example of such "impact" research.

The second perspective emphasized the family's active processes of perceiving, valuing, deciding, and acting on the spatial environment in order to understand why families may be dissatisfied with their housing, alter their residential environments, move, or alter family composition to "fit" existing housing. A conceptual scheme developed by Morris and Winter (1975) was presented, linking cultural and family values to family decision-making and environmental constraints with three kinds of outcomes predicted: residential mobility, residential adaptation, or family adaptation. If residential mobility does occur, then family adjustment to a new spatial environment must take place. Voluntary control over changes in the spatial environment, it was argued, is important in determining the meaning attached to such changes.

REFERENCES

Bell, W. Social choice, life styles and suburban residence. In W. Dorbriner, ed., *The Suburban Community*. New York: Putnam, 1958.

Berger, B. M. *Working Class Suburb*. Berkeley: University of California Press, 1960.

Blood, R., and Wolfe, D. *Husbands and Wives: The Dynamics of Married Living*. New York: Free Press, 1960.

Brolin, B. C., and Zeisel, J. Mass housing: Social research and design. *Architectural Forum*, July-August 1968, pp. 66-70.

Burchinal, L. G., and Bauder, W. W. Adjustments to the new institutional environment. In *Family Mobility in Our Dynamic Society*. Ames, Iowa: Iowa University Press, 1965.

Calhoun, J. A. "Behavioral sink." In Eugene Bliss, ed., *Roots of Behavior*. New York: Harper and Row, 1962. (a)

————. Population density and social pathology. *Scientific American* 206 (1962): 139-146. (b)

Campbell, A., Converse, P. E., and Rodgers, W. L. *The Quality of American Life: Perceptions, Evaluations and Satisfactions*. New York: Russell Sage Foundation, 1976.

Chandler, M. J., Koch, D., and Paget, K. Developmental changes in the response of children to conditions of crowding and congestion. In H. McGurk, ed., *Ecological Factors in Human Development*. New York: North Holland, 1977.

Choldin, H. The response to migrants of the receiving community. In *Family Mobility in Our Dynamic Society*. Ames, Iowa: Iowa University Press, 1965.

Christian, J. The pathology of overpopulation. *Military Medicine* 128 (1963): 571-603.

Christian, J., and Davis, D. Social and endocrine factors are integrated in the regulation of growth of mammalian populations. *Science* 146 (1964): 1550-1560.

Cohen, S., Glass, D. C., and Singer, J. E. Apartment noise, auditory discrimination and reading ability in children. *Journal of Experimental Social Psychology* 9 (1973): 407-422.

Dennis, W., and Najarian, P. Infant development under environmental handicap. *Psychological Monographs* 71 (1957), no. 436.

Dubos, R. *Man Adapting*. New Haven: Yale University Press, 1965.

Fabun, D. *Dimensions of Change*. Beverly Hills, Calif.: Glencoe Press, 1971.

Festinger, L. *A Theory of Cognitive Dissonance*. Palo Alto: Stanford University Press, 1962.

Festinger, L., Schacter, S., and Back, K. *Social Pressures in Informal Groups: A Study of Human Factors in Housing*. New York: Harper and Row, 1950.

Freedman, J. L. *Crowding and Behavior*. San Francisco: W. H. Freeman, 1975.

Fried, M. Grieving for a lost home. In L. Duhl, ed., *The Urban Condition*. New York: Basic Books, 1963.

Fried, M., and Gleicher, P. Some sources of residential satisfaction in an urban slum. *Journal of American Institute of Planners* 27 (1961): 305-315.

Gans, H. Effects of the move from city to suburb. In L. Duhl, ed., *The Urban Condition*. New York: Basic Books, 1963.

Goldstein, S. *Patterns of Mobility, 1919-1950, the Norristown Study*. Philadelphia: University of Pennsylvania Press, 1958.

Goodman, J. Local residential mobility and family housing adjustments. In J. N. Morgan, ed., *Five Thousand American Families—Patterns of Economic Progress*. Vol. 2. Ann Arbor: Institute for Social Research, University of Michigan, 1974.

Greenfield, R., and Lewis, J. F. An alternative to a density function definition of overcrowding. In J. Pynoos, R. Schafer, and C. Hartman, eds., *Housing Urban America*. Chicago: Aldine, 1973.

Gutman, R. Population mobility in the American middle class. In L. Duhl, ed., *The Urban Condition*. New York: Basic Books, 1963.

Hartman, C. Social values and housing orientations. *Journal of Social Issues* 19 (1963): 113-131.

Hess, R. D., and Handel, G. *Family Worlds: A Psychosocial Approach to Family Life*. Chicago: University of Chicago Press, 1974.

Inman, M., and Melson, G. F. Family social environment and activity spaces in married student apartments. *Housing Educators Journal*, Proceedings of 1977 Annual Conference, pp. 63-69.

Janis, I., and Mann, L. *Decision-Making*. New York: The Free Press, 1977.

Lander, B. *Towards an Understanding of Juvenile Delinquency*. New York: Columbia University Press, 1954.

Lansing, J. B., Marans, R. W., and Zehner, R. B. *Planned Residential Environments*. Ann Arbor: Institute for Social Research, University of Michigan, 1970.

Lawton, M. P. Public behavior of older people in congregate housing. Proceedings of the Second Annual Conference of the Environmental Design Research Association, Pittsburgh, 1970.

————. *Planning and Managing Housing for the Elderly*. New York: Wiley, 1975.

McCarthy, D., and Saegerts, S. Residential density, social overload, and social withdrawal. *Human Ecology* 6 (1978): 253-272.

Melson, G. F. The home as a sex-typed environment: Implications for marital conflict. Paper presented to the National Council on Family Relations, 1976.

Melson, G. F., Inman, M., and Kemp, P. Perceived environmental stress and family functioning in married student families. In S. Weidemann and J. Anderson, eds., *Priorities for Environmental Design Research*. EDRA 8, 1978, pp. 175-181.

Mitchell, R. E. Some social implications of high density housing. *American Sociological Review* 36 (1971): 18-29.

Morris, E. W., and Winter, M. A theory of family housing adjustment. *Journal of Marriage and the Family* 27 (1975): 79-88.

————. *Housing, Family and Society*. New York: Wiley, 1978.

Mussen, P. H., Conger, T. T., and Kagan, J. *Child Development and Personality*, 4th edition. New York: Harper and Row, 1974.

Newman, O. *Defensible Space: Crime Prevention Through Urban Design*. New York: Macmillan, 1972.

Rutter M., and Madge, N. *Cycles of Disadvantage*. London: Heinemann, 1976.

Shannon, L. Occupational and residential adjustment of rural migrants. In *Labor Mobility and Population in Agriculture*. Ames, Iowa: Iowa State University Press, 1961.

Spitz, R. A., and Wolfe, J. M. Anaclitic depression: An inquiry into the genesis of psychiatric conditions in early childhood, II. In A. Freud et al., eds., *The Psychoanalytic Study of the Child*. Vol. II. New York: International University Press, 1946.

Stokols, D. The experience of crowding in primary and secondary environments. *Environment and Behavior* 8 (1976): 49-86.

Wachs, T. D., Uzgiris, I. C., and Hunt, J. M. Cognitive development in infants of different age levels and from different environmental backgrounds: An exploratory investigation. *Merrill-Palmer Quarterly* 17 (1971): 283-317.

Wattenberg, B. T. *The Real America.* New York: Capricorn Books, 1976.

Whyte, H. W. *The Organization Man.* New York: Simon and Schuster, 1956.

Wilmott, P., and Young, M. *Family and Class in a London Suburb.* New York: Humanities Press, 1960.

Wilner, D. M., Walkley, R. P., Pinkerton, T., and Tayback, M. *The Housing Environment and Family Life: A Longitudinal Study of the Effects of Housing on Morbidity and Mental Health.* Baltimore: Johns Hopkins Press, 1962.

Wilner, D. M., and Walkley, R. P. Effects of housing on health and performance. In L. Duhl, ed., *The Urban Condition.* New York: Basic Books, 1963.

Yancey, W. L. Architecture, interaction, and social control. *Environment and Behavior*, March 1971, pp. 3-21.

Yockey, K. M. Space norms and housing satisfaction in low income families. *Housing Educators Journal* 3 (1976): 2-10.

Change and
Stability in
Family Ecosystems

12

Families pull up stakes and move, separate and divorce, change jobs, have children, rethink their lives and strike off in new directions, lose their feelings of efficacy and sink into depression. Family life may be viewed as the sum of many changes, some self-initiated, some imposed from without. Within the family unit, individuals change constantly in the push and pull of intimate interaction.

Yet families also cling to what is known, tried and true. They transmit the values of their culture to their children, pass on many of the same attitudes, form links of continuity with contemporaries and with previous generations. Parents are concerned with their responsibility as shapers of the next generation. Within the family, unwritten rules of behavior in the form of roles structure interaction to make it predictable.

Change and stability are dual themes of family-environment transactions. This chapter presents a framework within which these twin pillars may be understood. In short, we will argue that optimal levels of stimulation are sought by the family. These adaptation levels guide both the search for change and the quest for stability. Families attempt to "fine tune" their environment to such adaptation levels. Because of both environmental pressures and family interaction demands, such fine tuning is imperfect and subject to breakdown. The concept of stress is introduced to illustrate such dysfunction in family-environment adaptation and is discussed more fully in Chapter 13.

STABILITY: THE CONCEPT OF ADAPTATION

Chapter 2 spoke of the family, and the individual within the family, in transaction with the environment as *adapting to its environments*. By adaptation is meant "the process of establishing and maintaining a relatively stable reciprocal relationship with the environment" (Brody, 1969). Such a reciprocal relationship implies a "fit" between the functioning of the system—be it individual or family unit—and the functioning of the environment of which the system is a part.

"Fit" means that the *demands* of a system are met by adequate *supplies* of resources from the environment, or it may mean that environmental demands are satisfied through system supplies. In this second case, we speak of *environmental press* exerted upon a system.

System Demands

What are system demands? The *needs* of an individual family member might be considered system demands upon his or her family environment. Young children have obvious needs for physical care, adequate nutrition, cuddling, and security. In addition, they have less obvious needs to test and challenge their environment, to define themselves as separate human beings, and to enhance their self-esteem.

Personality characteristics also may be considered individual system demands. Differences in temperament and style place requirements on interacting others to respond appropriately, to "match" rather than "mismatch" tempos. We may conceive of personalities as also differing in their *range and intensity of demand characteristics*. What others perceive as an easy-going personality is one in which system demands in terms of personality characteristics are not high, while those that exist are relatively easy to meet. By contrast, the "difficult" personality may be thought of as one with strong demands, for example, an unusually high need for companionship or novelty or one with contradictory demands such as an active, exploratory style together with high sensitivity to change. Individual differences in *values* may be thought of in this context as a system demand. Based on values, individuals develop expectations concerning the behavior of others and formulate plans to reach goals. For example, if one values personal freedom above all else, this will lead to expectations that others not interfere and to decisions which maximize autonomy.

Spacing as a preferred pattern of stimulation regulation also varies in individuals. It, too, constitutes an individual system demand. A person who needs to be given plenty of psychological and physical room may be said to "demand" these characteristics of his or her environment.

When one shifts perspective to view the family as the system in its environmental surroundings, demands may also be identified. If a family system is to persist, it demands a certain minimal level of communication, integration, solidarity, flexibility, and congruence of images from its members. A particular mix of change and constancy is needed. The need to maintain and enhance self-esteem may be considered a basic system demand for both the individual and the family system.

Family members must feel some identification with the family as a group. They must have some sense of emotional closeness, even if it is laden with conflict. There must be some agreement between individual and family values and between those values and the means chosen to realize them. Of course, families vary enormously in the degree to which they exhibit organization, cohesiveness, or identification. However, it is likely that all family systems share these characteristics to some degree.

For families with children, a major family function is *nurturant socialization*, a term used by Reiss (1965) to indicate the process of transmitting culture to the young while fulfilling their emotional and physical needs. Thus, a basic system demand for most families is an environmental context that makes nurturant socialization possible.

Identifying family system demands is always more complex than doing so on the individual-system level, since every family consists of an often unstable, shifting web of individual systems. Moving in and out of the nuclear family group are kin connections and surrogate family members, those whose ties sometimes seem thicker than blood.

Complicating matters further, all systems have a rhythm of change and development. Within families, individuals often change at uneven rates. Periods of high demand may coincide, overloading the family system with needs even the most beneficent environment cannot meet. Often, too, individual systems make contradictory demands on each other. The adolescent daughter needs to test and wants reassurance about her own attractiveness. A wife caught up in new-found independence and work success collides with her over-the-hill executive husband yearning to abandon the rat race for quiet domesticity. Such coincidences of clashing demands make system-environment fit or adaptation difficult.

Environmental Demands

Just as individual and family systems may be thought of in terms of sets of demands upon surrounding environments, these environments themselves place certain demands upon both individual and family unit.

First, environments may be understood as settings with rules for appropriate behavior. So environments demand that those entering them have learned how to act "correctly" and insist that they conform to their expectations. The classroom environment, for example, includes rules about appropriate language, dress, seating, and deference to authority. Of course, such environment demands are not static. Keeping to the classroom example, many innovations in education, such as open classrooms and alternative schools, arose because environmental demands were not fitting the needs of many participants. Interestingly, however, once such innovations become going concerns, they develop their own set of fairly rigid rules. One alternative school's unwritten dress code might read, "NO ties or jackets allowed." A particular work environment, such as an office, may demand promptness, organization, delegation of authority, and impersonal interactions from those who function in it.

The level and type of stimulation in an environment constitutes a set of demand characteristics. Environments with high levels of stimulation require abilities to process stimulation quite different from less stimulating environments. Environments whose level of stimulation changes rapidly demand greater flexibility than relatively unchanging surroundings. Environments that contain a great deal of contradictory, ambiguous information demand information-processing skills that go untested in a simpler setting.

System Supplies

Those resources used to meet environmental demands may be called system supplies. When the family is viewed as the environment within which the individual system functions, system supplies may be considered as any characteristics of the individual that have the potential of facilitating his or her functioning in that environment. The individual's capacity for responsiveness to others, for organizing and making a meaningful understanding of the world, and for adapting to changes in others are important individual system supplies of particular relevance to the family environment. The constitutional capacities of the individual are another set of system supplies. The robust, outgoing, assertive, and flexible personality appears, in a culture that values these traits, to be better supplied to deal with environmental demands than a more passive, irritable, and rigid personality.

For example, in Chapter 8 we characterized the malnourished infant as apathetic, underweight, and physically unappealing. Such a baby lacks in full measure the ample supplies of social responsiveness and effective distress signals which ensure that a caretaker will come near and will attend to the infant's needs. Thus, research indicates that malnourished infants are apt to have increasingly unresponsive caretakers.

Perceiving, spacing, deciding, and valuing are means by which environmental demands and system supplies, system demands and environmental supplies are reconciled. This mutual adaptation is represented schematically in Figure 12.1.

Earlier chapters have provided numerous examples of such adaptation. Family members living in polluted settings come to perceive brown-gray as the sky's normal color. Environmental

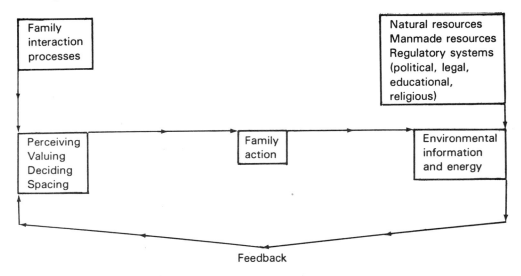

Figure 12.1. Schematic representation of family-environment adaptation.

conditions of high air-pollution, whose roots may be traced to the resource-use policies of regulatory systems, affect family members' abilities to extract and transform environmental energy. Specifically, here both perceiving and valuing have been affected. Long exposure to polluted air may result in perceptual and value changes.

Family extraction and use of nutritional energy may be viewed within the same framework. The provision of nutrient energy to the family is constrained by food type and availability, which in turn depends on what family members, usually the mother, perceive as suitable and value as desirable. These active processes are themselves tied to the family's nutrient resource base. In such a way, the extraction of nutrients can be viewed as family-environment interdependence and adaptation.

Family organization of the spatial environment provides another example. Family members have spatial needs, values, and perceptions that have been discussed under the concepts "personal space," "territoriality," and "privacy." When the family is viewed as a unit, the home is seen to carry special significance as the spatial incarnation of family identity. These concepts indicate that the family attempts to fashion its spatial environment in the light of its interaction processes. At the same time, the spatial environment itself—and we have considered crowding and functional distance from other families as examples—exerts an influence on family behavior. Just as exposure to air pollution may result in adaptational changes, so may living in high- or low-density environments. Rural migrants to an urban center have been found to perceive higher noise and pollution levels than migrants from other cities (Wohlwill and Kohn, 1973). Cultural differences in personal space and preference for contact with others may be partially rooted in such differences of adaptation level. Long-time urban dwellers become accustomed to densities perceived as crowded by their country cousins.

Such differences in adaptation level as a function of experiencing differences in environmental conditions come about through a psychological process called *habituation*. Habituation refers to *a decrement in responding upon repeated presentations of a stimulus*. For example, if a light flashed on in front of you, you would undoubtedly sit up and take notice. Gradually, if the light appeared repeatedly and at regular intervals, you would come to expect its occurrence, cease to take as much notice of it, and in effect, become *habituated* to it. The light changes from a distinctive stimulus to a relatively neutral one.

Environments may also be characterized in terms of their overall level of stimulation. Family members differ as individuals and as groups in preferred level and pace of stimulation. They will act *on* the environment in the attempt to regulate stimulation at the desired pace. At the same time, environmental conditions, many of which are out of family control, will exert influence on the family and stimulate change within it to increased tolerance or positive desire for a greater (or lower) stimulation level.

Changes within individuals prompt reciprocal changes in other family members and overall shifts in the family system as a whole. Families differ in presenting a relatively fluid or rigid environment to which members must adapt. A rigid environment implies a family in which conformity and unbending rules override individual developmental change, while a fluid environment is more accepting of change and ambiguity. Just as the family unit is affected by its ecological setting, so are individual family members affected by the micro-ecology of their family group. In both cases the unit (family or individual) is in an adaptive relationship to its environmental surround.

These examples illustrate several important characteristics of family adaptation.

Interdependence

Change in the family prompts attempts to change environmental conditions; change in the environment prompts similar family change. Change in the individual demands changes in other family members. We have seen this principle illustrated in earlier chapters. Families attempt to change their spatial environment by moving or modifying it. A major predictor of such changes is change in family composition brought about through additions to the family (births) or decreases (deaths, divorce, children moving out). These family changes bring about a discrepancy or disequilibrium in family-environment adaptation and lead to attempts to make appropriate environmental changes to restore equilibrium.

When nutrient energy is considered, the same interdependence obtains. Demographic changes in the family such as later marriage, increased maternal employment outside the home, and larger percentage of singles are associated with changes in food habits. People are eating less at home and more at fast-food restaurants. The role of the mother as "gatekeeper" of the nutritional status of her family may be diminishing. The symbolic significance of meal times may have changed.

Considering environmental changes, anthropological accounts show how changes in food supply are related to changes in social organization. Groups whose economy is pastoral, based on grazing animals on dry grassy lands, are likely to be independent roamers with strong clan loyalties. By contrast, the farmer, tied to a fixed land area, is under community control and social pressure. While individuals differ widely, as a group, pastoral people have been found to be more open emotionally, more direct, and more positively tied to their social unit than farming groups (Goldschmidt, 1974).

Closer to home, we have seen how food quality and availability affect family members' abilities to develop as individuals and to relate to one another. Poorly nourished children are at risk for both proper intellectual and social development. More than that, the family as an interdependent, intimate group is affected. Its ability to act on the environment effectively is impaired. Thus, changes in family processes affect management of nutrient energy, while changes in nutrient supply affect the organization of family life.

Consumer behavior provides another example of interdependence, this time between family interaction-processes and environmental information. Changes in the family, such as increased education and income, equip its members to consume different, perhaps better products, to process more information about products and in general to engage in more intelligent consumer behavior. By "intelligent" is meant behavior that facilitates the reaching of family goals. In turn, changes in the environment of consumer products and availability prompt changes in the family. Level of information, the character of advertising, the appearance of new products and disappearance of old ones, changes in governmental regulations, all cause adjustments in family consumer behavior. Again, many of these consumer product changes come about through the operation of forces—political, legal, economic—largely outside the influence of the family.

The spatial environment, the extraction of nutrient energy, consumer behavior—in each instance, interdependence is illustrated by the mutual adjustments that change in either family or environmental conditions bring about. In each case, environmental conditions are shown to be influenced by a nested series of systems that play a role largely independent of the family.

When the level of analysis is shifted so that the family is now the "larger" environment and the individual the unit, the principle of interdependence is equally apparent.

Parent-child relations are a good illustration of this. It has long been recognized that parents have enormous impact on their children's development. The kind of discipline parents use, the quality of their attention toward the child, their stimulation of the child's maturing cognitive capacities, indeed, almost every aspect of their behavior affects the pathways of the child's later development (Clarke-Stewart, 1977).

Increasingly, however, researchers have come to appreciate the degree to which children affect their own development. They now recognize that children determine parental behavior as parents determine children's. From the beginning, parents behave differently toward children based on child characteristics such as sex, "cuddliness," and birth order. Furthermore, as the parent cares for the infant, the degree to which the infant can respond to parental efforts will determine whether the parent is becoming closely attached to the child, taking increasing pleasure in his or her company, or whether frustration and feelings of incompetence are building. Infants and children differ greatly in their "readability," that is, how easily adult observers can interpret the inarticulate child's state. Children also differ from the outset in "state manipulability," the ease with which they respond to parental efforts to soothe or stimulate them. The colicky baby, for example, suffers from a nearly complete breakdown in state manipulability (Bell, 1977). Nothing parents do seems to alleviate the infant's suffering. The poor success such parents feel takes a severe toll on their subsequent ability to behave effectively.

Many other characteristics of the child have an impact on the parents. Children differ greatly in their responsiveness to others, their assertiveness, and their competence. Bell and Harper (1977) have suggested that parents have upper and lower levels of tolerance for various child behaviors. Parental actions are determined by the kinds of behaviors shown by the child. For example, a very quiet, passive, and dependent child exceeds parental lower limits for assertiveness and parents will try to stimulate and encourage the child's activity. The extremely active, aggressive child may exceed parental upper limits, and parents will try to tone down this child, perhaps by discipline or other restrictions. The central theme is that parental behavior is keyed to that of the child.

Interdependence means mutual influence among family members, but it does not necessarily imply the degree of influence is always distributed in a fifty-fifty fashion. After all, parents generally have explicit goals for their children, and they try to engineer their actions so that these goals can be reached. The adult is much more mature than the child. Within an overall reciprocal framework, parents may, at times, exert relatively more control over their children. At other times, children may be calling the shots. Even when the child is very immature, the amount of child control uncovered by research is surprising. The infant or young child starts approximately 50 percent of all parent-child interactions (Bell, 1971).

Developmental change implies constant mutual adjustment and influence within the family. As children mature, they make new demands on parental conceptions of them. Historical changes and social currents, such as the women's movement, send shock waves through the family in the form of changes in adult self-definition. Developmental crises are not the privilege of adolescence, but may continue throughout adulthood. Hence, individual change on the part of *all* family members demands reciprocal changes.

The Adaptation Level

What underlies this process of mutual change and adjustment? One concept that helps explain what has been termed "person-environment fit" is that of that *adaptation level*. This concept was developed by Helson (1964) and first applied to studies of stimulus perception. Consider, for example, that you are blindfolded and an experimenter touches your hand with different materials varying in heat from ice to fire. You are asked to report your sensations. More than that, you are asked to do so *relatively*, by ranking each item from hottest to coldest and by saying how much hotter or colder each is from the other. Participants in such an experiment soon discover that their judgments are affected and organized by the temperature that seems to them to be "neutral," that is, neither perceptibly hot nor cold. Then materials which are felt to be progressively above this neutral point are perceived as hot and those below as cold. Such a neutral point is called an "adaptation level" (AL). Whether temperature or any other environmental characteristic is considered, it is evident that everyone does not have the same AL. For some people the soup is nice and hot; for others, it is lukewarm.

A second characteristic of the AL is its responsiveness to change. We may say that the AL is both relatively enduring and changing. It is relatively enduring in that it reflects early experience, constitutional predispositions, and habits. It acts as a goal, stimulating behavior, but the AL is not static. Environmental conditions change; for example, changing to a hotter climate may lead to a slight upward shifting of the AL so that formerly "warm" weather is now perceived as neutral. Developmental changes in the individual, particularly changes in receptor capacities with aging, may bring about changes in AL largely independent of environmental conditions.

The AL is also not static because individuals operate in diverse situations varying in stimulus level. Particularly in modern industrialized societies, people are accustomed to moving in and out of widely different contexts. The urban worker may wake in the morning, ride a packed subway, work in an office with a small group, eat lunch alone, drop in later at a party, jog in a nearly deserted park. Such a day is composed of many worlds, each differing in "appropriate" stimulation level. A subway car with fifty people seems almost empty, but the same fifty people on the jogging path make for an intolerable crowd. The convivial noise level of the party is impossible distraction at the office. Each behavior setting has rules, many unwritten, about appropriate behavior and appropriate stimulation. Learning to operate in differing behavior settings implies that differing adaptation levels are also learned, each felt to be appropriate to its setting.

This relatively enduring, yet also changing, AL may be likened to the setting on a thermostat. When the temperature falls below or above the setting, the heating or cooling mechanism is activated. Similarly, when environmental conditions depart from a person's AL, this prompts behavioral changes designed to restore the old balance. Such changes may involve actions on the environment, changes of the AL itself, or both.

The individual may be thought to have an AL, or optimal level for stimulation (Wohlwill, 1974), which regulates the extracting and processing of environmental information and energy. So, too, the family as both a collection of individuals and as a unit formed from them with its own character, may be conceived of having an AL, or more properly, a number of them for different behavior settings. The concepts of family perceptual style, family theme, family decision-making style, spatial organization of the family home, all share a common reference to a level, type, organization, and pace of environmental stimulation to which the family is adapted. Because the family has both individual and group characteristics, ALs of individual family members and the family AL are likely to differ. A dynamic tension between such ALs exists, with the achievement of coherence or coexistence among them one of the challenges of family interaction.

Enhancing the Self

The Adaptation Level concept may be thought of as an individual or family characteristic which, at the same time, depends upon environmental conditions and the individual's or family's history of environmental transactions. This dual nature of adaptation is most important. It is not only a matter of adapting *to* environmental conditions, but just as much a matter of doing so while maintaining and enhancing one's self-image. The AL concept calls attention to the fact that people differ in the rate, level, and kind of environmental stimulation they seek and avoid. It is likely, however, that the need to maintain internal integrity in the face of environmental demands is universal.

Adaptation as a Value-Free Concept

The mutual interdependence of family and environment, and the operation of the AL as a mechanism of adaptation, should not lead to the mistaken impression that adaptation is "good." The question of values is a separate one. Families can adapt to conditions that are actually physiologically harmful. It is an unfortunate truth that people often prefer what is bad for them. Moreover, families may adapt to adverse environmental conditions by developing destructive, abusive interaction patterns. An individual may adapt to the demands of his or her family at the cost of personal development, stunting potential growth in the name of stability. Such patterns achieve their own kind of equilibrium and may be extremely resistant to change. Hence, adaptation is value-free and does not necessarily denote a "successful" individual or family.

Adaptation as Distinct From Adjustment

Adaptation may be distinguished from *adjustment*. Adjustment may be defined as behavior change that modifies stimulus conditions. Wohlwill (1974) has used the temperature example to illustrate the distinction between the two concepts. If an American visiting Britain in the winter feels uncomfortable in the lower indoor temperatures and so puts on an extra sweater, we may say that he has made an *adjustive* response. But if, after a prolonged stay in England, he no longer experiences indoor temperatures as uncomfortable, we may say he has become adapted to them.

Thus, adjustment implies no change in how the environment is perceived, while adaptation involves a perceptual shift. Adjustment is often a response to short-term changes, while adaptation carries long-range implications.

The Limits of Adaptation

A thermostat may be set to a desired temperature; then discrepancies between actual and desired environmental conditions are sensed automatically and immediately the equilibrium is restored. Not so with family-environment or individual-family interdependence. It is most appropriate to think of the thermostat analogy as an *ideal* or theoretically perfect regulatory system, one that human families never achieve.

Some sources of imperfection lie primarily within the family. A thermostat, if working properly, is a fail-safe environmental sensor. As earlier chapters on perceiving demonstrated, family members wear the glasses (and sometimes blinders) of perceptual styles, which they elaborate into family themes. Thus, environmental change is selectively processed. Some environmental information is ignored, other information given exaggerated emphasis. Some families take account of the consequences of previous actions (in other words, use feedback) while others have a more restricted time focus. Similarly, families vary in their receptivity to information about changes in individual members. Some impose their images or conceptions of each other regardless of contradictory information, while more "open" families periodically reevaluate each other as changed beings.

Such differences form part of an *adaptational style* (Murphy and Moriarty, 1976). In addition to variations in information processing, its components include constitutional predisposition for feedback from previous efforts at adaptation.

Constitutional predisposition. Chapter 4 documented differences in early temperament and perceptual style, which interact with environmental experiences. From the beginning, temperament affects one's tolerance for stimulation and, hence, adaptation level. Moreover, some temperaments, it has been found, have particular difficulty in adapting to changing environmental conditions. For example, the highly active baby who is at the same time extremely sensitive to stimulation will experience a "push-pull" conflict in adapting to its environment (Murphy and Moriarty, 1976). As mentioned earlier, some individuals are difficult for others to "read." The meaning of changes in such individuals are difficult to interpret, and hence it is unclear how to respond appropriately to them.

Past efforts at adaptation. Adaptation styles in individuals and families are affected by their history. How has the individual or family met previous challenges, the challenges of internal changes such as physical growth, situational changes such as a new teacher, larger environmental transformations such as a geographical move, unforeseen crises such as a death in the family or natural disaster? Successful weathering of such challenges builds increasing competence and confidence in future adaptational efforts. Feelings of failure breed a sense of helplessness.

The Family as a Small Group

The nature of the family as a small group is a further limit to the mutual adaptation of family and environment. Individual styles must somehow be integrated. Needs for separation and individuation must be reconciled with group needs for unity. The fact of intimate interaction over a long period means that conflict will be an inevitable accompaniment to family life. The family as an adaptor to environmental conditions is constrained by the organizational demands and tensions of family life.

These organizational demands and tensions are likely to increase with the size of the family group. Each additional family member adds to the complexity of the group and makes added conflict more likely. While some extol the virtues of the "big, happy family" (Bossard and Boll, 1956), most evidence (Schooler, 1972; Heiss, 1975) supports the view that, as the number of relationships within a family multiplies, so do the opportunities for conflicting demands, loyalties, interests, and goals. As a result, parents in large families tend to be more inflexible and controlling with their children, who in turn receive less education, make less money as adults, and are somewhat more frustrated and dissatisfied than those from smaller families.

Skills

Adaptation is further limited by family members' *skills*. In earlier chapters, education and income have repeatedly surfaced as variables affecting ability to extract and manage environmental resources, skill in information processing, decision making, consumer behavior, etc. All this evidence may be summed up in the following generalization: Education and income are important family *resources* for equipping the family to engage in adaptive, goal-directed transactions with the environment. Education in particular provides its possessor with increased information-processing skills, more cognitive categories and greater analytic abilities. Because of this, education is strongly associated with the feelings of an internal locus of control, the sense that environmental forces can be directed and modified to conform with one's goals. When values are considered, amount of education is positively correlated with values emphasizing self-actualization rather than obedience to social forces. While we have placed education and income in the category of "family characteristics," it is important to note that a family's social position is determined by many elements outside the family's control, including the social position of preceding generations. The label of "family characteristic" should not imply that educational and income levels are wholly within the family's control.

Environmental Constraints

Up to now, this discussion of the limits of family adaptation processes has centered on constraints lying within the family itself. However, limits on adaptation also exist outside the family. Environmental characteristics may make family adaptation difficult if not impossible. What we know about family processes leads to the conclusion that human limits exist for amount, range, and pace of environmental change. Humans are adapted as a species to a specific range of environmental conditions (e.g., temperature) and cannot survive outside it. Social change may proceed at a pace too rapid for even the most adept coper.

Adaptation is never a matter merely of adaptational style. It also depends on the social institutions that aid adaptive responses, on cultural incentives for certain adaptational strategies, on educational institutions that train relevant coping skills, and on social supports for families in crisis situations (Mechanic, 1974). Do families experiencing environmental upheaval when a family member suddenly dies find community support, or must they go it alone? Do long years of educational training outfit the graduate to cope with current occupational and social demands?

Are families encouraged by governmental institutions such as the welfare system to cope actively with their environment, or do they learn helplessness? The social milieu of the family can strain or support its adaptive capacities.

A family's position in society determines its access to environmental supplies. Minority-race status can act to bar advancement, putting an arbitrary ceiling on how far effort and ability will be rewarded with proper compensation. Characteristics of family members such as sex and age further determine how environmental resources will be allocated and opportunities given. The focus of much of the women's movement and activist groups of senior citizens, such as the Gray Panthers, is on ensuring that such environmental obstacles are removed.

Some environmental constraints operate selectively on certain groups, such as blacks, who are often denied equal access to resources. Others are more pervasive, affecting almost everyone. As an example of such universal environmental constraints on adaptation, let us consider in greater detail one environmental characteristic, rate of change. Popular attention to the demands of rapid environmental change on both individuals and families was stimulated by the publication in 1970 of *Future Shock* by Alvin Toffler. This bestseller described contemporary life in highly industrialized countries as beset by an ever-accelerating pace of change in the rate of economic growth of nations, technological innovation, the explosion of accumulated information, and life generally. Toffler argued that, as a result, transience has invaded our values and life styles, creating a throwaway, disposable culture with "hurry-up," easily terminated friendships, designed for people chronically on the move.

Accelerated rates of change create, in Toffler's view, mass susceptibility to a condition he calls "future shock," "the distress, both physical and psychological, that arises from an overload of the human organism's physical adaptive systems and its decision-making powers. Put more simply, "future shock is the human response to over-stimulation" (p. 326).

Future shock arises because of inherent limitations in the human ability to process new information. Sherlock Holmes must have had such limits in mind when, in response to Dr. Watson's telling him the earth went around the sun, he said that he hadn't known that and would forget it since he couldn't clutter up his mind with facts! In a classic article, "The Magical Number Seven Plus or Minus Two," Miller (1956) concluded that in the absence of any generative rules, no more than seven items of information such as digits, nonsense syllables, or things on a list could be stored in memory and recalled for use.

If the brain must work with small chunks of information, then accelerated diversity and change present more information than can possibly be retained and made available for intelligent choice. Hence, the paradoxical prediction that the greater the diversity and rate of change, the more diminished is individual freedom.

It is important to point out that Toffler does not indict change per se. It is universally recognized that change is as necessary to life as stress and adaptation. The issue here is how much and how often. What Toffler is arguing is that an optimal rate of change exists, that limits to adaptability exist, and that highly accelerated change takes both a physical and psychological toll.

The effects of this accelerated rate of change upon the family have been the subject of much debate. In an age of transience and impermanence, perhaps the family assumes new importance as the one bastion of acceptance and security, the one portable relationship. In this view, the more novel the environment, the more important the family as haven from the turbulence. Bennis and Slater, in their book *The Temporary Society* (1968) feel that the increase of temporary, transitory systems requires that personal relationships grow and break off rapidly. This social "turnover" places great burdens on family relationships to fulfill needs for acceptance, permanence, and trust.

Others argue that the family is just as vulnerable as any other institution to the ravages of change. Since new experiences, new jobs and new relationships always beckon, so, too, the family as the most important of relationships can be broken for something better just over the horizon, or around the bend.

Thus, Toffler predicts that in a society characterized by accelerated rates of change, it is increasingly unlikely that a couple can continue to "grow together," that is, to match their own rates of change and development. Since this sense of mutual growth appears to be tied into what many characterize as a successful marriage, Toffler sees serial marriage as increasingly more likely. Couples may delay marriage, first living together in a trial-marriage situation. After entering upon a formal marriage, they may terminate their union at critical junctures in their mutual development, at the start of the empty-nest period, when the children leave home, or later when one member of the couple retires from work. These junctures mean particularly radical changes for family functioning and, hence, will be pressure points stimulating new marital unions.

One might also predict that accelerated rates of technological and social change would create ambiguity and potential conflict in family functioning within any one of these predicted serial marriages. The sources of such ambiguity are many. First, family members are exposed to a bewildering barrage of messages about proper marital relations and childrearing. From experts and nonexperts, they are urged to be pals with their kids, uphold strict standards, or combine warmth and firmness in some unspecified way. It is not clear whether parents should encourage independent strivings by allowing children to make their own decisions or avoid the pitfalls of permissiveness by firmly laying down the law. In the fifties one examination of changes in child-guidance literature "fads" (Wolfenstein, 1955) indicated a shift from strict upbringing to a "fun morality" of permissiveness. A more contemporary update of that study might show attempts to correct excesses made in the name of permissiveness. The latest advice often urges the parent to be both warm *and* firm, although precisely how to communicate both qualities simultaneously is usually not specified.

The marital relationship similarly is dissected by experts. How-to books, most conspicuously on the sexual aspect of marriage, abound. Love and companionship are central but hard-to-measure functions of contemporary marriage; hence, it is very nearly impossible for the couple to gauge when they are "successful." The role of the expert is often to tell the couple which of its behaviors—for example, fighting fair—are signs of progress toward a certifiably successful relationship.

In addition to the confusion of messages about marriage and childrearing in an era of rapid change, other adverse consequences for the family exist. Social change may not (and indeed probably will not) affect all family members equally. Particularly if the wife remains at home, she may be less exposed to the impact of changing events than her husband.

Rapid change implies discontinuity between generations. Traditionally, parents could train their children to adopt behaviors likely to ensure their effective functioning as adults. This was because parents could safely predict that their children's future life as adults would not be much different from their own. In a "future-shocked" society, however, parents can no longer be sure just what behaviors, values, and skills will be most important to their children. The children must construct their own identity.

While aspects of contemporary life fit Toffler's picture of the future-shocked society, it is overdrawn as a severe challenge to family adaptive capacities. For one thing, many Americans stay put, value roots, and enjoy stable family networks and predictable community surroundings. The country is too diverse to be easily characterized with a few broad strokes.

Moreover, even in situations of rapid change, there are certain strengths within families that cushion adverse effects to some extent. Evidence of family functioning during periods of social upheaval sometimes finds the family remarkably resistant. Robert Blood (1972) tells of journeying to postwar Japan to study the disruptive effects of the war and its aftermath on Japanese family life only to drop the research because the patient appeared to be doing fine!

Because the family is the most decentralized, smallest unit of social organization, it is most resistant to change, both planned and unplanned. Moreover, since most children become parents themselves, the revolutionary ardor of the young is sure to cool, and the rebel soon becomes the conservative. Those who would "never trust anyone over thirty" have now to choose between self-distrust and reevaluation of old ideas. The cyclical nature of the family from generation to generation ensures that every swing of the pendulum will be matched eventually by a swing back. This creates a kind of long-range stability and the likelihood that family life will not differ too radically a hundred years from now (Blood, 1972). Not only does the family have built-in sources of stability in the face of rapid change, but it may be the one institution in society that can absorb and respond to changes effectively. Vincent (1966) has emphasized what he calls the *adaptive function* of the family. The family responds to changes both externally and from within. It also contributes to change in the society by socializing the young to new roles. In Vincent's view, the family is not buffeted by societal changes, but rather is the agent through which such change comes about.

THE POSITIVE NEED FOR CHANGE

A discussion centered on the family's adaptation to the environment, its equilibrium-seeking tendencies, and its susceptibility to "future shock" can lead to a mistaken view of the family as change-resistant. Yet common sense tells us that change is the stuff of life. The search for novelty can be as compelling as the retreat from overstimulation. Conflict and disequilibrium are as natural to existence as homeostasis.

How may both these truths be reconciled? At this juncture we must add another concept to that of AL, namely, *adaptation range*. Recall that the AL was described as a theoretically neutral point of stimulation. Keeping this in mind, the adaptation range may be defined as a range of stimulation both above and below the AL to which the individual (or family) is adapted. That is, the individual possesses behaviors that enable him or her to engage in goal-directed activity within this range. He or she feels positive affect when operating within this range. As stimulation increases further on either side of the adaptation range, the individual's behavioral capacities are diminished, and feelings of discomfort, frustration, and stress are likely to occur. We may think of the adaptation range as the upper and lower limits of tolerance for stimulation.

The relation between AL, adaptation range, and affect is depicted in Figure 12.2. The notion of adaptation range, then, is another way of stating that change in stimulation (but not too much) is positively valued and indeed actively sought.

How much, however, is "too much"? This is a question impossible to answer generally. Just as AL differs within and among families and is a product of constitutional predispositions, developmental changes, and environmental influences, so the same may be said for adaptation range. The AL differs by behavior setting and so, too, does the adaptation range. Specification of either can come only after close examination of family processes—perceiving, spacing, valuing, and deciding—as well as family history.

RANGE OF ADAPTATION

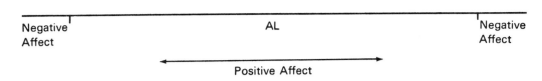

Figure 12.2. Adaptation level (AL) and range of adaptation.

A number of examples taken from earlier discussions will illustrate this point. We have noted differences in perceptual style in terms of preferred level of stimulation and pace of stimulation change. When discussing values, we have seen that some give primacy to individual development while others emphasize traditionalism and conformity. A component of decision making was amount of preferred risk-taking. Taken together, these variations in perceiving, valuing, and deciding have a common reference to size of adaptation range. The risk-taking individual with an "augmenter" perceptual style and high valuation on self-development has a wider adaptation range than another whose perceptual style is "reducer," whose values emphasize conformity and who sticks to "safe" decisions.

Jessie Bernard has contrasted the term *eustress* to distress (1968). Eustress is associated with excitement, adventure, thrills. It is sought-after risk and change. It becomes an avenue by which physical energy is consumed (e.g., sports). Who are the seekers after "eustress"? Bernard believes that eustress-seeking is released only when other, more basic needs are satisfied. Hence, eustress is likely to be higher among the affluent, who have more disposable time and who can afford the often expensive pursuit of adventure.

When the family is substituted for the individual as the unit of analysis, the same may be said. For the family, its adaptation range is a dynamic product of the interaction of the ranges of its members. We may search for indications of its character by examining what has been called "family theme" or "family perceptual style," its tolerance for diversity, its valuation of change.

In discussing the mutual influence that parent and child exert upon one another, Bell's concept of parental upper and lower levels of tolerance for child behaviors was presented. This is the adaptation range in different dress. Parents differ in their placement of these upper and lower limits. For one parent, an unacceptably withdrawn and passive child is to another acceptably quiet. The placement of these limits reflects parental values, which in turn reflect the family's linkages to the wider society. Social class is one such linkage thought to be important. Middle-class parents appear to be more permissive, tolerate a wider range of behavior in their child, and are more accepting of change.

The fact of class membership does not explain why these differences occur. Moreover, there are group differences that tend to obscure differences between individual families. Are lower-class parents more frustrated in their dealings with the outside world and hence, less tolerant of changes within the family world? Do lower-class parents see child expressiveness as possibly threatening to a child who may be taking orders rather than giving them? Existing research does not enable us to answer these questions. It is likely to be more beneficial for future research to ask what specific behaviors of parents are related to tolerance for change and indeed, change-seeking, rather than to rely on global categories like social class. The adaptation range of the individual and of the family sets goal-directed behavior and thus determines the ratio of change seeking to adaptation to change.

Changing System Demands

Change may be self-initiated as the result of changes in system demands. Considering the individual system first, it is evident that the developing child makes changing demands for stimulation, contact, reassurance, and challenge from other family members. Knowledge of broad developmental patterns makes some of these changes relatively predictable. The young child who can crawl will demand more freedom of exploration than the baby who still only sits up and watches. Yet these broad patterns can obscure individual differences in change. For example, it is an accepted truism that the biological changes of puberty will be accompanied by increased demands for autonomy and testing of individuality. Yet, as experts on adolescence have pointed out (Adelson, 1979), such new demands do not necessarily characterize all or even most adolescents, some of whom may require more nurturance and reassurance from parents than ever before.

Changes in individual system demands characterize adults as well. It is now appreciated that adult development is better described by jagged peaks and valleys than a smooth plateau. Adult change is less tied to biological and maturational factors and more linked to important life experiences. Menopause is likely to bring about fewer changes in a woman's life than separation from her husband or a career involvement. Many of these changes in system demands are self-initiated, reflecting changes in values rather than responses to environmental conditions.

Family systems also change voluntarily. Dissatisfaction with some element of family life, for example, housing, may lead to attempts to change the dwelling. The more information family members acquire about the range of possibilities open to them, the more they may be expected to revise their expectations. Hence, increased education may lead to greater dissatisfaction.

Changing System Supplies

Changes also occur in system supplies, on both the individual and family system levels. An individual's skills and abilities to some degree unfold in a regular sequence of qualitatively different stages. In the realm of cognitive functioning, Piaget describes the gradual emergence of abstract *schemas* or mental representations by which the young child learns to understand the world. He emphasizes that the thought processes of the young child are not rudimentary versions of adult thought, but have unique characteristics.

Emphasis on a sequential unfolding of individual skills may obscure abrupt, multi-directional changes that also occur. Particularly where emotional functioning and interpersonal relations are concerned, individuals may change from autonomous to fearful, from concerned to resentful. Such changes may be in response to environmental changes beyond the adaptive capacities of the individual, as when a crisis like divorce strains the functioning of family members (Hetherington, Cox, and Cox, 1977). Or they may be less easily traced to environmental conditions, but rather seen as outward manifestations of an inner dynamic.

Changes in family system supplies come about as changing individuals affect patterns of communication, feelings of cohesiveness, and sense of family identification. Falling and rising levels of resources, such as income, directly affect the family's ability to transact with the environment and indirectly have impact on patterns of family interaction. A father faced with unemployment may find his usual patience at home taxed.

Families often set out to change their system supplies deliberately through their decisions about more or less education for members, this job or that. The resolution to better oneself is a shorthand way of describing a variety of decisions about changes in system supplies.

STRUCTURING ONE'S OWN ENVIRONMENT

Change as a positive force may be illustrated in the creativity involved in structuring one's own environment. The professional architect and planner see the physical environment as a set of possibilities, not as givens. An approach that appeals to many of the most creative environmental planners is the *megastructure*, a three-dimensional matrix-system for the containment of human activities—living, working, playing, worshipping, governing. The ideal of the megastructure is that of a neutral container, one which permits the additive inputs and mutual feedback of individuals and the community, acting as a supportive framework in which goals may be pursued (Kepes, 1972). In this view, environments are seen as vehicles by which the human relation to ecosystems is expressed. Paolo Soleri (1973) advocates *archologies*, architectural entities that are ecologically relevant. The way we construct and change our environment reflects our feelings of connectedness to natural and man-made ecosystems. At the same time, living in an environment emphasizes one kind of relationship and ignores others.

While professionals think in global terms, family members also express their creativity by changes made upon their spatial environment. When spaces are rearranged, colors changed, objects added and removed, feelings and interaction patterns subtly change also.

More than expressing creativity, families act on their environment where possible to better the fit between their demands as a system and the supplies they feel their setting provides. In research the present author conducted with M. Inman, one goal was to identify changes in family behavior occasioned by a perceived lack of fit between system needs and environmental demands. The families studied were married students with at least one child. Each family lived in a unit of married student housing that most residents felt lacked adequate space for their needs. Since it was impossible to directly modify the physical structure, many families responded by:

1. Becoming less concerned about maintenance
2. Establishing house rules for children
3. Setting up a schedule
4. Assigning household tasks
5. Becoming more inhibited about lovemaking
6. Socializing less with neighbors

When the environment resists modification, changes in family behavior are dominant. When environmental constraints are removed, it is likely that families would attempt to change housing conditions by moving or altering the dwelling (see Morris and Winter's theory in the chapter on housing).

SUMMARY

The twin themes of change and stability within the family as ecosystem have been portrayed within the framework of adaptation levels (AL) and adaptation range. The family maintains an adaptive relationship to its environments, characterized by interdependence. Changes in family characteristics prompt attempts to modify environmental characteristics, while changes in environmental conditions stimulate family responses. Similarly, when the family is considered the surrounding environment to which individual family members adapt, the same picture of mutual change emerges.

The organizing principle underlying such interdependence is the existence of ALs, theoretically neutral points of stimulation and adaptation ranges, stimulation levels above and below the AL that are experienced as positive. The family as a goal-directed ecosystem seeks to maintain its functioning within its adaptation range. Individual family members, too, attempt to be thus adapted to the family environment.

The process of adaptation is imperfect both because of conditions within the family and outside it. Individuals and whole families differ in the accuracy with which they perceive and use environmental information. Some families see themselves as little able to affect their lives. For others, a predominantly present-time orientation blinds them to considering future consequences. Families differ in the extent to which coping processes, focussed on the active understanding and mastery of the environment, are nurtured. Families differ widely in the possession of coping resources of education, income, and social support. Rigid family expectations create an environment unresponsive to individual changes.

Environmental constraints on family adaptation are also important. Environments must provide institutions, incentives, and training to support individual and family efforts at adaptation. The phenomenon of overly rapid and contradictory change has been argued to produce "future shock," which impairs individual and family functioning. While such a portrait may not give sufficient emphasis to the inherently stabilizing tendencies of the family, it is nonetheless true that environmental change beyond the limits of the family's or individual's adaptation range is common.

Individual and family systems are also characterized by the positive need for change. As individuals develop they make new demands upon other family members. Family systems, too, decide to initiate change when family needs or values change. The level of family "supplies" in the form of income, material resources, and intangible assets is always fluctuating to some degree. These changes affect their ability to meet environmental demands.

Where possible, families are actively interested in structuring their environment to fit their needs. When environmental characteristics resist modification, changes in family behavior may occur.

REFERENCES

Adelson, J. Adolescence and the generalization gap. *Psychology Today* 12 (1979): 33-37.

Bell, P.. Q. Stimulus control of parent or caretaker behavior by offspring. *Developmental Psychology* 4 (1971): 63-72.

————. Contributions of human infants to caregiving and social interaction. In E. M. Hetherington and R. D. Parke, eds., *Contemporary Readings in Child Psychology*. Highstown, N.J.: McGraw-Hill, 1977.

Bell, R. Q., and Harper, L. *Child Effects on Adults*. Hillsdale, N.J.: Lawrence Erlbaum Associates, 1977

Bennis, W., and Slater, P. *The Temporary Society*. New York: Harper and Row, 1968.

Bernard, J. The eudaemonists. In S. Z. Klausner, ed., *Why Man Takes Chances*. Garden City, N.Y Doubleday, 1968.

Blood, R. *The Family*. New York: The Free Press, 1972.

Bossard, J. H. S., and Boll, E. S. *The Large Family System*. Philadelphia: University of Pennsylvania Pres. 1956.

Brody, E. B., ed. *Behavior in New Environments: Adaptation of Migrant Populations.* Beverly Hills, Calif.: Sage Publications, 1969.

Clarke-Stewart, A. *Child-Care in the Family.* New York: Academic Press, 1977.

Goldschmidt, W. Ethology, ecology and ethnological realities. In G. V. Coelho, D. A. Hamburg, and J. A. Adams, eds., *Coping and Adaptation.* New York: Basic Books, 1974.

Heiss, J. *The Case of the Black Family: A Sociological Inquiry.* New York: Columbia University Press, 1975.

Helson, H. *Adaptation-Level Theory.* New York: Harper and Row, 1964.

Hetherington, E. M., Cox, M., and Cox, R. Beyond father absence: Conceptualizations of effects of divorce. In E. M. Hetherington and R. D. Parke, eds., *Contemporary Readings in Child Psychology.* New York: McGraw-Hill, 1977.

Kepes, G., ed. *Arts of the Environment.* New York: George Braziller, 1972.

Mechanic, D. Social structure and personal adaptation: Some neglected dimensions. In G. V. Coelho, D. A. Hamburg, and J. A. Adams, eds., *Coping and Adaptation.* New York: Basic Books, 1974.

Miller, G. The magical number seven plus or minus two. *Psychological Review* 63 (1956): 81-97.

Murphy, L. B. and Moriarty, A. E. *Vulnerability, Coping and Growth From Infancy to Adolescence.* New Haven: Yale University Press, 1976.

Reiss, I. J. The universality of the family: A conceptual analysis. *Journal of Marriage and the Family* 27(1965): 443-453.

Schooler, C. Childhood family structures and adult structures. *Sociometry* 35 (1972): 255-269.

Soleri, P. *The Bridge Between Matter and Spirit Is Matter Becoming Spirit.* Garden City, N.Y.: Doubleday, 1973.

Toffler, A. *Future Shock.* New York: Random House, 1970.

Vincent, C. E. Familia spongia: The adaptive function. *Journal of Marriage and the Family* 28 (1966): 29-36.

Wohlwill, J. Human adaptation to levels of environmental stimulation. *Human Biology* 2 (1974) 127-147.

Wohlwill, J., and Kohn, I. The environment as experienced by the migrant: An adaptation level approach. *Representative Research in Social Psychology* 4 (1973): 135-164.

Wolfenstein, M. Fun morality: An analysis of recent American child-training literature. In M. Mead and M. Wolfenstein, eds., *Childhood in Contemporary Cultures.* Chicago: University of Chicago Press, 1955.

13

Stress

The interplay of change and stability as families adapt and readapt to environments formed the theme of Chapter 12. In this chapter stress in family-environment relations is examined. The phrase "coping with stress" is often heard in connection with individuals and families. Certain environmental conditions such as poverty or social upheaval are thought to make the lives of people caught in them stressful ones. Attention may be directed at changing the environment or at providing resources to help the family cope with adverse conditions.

The concept of stress has been defined in varying, sometimes contradictory, ways. For some it is a stimulus or event, or perhaps a cluster of events or stressors. In this view, stress consists of stressful life events such as death of a loved one, war, famine, sickness, or parental mistreatment. Such events may be isolated, discrete occurrences, such as an illness, or they may be diffuse, ongoing conditions such as a "depriving" environment. Another view defines stress as an inferred internal state of an organism who reacts to certain events, particularly those involving new and demanding stimuli. For example, one definition states that stress is a "state where the well-being or integrity of an individual is endangered and he must devote all his energies to its protection" (Cofer and Appley, 1964).

Stress also has a physiological component and some (Selye, 1956) have viewed stress primarily in terms of the biochemical body changes associated with it. These variations in terminology and approach lead to confusion when the term *stress* is applied.

DEFINING STRESS

What has been said thus far about "future shock" and adaptation range would lead us to consider stressful events or conditions as those which lie outside the individual's or family's range of adaptation. Wesley Burr, a major theoretician of the family (1973), states that stressor events are those outside the family system's normal range of functioning. They are relatively unexpected and seem to call for new, unpracticed responses. For example, for a man beset by chronic unemployment, being fired is not a novel event and one that probably would not constitute a stressor event for him and his family. However, long-term unemployment or the sudden windfall of a high-status, secure position may both be unusual occurrences for which this family system is unprepared.

Thus, events are stressful to someone because of the *meanings* assigned to those events. Reuben Hill, who has written extensively on families under stress (1949; Hill and Hansen, 1962;

Hansen and Hill, 1964), emphasizes that the severity of a crisis depends upon the meanings assigned to it, the way it is defined and understood by those experiencing it. At least three different definitions of the same crisis situation may coexist: that of the impartial observer, that of the community, and that of the family itself. The hallmark of stress is the disturbance of equilibrium in the system. Stress is here defined relative to experiences within the range of adaptation; hence, understanding stress implies understanding the context of an individual's or family's history. For example, if a family is adapted to a particular range of environmental changes, increases or decreases in the number and type of changes, even if positive ones (inheriting a lot of money) would be predicted to be stressful. Although most writers use the term *stress* to refer only to negative states, according to our definition any disturbance of equilibrium, produced by joyous or distasteful events, may be stressful. Popular wisdom confirms the potentially stressful effects of positive disturbances in equilibrium with tales of instant millionaires whose lives fall apart.

An interesting body of research, known as life-changes research, shows that even positive changes such as a desired marriage or a longed-for child may be viewed as stressors as well. This is built around the concept already met in "future shock," that excessive change per se, whether in a positive or negative direction, requires adaptive reactions from the body and mind that take a toll on the organism. If changes mount within a limited time and exceed the adaptation range, the individual is likely to show signs of wear and tear in physical and mental symptoms.

Table 13.1 shows the life-changes chart developed by Thomas Holmes and Richard Rahe. Note that changes are rated for the potential impact, with "death of spouse" being the most disruptive. The reader might like at this point to fill out the chart in order to see the magnitude of life changes that have occurred personally within the last year. In an impressive body of research, magnitude of score has been related to onset of a variety of adverse consequences, particularly mental and physical illness during the following two years after assessment, for example, sudden cardiac death, fractures, onset of pregnancy, onset of leukemia in children, and incarceration in a federal prison (Holmes and Masuda, 1974). Thus, results from the life-changes chart show that individuals who experience too many changes within a limited period show evidence of stress.

THE POSITIVE SIDE OF STRESS

It should not be assumed that stress is always a negative experience, and hence something one should work to eliminate. Moderate amounts of stress alert the mind and body to danger, mobilize resources, and prepare the individual to engage actively with the environment. Stress is a natural, indeed indispensable, part of life. A certain amount of stress, in the form of challenge and excitement, is often sought after, not avoided. Jessie Bernard (1968) has traced what she terms *eustress*, positive tension-seeking as a theme in literature, sports, and leisure.

When families make new demands upon their members or upon the environment, they may be seeking to shake up a quiescent adaptation level. They take on stress as part of the price of arriving at a new, more satisfying adaptation in the future, and this price is often paid willingly. One should not assume that families necessarily flee from stressful experiences.

STRESS AS SYSTEM-ENVIRONMENT INTERACTION

While stress is a psychological state relative to the individual or family system's adaptation range, it is not entirely in the head. Certain environmental events are thought to lie outside almost anyone's range of adaptation and hence may be identified as stressors. The human species is limited in its ability to process stimulation. Hence, as levels of stimulation rise beyond these levels

TABLE 13.1 LIFE-CHANGES CHART

1	Death of spouse	100
2	Divorce	73
3	Marital separation	65
4	Jail term	63
5	Death of close family member	63
6	Personal injury or illness	53
7	Marriage	50
8	Fired at work	47
9	Marital reconciliation	45
10	Retirement	45
11	Change in health of family member	44
12	Pregnancy	40
13	Sex difficulties	39
14	Gain of new family member	39
15	Business readjustment	39
16	Change in financial state	38
17	Death of close friend	37
18	Change to different line of work	36
19	Change in number of arguments with spouse	35
20	Mortgage over $10,000	31
21	Foreclosure of mortgage or loan	30
22	Change in responsibilities at work	29
23	Son or daughter leaving home	29
24	Trouble with in-laws	29
25	Outstanding personal achievement	28
26	Wife begin or stop work	26
27	Begin or end school	26
28	Change in living conditions	25
29	Revision of personal habits	24
30	Trouble with boss	23
31	Change in work hours or conditions	20
32	Change in residence	20
33	Change in schools	20
34	Change in recreation	19
35	Change in church activities	19
36	Change in social activities	18
37	Mortgage or loan less than $10,000	17
38	Change in sleeping habits	16
39	Change in family get-togethers	15
40	Change in eating habits	15
41	Vacation	13
42	Christmas	12
43	Minor violations of the law	11

Reprinted with permission from *The Journal of Psychosomatic Research*, vol. 11 by Thomas Holmes and Richard Rahe, "The Social Readjustment Rating Scale." © 1967 Pergamon Press, Ltd.

of tolerance, one may predict that most individuals will experience stress. The amount and nature of that stress will, of course, depend upon prior experience with the stressor, temperament, styles of perceiving, and the like. Excessively high or excessively low levels of environmental stimulation have been studied in relation to stressors such as noise, rate of change (see Life-Changes Scale), and amount of cognitive information to be processed.

NOISE

Modern cities are characterized by a constant din. Many workers spend their day bombarded by high noise-levels. What are the short- and long-term effects of noise as a stressor? What dimensions of the noise stimulus are most important—intensity, range, regularity, control? Glass and Singer (1972) have been most active in attempting to find answers to these questions. They found that high-intensity noise did impair performance on complex tasks, particularly if the noise was intermittent and unpredictable. Inability to anticipate and control stimulation appears here, as in much other research, as a critical factor in determining its effects.

While Glass and Singer used a laboratory situation to measure the stressful effects of noise, it is likely that their results apply to natural settings. Recall that Chapter 11 reported other research conducted by Cohen with Glass and Singer measuring the effects of naturally occurring noise levels on children's auditory discrimination and reading achievement. The fact that this research also found impairment supports the validity of the laboratory results.

Laboratory investigations of noise as a stressor generally measure short-term effects only. The Cohen, Glass, and Singer field study, however, uncovered evidence of long-term impairments. Children who had lived in a noisy apartment building for more than four years had poorer reading achievement scores than those who had lived there for a shorter time (Cohen, Glass, and Singer, 1973). Thus, adaptation to noisy conditions may result in long-range impairment of which the individual may be unaware.

STIMULATION DEPRIVATION

It should be remembered that levels of stimulation *below* as well as above one's adaptation range are likely to be stressful. Thus, too little stimulation may be as aversive as too much. This has been amply demonstrated in experimental studies of isolation and stimulation deprivation. In the typical experiment, a volunteer spends a certain amount of time in a barren room acoustically sealed off from the outside world. Even fingers may be taped to prevent kinesthetic stimulation. The effects of such an environment are predictably severe. Afterwards, individuals hallucinate, report feelings of bodily strangeness, cannot concentrate, and cannot solve even simple problems.

The effects of stimulus deprivation have been demonstrated, not only experimentally, but also in naturally occurring cases. In the 1940s and 1950s, the shocking effects of a severely depriving institution on the development of young children were documented (Spitz and Wolff, 1946; Dennis, 1960; Dennis and Najarian, 1957). In the absence of a cognitively stimulating and nurturing setting, the growth of many children was retarded. Moreover, sickness and death rates were high despite adequate sanitation, hygiene, and nutrition.

Support for the importance of adequate stimulation, particularly during the sensitive period of early development, also came from animal research conducted by Harlow and his associates (Harlow and Zimmerman, 1959). They demonstrated the adverse effects of stimulation deprivation on the later adult functioning of monkeys. Other work with monkeys indicated that even the normal maturation of perceptual apparatus required environmental stimulation (Riesen, 1947). Monkeys whose eyes had been taped shut for the first six months of life did not recover their sight later.

Stimulation deprivation in adulthood also appears to have extreme consequences. Studies of brainwashed American prisoners during the Korean war revealed that they had been placed in the dark away from other persons or sounds, deprived of any objects or information. Often they did not know if it was day or night. Their only contacts were when food was brought or when they were interrogated. Under these conditions many prisoners had mental breakdowns, losing motivation to do anything. Some died from apparent loss of will to live (Segal, 1957).

Animal studies, together with results from laboratory and naturally occurring deprivations, amply demonstrate the negative consequences of extreme stimulation deprivation. It is likely also that milder forms of stimulation deficit are experienced as somewhat stressful. The urban dweller finds the peacefulness of the country irksome and longs for the familiar roar of the elevated train.

Low levels of social stimulation may be associated with feelings of isolation and alienation. This is supported by findings that individuals living alone are more likely to be admitted to mental hospitals than those living with others (Kahn and Perlin, 1967).

SENSORY OVERLOAD

Since humans are inherently limited in the amount of environmental information they can absorb, environments overloaded with sensory information are likely to produce stress. Milgram (1970) has characterized large cities as such overloaded environments and demonstrated in a series of field studies various strategies used by individuals to reduce the overload. For example, because of too much stimulation, city dwellers are less likely to be responsive to others, preferring superficial relationships and avoiding involvement with strangers. They may be less likely to come to the aid of a stranger in distress than residents of smaller communities (Latané and Darley, 1970).

Because there is too much stimulation to process, city dwellers develop norms of impersonality, aloofness, and noninvolvement. They interact with each other as strangers; they develop blasé attitudes toward the bizarre and deviant. These patterns of social relations are viewed by Milgram as a necessary adaptation to the demands of city life.

This view of city life as inherently overloaded and hence stressful may be exaggerated, however. Wide individual differences in adaptation range make it likely that the "overloaded" character of city life and its impersonality may be attractive to some individuals who appreciate its anonymity and stimulation. Besides, considerable variation exists within the largest and most crowded city in friendliness and helpfulness.

TEMPERATURE

Heat as a stressor has been the focus of some interest, particularly since the phenomenon of urban rioting during summer heat waves. Room temperature has been shown to interact with other characteristics in affecting feelings of crowdedness. Warm rooms are likely to feel more crowded than cool ones when amount of space or number of persons remains unchanged (Griffitt and Veitch, 1971). When individuals change to environments whose temperature and humidity differ from their adaptation levels, they may experience a variety of stresses. An investigation (Edholm, 1953) of soldiers stationed in New Guinea, a tropical climate with consistently high temperature and humidity, found decreases in body weight, blood pressure, energy, and general well-being.

OVER- AND UNDER-MANNED SETTINGS

Wicker and his associates (1972, 1973) have developed the concepts of over-, adequate, and under-manning. They refer to the optimal number of persons required for the performance of essential roles in maintaining a setting. This optimum is derived from cultural norms. A setting containing too few people to fill all essential roles is said to be *under-manned*, while an environment with an excess of persons-to-roles ratio is *over-manned*.

When under-manning exists, people are forced to handle a number of roles at once. The under-manned setting makes a greater claim on them, investing them with more responsibility than they might have in adequate or over-manned settings. For example, the single parent feels as though he or she needs to perform both maternal and paternal roles. Severely under-manned settings may lack what Wicker calls the *maintenance minimum* of persons to keep the setting going, while the severely over-manned setting may contain so much excess population that they threaten the functioning of the setting as well. Changes in settings from under- to over-manning or the reverse constitute a potential stressor. If the setting is to persevere, adaptive responses must be made. For example, when a setting becomes severely over-manned, new applicants hoping to gain entry to it may encounter difficulties. When colleges are flooded by applicants, standards for admission tend to rise. When under-manning threatens to deplete the setting, admission standards are likely to be relaxed.

The behavior setting of the family home may be characterized by over- and under-manning as well. When family size increases but space in the home does not, the family may deal with this over-manning by trying to expand or change dwellings, limit new family members or encourage older family members to strike out on their own. When family size drops through divorce, separation, or death, other family members may be pressed into service to take on additional roles. The eldest son may feel himself the "man of the house" in his father's absence. A grandmother may help her divorced daughter out with regular child care.

Research on magnitude of life changes, stimulation overload, stimulation deprivation, noise, temperature, and over- and under-manned settings tend to focus on group differences in stress level as a function of exposure to a particular stressor. Yet, adaptation level and adaptation range are attributes of the individual and family and hence subject to wide variation. A stressful life event for one person is interpreted differently by another. Indeed, investigations of stress have consistently identified two groups of people, the vulnerable and the buffered.

THE VULNERABLE AND THE BUFFERED

One cannot simply conclude that lots of life change will lead inexorably to physical illness or "doing time" in prison. In other studies of reactions to stressful events (Hinkle, 1974), the results show that while many people do react in the predicted way with both mental and physical impairment, two groups of individuals do not. Studies of varieties of stress situations have repeatedly found that among those exposed to the severest stresses, a minority appear relatively unaffected by the severity of their life experiences.

Not only that, they seem to be thriving. E. James Anthony has been studying children of schizophrenic parents (1974). In his work, he identified a group of children socially at ease, active masterers of their environment, autonomous, yet ready to help others. These "superkids" appeared somehow insulated from life's adversities. A graphic description of just such a person (here an adult) emerges from the following portrait:

> Mrs. X was the daughter of an alcoholic longshoreman and a teenaged immigrant girl. She had been born into a household of great poverty, constant conflict, and much turmoil. Four of her nine siblings had died in infancy of infection and apparent malnutrition. When she was three years of age, her father had deserted his family. When she was five years of age, she had been placed in an orphanage by community action because her

mother was neglecting her and been adjudged unfit to raise her. She had had a barren childhood in orphanages. When she was 13, she had been put out to work as a servant. At the age of 16 she had left the place at which she was working and had lived, as she put it, "all around the town" with another teenage girl. During this time she had had a number of casual sexual attachments and many jobs. When she had obtained her present job as a telephone operator, she was 23 years old. At the age of 27 she had married a chronically ill, neurotic plumber's helper, whom she had had to support thereafter. They had no children. He had died in her arms of a massive gastric hemorrhage when she was 44 years old. Thereafter, she lived alone as a widow. At the age of 54, when we examined and interviewed her, we found her to be a well-liked and highly respected employee. She had had only two episodes of sickness disability in 31 years. The only significant illness that we could uncover on extensive questioning and examination had been a few colds. However, she said she did have a few days of "nervousness" after her husband's death.*

To some observers Mrs. X may seem emotionally shallow, self-centered, lacking capacity to feel not only the joys but also the sorrows of the human condition. Other students of such "insulates" from stress emphasize their tension-management skills (Antonovsky, 1974). Anthony (1974) shows that those offspring who avoid being engulfed by their parents' mental illness by remaining detached and aloof from them resist identifying with pathological parental examples.

Those adults who appear insulated from stress may possess a variety of what have been called "resistance resources," including a network of supportive friends and family who help them withstand the negative effects of adverse life circumstances. It is also likely that the buffered have highly developed coping skills. Finally, the possibility of some genetic basis for flexibility or plasticity in the face of environmental change cannot be ruled out (Dobzhansky, 1962).

A second group also appears to contradict a simple relation between magnitude of life changes and strain. This group consists of those who seem to have rather benign histories with few, if any, disruptive life events. Their lives have gone smoothly and uneventfully and yet, based upon physical and mental symptoms, they seem under severe strain.

It has been suggested that since some individuals are predisposed to various physical and mental strains, relatively minor stressful life events can increase their susceptibility markedly to major strains, while to a more "robust" group, these minor stressors would have little effect. Another possibility is that such vulnerable individuals lack the resistance resources that appear to insulate others. Many children lack the ability to conceptualize a distressing situation and develop plans for coping with it. Hence, as a group, they are more vulnerable than adults.

Not only individuals, but certain family systems may be more vulnerable to stress than others. Angell (1936), in an early study of families' responses to the Great Depression, was the first to identify two characteristics of family systems as particularly important: *adaptability* and *cohesiveness*. *Adaptability* refers to the system's ability to change its functioning in response to new demands without undue strife or psychological discomfort, while *cohesiveness* refers to the level of organization of the system. To the degree that family members function smoothly as a unit, and feel themselves to belong together more than apart, they may be said to be *cohesive*.

Thus, study of these two groups, the insulated and the vulnerable, illustrates the necessity of taking into account (a) perception of stressors, (b) coping strategies, psychological defenses and other sources of resistance to stress effects, and (c) possible genetic bases for flexibility in the face of environmental change.

---

* Reprinted with permission from Hinkle, 1974.

The "insulated" are relatively unaffected by the stressful events to which they have been exposed. (Photo by Natalie Leimkuhler.)

COPING WITH STRESS

Contrasting extreme groups such as the buffered and the vulnerable obscures the fact that coping with stress is central to all lives. What exactly is coping? One view defines it as "actions that make it possible for individuals (and families) to exploit, to understand, to master, to reshape, and to gain sustenance from their environment both inner and outer" (Haan, 1977). Such actions help the individual and family system recover from crisis by reducing distress and by reorganizing the system so that it may resume normal functioning. This does not mean that families remove all conflict, internal and external, or that they return to the *status quo*, but simply that the disruption occasioned by a crisis is reduced to manageable proportions.

As Table 13.2 indicates, the coping process may be distinguished from *defense* or *fragmentary* processes, which do not result in active mastery of the environment. The coping individual or family is both purposive and flexible, future oriented, grounded in reality, accepting of disturbing feelings, and prone to think in an organized, relevant manner. As our previous discussion of the insulated and vulnerable indicated, coping capacity is enhanced by a stable, well-balanced physi-

TABLE 13.2 CONCEPTUALIZATIONS OF EGO: PROCESSES, FUNCTIONS, REGULATIONS

Properties of Ego Processes

Coping Processes	Defense Processes	Fragmentary Processes
1. Appears to involve choice and is therefore flexible, purposive behavior.	1. Turns away from choice and is therefore rigid and channeled.	1. Appears repetitive, ritualistic, and automated.
2. Is pulled toward the future and takes account of the needs of the present.	2. Is pushed from the past.	2. Operates on assumptions which are privatistically based.
3. Oriented to the reality requirements of present situation.	3. Distorts aspects of present requirements.	3. Closes system and is nonresponsive to present requirements.
4. Involves differentiated process thinking that integrates conscious and pre-conscious elements.	4. Involves undifferentiated thinking and includes elements that do not seem part of the situation.	4. Primarily and unadulteredly determined by affect needs.
5. Operates with the organism's necessity of "metering" the experiencing of disturbing affects.	5. Operates with assumption that it is possible to magically remove disturbing feelings.	5. Floods person with affect.
6. Allows various forms of affective satisfaction in open, ordered and tempered way.	6. Allows gratification by subterfuge.	6. Allows unmodulated gratification of some impulses.

Reprinted with permission from Haan, 1977, p. 36

ology, by resources of social and material supports, and by previous positive coping experiences that build confidence in one's future efforts. The development of individuals able to actively master their environment is a major goal of family life. However, it must be emphasized that no one, is, or should be, wholly a coper. Rather, elements of coping, defending, and fragmentary processes occur in everyone in different combinations. These three processes, taken together, may be thought of as various *strategies of adaptation* (White, 1974). Although they are most evident in times of crisis, the slings and arrows of daily existence involve adaptational strategies as well.

In real-life stress situations, adaptation is almost always a judicious mix of strategies. Coping is not always desirable. In an extremely disturbing crisis, as when facing death or multiple injury, denial, tuning out, and retreating from mastery may have the beneficial effect of buying time to tame feelings, reorganize thoughts, and, most important, reestablish self-esteem.

Keeping these qualifications in mind, it is nevertheless true that the development of individuals and families who may be broadly characterized as coping is a positively valued outcome of family life. The skill of coping is affected, not only by environmental resources, but just as strongly by family interaction. Coping in children may be nurtured or stifled by parents. Coping by spouses is similarly affected.

How does family behavior affect coping ability? Haan has suggested two distinct styles of childrearing: *contravention* and *facilitation*. Parents who are contraveners feel they, as responsible parents, need to shape their child to be an effective adult and so exert pressure on the child to conform. The facilitator, by contrast, sees the child as responsible for his own development. Parent-child relations are one of mutual exchange. The parent expresses his wishes and feelings to the child, who is expected to make his or her own decisions. Such parents tolerate uncertainty. They accept the fact that, at times, particularly during adolescence, their child's development will be rocky and even socially unacceptable.

Haan cites evidence that facilitation is more likely to produce coping adults than contravention. Facilitation allows the developing child to take self-responsibility, to test the environment while learning to accept negative consequences and profit from them. Although these concepts of contravention and facilitation were developed to explain how coping may be nurtured in children by their parents, they might apply as well to other family interactions, such as those between husband and wife. The spouse who holds fairly unyielding expectations about correct marital and parental roles may be contrasted to one who expresses personal views openly but accepts disagreements graciously.

Others have identified the contravention-facilitation distinction using other terms. Intrusive, *authoritarian*, controlling parents have been contrasted to *permissive* parents. Baumrind (1967) has further refined this distinction. Based on observations of three- and four-year-old children, she was able to identify particularly competent ones. These children were mature, content, independent, realistic, self-reliant, explorative, friendly, and assertive. What kind of parents did such competent children have? Baumrind found that competent children tended to have parents who were warm, loving, supportive, conscientious, and good communicators. To this extent, they appeared to be facilitators in Haan's sense. Yet, they were *also* controlling and demanded mature behavior from their offspring. While respecting their child's independence, they held firm to their convictions about what was right, explaining their reasoning to the child, yet insisting upon proper behavior. To this parental pattern, Baumrind gave the term *authoritative* and contrasted it to both *authoritarian* (controlling without love or warmth) and to *permissive* (noncontrolling but warm).

It is important to point out that neither the research of Haan nor that of Baumrind show that certain parental childrearing styles *cause* competence in children. The association they found could also be explained as a parental response to an already competent child. It is easier to be warm and to enforce clear standards with a child who is friendly, competent, and self-reliant than one who is hostile, passive, and dependent. This latter explanation does not, of course, illuminate the original source of the child's competence. The system properties of the family require one to view parent-child relations as with other familial relations as complex chains of mutual influence.

On the part of all family members, competence in coping with stress is enhanced by recognition of uniqueness and individual change. Parents start out with expectations for the child—"She will be the dancer I never was." Spouses begin life together with such expectations as well—"She will be a devoted mother to our kids, just as my own mother was." How receptive are family members to information disconfirming these expectations? As individuals change, how readily do other family members revise their images of one another? Coping is associated with *openness* of the family system to new information from within (changes in individual members) and without (changes in environment external to family unit).

Family members influence each other's coping styles not only by what they do to each other, but by what they do for themselves. Parents are watched as they attempt to cope in moments of stress, modelling resilience or vulnerability.

The "crisis-prone" family has been identified (Koos, 1946) and contrasted with the family competent at meeting crises. Interestingly, the distinctions of class, income, and occupation (environmental resources) do not enable us to predict totally the resiliency of a family under stress. Attributes of *family functioning* are also important. Families competent at meeting crises have been found to have a nonmaterialistic value orientation, to perceive emotional problems as appropriate family concerns, to identify accurately family problems and hold egalitarian leadership patterns. Competent families were cohesive, with open communication and rational decision-making. Furthermore, they had ways of handling inevitable tensions among family members (Hansen and Hill, 1964; Hill, 1965).

It has been suggested that a moderate amount of consultation about decisions is optimal for coping with a crisis (Burr, 1973). Too much agonizing over every move might paralyze the family from taking swift action, while too little consultation would anger and alienate.

As the family tries to come to some understanding of the events that have produced stress, the kind of conclusions they reach will affect their ease of recovery. Families who tend to *externalize blame*, to shift it onto others rather than themselves, appear to recover from stressful experiences more readily than those filled with guilt and self-accusation (Hansen, 1965). A wage earner who has been fired retains his or her self-respect more readily if management or even bad luck can be the culprit.

The family, through the participation of its members, is linked to many extrafamilial systems. First, the nuclear family has kin and quasi-kin relationships that can cushion it against stress. For example, the adaptation of Appalachian migrants to an industrial work-situation was studied as an example of a stress situation (Schwarzweller and Crowe, 1969). The investigators found that many migrant families were able to use the wider family support system as a "haven of safety" against the ravages of nearly total change.

The degree to which a family has frequent, intense, and useful interactions with relatives has been termed *extended familism* (Winch and Greer, 1968). Hansen and Hill (1964) have suggested that extended familism is a useful family asset in meeting long-term crises, but may be detrimental for short-term ones. Why should this be so? Let us imagine a short-term family crisis. In the Jacoby family, twelve-year-old Myra has suddenly run away. After a frantic night's search, she is located at a friend's house. The involvement of aunts, uncles, and "cousins by the dozen" might make it more, not less, difficult for the Jacoby parents to understand their daughter's behavior and to intervene appropriately. What might be support and resources in a crisis of long duration—such as a death in the family—becomes meddlesome obstruction in the short run.

Both nuclear family and kin network are tied, of course, to regulatory systems—educational, political, legal—which have received repeated emphasis in earlier chapters. Rapid change in these systems is one source of environmental demand on the family. Often multiple demands conflict. For example, long years of specialized education, a demand of the educational system, may be incompatible with employment opportunites demanding flexibility of skills. On the other hand, family participation in regulatory systems may enhance coping skills. When family members possess the resources available in such systems—higher education, political power, legal advantages—they may be able to use these resources to regulate change and cope with stress. For example, it has been suggested (Burr, 1973) that a wife's participation in activities outside the home may make recovery from crisis somewhat easier for the family.

In addition to the demands regulatory systems make and the resources they provide, they impinge upon family coping in yet another way. Increasingly, successful coping requires concerted group effort aimed at making an impact on the environment (Mechanic, 1974). Individual families can do little to reduce pollution, provide better health care and day-care services, or make education more relevant to occupational demands. Individuals both within and outside family contexts must possess the ability to function effectively in groups dedicated to change. A person's knowledge and skill in maneuvering through these regulatory systems in concert with others is a dimension of coping not less important than accuracy of information processing or temperament.

FAMILY CRISES

Family adaptability to stress is not static, however. The perspective of the family life cycle emphasizes the discontinuity of stages. New demands, new stresses appear as the family makes a transition from one stage to the next. The family that weathers the pre-child "honeymoon" period may be hard hit by the advent of the first child, while another family unruffled by child care cannot cope with adolescent rebellion. Research on families through the life cycle does not identify any central core of competencies that persists through disparate crises. Rather, new coping skills are required for each critical transition.

The idea of *developmental tasks* illustrates that some events assume greater primacy during some periods of the family life cycle as compared with others. For example, the childrearing stage of the family life cycle is one in which the following developmental tasks predominate: expanding the communication system, establishing a philosophy and method of childrearing, adjustment of space, income allocation, reorganization of routine and responsibility, maintenance of morale. It stands to reason that when the family system is most focussed about the child, a life change, such as death of that child, would disrupt the family more completely than would the same change during the "empty nest" period after the child has left home and been established independently.

Indeed, there is some indication that death is in general most disruptive when the deceased had an active, central position in the concerns of those around him. The middle-aged father cut down in his prime may leave an economically dependent wife and children as well as aging parents, and his loss may require a host of adaptations not necessary when death takes an individual gradually removed from responsibility through advanced age and illness (Blauner, 1966). Thus, it stands to reason that disruptions in life events central to particular developmental stages of the family will be more strongly felt than disturbances of more peripheral events.

In addition, it has been suggested (Rodgers, 1973) that particular periods in the family career are stress-prone due to fluctuating levels of what have been called *resistance resources*. For example, the early childrearing period is one in which new financial, physical, and emotional demands are being made on both husband and wife precisely at a time when their income may be curtailed because of termination of the wife's outside employment. Thus, it is not surprising that families with young children indicate themselves more dissatisfied with jobs, level of living, most worried over the financial cost of children than families with adolescents or "launched" children.

DIVORCE, SEPARATION, AND FAMILY BREAKDOWN

Divorce is almost always a stressful crisis that disturbs the adaptation of the family system and requires reorganization at a new level of adaptation. Although a great deal of attention has been devoted to the effects of divorce on children, it is clear that the family system as a whole undergoes stress and eventual restabilization. As Chapter 3 indicated, the rising incidence of divorce makes this an increasingly predictable crisis for many families. In 1974 an estimated one of every six children was living with a single parent, almost always the mother and almost always as a result of divorce or separation.

Hetherington and her associates (1977) have conducted a study of the two-year period following divorce in a number of families, tracing the pattern of disequilibrium, stress, reorganization, and eventual stability within a new family system. The research documented the stressful aspects of divorce. For example, among divorced families, in comparison to intact controls, economic hardship was more evident. Divorced couples, especially women, reported a disruption of their social life, which had previously been organized around couples. Even two years after divorce, happiness, self-esteem, and feelings of competence were lower among divorced parents than among their nondivorced counterparts. In general, the lives of divorced families were quite disorganized, particularly during the first year after divorce. Pick-up meals were eaten at irregular times, bedtime was unpredictable, and the children were often late for school.

Parent-child relations also suffered. Divorced parents communicated less well, were less affectionate, made fewer maturity demands and were more inconsistent than were nondivorced parents. The poor parenting patterns reached their peak a year after divorce and gradually subsided, so that by the end of the second year, evidence of a new adaptation level was found.

The severity of divorce as a crisis depended to some degree on certain characteristics of the divorcing adults and their relationship. When agreement about disciplining the child and support in childrearing persisted despite the divorce, disruption in family functioning was less extreme and the period of recovery was briefer. Emotional maturity in both the mother and father was related to coping ability. External support systems, such as grandparents and friends, helped the mother manage to keep the household going. In Wicker's terms, these people could be pressed into service to fill the void in a newly *under-manned* setting.

Hetherington's study examined only white, middle-class families. Hence, the impact of divorce was not compounded by economic deprivation, racial discrimination, malnutrition, or lack of medical attention. Since poor, nonwhite, and young families are more likely to be divorced or separated than their more affluent, white counterparts, in most cases, disruption to the family system is more extreme than the picture painted by the Hetherington study.

REMARRIAGE—THE RECONSTITUTED FAMILY

When divorced persons remarry, as the majority of them do, the new family system that comes into being is called the *reconstituted* or "blended" family. The early years of such a family system are likely to be characterized by difficulties, as formerly separate family units must be integrated into a new whole. A complex network of relationships—natural parents, stepparents, siblings, stepsiblings, half siblings, sets of grandparents for every child—make this integrative task extremely complex. Thus, it is perhaps not surprising that such families are overrepresented in populations at child psychiatric clinics (Kalter, 1977).

The task of structuring a new family system may be challenged by resentful teenagers who threaten, "Watch out or I'll go live with my other parent," by sexual attraction between stepsiblings or between stepfather and stepdaughter, by persistent parent-child closeness that seems to exclude new family members, or the difficulty of establishing a parental relationship between stepparent and child without threatening disloyalty to the natural parent (Whiteside and Auerbach, 1978). Just as the process of divorce was one of disruption and restabilization of the family, so does the reconstituted family appear to go through an extended period of reorganization.

INDIVIDUAL TRANSITIONS

Just as periods in the family's life cycle are particularly vulnerable to stress, so are certain times within the life of the individual. One can conceptualize the individual life cycle as a series of transitions that disturb the equilibrium of the system and result in new patterns of organization.

From family to school. During early childhood, children gradually widen their world from parents and siblings to include neighborhood playmates, visits to relatives and family friends, trips to the store, movies, circus. While this process is continuous, a more marked transition is evident when children begin regular schooling. The teacher becomes an important adult figure, classmates move from the status of occasional playmates to important elements in the child's social world. The expectations of school are in some senses distinctive ones. For the first time, children may be expected to memorize material and be tested on it. Learning skills are emphasized and consciously taught. The setting of the school carries its own rules for appropriate behavior. In addition, there may be significant differences between the values and practices of the home environment and that of the school. Longitudinal research confirms that discontinuity in development is most likely during the family-to-school transitional years than before or after, particularly when the expectations of school and home conflict. For example, dependency in boys and aggression in girls are both apt to decrease at this time (Kagan and Moss, 1962). This has been interpreted as a result of the school environment's discouragement of masculine dependency and feminine aggression.

Adolescence. Early adolescence (ages twelve to fifteen) has been singled out as a time when far-reaching biological changes coincide with culturally imposed social pressures (Hamburg, 1974). The twelve-year-old boy, beset by mood swings, suddenly does not recognize his own body. At the same time, the discontinuous environment of the junior high school, with its sharp increase in academic pressure, imposes heavy performance demands. To make matters worse, parents often treat the transition into junior high as a sign that their child is now an adolescent and expect instant maturity.

Establishing identity. Erikson has called attention to the task of establishing identity as a prelude to effective adult functioning. He described the "identity crisis" occasioned by the youth's reevaluation of his or her past and expectations for the future. Erikson sees the formation of identity as a product of the *interaction* of self and society. Society must provide meaningful roles for young people to assume; at the same time, they must integrate their childhoods in a new fashion to function autonomously outside their family. The crisis nature of this transition is indicated by the *moratorium* it sometimes engenders. This is a "time-out" period of experimentation or drifting during which various adult roles are tentatively tried on. The no-longer-a-child, not-yet-an-adult swings from assertions of independence to lapses of dependency. This is particularly difficult for the parents who at the same time are experiencing a transition of their own. They must learn to "let go," recasting but not destroying their old relationship. At the same time, the marital bond may become more salient for them as the focus shifts away from child-rearing tasks.

Wide individual variation in passage through this period exists. For many, continuity is the hallmark, with little disruption of the pattern of previous existence. For others it is a stormy wrestling with the basic question, "Who am I?"

Transition to parenthood. The advent of the first child characteristically disturbs the equilibrium of both the family system and individual identities. Alice Rossi (1968) has called our attention to the difficult nature of this crisis. Strong societal pressures to view the coming baby in idyllic terms collide with the realities of an often uncomfortable pregnancy, disruption of schedules, new and incessant demands. In addition, most new parents are thoroughly unprepared for the role they are expected to take on with such gusto. In the age of isolated, nuclear families, fewer and fewer adults have experience caring for young children or even observing their care before they themselves become parents. For the first time, one is faced with an unconditional, lifetime dependency relationship, from which there is no time-out and no means of termination. The overwhelming nature of this transition makes it among the most difficult to handle.

Again, both parental and infant characteristics are likely to be important in ameliorating or intensifying the experience. The changes occasioned by the first child are less significant than the interpretations given those changes by the new parents. A relatively minor adjustment can be perceived as a nearly intolerable change of crisis proportions, or it can be taken in stride (Jacoby, 1969). Most parents eagerly await their first child and take great pleasure in its appearance. Their investment of care pays dividends of attachment. The crisis nature of the transition to parenthood is modified by interpretations of the event and the counterbalancing force of positive feelings.

Most studies on the transition to parenthood note class differences in its severity. Middle-class couples are likely to experience parenthood as more of a crisis than lower-class couples. Some have interpreted this as indicating the greater familistic orientation or perhaps the less intense marital bond of working-class families (Jacoby, 1969). In addition, middle-class parents, particularly mothers, may have greater expectations for their child. They may see their role as crucial in forming the child's cognitive capacities for later achievement. Many books on parenting (see White, *The First Three Years*) encourage the view that parenting is an arduous, high-risk task for which the novice must be well equipped. Hence, fear of failure and general anxiety over doing a good job are likely to be greater among middle-class families.

Such crisis points are not confined to the early years. The entire life cycle may be viewed as a succession of significant landmarks, whose passage is rarely negotiated in total ease.

Midlife transitions. Recent investigations of adulthood (Levinson, 1978) have described this period as one in which the developing individual-system's equilibrium is periodically disturbed. As a result of these transitions, the individual must reorganize his or her life and achieve a new stability. Levinson (1978) in his study of middle-aged men identified an age thirty and age forty transition. Levinson believes that, for many men, these transitions are painful times, *crises*, during which the structure of their lives is no longer adequate yet before a new, more acceptable structure

Levinson (1978) has written about the "midlife crisis" of men about age 40. (Photo by Natalie Leimkuhler.)

has been formed. At thirty, for example, many men evaluate the occupational and emotional choices they made during the more provisional twenties, with the sense that time is running out. The need for more lasting commitment may be stressful. At about age forty—these time markers are loosely employed to denote an age range of about five years—what Levinson calls the *midlife transition* or *age forty crisis* occurs for most men. During this time a man evaluates the commitments he has earlier made and asks: "What have I made of myself? What have I accomplished? Did I live up to the dreams of my youth?" Again, while a minority of men Levinson studied experienced this as a relatively smooth transition, for the majority it was a moderate-to-severe life crisis, in which nearly every aspect of their lives was questioned.

These time markers appear to be important because, in our society especially, adults evaluate themselves as "on-time" or "off-time" in reaching certain landmarks. For example, women who pass their thirtieth birthday unmarried have traditionally been viewed as "late" for the landmark of marriage. Men who are still experimenting with occupational goals at age thirty sense this same "lateness." Note that Levinson studied only men in his depiction of age thirty and age forty crises. It is likely that women, with their up-to-now different investment in work identity, would experience developmental changes in adulthood according to a different rhythm. Sheehy's popular book *Passages* suggests that the timing of female developmental peaks and valleys will depend greatly on the timing of choices a woman makes. Those women who placed heavy emphasis on career achievement during early adulthood may experience a midlife crisis of "switching gears" as they attempt to focus on their nurturant side, while women who invested primarily in nurturance through raising a family find at midlife they have forty years in which to explore other facets of their personalities.

FACTORS AFFECTING THE PERCEPTION OF STRESS

Personal responsibility. In addition to life-cycle differences in the perception of life events as stressful, it is likely that the type of stressful change is significant as well (Kellam, 1974). Earlier the distinction between external and internal locus of control was emphasized (Rotter, 1966) in connection with styles of perceiving the environment. Since the perception of stress is a type of environmental perception, it is not surprising that locus of control might be important here as well. It is likely that fateful events over which the individual perceives no control would have different impact compared to events for which it is possible to take responsibility. For example, in one study (Kellam, 1974) the impact of a fateful life change—family residential move—and a personal responsibility one—academic failure—on the young child was compared. The first type tended to increase the child's adaptive capacity to deal with a later crisis, such as losing a teacher in the middle of the year, while personal failure tended to decrease adaptiveness, perhaps by dampening self-concept. Coping with environmental demands must not only result in restoring "person-environment fit" or equilibrium, but also preserve and enhance self-image while fostering conditions for further development.

Cultural norms. To a certain extent, cultural norms define what experiences are likely to be perceived as stressful. Such norms give meaning to experience, defining what is proper, what should be occurring. To the extent that an individual or family subscribes to these norms, failure to live up to them will be perceived as stressful. Being "on time" for certain developmental landmarks such as marriage, parenthood, and occupational choice is one kind of cultural norm. It is evident that cultural norms themselves are changing. In addition, considerable variety exists in the extent to which people subscribe to norms.

There is less agreement than previously about a "proper" time for marriage, or if to marry at all. One aspect of the mid-life changes which Levinson and Sheehy describe is the periodic reevaluation of *personal norms* in relation to cultural ones.

Life context. Although it is sometimes useful to identify specific stressful aspects of the environment or the developing individual or the changing family, in reality events are not experienced in isolation, but rather in the context of one's total life. A stressful event such as malnutrition tends to occur, as was seen in Chapter 8, in an environment also characterized by low income, poor housing, inadequate sanitation, infrequent medical attention, uncontrollable sensory stimulation, and unstable home conditions. Stress is not simply additive but a product of the complex interaction of all aspects of the environment. Intervention that attacks only one component is less successful than broad-based efforts.

Individual differences. A direct implication of the adaptation range and family environment transaction concepts is the view that stress results more from a *mismatching* of individual system with environmental stimulation than in absolute levels of environmental conditions. This statement must be qualified by the earlier discussion in this chapter of certain *potential* stressors that generally lie outside most adaptation ranges.

COMPETENCE THROUGH AWARENESS

Family members can become more competent in transacting with environments by improving certain kinds of awareness. *Ecological awareness* is one example. The resources the family uses to produce its own human resources are limited. Resource use in one sphere of the global ecosystem has repercussions through the rest. Ecological awareness means accepting limits to human intervention in the system of energy exchanges called life. This is particularly difficult in cultures like our own with a strong mastery-over-nature orientation. Yet research on energy management suggests that once such an orientation is supplanted by greater ecological consciousness, behavior patterns change. Programs of fuel conservation are then more likely to succeed.

Ecological awareness also means understanding how family behavior is linked to its natural resource base. How people feed and house themselves affects how they communicate, with what goals they raise their children, and by what values they structure their lives.

Finally, ecological awareness encompasses understanding the links between families and the many systems in which they participate—legal, political, educational, occupational, religious. These systems regulate behavior and hence act on the family. At the same time, family members participate in such systems. In important role positions, they determine and direct their policy. Yet, from the standpoint of the family, the impact of these many extra-familial institutions is likely to be contradictory. For example, high energy consumption may be implied by one's job performance, turning out new cars at the factory, while at the same time, political and educational institutions are emphasizing conservation. Other segments of industry continue to push high consumption as the way to economic prosperity, while at Sunday worship, the importance of global responsibility is stressed. The family at the intersection of these mixed messages receives no clear direction.

A type of awareness related to the ecological is *consumer awareness*. In recent years consumer organizations and advocates have sprung up to champion the cause of the unwittingly duped consumer. At the same time, attention is being paid to consumer education as a means of increasing the ability of the consumer to be his or her own advocate. How is this to be done? The ecosystem framework can give us some guidelines. First, merely increasing the volume of information does not educate. Information must be in manageable chunks. Secondly, consumer information is significant as it is processed through perceptions, values, and patterns of decision making. A study by Lenahan et al. (1973) is a good illustration of this point. The investigators were interested in consumer awareness, understanding, and use of nutritional labels on food products. Investigating a national probability sample, they found that 25 percent of the respondents were aware of the labelling, 15 percent understood it, and only 10 percent actually used it. Thus, information designed to make the food consumer better informed went unused by 90 percent of them. Should one then conclude that nutritional labelling has been a resounding failure? The authors say no. Their results revealed that for consumers, indirect nonfood-related benefits of nutritional labelling were perceived as important. Specifically, consumers saw labelling as evidence that food producers and distributors were being held accountable for their merchandise. With the disappearance of the trusted corner grocer, the authors argue, food purchases have become impersonal. No basis for trusting advertising claims exists. At the same time, changes in the family, such as increased dual employment, have made food purchases more hurried. In such a context, nutritional labelling helps restore a sense of trust in food suppliers, a benefit more important than simply informational content.

Understanding the ways in which consumer behavior reflects values and interaction patterns is a second path to greater awareness. Changes in consumption activities may bring about changes in other spheres of life. For example, it has been suggested (Nicosia and Mayer, 1976) that as eating in restaurants becomes more and more common, enforcement of religious dietary regulations will be more difficult, and this will prompt changes in religious life. These same eating-out habits may also be expected to change family interaction patterns organized around shared meals.

Not only does consumer behavior change other areas of life, but values themselves structure consumption. Values of frugality, savings, and delay of gratification lead to one pattern while orientation toward the present, hedonism, and expressiveness lead to another. One analysis (Nicosia and Mayer, 1976) suggests that as the cultural values of freedom of choice, individual achievement, and egalitarianism become weaker in occupational and government institutions organized around unions, seniority, and centralization, they become "deflected" or diverted into consumption behavior. In other words, people now tend to express their individuality and strivings through their consumer behavior because they can no longer do so at work or through government. Although this idea is highly speculative, it does provide an explanation for the proliferation of products for marketed life styles.

IMPROVING SKILLS

The family ecosystem's emphasis on transactional processes, adaptation and self-direction has implications for both families and those whose work directly affects them. The architect, interior designer, and city planner design environments for family life; the nutritionist plans food consumption patterns; the teacher, social worker, or psychologist direct their attention to family interaction. To those who design spatial environments, we have emphasized how the physical setting affects the perceptions, values, attitudes, and interaction possibilities of those found in it. Space is an important means of regulating stimulation, of achieving an optimal balance between separateness and connectedness. Therefore, a setting which allows for user "fine-tuning" to maintain that shifting balance is necessary. As one architect put it, we need to look for "people patterns in the blue prints" (Deasy, 193).

To the nutritionist, the ecosystem approach stresses how bound up are values, culture, and interaction patterns with food consumption. Cultural food taboos are a striking example of this. Less obvious is the influence that a mother's needs, attitudes, and motivations have on the quality of food provided her child. For children, food sometimes becomes a symbolic language with which to express anger, resentment, or the desire for autonomy. Because of this larger significance of food, attempts to provide clear information about proper nutrition without at the same time dealing with motivations, needs, and values often fail to achieve their objectives, or fulfill other unnoticed needs. As the earlier discussion of nutritional labelling showed, such increased information was not used as intended to make food purchasers more informed, but to increase trust in the accountability of large food producers and distributors.

To the teacher or social worker, the ecosystem approach underlines the significance of family perceptions, values, and interaction patterns in determining transactions with the environment. The importance of self-direction implies that help to families which does not permit them to help themselves is little help at all. Social-welfare programs often put families in the position of receivers of what society doles out. Despite good intentions, this method of aid reinforces an external locus of control, the belief that events happen to the family from external sources rather than from self-direction. It leads, too, to family adaptation to change in terms of reduction or increase in family demands and supplies rather than attempts to change environmental demands and supplies.

The ecosystem approach also implies that families will differ in optimal rates of change and stimulation. Stress must be defined relative to the meaning of situations for the family itself. Therefore, both teaching about and assistance to families should be centered on the theme of diversity. The question that then arises is: How can we find out about particular families, their transactional processes, their adaptation range, and their methods of coping with stress? Information concerning family processes of perceiving, valuing, spacing, and deciding may be coupled with detailed information concerning the family environment. Rather than studying family patterns or environmental conditions in isolation, we always consider them in relation to each other. It is the *fit* between family system demands and environmental supplies, between system supplies and environmental demands, that is significant in understanding the process of adaptation.

If the goal is bettering *fit*, we can explore ways in which families can be helped to modify environmental conditions to better suit their demands. When this is impossible, strategies for changing family demands or supplies in relation to environmental conditions can be employed.

SUMMARY

The concept of stress was defined as environmental stimulation outside an individual's or family's adaptation range. While stress is relative to the meanings assigned to a situation, some environmental conditions, lying outside the adaptation ranges of most, are generally regarded as stressors. Excessive noise, stimulation deprivation, and stimulation or information overload were briefly considered.

Not everyone reacts to extremes in environmental stimulation in the same manner. "Vulnerable" individuals and families experience stress in relatively benign circumstances, while the "insulated" or "buffered" seem immune to even extremely harsh environmental conditions. Wide differences in adaptation range distinguish these groups. In addition, differences in resistance resources in the form of material and social supports, or in coping skills probably differentiate these two groups. Finally, one cannot rule out the role played by constitutional differences which may predispose some to stress while making others resilient.

Periods in the individual and family life-cycle may be characterized as particularly prone to stress. Transition periods such as adolescence or parenthood require reorganization of the family system. The passage through adulthood appears to be a stormy one, with age thirty and age forty crises experienced by many men. Changes in the family system through divorce or remarriage generally involve a lengthy period of destabilization, disorganization, and eventual restabilization at a new adaptation level.

Since adaptation is seen as the process of maximizing *fit* between system and environment, family adaptation might be enhanced by supports given the family to increase their competence in modifying the environment to their needs. Programs of ecological and consumer awareness, as well as awareness of family dynamics and value clarification, are relevant here. Skills aimed at directly attacking environmental problems through group action are useful. Environmental competence as a goal for family systems allows them to be active environmental creators rather than passive reactors.

REFERENCES

Angell, R. C. *The Family Encounters the Depression.* New York: Scribner's, 1936.

Anthony, E. J., and Koupernik, C., eds. *The Child in His Family: Children at Psychiatric Risk.* Vol. 3. New York: Wiley, 1974.

Antonovsky, A. Conceptual and methodological problems in the study of resistance resources and stressful life events. In B. S. Dohrenwend and B. P. Dohrenwend, eds., *Stressful Life Events: Their Nature and Effects.* New York: Wiley, 1974.

Baumrind, D. Child care practices anteceding three patterns of preschool behavior. *Genetic Psychological Monographs* 75 (1967): 43-88.

Bernard, J. The eudaemonists. In S. Z. Klausner, ed., *Why Man Takes Chances.* Garden City, N.Y.: Doubleday, 1968.

Blauner, R. Death and social structure. *Psychiatry* 29 (1966): 378-394.

Burr, W. R. *Theory Construction and the Sociology of the Family.* New York: Wiley, 1973.

Cofer, C. N., and Appley, M. H. *Motivation: Theory and Research.* New York: Wiley, 1964.

Cohen, S., Glass, D. C., and Singer, J. E. Apartment noise, auditory discrimination and reading ability in children. *Journal of Experimental Social Psychology* 9 (1973): 407-422.

Deasy, C. M. People patterns in the blueprints. *Human Behavior,* August 1973, pp. 8-15.

Dennis, W. Causes of retardation among institutional children: Iran. *Journal of Genetic Psychology* 96 (1960): 47-59.

Dennis, W., and Najarian, P. Infant development under environmental handicap. *Psychological Monographs* 71 (1957): 436.

Dobzhansky, T. *Mankind Evolving.* New Haven: Yale University Press, 1962.

Edholm, O. G. Tropical fatigue. In W. F. Floyd and A. T. Weford, eds., *Symposium on Fatigue.* London: H. K. Lewis, 1953.

Glass, D. C., and Singer, J. E. *Urban Stress.* New York: Academic Press, 1972.

Griffitt, W., and Veitch, R. Hot and crowded: Influences of population density and temperature on interpersonal affective behavior. *Journal of Personality and Social Psychology* 17 (1971): 92-99.

Haan, N. *Coping and Defending: Processes of Self-Environment Organization.* New York: Academic Press, 1977.

Hamburg, B. Early adolescence: A specific and stressful stage of the life cycle. In G. V. Coelho, D. A. Hamburg, and J. A. Adams, eds., *Coping and Adaptation.* New York: Basic Books, 1974.

Hansen, D. A. Personal and positional influence in formal groups: Propositions and theory for research on family vulnerability to stress. *Social Forces* 44 (1965): 202-210.

Hansen, D. A., and Hill, R. Families under stress. In H. T. Christensen, ed., *Handbook of Marriage and the Family.* Chicago: Rand McNally, 1964.

Harlow, H. F., and Zimmermann, R. R. Affectional responses in the infant monkey. *Science* 130 (1959): 421-432.

Helson, H. *Adaptation-Level Theory.* New York: Harper and Row, 1964.

Hetherington, E. M., Cox, M., and Cox, R. Beyond father absence: Conceptualization of effects of divorce. In E. M. Hetherington and R. D. Parke, eds., *Contemporary Readings in Child Psychology.* New York: McGraw-Hill, 1977.

Hill, R. *Families Under Stress.* New York: Harper and Bros., 1949.

————. Challenges and resources for family development. In *Family Mobility in Our Dynamic Society.* Ames, Iowa: University of Iowa Press, 1965.

Hill, R., and Hansen, D. A. The family in disaster. In G. Baker and D. Chapman, eds., *Man and Society in Disaster.* New York: Basic Books, 1962.

Hinkle, L. E. The effect of exposure to culture change, social change, and changes in interpersonal relationships on health. In B. S. Dohrenwend and B. P. Dohrenwend, eds., *Stressful Life Events: Their Nature and Effects*. New York: Wiley, 1974.

Holmes, T. H., and Masuda, M. Life changes and illness susceptibility. In B. S. Dohrenwend and B. P. Dohrenwend, eds., *Stressful Life Events: Their Nature and Effects*. New York: Wiley, 1974.

Holmes, T. H., and Rahe, R. H. The social readjustment rating scale. *Journal of Psychosomatic Research* 11 (1967): 213-218.

Jacoby, A. P. Transition to parenthood: A reassessment. *Journal of Marriage and the Family* 31 (1969): 720-727.

Kagan, J., and Moss, H. A. *From Birth to Maturity: The Fels Study of Psychological Development*. New York: Wiley, 1962.

Kahn, R., and Perlin, S. Dwelling unit density and the use of mental health services. *Proceedings of the 75th Annual Convention of the American Psychological Association*, 1967, pp. 175-176.

Kalter, N. Children of divorce in an outpatient psychiatric population. *American Journal of Orthopsychiatry* 47 (1977): 40-51.

Kellam, S. Stressful life events and illness: A research area in need of conceptual development. In B. S. Dohrenwend and B. P. Dohrenwend, eds., *Stressful Life Events: Their Nature and Effects*. New York: Wiley, 1974.

Kepes, G., ed. *Arts of the Environment*. New York: George Braziller, 1972.

Koos, E. L. *Families in Trouble*. New York: Kings Crown Press, 1946.

Langner, T. W., and Michael, S. T. *Life Stress and Mental Health*. New York: Free Press, 1963.

Latané, B., and Darley, J. *The Unresponsive Bystander*. New York: Meredith, 1970.

Lenahan, R. J., Thomas, J. A., Taylor, D. A., Call, D. L., and Padberg, D. I. Consumer reaction to nutritional labels on food products. *Journal of Consumer Affairs* 7 (1973): 1-12.

Levinson, D. *The Seasons of a Man's Life*. New York: Knopf, 1978.

Mechanic, D. Social structure and personal adaptation: Some neglected dimensions. In G. V. Coelho, D. A. Hamburg, and J. A. Adams, eds., *Coping and Adaptation*. New York: Basic Books, 1974.

Milgram, S. The experience of living in cities. *Science* 167 (1970): 1461-1468.

Neugarten, B. Continuities and discontinuities of psychological issues into adult life. *Human Development* 12 (1969): 121-130.

Nicosia, F. M., and Mayer, R. N. Toward a sociology of consumption. *Journal of Consumer Research* 3 (1976): 65-75.

Riesen, A. H. The development of visual perception in man and chimpanzee. *Science* 106 (1947): 107-108.

Rodgers, R. *Family Interaction and Transaction: The Developmental Approach*. Englewood Cliffs, N.J.: Prentice-Hall, 1973.

Rossi, A. Transition to parenthood. *Journal of Marriage and the Family* 30 (1968): 26-39.

Rotter, J. Generalized expectancies for internal versus external control of reinforcement. *Psychological Monographs* 80 (1966), no. 1.

Schaie, K. W. A field-theory approach to age changes in cognitive behavior. *Vita Humana* 5 (1962): 129-141.

Schwarzweller, H. K., and Crowe, J. M. Adaptation of Appalachian migrants to an industrial work situation: A case study. In E. B. Brody, ed., *Behavior in New Environments: Adaptation of Migrant Populations*. Beverly Hills, Calif.: Sage Publications, 1969.

Segal, J. Correlates of collaboration and resistance behavior among U.S. Army POWs in Korea. *Journal of Social Issues* 55 (1957): 197-201.

Selye, H. Stress and psychiatry. *American Journal of Psychiatry* 115 (1956): 423-427.

Sheehy, G. *Passages: Predictable Crises of Adult Life*. New York: E. P. Dutton, 1976.

Spitz, R. A., and Wolff, K. M. Anaclitic depression: An inquiry into the genesis of psychiatric conditions in early childhood, II. In A. Freud et al., eds., *The Psychoanalytic Study of the Child*. Vol. II. New York: International Universities Press, 1946.

White, R. W. Strategies of adaptation: An attempt at systematic description. In G. V. Coelho, D. A. Hamburg, and J. A. Adams, eds., *Coping and Adaptation*. New York: Basic Books, 1974.

Whiteside, M. F., and Auerbach, L. S. Can the daughter of my father's new wife be my sister? Families of remarriage in family therapy. *Journal of Divorce* 1 (1972): 271-283.

Wicker, A. W. Undermanning theory and research: Implications for the study of psychological and behavioral effects of excess populations. *Representative Research in Social Psychology* 4 (1973): 190-191.

Wicker, A. W., McGrath, J. E., and Armstrong, G. E. Organization size and behavior setting capacity as determinants of member participation. *Behavioral Science* 17 (1972): 510.

Winch, R. F., and Greer, S. Urbanism, ethnicity and extended familism. *Journal of Marriage and the Family* 30 (1968): 40-45.

Glossary of Terms

ACCULTURATION—the process of gradually adopting the values and behaviors of a culture.

ADAPTATION—the process of establishing and maintaining a relatively stable reciprocal relationship with the environment.

ADAPTATION LEVEL (AL)—a theoretically neutral state of stimulation at which the individual or family system is at its customary level of functioning.

ADAPTATION RANGE (AR)—stimulation above and below the AL; a range within which the individual or family system habitually functions.

ADJUSTMENT—minor behavioral or physiological changes that modify stimulus conditions.

AUGMENTER PERCEPTUAL STYLE—characteristic preference for relatively low levels of stimulation. Contrasted to *reducer* perceptual style.

AUTHORITY—beliefs concerning proper exercise of power.

BEHAVIOR SETTING—concept developed by Roger Barker to indicate all aspects of a physical setting together with expectations for behavior within that setting.

BODY-IMAGE BOUNDARIES—the concept of the body as having definite limits or boundaries that separate it from the outside world.

CENTRAL-SATELLITE DECISION LINKAGE—the relation between a major decision and other related but lesser decisions.

COGNITIVE DIFFERENTIATION—the degree to which the categories used to organize stimulation are complex (e.g., differentiated) or simple.

COGNITIVE MAP—a mental representation of a physical setting.

CONSTANCY FEEDBACK LOOP (or negative feedback loop)—the process designed to maintain the stability of a system in response to environmental changes.

CONSTRAINTS—factors that restrict an individual's or family's behavior.

CONSUMER SOCIALIZATION—the process by which consumer attitudes and behaviors are transmitted, particularly to children.

CONTRAVENTION—a style of childrearing whereby parents feel responsible to shape their children to be effective adults and so exert pressure on them to conform (see Haan). Contrasted to *facilitation* .

COPING—actions that make it possible to understand and master the environment.

CROSS-SECTIONAL RESEARCH—an investigation of two different groups during the same time period.

CROWDING—psychological feeling of discomfort due to perception of inadequate space to achieve goals.

CULTURE—a system of rules, standards, and values for behavior, interaction, and living conditions.

DECISION MAKING (deciding)—the process by which information is transformed into actions.

DEFENSES (against stress)—responses that reduce stress but do not result in active mastery of the environment.

DEFENSIBLE SPACE—a physical setting, usually residential, about which occupants feel a sense of control and ownership.

DEVELOPMENTAL TASKS—characteristic changes in behavior and attitudes brought about by characteristic changes in the individual or family system (e.g., the developmental tasks of adolescence include establishing a sense of independent identity).

DEVIATION AMPLIFYING CAUSAL LOOP (or positive feedback loop)—the mechanism that responds to changes in the state of a system by causing still further changes; mechanism for building in variety and change.

DOMINANCE HIERARCHY—ranking of individuals within a group with respect to privileges others in that group accord them.

ECOLOGICAL NICHE—the place of an organism within its environment.

ECOLOGY—the pattern of relations between organisms and their environment; also the scientific study of the relations of living organisms with each other and with the environment.

ECOSYSTEM—the complex of a system and its environment considered as a unit.

ENERGY FLOW—the path by which solar energy is transformed into other energy forms.

ENVIRONMENT—everything outside a system of interest (e.g., the individual system within a family environment; the family system within a housing environment).

ENVIRONMENTAL PRESS—demands of an environment exerted upon a system.

EQUILIBRIUM—preferred state of a system; it tends to be maintained when disturbed.

ETHOLOGY—the scientific and objective study of animal behavior.

EXOSYSTEM—social structures that impinge on or encompass the immediate settings of an individual.

EXPRESSIVE ROLE—role specializing in nurturing and emotional areas of family functioning. Contrasted to *instrumental* role.

FACILITATION—style of childrearing whereby parents see the children as responsible for their own development. Contrasted with *contravention*. (see Haan.)

FAMILISM—value placed on family life. Contrast to "careerism," value placed on occupational success.

FAMILY—a semi-closed, mutually interacting system of individuals characterized by long-term, intimate, reciprocal relationships, usually of blood, marriage, or adoption.

FAMILY ENVIRONMENT—a composite measure of dominant family values and concerns. (see Moos.)

FAMILY LIFE-CYCLE—view of stages of family life in terms of changing composition of the family and changes in goals that accompany these changes in composition.

FAMILY STRATEGY—recurring patterns of interactions within a family. (see Kantor and Lehr, 1975.)

FAMILY THEME—basic issues around which a family is organized, fundamental concerns to which it repeatedly returns. (see Hess and Handel.)

FEEDBACK—the process by which an individual or family system uses information concerning its own actions to direct its subsequent functioning.

FIELD INDEPENDENCE/DEPENDENCE PERCEPTUAL-COGNITIVE STYLE—tendency to use internal cues (field independence) versus external cues (field dependence) in making a judgment based on conflicting perceptual evidence from the environment and from within oneself.

HOMOGAMY—the tendency for persons with similar characteristics to marry one another.

IMPULSIVE/REFLECTIVE PERCEPTUAL-COGNITIVE STYLE—when one is engaged in problem solving, the tendency to pause to consider and assess the quality of thinking (reflective) rather than accept and report the first hypothesis produced (impulsive).

INFORMATION OVERLOAD—more information than a system has the capacity to process.

INSTRUMENTAL ROLE—within the family, the role that specializes in relations with external systems (e.g., work, economy) and task-oriented behaviors. Contrasted with *expressive* role.

KIBBUTZ (pl. = kibbutzim)—Israeli collective settlement whose methods of childrearing and work organization have attracted wide interest.

KWASHIORKOR—a disorder often resulting in death, produced by severe protein-calorie malnutrition.

LOCUS OF CONTROL—tendency to perceive the causes of events as external to the individual or family (e.g., *external* locus of control) or internal (e.g., *internal* locus of control).

LONGITUDINAL RESEARCH—investigation of development by examining the same individuals at repeated intervals over time.

MACROSYSTEM—overarching institutions of a culture, such as religious, political, economic, and educational systems.

MALNUTRITION—an inadequacy of certain nutrients in a diet (e.g., protein malnutrition).

MESOSYSTEM—those immediate settings regularly involving an individual.

MICROSYSTEM—the immediate setting of an individual.

MIGRATION—long-distance and relatively permanent change of residence.

NEED-HIERARCHY—a set of needs ranked in order of importance.

NORMS—a set of standards about appropriate behavior (e.g., cultural norms concerning housing).

NUTRITION—process by which individual takes in and uses food.

OBSERVATIONAL LEARNING—acquiring new behavior by watching it performed by another.

ORCHESTRATION DECISIONS—important, infrequent policy decisions. (Contrasted to *instrumentation* decisions—frequent decisions involving tactics and administration.)

PERCEIVING—the process by which environmental information is registered by the senses, organized and made available for use.

PERSONAL SPACE—an individual's or family's preferred distance from others.

PRIVACY—selective control over access to the self or to one's group; management of the boundary between self and environment.

RESIDENTIAL MOBILITY—change of dwellings.

RESIDENTIAL PROPINQUITY—distance between dwellings.

RESISTANCE RESOURCES—material or psychological assets that help an individual or family respond to stress.

ROLE—a set of unwritten rules that specify appropriate behavior for certain situations or relationships (e.g., father role, consumer role).

SCHEMA—mental representation.

SELF-ACTUALIZATION—development of one's fullest potentiality as a human being.

SOCIALIZATION—the process by which a culture's values and attitudes are transmitted, especially to children.

SPACING—the process by which a sense of separateness balanced by connectedness is maintained. Distance regulation.

STARVATION—life-threatening deficit of nutrients.

STIMULUS OVERLOAD—stimulation exceeding one's capacities to absorb it.

STRESS—feelings of discomfort caused by stimulation outside one's adaptation range.

SYSTEM—Interdependent parts in interaction.

TEMPERAMENT—characteristic mode of emotional response.

UNDERNUTRITION—deficiency in total number of calories needed to sustain body weight and well-being.

VALUES—enduring beliefs that specific modes of conduct or end-states are personally or socially preferable.

VALUING—use of standards by which perceived information is selected and used.

VALUE-ORIENTATION—values linked to beliefs and attitudes to form means of explaining experience.

VICARIOUS REINFORCEMENT—the act of being rewarded indirectly; as when observing a model being rewarded for a behavior acts as a reward to the observer for performing that same behavior.

Index